More Praise for
Across the Aisle

My friend, the late Congressman G.V. "Sonny" Montgomery, was a true champion for U.S. servicemen and women. His persistent and tireless efforts to enact permanent education assistance legislation, known for its namesake as the "Montgomery GI Bill," have created opportunities to develop and enrich the lives of countless veterans since its enactment in 1987. I was honored to work closely with Congressman Montgomery on this important piece of legislation and greatly respected his ability to reach across the political aisle, generational divides, and state lines to fight for and provide this well-crafted legislation.
—*Bill Cohen*
Former Secretary of Defense, U.S. Senator & Member of Congress

This magnificent case study brought happy tears. I had the distinct privilege of working with Congressman Sonny Montgomery from 1983-1987, as he carefully forged the necessary strength to achieve the enactment of the Montgomery GI Bill. I had the honor of telling him in a Congressional legislative hearing that the Army was so in favor of the GI Bill that we would pay for it. It changed the Army forever.
—*Lt. General Robert M. Elton, U.S. Army (Ret)*

In many respects, military service represents America's most fundamental—and longstanding—form of national service. I personally honor that service and commend to America's numerous civilian-volunteer organizations Sonny Montgomery's wonderful lessons in leadership.
—*Colonel Robert L. Gordon, III, U.S. Army (Ret)*
Chief Brand Officer and Senior Vice President for Civic Leadership, Boston City Year

Across the Aisle is a fitting tribute to legislative brilliance and inspired vision of Sonny Montgomery, combat veteran and life-long supporter of national security. His GI Bill created an enduring basis for the All-Volunteer Force and assures America's security for the foreseeable future. Generations of troopers and their families have Chairman Montgomery to thank for uplifting educational opportunities established by the Montgomery GI Bill.
—*General John Wickham, U.S. Army (Ret)*

Sonny Montgomery was an exceptional leader who was one of the unsung national heroes in recognizing and rewarding our military veterans. Kehrer and McGrevey have done a masterful job at describing the background and historic significance of the Montgomery GI Bill. If you are interested in Veteran's affairs and politics, this book is a must read.
—*Kirk Shultz*
President, Kansas State University

The emergence of our nation's modern-day community colleges is closely intertwined with the Sonny Montgomery GI Bill. *Across the Aisle* is a detailed account of this landmark legislation and Sonny's unfailing determination to provide America's military men and women with the education and training worthy of their service and sacrifice.
—*Clyde Muse*
President, Hinds Community College, Mississippi

For 26 years, The Montgomery GI Bill has produced untold numbers of teachers, engineers, business leaders, physicians, lawyers, first-responders, the full range of technologists, and countless other professionals. If students read only one book on the art of legislative leadership, this is the one I would recommend.
—*Jack Quinn, President*
Erie Community College of the State University of New York
Past Chairman, Subcommittee on Economic Opportunity
Committee on Veterans' Affairs, U.S. House of Representatives

Creation of the New GI Bill remains an example of how major legislative achievements are possible when Democrats and Republicans work together toward a common goal. This is something that couldn't happen today given the bitter partisan fighting over almost everything and it wouldn't have happened in 1987 without G.V. "Sonny" Montgomery, whose ability to form alliances with almost anyone willing to listen made him one of the last legislative giants.
—*Rick Maze*
Congressional Editor, Army Times
Author, "Insider's Guide to the New GI Bill"

I remember when Sonny came to Congress. I was the only Army National Guardsman until Sonny came, and he was a wonderful addition. We were both World War II veterans and became close friends. This friendship grew even stronger when President Reagan named me Secretary of the Army. I could not have had a stauncher ally than Sonny. We were in constant communication. No one knew more members of Congress on either side of the aisle, and none was more respected than Sonny. Only a few in the gym crowd were aware that President George H.W. Bush—during his presidency—kept his gym gear in Sonny's locker. The All-Volunteer Force in the 1970s became a major instrument of national security policy. It was defined by implementing legislation, but it was Sonny, and the Montgomery GI Bill, that made it work. I know because I was there. It had to succeed in the Army and it did because of Sonny.

—*John O. Marsh, Jr.*
Secretary of the Army, 1981-1989

Representative Sonny Montgomery and his "team-of-many"—inside and outside of government—created a permanent, GI Bill educational assistance program that has paid for itself many times over. Mr. Montgomery's learning-friendly case study is a tribute not only to his foresight but also to the 2.6 million engaging and resourceful members of our military who have made the Montgomery GI Bill such a resounding success.

—*Anthony J. Principi*
Secretary of Veterans Affairs, 2001-2005

Few entitlement programs provide a return-on-investment at the level of the Montgomery GI Bill. The government return is slightly more than $2.5-to-$1 and the private return is $8.6-to-$1. In a highly reader-friendly way, *Across the Aisle* expertly chronicles the bill's long legislative journey.

—*Tim Penny*
Member of Congress Representing Minnesota's 1st District
Member, Committee on Veterans' Affairs, 1983-1995
Senior Fellow, University of Minnesota
Author of "Common Cents: A Retiring Six-Term Congressman Reveals How Congress Really Works and What We Must Do to Fix It"

Students and others who read *Across the Aisle* will gain an insider's perspective on the challenges that face passage of comprehensive legislation. The innovative approach in the book is striking. The visual content of persons, documents, and news articles helps students have an expanded context that should help make the reading become more "real."

—*Dan Doyle*
Professor of History and Fulbright Scholar
Pennsylvania College of Technology/The Pennsylvania State University

Across the Aisle is an amazing historical account of the Montgomery GI Bill. The meticulous research and remarkable accuracy in preparing this extraordinary book should make it a class case study on the legislative process.

—*Dale Jones, Ph.D.*
Associate Professor of Public Administration
Director, National Homeland Security Project
President, College of Humanities and Sciences Faculty Council
Virginia Commonwealth University

Transitioning to the All-Volunteer Force was the most important change the Army made since World War II; the Montgomery GI Bill was the policy vehicle that allowed this to happen.

—*Colonel Michael Meese, Ph.D.*
Head, Department of Social Sciences, U.S. Military Academy

The Montgomery GI Bill, through its laser-like focus upon education and training, has profoundly impacted for the better America's ongoing ability to compete globally. *Across the Aisle* brilliantly captures the story behind this legislation, detailing from many perspectives both its enactment and its extraordinarily positive—and somewhat under appreciated—contribution to the development of our nation's workforce.

—*Paul Roitman Bardack, ESQ*
Director, George Mason University Center
for Online Workforce Development, Fairfax, VA

ACROSS THE AISLE

The Seven-Year Journey
of the Historic Montgomery GI Bill

A case study in the art of legislative leadership

Montgomery GI Bill
The Legacy of Service: The Future of Freedom

By G.V. "Sonny" Montgomery

Member of Congress—1967-1997
Chairman—Committee on Veterans' Affairs 1981-1995

With Darryl Kehrer and Michael McGrevey

University Press of Mississippi, Jackson, in association with Mississippi State University

Across the Aisle: The Seven-Year Journey of the Historic Montgomery GI Bill

© 2010 Mississippi State University

www.upress.state.ms.us

The University Press of Mississippi is a member of the Association of American University Presses.
Manufactured in the United States of America

Library of Congress Cataloging-in-Publication Data
Montgomery, G.V. (Gillespie V.)
Across the Aisle: The Seven-Year Journey of the Historic Montgomery GI Bill/by G.V. "Sonny" Montgomery;
with Darryl Kehrer and Michael McGrevey.
p.cm.
Includes bibliographical references and index.
ISBN 978-1-60473-965-7 (cloth: alk. paper)
ISBN 978-1-60473-966-4 (pbk.: alk. paper)
ISBN 978-1-60473-967-1 (ebook)

I. Veterans—Education—Law and legislation—United States—History.
2. Kehrer, Darryl W.
II. McGrevey, Michael, III. Title.

KF7749.E3M66 2010

343.74'01130262—de22   2010037934

Covers and Book Design: Kim Gianakos

MANUSCRIPT NOTE

Across the Aisle author G.V. "Sonny" Montgomery died on May 12, 2006, at age 86. Mr. Montgomery guided the book's 16-chapter broad outline in mid-2005. He reviewed multiple drafts of Chapters 1 through 6 and 12 through 16 during fall 2005 and early 2006. We created Chapter 17 later by dividing Chapter 16 into two chapters.

Mr. Montgomery did not review Chapters 7 to 10 prior to his passing. The last chapters drafted—7 to 9—reflect the 1984 debate in the U.S. Senate. We drew these chapters nearly verbatim from the *Congressional Record*. Also, at Mr. Montgomery's direction, we took extra time to coordinate the development of those chapters with former Senator John Glenn's staff by sharing two early drafts with him in 2005 and 2006. Lastly, Chapter 10 on the 1984 House-Senate Conference Committee was informed by Chapter 4 of the 2003 book, *Sonny Montgomery: The Veterans Champion*, as well as from numerous interviews.

TABLE OF CONTENTS

FOREWORD

Dear Sonny – Memories of a great day, but can't you get some bigger letters?

Geo Bush

Vice President George H.W. Bush, Barbara Bush, and G. V. "Sonny" Montgomery at the 1981 dedication of the G.V. Montgomery National Guard Complex in Meridian, Mississippi.

The late Sonny Montgomery was my friend. We both were elected to Congress in 1966, and we were friends from that day forward.

The story of the GI Bill that bears Sonny Montgomery's name is a wonderful lesson for America's students in how to write a good law. In this book, Sonny tells the story in his own words.

The Montgomery GI Bill that Congress created in 1987 has helped make our All-Volunteer military the best in the world. America's sons and daughters who serve in our military represent the very best in character, commitment, and resolve in protecting our homeland. Many of them recognized the value of educational benefits and joined our military, in part, to qualify for these benefits at the conclusion of their service to America.

As students, you'll relive and participate in the actual public debate on the bill and learn the art of legislative leadership. You'll learn how Sonny's powerful listening skills, down-home friendliness, vision, and old-fashioned perseverance created a diverse, goal-oriented team—inside and outside of government—committed to creating a quality GI Bill for America's youth. You'll learn, too, that the Montgomery GI Bill helps America in many ways, including postsecondary education and training opportunity, national security, workforce and youth development, economic vitality, and civic leadership.

I suspect you'll enjoy traveling the long legislative road with Sonny as your escort and mentor as much as I've enjoyed—and valued—his friendship and counsel.

George H.W. Bush
41st President of the United States

ACKNOWLEDGMENTS

Like the legislative journey, our review process also included a valued team. We are grateful to The Montgomery Institute, a non-profit economic development firm in Meridian, MS, for initiating this book and its financial support. We circulated the draft manuscript to a generous team of readers, many of whom were there as Hill staffers helping to shepherd the legislation for all seven years of the legislative journey. These included Mack Fleming, Jill Cochran, Patrick Ryan, Jim Holley, Beth Kilker, Debbie Smith, Kim Wincup, and Bob Cover in the House; and Jim Dykstra, Jonathan Steinberg, Ed Scott, and Babette Polzer in the Senate. Many reviewed it line by line, and we received many helpful comments.

Readers who were there for part of the legislative journey or reviewed the manuscript given their expertise included Dan Nyseth, Al Bemis, Marcelle Habibion, Dale Jones, Anthony Principi, Don Sweeney, Chris Yoder, Bill Brew, Bill Susling, Mary Ann Settlemire, Bo Maske, Anne Campbell, Capt. Joe Foster, Fred Pang, Michael Musheno, John M. Bradley III, Andrea Baridon, Adam Jones, Christina Roof, and Heather Freitag.

We thank former members of Representative Montgomery's staff: André Clemandot, Kyle Steward, Louise Cave, and Nancy Sullivan.

We thank those who graciously opened their classrooms to field-test the draft manuscript, including Colonels Russ Howard, Rob Gordon, and Michael Meese, and Majors Darrell Driver and Shannon Lyerly at West Point; Professor Suzanne Mettler at The Maxwell School, Syracuse University; Professor Marty Wiseman at the Stennis Institute of Government, Mississippi State University; Lt. Colonel Anne Campbell and Professor Fran Pilch at the U.S. Air Force Academy; Professor Tim Penny at Winona State University, and Bill Rhatican at West Potomac (VA) High School. Kim Gianakos, Ad Astra LLC, brought the visuals to life for the field test in a way that resonated with students.

We thank Julie Kimbrough, William Mahannah, Larry Surratt, and staff at the Law Library of the Library of Congress, Washington, D.C.; Tom Dodson, Tom Burch, Charles Glasgow, Susan Sokoll, Susan Hill, and Bruce Edwards at the Legislative Reference Library of the Department of Veterans Affairs, Washington, D.C.; Richard Sommers at the U.S. Army Military History Institute, Carlisle, PA; and Dieter Stenger at the U.S. Army Historical Center, Ft. McNair, Washington, D.C.

Keith Wilson, Dennis Douglass, Ted Van Hintum, Karen Patton, Lynn Nelson, James Palanchar, Michael Yunker, and Devon Seibert of the VA's Education Service furnished program usage information and technical data.

We are grateful to the The Woodrow Wilson National Fellowship Foundation, Princeton, NJ. The Foundation named Darryl Kehrer and Marcelle Habibion Public Service Fellows in 1992, representing the U.S. Department of Veterans Affairs, thus funding initial research for the book. David Walton assisted.

Bonny Paez Garrido helped with the research, organized the visuals and footnotes, helped type the draft manuscript, and performed many other tasks. West Point Cadet Matthew Price helped with manuscript preparation and research during a summer internship, and Ryan Thompson helped locate needed documents.

Monica Parkzes at Army Times Publishing Co. found needed articles for us.

The careful and uniquely creative eye of Kim Gianakos made the visuals a value-added part of the manuscript. Kim created the book's chapter and page formats/design and inserted the visuals with great care. We are very indebted to her and her business partner, Kelly B. Smith, who meticulously edited the early page proofs and checked hundreds of sources.

We are especially grateful to House Committee on Veterans' Affairs staff members Jill Cochran and Beth Kilker, both of whom had the foresight to create a seven-year, internal historical file on the Montgomery GI Bill's development. This file proved very useful. Debbie Smith and Jim Holley coordinated our access to the internal file, and Richard Fuller provided valuable information from the early 1980s.

Many persons at Mississippi State University furnished assistance, including Dean of Libraries Frances Coleman, Michael Ballard, Ryan Semmes, Kyle Pippins, Ophelia Mitchell, Debbie Walker, Andrew Rendon, Lorene Cox, Peggy Jo Hurst, Frank Wills, Lamarris Williams, Marty Wiseman, and Stennis-Montgomery Student Association members Edward Sanders and Christen Reeves. Ashleigh Murdock and Kelly Agee skillfully checked endnote sources and edited the first draft of the manuscript.

John V. Sullivan, Bob Cover, Pierre Poisson, Kim Wincup, Jack Marsh, Charles Johnson, John Brizzi, and Gay Topper furnished valued advice on legislative history matters. Fred Beuttler, Michael Cronin, and Anthony Wallis, of the House Historical Office, accessed numerous visuals and furnished guidance on relevant aspects of House tradition and procedure. Heather Moore of the Senate Historical Office provided pictures of former senators.

Al Bemis, Jim Holley, Dale Jones, Anne Campbell, Ross Trower, Bob Foglesong, Kingston Smith, Rob Gordon, and Michael Meese encouraged the book's writing so as to benefit future generations. Bill Scaggs, former president, and Aida Reeves, office manager at The Montgomery Institute, furnished valued support.

Lastly, we do not suggest that this is the complete history of the Montgomery GI Bill's genesis, legislative journey, or implementation. But we do believe (1) our careful quoting of debate at the actual time in the legislative cycle during which events occurred/were documented; (2) our many interviews with persons who witnessed first-hand the policy development process; and (3) our extensive review of source documents generated before/during/after enactment allow us to suggest we have told the story as accurately as possible.

—Darryl Kehrer & Michael McGrevey, October 2010

SONNY'S CAST OF CHARACTERS

Principal (but not all-inclusive) persons/organizations that shaped the Montgomery GI Bill's 1987 enactment included the following:

EXECUTIVE BRANCH

Vice President George H.W. Bush

Vice Admiral Dudley Carlson, U.S. Navy

Lieutenant General Earnest Cheatham, U.S. Marine Corps

Lieutenant General Bob Elton, U.S. Army

Lieutenant General Thomas Hickey, U.S. Air Force

Secretary of the Army John Marsh

General Edward "Shy" Meyer, U.S. Army

General Max Thurman, U.S. Army

Chief Benefits Director, John Vogel, Veterans Administration

General John Wickham, U.S. Army

LEGISLATIVE BRANCH

Senator Bill Armstrong (R-CO)

Representative Beverly Byron (D-MD)

Senator Bill Cohen (R-ME)

Senator Alan Cranston (D-CA)

Representative Ronald Dellums (D-CA)

Representative Wayne Dowdy (D-MS)

Representative Bob Edgar (D-PA)

Representative Lane Evans (D-IL)

Senator John Glenn (D-OH)

Representative John Paul Hammerschmidt (R-AR)

Representative Marcy Kaptur (D-OH)

Senator Edward Kennedy (D-MA)

Senator Spark Matsunaga (D-HI)

Senator Frank Murkowski (R-AK)

Senator Sam Nunn (D-GA)

Representative Tim Penny (D-MN)

Representative Christopher Smith (R-NJ)

Senator Alan Simpson (R-WY)

Representative Bob Stump (R-AZ)

Senator Strom Thurmond (R-SC)

Senator John Tower (R-TX)

COMMITTEES OF JURISDICTION

House Committee on Veterans' Affairs;
     and Subcommittee on Education, Training, and Employment

House Committee on Armed Services;
     and Subcommittee on Military Personnel and Compensation

Senate Committee on Veterans' Affairs

Senate Committee on Armed Services;
     and Subcommittee on Force Management and Personnel

Senate Committee on Budget

House Committee on Budget

House Committee on Rules

INTEREST GROUPS

Non Commissioned Officers Association of the United States (NCOA)

American Association of Community and Junior Colleges

American Association of State Colleges and Universities

American Council on Education (ACE)

Fleet Reserve Association

National Association of State Approving Agencies

National Association of Veterans' Program Administrators

American Association of Minority Veterans Programs Administrators

National Home Studies Council

Association of the United States Army

Navy League of the United States

The Retired Officers Association

Reserve Officers Association of the United States

National Association for Uniformed Services

National Guard Association of the United States

Naval Reserve Association

Enlisted Association of the National Guard of the United States (EANGUS)

Air Force Association

Air Force Sergeant's Association

Marine Corps League

National Military Wives Association

Disabled American Veterans (DAV)

Paralyzed Veterans of America (PVA)

Vietnam Veterans of America

Veterans of Foreign Wars of the United States (VFW)

The American Legion

AMVETS

Blinded Veterans Association

American Veterans Committee

MEDIA

P.J. Budahn, *Army Times*

Tim Carrington, *Wall Street Journal*

Adell Crowe, *USA Today*

Richard Halloran, *New York Times*

Otto Kreisher, *New York City Tribune*

Rick Maze, *Army Times*

Paul Smith, *Army Times*

George C. Wilson, *Washington Post*

SONNY'S TRAVEL TOOLS

I call *Across the Aisle* a visual (and participative) case study because, as students, you will study and take on the roles of scores of people who worked on the Montgomery GI Bill and shepherded it into law over seven years. You'll debate and discuss the bill just as we did, using words drawn from the actual legislative history.

These are words said or written, for example, in the House and Senate chambers, Congressional committees, press conferences, Congressional correspondence and reports, White House events and correspondence, newspapers, and staff papers.

SEE IT

I call this a visual case study because just as responsibility is the best teacher, to me, seeing is learning. I want to put a human face on the legislative process.

I've included several hundred visuals in the form of illustrations, quotations, and photos that I hope will bring the case study alive for you.

I've divided the case study into 17 chapters, many of which depict how the legislative road is filled with "potholes."

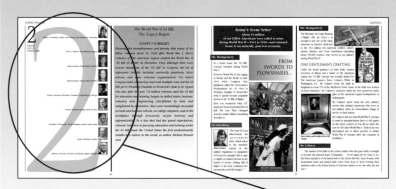

SAY IT

All of the substantive debate appears on the pages. **Sonny's Cast of Characters** tells you who is talking. By reading their words, you, in effect, say them for yourself.

HEAR IT

You'll hear the story from me firsthand, as I'm your host and guide in the form of moderator.

At the beginning of each chapter, you'll see **Sonny's Summary**—a useful overview—and **Sonny's Scene Setter.**

In Chapters 5 to 14, you'll also see the **Legislative Journey Guide**, which tells you where we are on the Legislative Journey chart on pages 10-11.

At the end of each chapter you'll see what I call **Sonny's Lessons Learned.**

Also at the end of that chapter is a section called **Worth Repeating**—featuring the most instructive statements.

SONNY'S LEARNING OBJECTIVES

Our goal is to:

- Learn the origins of—and factors that shaped—the Montgomery GI Bill and its relationship to the All-Volunteer Force;

- Learn the reality and challenge of writing the Montgomery GI Bill into law through problem identification, enactment, and implementation;

- Learn the prominent roles played by subcommittees and full committees functioning as "little legislatures;" and

- Learn the art of policy development, as practiced (as in "trial and error") by the legislative and executive branches and interest groups through visuals we hope will bring the case study to life for you.

U.S. House of Representatives

THE LEGISLATIVE JOURNEY

Congressman G.V. "Sonny" Montgomery and colleagues consult with military service branches/stakeholder groups.

H-1   Introduction of H.R. 1400 Veterans' Educational Assistance Act of 1981, the New GI Bill ....Feb. 28, 1981

H-2   House Veterans' Affairs Committee mark-up of H.R. 1400..May 19, 1981

H-3   House Armed Services Committee mark-up of H.R. 1400 with amendments ....May 11, 1982

H-4   Reintroduction of H.R. 1400 Veterans' Educational Assistance Act of 1983, the New GI Bill ....Feb. 20, 1983

H-5   House Veterans' Affairs Committee mark-up of H.R. 1400 ....May 12, 1983

H-6   Introduction of H.R. 5167 DoD Authorization Act, FY 1985, including New GI Bill Provision ....February 1, 1984

H-7   House Armed Services Committee mark-up of H.R. 1400 ....April 19, 1984

H-8   U.S. House of Representatives passage of H.R. 5167 ....May 31, 1984

H-9   U.S. House of Representatives passage of H.R. 5167 Conference Report, New GI Bill 3-Year Program............Sept. 26, 1984

President Ronald Reagan signs DoD Authorization Act, 1985

New GI Bill 3-Year Program

H-10   Introduction of H.R. 1085, New GI Bill Continuation Act ....Feb. 11, 1987

H-11   House Veterans' Affairs Committee mark-up of H.R. 1085 ....March 4, 1987

H-12   House Armed Services Committee mark-up of H.R. 1085 ....March 11, 1987

H-13   U.S. House of Representatives passage of H.R. 1085, as amended ....March 17, 1987

H-14   U.S. House of Representatives' acceptance of Compromise Agreement on H.R. 1085, as amended ....May 13, 1987

Speaker of House and President Pro Tempore of Senate

Signature on Enrolled Bill

President Ronald Reagan signs Montgomery GI Bill

1980 TO 1987

1980 • Departure

1979 and 1980 .... Introduction of S. 2020, S. 2596, and S. 3263*	S-1
Feb. 5, 1981 .... Introduction of S. 417 All-Volunteer Force Educational Assistance Act	S-2
Jan. 8, Mar. 7, and Aug. 3, 1983 .. Introduction of S. 8, S. 691, and S. 1747, New GI Bill	S-3
July 13, 1983............. Senate disapproval, Armstrong New GI Bill Amendment to DoD Authorization Act, FY 1984	S-4
May 31, 1984 .... Introduction/mark-up of S. 2723, Omnibus Defense Authorization Act, FY 1985	S-5
June 11-13, 1984 ...... Senate approval of Glenn Citizen-Soldier Pilot Education Program Amendment to S. 2723	S-6
June 20, 1984 .... U.S. Senate passage of S. 2723	S-7
Sept. 27, 1984 .... U.S. Senate passage of H.R. 5167 Conference Report, including New GI Bill 3-Year Program	S-8

Oct. 19, 1984 • Halfway Point

Jan. 6, 1987................ Introduction of S. 12, New GI Bill Continuation Act	S-9
Feb. 26, 1987 .... Senate Veterans' Affairs Committee mark-up of S. 12, as amended	S-10
April 30, 1987............ Senate Armed Services Committee mark-up of S. 12, as amended	S-11
May 8, 1987 .... U.S. Senate incorporation of S. 12 language into H.R. 1085, as amended	S-12
May 13, 1987 .... U.S. Senate acceptance of compromise agreement on H.R. 1085, as amended	S-13

May 19, 1987 • H.R. 1085, as amended

*Armed Forces Earned Educational Assistance Act, Veterans' Educational Assistance Act of 1980, and All-Volunteer Educational Assistance Act of 1980, respectively.

June 1, 1987 • Destination

1

SONNY'S CAST OF CHARACTERS

Honorable William "Bill" Cohen, Secretary of Defense, Senator (R-ME), and member of House of Representatives (R-ME)

Representative G.V. "Sonny" Montgomery (D-MS), Chairman, Committee on Veterans' Affairs

This is "Sonny:" Honorable Bill Cohen

SONNY'S SUMMARY

My friend Bill Cohen, a former Secretary of Defense, United States Senator, and Representative, graciously highlights in his own words my nearly 40 years in public life. This included 30 years representing Mississippi's Third Congressional District, chairing the Veterans' Affairs Committee for 14 years, and serving under seven presidents. Secretary Cohen also speaks about how we successfully worked together on national defense issues, even though he and I were from different generations, regions of the country, bodies of the legislature, and political parties. Senator Cohen's early leadership and long-term commitment to creating a permanent New GI Bill made a real difference.

Sonny's Scene Setter

Bill Cohen in Bangor, Maine,
and G.V. Montgomery in Meridian, Mississippi.

Mr. Cohen

Bill Cohen

Ladies and gentlemen, my name is Bill Cohen. You'll be joining G.V. "Sonny" Montgomery on the long and sometimes bumpy legislative road traveled by a measure that Congress enacted into permanent law in 1987…

THE REAL THING…

the All-Volunteer Force educational assistance program known as the "Montgomery GI Bill." The forerunner of the Montgomery GI Bill was the "New GI Bill" enacted in 1984, also under Sonny's leadership.

ABOUT SONNY

I'm honored that Meridian's Montgomery Institute and Mississippi State University have asked me to introduce Sonny Montgomery to America's government, public administration, public policy, and politics students.

Through a lifetime of public service, Mr. Montgomery has been able to work with persons in all branches of government and both political parties.

Indeed, when I was Secretary of Defense, a U.S. Senator and a Congressman, Sonny and I worked together, especially on the All-Volunteer Force educational assistance program that bears his name. His vision and leadership made a difference.[1]

It did not matter to Sonny that I was a Republican and he was a Democrat; or that I was a Senator and he a Congressman; or that I hailed from Maine and Sonny from Mississippi; or that he and I were from different generations. And it didn't, because Sonny's rural roots made him what we call a "workhorse" rather than a "show horse." Sonny knew how to work with people as a team and treat them

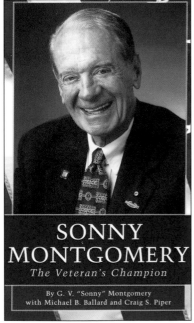

SONNY MONTGOMERY
The Veteran's Champion

By G. V. "Sonny" Montgomery
with Michael B. Ballard and Craig S. Piper

with respect. He had good ideas, and he was a powerful listener.

They say that "politics is the art of the possible."[2] I'm not sure it's just politics, though. I think that a good idea—one that stands or falls on its own merit—becomes the art of the doable.

Elected to the U.S. House of Representatives in 1966, G.V. Montgomery represented Mississippi's Third District in Congress for 15 terms, serving under seven presidents. His autobiography, *Sonny Montgomery: The Veteran's Champion*, provides a very personal history of his nearly 40 years in public life.[3]

Sonny during World War II.

Sonny's advocacy for veterans, the lodestar of his career, came from personal experience and conviction. During World War II, as a young lieutenant serving with the 12th Armored Division, he helped capture a German machine gun nest and earned the Bronze Star Medal for Valor.

He returned to duty with the 31st National Guard Infantry Division during the Korean Conflict. He had a long and distinguished career in the Mississippi National Guard, retiring with the rank of Major General. His military service spanned 35 years.[4]

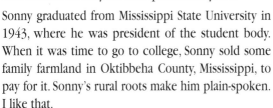

Sonny's senior portrait from Mississippi State University.

Sonny graduated from Mississippi State University in 1943, where he was president of the student body. When it was time to go to college, Sonny sold some family farmland in Oktibbeha County, Mississippi, to pay for it. Sonny's rural roots make him plain-spoken. I like that.

George H.W. Bush and Sonny were both elected to Congress in 1966. They were sworn in during the same ceremony in January 1967. They personally met later that day in the House gym.[5]

And they've been friends ever since.[6]

Sonny's bipartisan spirit and vision for the men and women of our military made it easy for me to work with him.

George H.W. Bush and Sonny as freshmen in Congress.

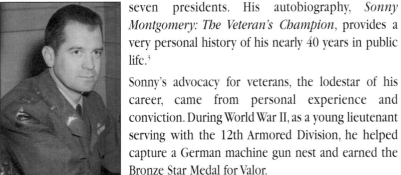

Sonny, First Lady Barbara Bush and President George H.W. Bush remained close friends throughout his life.

A champion of veterans, Sonny often visited soldiers in the field during the Vietnam Conflict.

Indeed Sonny spent each Christmas—from his freshman year in Congress in 1967 until the Vietnam Conflict ended in 1973—visiting our soldiers in the field.[7]

Sonny's portrait hangs in the Veterans' Affairs Committee hearing room in the House of Representatives. The National Guard Association of the U.S., the U.S. Court of Appeals for Veterans Claims and other organizations also display portraits of Sonny in their offices.

Thank you for the privilege of introducing Sonny Montgomery. I think you'll learn a good deal from him about the art of legislative leadership. Greatest luck to each of you.

Sonny's portrait at the National Guard Association of the U.S. in Washington, D.C.

ABOUT THE SECRETARY

Mr. Montgomery

BILL COHEN PERSONIFIES PUBLIC SERVICE...

Thank you, Mr. Secretary. I appreciate your kind words.

We have worked together on many legislative initiatives and especially on the Montgomery GI Bill.

Senator Cohen's early leadership and long-term commitment made a real difference. Indeed, working primarily with the Non Commissioned Officers Association of the United States and the National Association of State Approving Agencies as early as 1979, Senator Cohen introduced legislation that would create a better GI Bill to encourage educationally motivated young men and women to consider military service.[8]

Again in 1983, Senator Cohen and Senator Bill Armstrong (R-CO) introduced similar legislation and stood on the Senate floor making what they felt was a persuasive case for improved All-Volunteer Force education benefits, only to be narrowly defeated on procedural grounds.[9] Indeed, I believe Bill Cohen personifies public service. Bill Cohen served in the U.S. House of Representatives, the U.S. Senate, and on the President's cabinet. I think that's pretty extraordinary.

In 1974, during his very first term in Congress, *Time* Magazine named Bill Cohen as one of "America's 200 Future Leaders."[10]

Mr. Cohen attained national prominence as a freshman Republican Congressman when the House Judiciary Committee selected him to build the evidentiary base for the impeachment of President Richard Nixon. In the Senate, he served as Chairman of the Committee on Aging and Vice Chairman of the Select Committee on Intelligence.

After 18 years of distinguished leadership in the Senate, President Bill Clinton asked Senator Cohen to serve as Secretary of Defense. This represented another "first"—because it was the first time I know of in modern U.S. history a President chose an elected official from the opposite political party to be a member of his cabinet.[11]

Following 31 years of public leadership, Secretary Cohen leaves behind a record of unparalleled accomplishment, integrity, and respect.[12]

He leaves something else behind, too: an important part of the title of this book is our use of the word *journey!* On May 13, 1987—some eight years after he first introduced legislation—the Senate approved H.R. 1085 that created the Montgomery GI Bill by a vote of 89-0.

Noted Senator Cohen on the Senate floor in 1987, "the battle was not an easy one… .This is truly a historic day, and it is all the more remarkable when we consider how difficult the **journey** [emphasis added] has been… ."[13]

Mr. Secretary, your vision and durability played a special role in our informal team reaching its destination. And your vision continues today in international business.

Thank you again, sir.

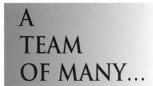

Working with then-Senator Cohen and a fabulous team of many people[14] over about seven years to create a permanent GI Bill educational assistance program for our youth proved to be a wonderful experience.

As I said on the House floor when the House passed the Montgomery GI Bill legislation March 17, 1987, I was one man on an informal team of people committed to making our "all-volunteer" military successful and offering post-service educational opportunity to our youth. It was a team effort and not really about me.[15]

When I say our informal team, I mean members of Congress, leaders from each military service, representatives of the veterans/military personnel[16]/higher education groups, certain members of the media, and some courageous leaders in the executive branch who all worked cooperatively to make the bill a reality.

THE JOURNEY

Here's how it started. We discontinued drafting 19-year-old men into our military in 1973.[17] By 1980, I thought our all-volunteer military concept would fail if we did not create a quality, post-military service educational scholarship as an incentive for our youth to serve, and to give them access to post-secondary education and training, as well.

My colleagues and I felt we would get better enlistees through an educational incentive than we could with, for example, a one-time cash bonus to enlist.

Monetary bonuses could be used to encourage our youth to serve in specific, hard-to-fill military occupational specialties; these especially included Army combat arms specialties—infantry, armor, artillery, and combat engineer.

We called this post-service educational incentive the New GI Bill. My colleagues and I began working on a New GI Bill in 1980 and introduced legislation to create it in 1981. It was a New GI Bill in that—for the first time—America would use the GI Bill to encourage youth to enlist voluntarily instead of drafting them. The New GI Bill was also a new concept because it would exist **permanently**, whether or not the nation was at war.

Senator Cohen, General Maxwell Thurman and Sonny in 1985.

The New GI Bill replaced a much weaker and less attractive program called the Post-Vietnam Era Educational Assistance Program, commonly known as VEAP, established January 1, 1977, in Public Law 94-502. VEAP proved largely unsuccessful because few service members signed up for it or used it. (We discuss VEAP later in our journey.)

Congress initiated the New GI Bill for a three-year period. It was limited to service members entering the military from July 1, 1985, to June 30, 1988.

As part of this 1985-1988 test program, America's youth responded to the New GI Bill in droves,[18] particularly those who scored in the upper quartiles on the Armed Forces Qualification Test.

In 1987, after extensive debate and a highly effective lobbying effort by parts of the higher education, the military personnel, and veterans communities, Congress made the New GI Bill the law of the land, as a permanent program. To my surprise, Congress named it after me. I was deeply honored.

But many people shared and guided our vision for this different kind of GI Bill program. In many respects, the Montgomery GI Bill represents the first permanent GI Bill in the history of our republic.[19]

As I see it, the story of the Montgomery GI Bill is one of national purpose, initiative, and opportunity.

Since 1985, more than 2.3 million former servicemen and women have used it for post-military education and training.[20]

Currently, as private citizens, these veterans represent valued leaders of our domestic economy as teachers, engineers, doctors, bankers, pilots, law enforcement officials, firefighters, small business owners, public servants, and many other professions.

Folks, I'd like each chapter's "lessons learned" to speak to the realities of writing laws rather than generalities associated with legislative theory. What did you learn in this chapter?

INITIATIVE AND OPPORTUNITY...

1

Sonny's Lessons Learned

I'd say what I'd want you to learn is the way Senator Bill Cohen and I worked together for seven years, even though Mr. Cohen and I were different in so many ways. We came from different political parties, parts of the legislature, regions of the country, and generations. Success requires reaching out to people. And it worked both ways—me to Mr. Cohen, and he to me. We all get things done through and with others, especially in a democracy.

Worth Repeating

"Sonny's rural roots make him plain spoken.
I like that."

—*Honorable Bill Cohen*

"Indeed, working with
the Non Commissioned Officers Association
of the United States and the
National Association of State Approving Agencies
as early as 1979, Senator Cohen introduced
legislation that would create a better GI Bill
to encourage educationally motivated
young men and women
to consider military service."

—*G. V. "Sonny" Montgomery*

"Bill Cohen served in the U.S. House of
Representatives, the U.S. Senate,
and on the President's Cabinet."

—*G. V. "Sonny" Montgomery*

"In 1974, during his very first term in Congress,
Time Magazine named Bill Cohen as one of
'America's 200 Future Leaders.'"

—*G. V. "Sonny" Montgomery*

"Following 31 years of public leadership, Senator
Cohen indeed leaves behind a record of unparalleled
accomplishment, integrity, and respect."

—*G. V. "Sonny" Montgomery*

WHAT'S NEXT

Let's move to both the origin and unique history of the World War II GI Bill of Rights. My colleagues and I like to think of the Montgomery GI Bill as the modern day version—and "direct descendant"—of this hugely successful education and training program that we'll learn about in Chapter 2.

2

SONNY'S
CAST OF
CHARACTERS[1]

Milton Greenberg, Author and Provost, The American University

Harry Colmery, The American Legion

Representative Edith Rogers (R-MA)

Representative Dewey Short (D-MO)

Robert Maynard Hutchins, President, University of Chicago

Senator Bennett Champ Clark (D-MO)

Franklin D. Roosevelt, 32nd President of the United States

James Michener, Author

Anthony Principi, Secretary of Veterans Affairs, 2001-2005

The World War II GI Bill: The Legacy Begins

SONNY'S SUMMARY

Knowing the unemployment and poverty that many of his fellow veterans faced in 1918 after World War I, Harry Colmery of The American Legion drafted the World War II "GI Bill of Rights" in December 1943. Although there were several champions of the "GI Bill" in Congress, the list of opponents initially included university presidents, labor unions, and some veterans' organizations. Not before Congress held 22 hearings and took multiple votes did the GI Bill get to President Franklin D. Roosevelt's desk to be signed into law. After the war, 7.8 million veterans used the GI Bill for education and training, largely in skilled trades, business, industry, and engineering. Disciplined by duty and enlightened by experience,[2] they were resoundingly successful at trade and business schools, on college campuses, and in the workplace through structured, on-job training and apprenticeships. In a law that had few grand expectations, veterans' initiative in pursuing education and training under the GI Bill made the United States the first predominantly middle-class nation in the world, as author Michael Bennett said.

Mr. Montgomery

In a broad sense, the "GI Bill" concept emerged during World War I.[4]

However, World War II was raging in Europe and the Pacific in June 1944 when Congress sent legislation called the Servicemen's Readjustment Act of 1944 to President Franklin D. Roosevelt's desk. It quickly became popularly known as the "GI Bill of Rights."

Have you wondered what "GI" stands for? In his book titled *The GI Bill: The Law That Changed America*, author Milton Greenberg describes it.

Dr. Greenberg

Milton Greenberg

"The term GI is an abbreviation for 'government issue,' which refers to the standardization of the military regulations or equipment (GI boots, for example). But it came to signify an enlisted person in any branch of service. Adding 'Bill of Rights' to the term combined two enormously powerful images." [5,6]

FROM SWORDS TO PLOWSHARES…

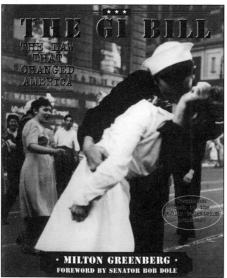

★ MILTON GREENBERG ★
FOREWORD BY SENATOR BOB DOLE

Mr. Montgomery

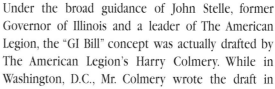

The 8th Army[7] Air Corps Museum ("Mighty 8th Air Force") in Georgia is just one of the many museums in America dedicated to the 15.6 million GIs, American soldiers, sailors, airmen, Marines, and Coast Guardsmen—including about 350,000 women—who served in our military during World War II.[8]

ONE GENTLEMAN'S CRAFTING

Under the broad guidance of John Stelle, former Governor of Illinois and a leader of The American Legion, the "GI Bill" concept was actually drafted by The American Legion's Harry Colmery. While in Washington, D.C., Mr. Colmery wrote the draft in longhand in room 570 of the Mayflower Hotel. Some of the draft was written on hotel stationery.[9] Mr. Colmery's extensive drafts are now preserved under glass at The American Legion headquarters in Indianapolis.

Harry Colmery and his drafts of the GI Bill concept.

Mr. Colmery knew from his own military service that ordinary Americans who serve in our military often do extraordinary things in service to their nation.

Mr. Colmery did not want World War II veterans to stand in unemployment lines or sell apples on the street corners, as was all too often the case in 1918 after World War I.[10] Indeed, he was determined not to allow poverty to define World War II veterans after the cessation of hostilities.[11]

Mr. Colmery

"…The burden of war falls on the citizen soldier who has gone forth, overnight to become the armored hope of humanity… . Never again, do we want to see the honor and glory of our nation fade to the extent that her 'men of arms,' with despondent heart and palsied limb, totter from door to door, bowing their untamed souls to the frozen bosom of reluctant charity, as we saw after the last war." [12]

Mr. Montgomery

One of the principal legislative architects of the World War II GI Bill of Rights was Representative John Rankin (D-MS),[13] and Chairman of the House Committee on World War Veterans' Legislation.[14]

Michael Bennett, author of *When Dreams Came True—The GI Bill and The Making of Modern America*, had the following to say about Mr. Rankin, who also co-authored legislation creating the Tennessee Valley Authority and the Rural Electrification Authority.

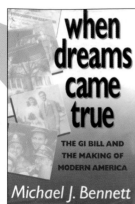

Mr. Bennett

"Rankin was one of the most effective legislators in the history of the House; a master of parliamentary procedure; a brilliant, if vicious orator; a staunch proponent of public electrical power for the poor; and a defender of both servicemen/women and veterans, although not a veteran himself. He was not bashful about making himself heard."[15]

John Rankin

Mr. Montgomery

Author Bennett also quoted Russell Whelan's July 1944 article in the magazine *The Nation*, titled "Rankin of Mississippi:"

Mr. Bennett

"Rankin made more speeches devouring more minutes than anyone in Congress. When he was in full oratorical flight, a bony arm is thrust upward the skylight, the strands of the grey mop began to wave like reeds in a gale, and the chords of the Tupelo calliope [pronounced cal **eye** o pee] are tweaking every solar plexus in the place.[16]

"Rankin generally was a strong supporter of states' rights but not when it came to a GI Bill and 'the Federal government that these boys were representing on the battlefield.'[17]

"Although a supporter of segregation common in the South at the time, Rankin wanted 'to protect the rights of smaller schools, including some Negro institutions.'[18]

"Indeed, when the American Council on Education initially opposed the GI Bill due to perceived, excessive federal control of education policy[19] and other reasons, Rankin's reaction was extreme. It transfigured him into a champion of unrestricted access to education—even for blacks."[20]

ONE LADY'S PERSUASION

Mr. Montgomery

Edith Rogers

Another prime mover of the bill in the House of Representatives was Republican Edith Rogers of Massachusetts, the ranking member of the Committee on World War Veterans' Legislation (that Congress after World War II would rename as the Committee on Veterans' Affairs).

During World War I, Mrs. Rogers traveled to Europe with the Women's Overseas Service inspecting field hospitals. She authored the legislation creating the Women's Auxiliary Army Corps, later known as the Women's Army Corps.[21]

The sixth woman elected to Congress, Mrs. Rogers served in the House from 1925 to 1960—35 years.

Her portrait, in which she was wearing her trademark rose, still hangs above the chairman's seat in the subcommittee hearing room of the House Committee on Veterans' Affairs.[22]

Mrs. Rogers took on the president of Harvard and others who portrayed the proposed GI Bill as a "special interest" of a lobbying group, The American Legion. Said Mrs. Rogers on the House floor…

Mrs. Rogers

"With reference to the educators calling The American Legion a powerful lobby, I think the American press is as strongly behind this measure as is the American public. It seems to me it is an all-over-the-country lobby."[23]

Mr. Montgomery

Illustrative of some of the initial opposition in Congress to the GI Bill is the statement of Representative Dewey Short of Missouri:

Mr. Short

"Have we gone completely crazy? Have we lost all sense of proportion? How are you going to pay for this bill? You [members] think you are going to bribe the veteran and buy his vote, you who think you can win his support by coddling him and being a sob sister with a lot of silly, slushy sentimentality[24] are going to have a sad awakening."[25]

Dewey Short

Mr. Montgomery

The "awakening" instead was a happy one.

Notwithstanding the ultimate success of the World War II GI Bill in making the United States the first predominantly middle-class nation in the world,[26] Milton Greenberg further summarizes the opposition to the bill... [27]

" ... THE FIRST PREDOMINANTLY MIDDLE-CLASS NATION IN THE WORLD... "

—*Author Michael Bennett*

Dr. Greenberg

"Other veterans' organizations [than The American Legion] dedicated to the disabled veterans feared that funds would be diverted from the most needy. Unions enjoying the protection of closed shops were cautious, and bankers feared government involvement in loans. And racial discrimination, legally commonplace at the time, including segregated military forces, became an issue regarding opportunities for black veterans."

Mr. Montgomery

Students, we are focusing on the education and job training part of the WW II GI Bill because it represented economic empowerment. But the WW II GI Bill also included benefits to allow a veteran to receive medical care, vocational rehabilitation, loans for purchasing homes and starting small businesses, job placement, unemployment compensation, and other forms of assistance.[28]

Robert Maynard Hutchins, president of the University of Chicago, was one of the most vocal opponents of the World War II GI Bill legislation.

Mr. Hutchins

"Colleges and universities will find themselves converted into educational hobo jungles. ... Education is not a device for coping with mass unemployment."[29]

Robert M. Hutchins

Mr. Montgomery

As we will discuss in Chapter 3, Cloyd Marvin, a World War I veteran and president of George Washington University during World War II, and Selma Borchardt,[30] president of the American Federation of Teachers, disagreed with Hutchins.[31]

So did Senate Majority Leader Ernest McFarland (D-AZ) and Senate Finance Subcommittee Chairman Bennett Champ Clark (D-MI). Noted Senator Clark:[32]

Ernest McFarland

Mr. Clark

"... The men and women who compose our armed forces not only hold the safety of our republic in their hands on the battlefronts today; they will hold its destiny for a generation to come... .

"By the time this war is over... more than 13,000,000 of our finest men and women will have seen service in our armed forces. They represent the cream of our human resources, the very backbone of our nation. This republic can ill afford to lose their skills and leadership.

Champ Clark

"Yet that leadership and those skills have been rudely interrupted by war. Education has been halted, the men to whom we must look for the future of business, commerce, industry, and agriculture have been torn from their civilian posts... .

"We must recapture those skills and that leadership... . I regard the GI Bill of Rights, passed by the Senate last week... as one of the most important measures that has ever come before Congress."

ONE CONGRESSMAN'S SCAMPER

Mr. Montgomery

Indeed, following fully 22 public hearings in the House[33] and extensive debate, it took a midnight scamper back to the capitol by Representative John S. Gibson (D-GA) to break a 3-3 vote deadlock in a House-Senate Conference Committee on the proposed GI Bill.[34]

'44 Model Paul Revere Rides to Washington to Save Rights Bill

Daring Dash from Southern Georgia, Through Rain and Darkness, Saves Legislation

All the elements of a motion picture play — drama, suspense, a wild drive across country at night through a driving rain, an airplane flight, and the surprise finish that made right and justice triumphant —were part of the closing sessions of the joint Senate-House conference committee when a compromise on The American Legion's Bill of Rights for War II veterans, acceptable to both houses, was agreed upon.

The leading character was Representative John S. Gibson, member of the lower House from Georgia's Eighth District. He was the 1944 model Paul Revere who rode through the night, braving dangers that the 1775 Paul could not dream

REP. JOHN S. GIBSON.

Folks, you may find interesting that some 40 years later it took a lot of hearings, too.

From 1980 to 1987, the House of Representatives alone had 19 hearings on the legislation to create the New GI Bill that Congress later named the Montgomery GI Bill.

These 19 hearings from 1980 to 1987 included 12 by the Armed Services Subcommittee on Personnel and Compensation and seven by the Veterans' Affairs Subcommittee on Education, Training, and Employment."[35]

President Franklin D. Roosevelt signs the GI Bill in 1944.

When signing the WW II GI Bill some two weeks after D-Day, President Roosevelt probably did not anticipate the GI Bill would become arguably "the most successful piece of domestic legislation since the Homestead Act of 1862."[36]

As he signed the original GI Bill in 1944, Roosevelt said the legislation…[37]

President Roosevelt

"[G]ave emphatic notice to the men and women of our armed forces that the American people do not intend to let them down."[38]

Mr. Montgomery

How do you think soldiers, sailors, airmen, and Marines learned about the GI Bill in the midst of war?[39]

ONE SAILOR'S STORY

Let me share with you the thoughts expressed by James Michener, the American novelist. Mr. Michener wrote at age 86:[40]

Mr. Michener

James Michener

"In 1944, while the war was still raging and I was on a lonely island in the distant South Pacific, the Navy informed us that a remarkable law had just been passed by Congress to reward those who were fighting.

"Its official title, the Servicemen's Readjustment Act of 1944, was rarely used because a popular simplification took over: the GI Bill.

"It said our nation, out of gratitude for the sacrifices being made by our men and women in arms, promised a free education, or assistance in finding a place in society when peace came, to every veteran.

"'A free college degree!' shouted the man who brought us the news.

"As a junior officer who saw thousands of military personnel in those years when I prowled the South Pacific, I saw the powerful effect[41] this offer had on various types of men.

"My friend Joe told me: 'I've always wanted to be a doctor,' and became one. Another was tired of working for others and wanted a business education so that he could start his own small factory, and would get both.

"I decided to take my chances at being a writer."

General Douglas MacArthur wades ashore during initial landings at Leyte, Philippines, October, 1944.

Mr. Montgomery

As the war neared conclusion, the GI Bill was there for the taking…[42]

All this at the very time that our sailors hung from every crevice of the *USS Missouri* to witness the Japanese surrender in Tokyo Bay…

Aboard the USS Missouri as the Japanese formally surrender.

The war was over. The sign below tells it all![43] The war was over for this guy in Times Square, too.

Families await their returning soldiers.

Celebrating war's end in Times Square.

The extent of selfless sacrifice was immense. As an example, 3,812 officers and men from the 8th U.S. Army Air Corps alone are buried at Cambridge, England.[44] Cambridge University donated the cemetery land on behalf of the British people.[45]

Folks, I want to take a few minutes now to describe for you—starting here and at the beginning of the next chapter—the profound effect the World War II GI Bill had on America.[46]

U.S. Cemetery, Cambridge, England.

I think it is important for you to know the bill's impact because, like Harry Colmery, I saw ordinary people do extraordinary things both during the war—while in combat—and after the war, in the classroom.

As Michael Bennett points out, the GI Bill's "unintended consequences were even greater than its intended purposes;"[47] veterans did not just pass through American higher education, they transformed it, as we'll discuss shortly.[48]

Veterans become students.

Of the 7.8 million veterans who used the GI Bill, 2.23 million attended colleges; 3.48 million attended other schools such as trade schools, business schools, and high schools; 1.4 million participated in on-job training; and 690,000 received institutional on-farm training.[49]

The results?

According to the Veterans Administration, the World War II GI Bill produced 2,600,000 skilled tradesmen and women, 1,375,500 businessmen and women, 451,000 engineers, 238,240 teachers, 175,000 scientists, 66,000 doctors, 22,000 dentists, and 12,000 nurses.[50]

What do you think, class? Pretty impressive, no?

10 NOBEL PRIZE WINNERS

Author Milt Greenberg notes at least 10 Nobel Prize winners were former GIs.[51]

Dr. Greenberg

"About 50 percent of the engineers who worked for the National Aeronautics and Space Administration (NASA) were veterans and I think many of whom, without the GI Bill, would not otherwise have gone to college.

"Spurred by wartime applications of science and technology, college-educated GIs contributed to a scientific revolution in television, computers, civil engineering, medicine, chemistry, physics, space exploration, and a continuing tradition of invention."[52]

Mr. Montgomery

Many of these individuals were the first in their families[53] to graduate from college or formal technical training. The Veterans Administration and the colleges/training institutions provided the opportunity, and the veterans provided the initiative—what Michael Bennett called "the American creed in action."[54] In 2000, Anthony Principi looked back, especially with respect to those who were enrolled in college-level training...

Mr. Principi

Anthony Principi (right) joins President George W. Bush (center) during a Washington ceremony honoring veterans.

"Veterans excelled in the classroom, ran the student governments, challenged professors, refused to wear freshman 'beanies,' began raising families, and some veterans did something that was seen as rather unusual—they went to school year 'round."[55]

Mr. Montgomery

I think these veterans at the University of Nebraska are good examples of the initiative Secretary Principi refers to. This was the case all across America.

World War II veterans flocked to schools like the University of Nebraska, taking pre-entry tests (left) and eventually registering for classes (below).

Sonny's Lessons Learned

Students, you'll hear a lot about unintended, negative consequences of laws and lawmaking; phrases like "those were not the results we [Congress] had in mind" or "instead of fixing it, Congress has created more problems."

Despite the best efforts of our elected representatives, unintended consequences do occur.[56] I think they most often occur when legislation addresses "symptoms" of problems—rather than the problems themselves.

But unintended consequences can be positive! I think author Michael Bennett best made this point: "The World War II GI Bill's unintended consequences exceeded its intended purposes." No one expected 7.8 million veterans to enroll in college and other forms of training, benefiting themselves and society alike.

The stated purpose of the World War II GI Bill was not to create a "learned society" or a "knowledge generation." Its purpose was simply to help millions of ex-GIs transition to civilian life after the war, avoiding serious unemployment.

Worth Repeating

"When [Representative Rankin] was in full oratorical flight, a bony arm is thrust upward the skylight, the strands of the grey mop began to wave like reeds in a gale, and the chords of the Tupelo calliope are tweaking every solar plexus in the place."
—*Author Michael Bennett*

"The World War II GI Bill produced 2,600,000 skilled tradesmen and women, 1,375,500 businessmen and women, 451,000 engineers, 238,240 teachers, 175,000 scientists, 66,000 doctors, 22,000 dentists, and 12,000 nurses."
—*Veterans Administration, 1969*

"Spurred by wartime applications of science and technology, college-educated GIs contributed to a scientific revolution in television, computers, civil engineering, medicine, chemistry, physics, space exploration, and a continuing tradition of invention."
—*Author Milton Greenberg*

"Veterans excelled in the classroom, ran the student governments, challenged professors, refused to wear freshman 'beanies,' began raising families, and some veterans did something that was seen as rather unusual—they went to school year 'round."
—*Anthony Principi*

WHAT'S NEXT

In the next chapter, we'll discuss the continued, unanticipated success of the World War II GI Bill of Rights, a law that worked beyond expectation.

3

*Cloyd Marvin, President,
George Washington University*

*Selma Borchardt, Vice President,
American Federation of Teachers*

James Conant, President, Harvard University

Nathan M. Pusey, President, Harvard University

*First Sergeant Willis Messiah,
Architecture Graduate,
The Catholic University of America*

Elmer Ellis, President, University of Missouri

Peter Drucker, Author

Suzanne Mettler, Professor, Cornell University

***Also featured in this chapter:
Edward Markey
Michael Bennett
Milton Greenberg
Anthony Principi***

The World War II GI Bill and Beyond:
The Legacy Continues

SONNY'S SUMMARY

The GI Bill was arguably our most successful domestic program ever. We'll learn from author Michael Bennett that part of "America's postwar motivation was fear; fear of another economic depression and what might happen to the country when we dumped 12 million troops into an economy potentially on the brink of bankruptcy when the mills of war stopped grinding." However, the $14.5 billion cost of the WW II GI Bill paid for itself by 1960 due to taxes paid on additional income earned by GI Bill graduates. These revenues helped fund the Marshall Plan's $12.5 billion to rebuild war-torn Europe. And author Peter Drucker will tell us "the GI Bill of Rights and American veterans' enthusiastic response to it signaled an unplanned shift to a knowledge society."

Mr. Montgomery

Let's hear from some educators, students, and government leaders about this enduring piece of legislation and its impact.[1] Twelve speakers will help us with this topic.[2]

If you learn about the effects of just one bill passed by Congress, I think the World War II GI Bill should be the one, because, arguably, it was the most successful ever.[3]

Each speaker has a different reference point on the legislation's design and depth. Legislation that ends up great doesn't always start great.

First, World War I veteran, Cloyd Marvin, 1943 president of George Washington University and chairman of the Commission of National Educational Associations [on postwar education], saw the bill's potential in what I would call a selfless way:[4]

Dr. Marvin

"Have in mind that today I am not speaking of colleges and universities. I am speaking of education. If that boy needs a six-month course on how to plant something in a technical school in Texas, or how to plant alfalfa in Wisconsin, let us make sure he gets it."

Dr. Cloyd Marvin

Mr. Montgomery

Second, Selma Borchardt, vice president, American Federation of Teachers, was also focused on the veteran:[5]

Ms. Borchardt

"When the first draft of the bill came before us we were simply shocked at many of the unfortunate provisions in it, and many of the vitally essential principles that were omitted from it. We are very happy to see that most of those unfortunate

Selma Borchardt

provisions have been deleted. For example, the original bill would have denied 93 percent of the men in the service the benefit of training by a stilted process of selection. That bill introduced provided that [only] those servicemen who were 'selected' should have training.

"The bill also provided that servicemen should be **assigned** [emphasis added] for training, thereby denying a man the right to determine for himself the kind of training he wanted.... We are grateful to you gentlemen for having eradicated many of the unfortunate provisions that were in the original bill.... We do feel there should be further recognition given to the fact that in every possible way that education is not limited to a classroom. I say this even though, or perhaps because, I speak as a teacher.

"... The original draft seemed to place great emphasis on the purely academic [classroom] approach.... The practical value of education cannot be measured in terms of credits of an approved education. We believe that something more real and more vital is needed. The bill does now—we are very happy to see the improvement—take formal recognition of the federal apprenticeship program."

Mr. Montgomery

Third, James Conant, president of Harvard University, had a close relationship with President Franklin D. Roosevelt because, as a world-class chemistry professor, Conant served as a key advisor on the Manhattan Project for developing the atomic bomb.

Initially, Dr. Conant was a strong advocate of IQ testing as a criterion for college admission and felt veterans would be an academic liability on campus.[6] However, in 1948, President Conant observed the following:

BEST IN HARVARD'S HISTORY

Dr. Conant

"The mature student body that filled our colleges in 1946 and 1947 was a delight to all who were teaching undergraduates.[7]

"For seriousness, perceptiveness, studiousness, and all other undergraduate virtues, the former soldiers and sailors were the best in Harvard's history."[8]

Dr. James Conant

Mr. Montgomery

Fourth, Nathan M. Pusey, who succeeded Conant as Harvard's president, agrees:

Dr. Pusey

"In the crash period that followed World War II, our university enrollment of veterans ran as high as 9,000 in one year… an able, mature, energetic, determined student body. Graduate school atmosphere became a common feature of the undergraduate campus."[9]

Nathan M. Pusey

Mr. Montgomery

Fifth, Edward Markey, who taught at Princeton University after World War II, shares his experiences:

Mr. Markey

"A college campus was an exciting place to be then. I was not much older than the students. They [veterans] were serious about their studies.

"And they all brought this important life experience to the campus. I remember one of the professors complaining about a vet in his world history class who challenged him on some point saying, 'don't tell me about China. I've been to China!'"[10]

Arriving on campus.

Mr. Montgomery

Folks, see in the next photo all the chevrons on the arm of First Sergeant Willis Messiah, who is standing in the center of the back row?

I bet Sergeant Messiah had been to places like China. And with his rank, one can be assured he was responsible for the lives and actions of a lot of fellow soldiers. Responsibility is a great—albeit stern—teacher.

Sixth, let's hear directly from Sergeant Messiah:

Mr. Messiah

"I served four years in the Army and studied architecture at Catholic University on the GI Bill.[11] I had a 40-year career in architecture. The GI Bill was a generous reward which many did not take advantage of. It was there for veterans, you just had to take advantage of it, but the key was that it was available."[12]

First Sergeant Messiah, back row, center, with his company.

>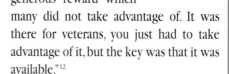
> "I HAD A 40-YEAR CAREER IN ARCHITECTURE."
> —*Former First Sergeant Willis Messiah*

Mr. Montgomery

Seventh, I suspect Dr. Elmer Ellis, president of the University of Missouri during World War II, agrees with architect Willis Messiah:

Dr. Ellis

"It is the virtually unanimous opinion of educators that assistance to veterans… for education after World War II was one of the most tremendous and far-reaching policies ever inaugurated by the government of the United States."[13]

> "… ONE OF THE MOST TREMENDOUS AND FAR-REACHING POLICIES EVER INAUGURATED… "
> —*Dr. Elmer Ellis president, University of Missouri*

Mr. Montgomery

Consider just a few notable World War II GI Bill users. In this group are President George H.W. Bush, President Gerald Ford, Chief Justice of the Supreme Court William Rehnquist, Senator Daniel Inouye, Senator Spark Matsunaga, actor Clint Eastwood, entertainer Ed McMahon, comedian Jonathan Winters, economist Arthur Brimmer, and humorist Art Buchwald.[14]

Clint Eastwood

INITIAL ANXIETY: ULTIMATE PROSPERITY

Eighth, I'd say author Michael Bennett described how an initial anxiety produced ultimate prosperity beyond what anyone reasonably could have expected:

> **"$14.5 BILLION COST... PAID BY ADDITIONAL TAXES ON INCREASED INCOME OF THE GI BILL RECIPIENTS BY 1960."**
> —*Author Michael Bennett*

Mr. Bennett

"America's post-war motivation was fear; fear of another depression and what might happen to the country when we dumped 12 million demobilized troops onto an economy potentially on the edge of bankruptcy when the mills of the war stopped grinding.[15]

"The $14.5 billion cost of the World War II GI Bill was paid by additional taxes on increased income of the GI Bill recipients by 1960. Without the prosperity and the social peace—engendered by the GI Bill—America could not have afforded the Marshall plan's $12.5 billion to rebuild war-torn Europe."[16]

Mr. Montgomery

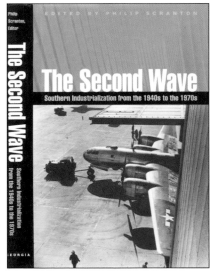

The war itself and the GI Bill revived the economy, especially in my part of the country.

What we refer to economically as the "first wave" of U.S. Southern industrialization lost momentum as the country toppled into the Great Depression in the 1920s. But with the postwar era came a revitalization of the South's industry.

As a Mississippian, I am proud to at least mention to you the book titled *The Second Wave: Southern Industrialization from the 1940s to the 1970s.*[17] The book documents Mississippi's contribution to the war effort and the surge of industry that followed the war.

Ninth, Anthony Principi, Secretary of Veterans Affairs from 2001 to 2005, helped America celebrate the GI Bill's 60th anniversary on June 18, 2004. The Secretary observed the following:

Mr. Principi

Sonny and Anthony Principi.

Principi and veteran Corporal Hector Delgado.

"The GI Bill made homes and a college education available to millions of Americans. By harnessing the drive of America's veterans, it created six decades of opportunity for the men and women who served in uniform. About 22 million veterans and service members have received more than $77 billion in GI Bill benefits for education and training since 1944. The GI Bill's home loan program has been used by [10 million] people for loans totaling $830 billion."[18]

Mr. Montgomery

Lt. Benjamin Callison

The cockpit of the B-17 fortress Callison flew in World War II.

Lt. Ben Callison of Loma, MT, flew 17 combat missions in the European theater and was decorated. After the war, Mr. Callison bought his first home through a VA home loan program. It was near the Los Angeles airport and cost $8,900.[19]

Tenth, Peter Drucker, author and pre-eminent authority on management and leadership, observed the following in 1993:

SHIFT TO A KNOWLEDGE SOCIETY

Mr. Drucker

Peter Drucker

"The GI Bill of Rights and the enthusiastic response to it on the part of America's veterans signaled the shift to a knowledge society.

"Future historians may consider it the most important event of the 20th century. We are clearly in the middle of this transformation [in 1993]; indeed, if history is any guide, it will not be completed until 2010 or 2020. But already it had changed the political, economic, and moral landscape of the world."[20]

Mr. Montgomery

Eleventh, let's hear again from Milton Greenberg, who served many years as provost at The American University in Washington, D.C. As Dr. Greenberg suggests, empower people and good things will happen.

Dr. Greenberg

"A permanent and vital legacy of the educational provisions of the GI Bill is a change in the very idea of who could be a university student. The sons of unemployed depression victims, the sons of immigrants, and the children of sharecroppers were just as smart as the children of wealthy and successful industrial leaders or descendants of those who arrived on the Mayflower. Older people could share classrooms with recent high school graduates and adults could go to school while married, raising children, and working at a job."[21]

> "... A CHANGE TO THE VERY IDEA OF WHO COULD BE A UNIVERSITY STUDENT."
> —*Milton Greenberg, The American University*

Mr. Montgomery

Twelfth and last, Dr. Suzanne Mettler, distinguished professor of political science at Cornell University, explains how the GI Bill's education and training provisions also produced yet another unintended consequence—civic and community leadership.

Dr. Mettler

Suzanne Mettler

"To appreciate the scope of the GI Bill's influence, we must consider that among men born in the United States in the 1920s—those of the generation in question—fully 80 percent were military veterans.[22]

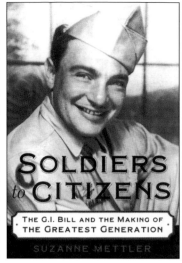

"I conducted surveys with over 1,000 World War II veterans. My analysis reveals that GI Bill beneficiaries became intensely involved in the civic renaissance that characterized our post-war democracy. Veterans who used the GI Bill belonged to 50 percent more civic organizations and participated in 30 percent more political activities/organizations than did non-GI Bill recipients.

"My book, *Soldiers to Citizens*, reveals that the positive effects of the GI Bill's education and training provisions were the results of the inclusivity, fairness, and transformative power of every aspect of this landmark social policy. The GI Bill users perceived that the government was for and about people like them and, as a result, they became more fully incorporated as citizens, and developed a capacity and inclination to be involved in civic and political life."[23]

KOREAN AND VIETNAM GI BILL PROGRAMS

Mr. Montgomery

Let's conclude this chapter with a few pictures from the Korean and Vietnam conflicts, because each produced opportunities through the GI Bill as well.

Soldiers during the Korean Conflict.

In 1952 Congress created a GI Bill education program, also a direct descendant of the WW II GI Bill, for veterans of the Korean Conflict.[24]

And in 1966 Congress created a GI Bill program for veterans of the Vietnam Conflict, retroactive to 1964.[25]

Marines in Vietnam.

POWs return from Vietnam.

Here's President Lyndon Johnson signing the Vietnam-era GI Bill with Congressmen Olin E. "Tiger" Teague of Texas at his side. Mr. Teague was one of the most highly decorated Army officers of World War II.[26]

Both Presidents Gerald Ford and Jimmy Carter signed into law legislation that provided improvements to the Vietnam-era GI Bill.[27]

President Lyndon Johnson

President Gerald Ford

President Jimmy Carter

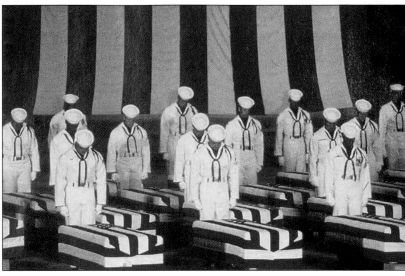
Honoring the fallen.

Almost 21 million veterans from all eras have used the GI Bill since World War II. It is an earned opportunity and a blue-chip investment for our country.

GI BILL RECIPIENTS

WORLD WAR II	7.8 MILLION
KOREAN CONFLICT	2.4 MILLION
VIETNAM CONFLICT	8.2 MILLION
MONTGOMERY GI BILL	2.3 MILLION

Lastly, I'd like you to know that Congress ensures that the spouses and children of U.S. servicemen and women who make the ultimate sacrifice (i.e. those who die in service to our nation) are eligible for up to five years of postsecondary education funded by the U.S. Department of Veterans Affairs.

For example, Mississippi State University student Jessica Maulding, daughter of the late Sergeant John Maulding (USMC), is one of the 67,620 dependent children and 11,513 widows or widowers of deceased or 100-percent disabled service members[28] who are using this VA program.

Jessica Maulding

Sonny's Lessons Learned

The World War II GI Bill represented one of Congress's shining moments because it simply unleashed the resolve of former GIs. Never underestimate the power of the human spirit, including in matters of public policy.

Worth Repeating

"... and what might happen to the country when we dumped 12 million demobilized troops onto an economy potentially on the brink of bankruptcy when the mills of war stopped grinding."
—*Author Michael Bennett*

"For seriousness, perceptiveness, studiousness and all other undergraduate virtues, the former soldiers and sailors were the best in Harvard's history."
—*James Conant, president, Harvard University*

"The $14.5 billion cost of the World War II GI Bill was paid by additional taxes on increased income of the GI Bill recipients by 1960. Without the prosperity and the social peace—engendered by the GI Bill—America could not have afforded the Marshall Plan's $12.5 billion to re-build war-torn Europe."
—*Author Michael Bennett*

"I served four years in the Army and studied architecture at Catholic University on the GI Bill. I had a 40-year career in architecture."
—*Sgt. Willis Messiah*

"The GI Bill of Rights and the enthusiastic response to it on the part of America's veterans signaled the shift to a knowledge society... ."
—*Author Peter Drucker*

WHAT'S NEXT

In the next chapter, we'll discuss the importance of Congressional committees in writing laws.

Knowing a bit about how committees work is necessary background to understanding the seven-year legislative journey of the Montgomery GI Bill.

4

*Charles W. Johnson, Parliamentarian,
U.S. House of Representatives*

*Colin Powell, former Secretary of State
and Chairman, Joint Chiefs of Staff*

Producing Legislative "Widgets:" Committees, Bills, and Bipartisanship

SONNY'S SUMMARY

Committees and subcommittees are like "little legislatures" because they take the lead in drafting laws in their areas of responsibility, such as veterans' affairs, armed services, international relations, judiciary, education/the workforce, and small business. When the subcommittee first—and then the full committee, second—approves a bill, the Committee sends it to the full body (House or Senate) for consideration. The subcommittee and committee of jurisdiction then remain very much involved in resolving differences in House- and Senate-passed bills. My approach as a committee chairman was not to take a bill to the House floor for a vote unless it had bipartisan support, meaning from both Republican and Democratic members of the committee. Bipartisanship produces mutual ownership, and I think often yields a better work product.

Mr. Montgomery

Before we track the seven-year legislative journey of what became known as the Montgomery GI Bill, let's talk about Congressional committees and their membership.

> **"COMMITTEES... TAKE THE LEAD IN WRITING LAWS INVOLVING THEIR SUBJECT-MATTER AREAS."**
> —G.V. "Sonny" Montgomery

In describing committees, we'll use and describe many terms or phrases. These include: "little legislatures," "legislative widgets," committee mark-up, committee report, reporting a bill, "Budget Act," annual budget resolution, mandatory (versus discretionary) spending, budget reconciliation, legislative whip, floor consideration, floor manager, suspension of the rules, vote stations, House-Senate conference committee, conference report, Joint Explanatory Statement, "four corners," enrolled bill, partisan, bipartisan, and "followership."

Committees are important.

Individual committees in the House and Senate typically cover about the same topics, including armed services, veterans' affairs, homeland security, international relations, small business, education and the workforce, judiciary, and transportation. These committees generally take the lead in writing laws involving their subject-matter areas.

In my experience, members of the House understandably would try to serve on a committee of importance to their constituents. Each member of the House typically serves on three committees. However, if a member serves on the Appropriations Committee, that's his or her sole committee assignment. Appropriating money to fund government agencies and public programs is serious business.

What committee to serve on?

If a member has military bases in his or her Congressional district, the member may want to serve on the Armed Services Committee.

If a member represents a farming

> **"EACH MEMBER OF THE HOUSE TYPICALLY SERVES ON THREE COMMITTEES."**
> —G.V. "Sonny" Montgomery

district, constituent interests might best be served on the Agriculture Committee.

If a member represents a highly developed area where traffic density is an issue, the member may wish to request a seat from his or her party's leadership on the Transportation Committee.

If a member represents a more rural area, the member may wish to sit on the Natural Resources Committee.

Each committee and subcommittee has both a "chairman," who is the presiding officer, and a "ranking member." The "chairman" is a member of the majority political party; that is, the party of the House or Senate that has the most elected members. The majority party has slightly more members on a committee, so it has more votes. The majority party "controls" the House or Senate and largely sets the legislative agenda.[1]

> **"THE MAJORITY PARTY HAS SLIGHTLY MORE MEMBERS ON A COMMITTEE, SO IT HAS MORE VOTES."**
> —G.V. "Sonny" Montgomery

The ranking member of the committee comes from the party in the House or Senate that is in the minority, meaning the political party that has fewer elected members. The minority party has slightly fewer members on a committee and thus has fewer votes.

When I served in the House, the Democratic Party was in the majority, and the Republican Party was in the minority.

But I didn't give a lick about a member's party affiliation. I felt I needed to work with members of both parties to be able to get anything done.

Have you heard the saying about when you have to carry out a daunting-type assignment? "When one's job is to 'eat the elephant,' we divide it up into 'steak-sized portions!'"[2]

Committees represent the "steak-sized" portions; and committees make the portions "bite-sized" by dividing the committee's work even further—and assigning it to subcommittees.

COMMITTEES: "LITTLE LEGISLATURES"

Committees and subcommittees are like "little legislatures" unto themselves because committees are where the "heavy lifting" occurs. It's where members of the committee, aided by the staff who are subject-matter experts, conceptualize, draft, think-through, revise, perfect, and mark-up (meaning vote on and approve) legislation.

In carrying out their work, prior to holding formal public hearings on planned legislation, committee and subcommittee staff members sometimes have informal work sessions with organizations—inside and outside of government—that are interested in the legislation.

Staff also obtain written cost estimates for a bill over one, five, and ten years from the Congressional Budget Office, which by law provides "nonpartisan budgetary information and analysis to Congress and its committees."[3]

Cost estimates are important because Congress uses the estimates to comply with the Congressional Budget and Impoundment Act of 1974 (also known as the Budget Act or Congressional Budget Act). Among other things, this act established the basic procedures of the annual Congressional budget process in regard to anticipated revenues and expenditures for programs and services administered by the U.S. government.

Said another way, the budget process "consists of procedures for coordinating Congressional revenue and spending decisions made in separate tax, appropriations, and legislative measures"[4] (including our New GI Bill/Montgomery GI Bill legislation). I might add that CBO cost estimates are one of the "legislative widgets" produced in writing a law that we'll discuss shortly.

A main committee vehicle in the annual Congressional budget process is the "budget resolution[5]—a concurrent [meaning House and Senate] resolution in which Congress establishes or revises its version of the federal budget's broad financial features for the upcoming fiscal year and several additional fiscal years. Like other concurrent resolutions, it does not have the force of law, but it provides the framework within which Congress subsequently considers revenue, spending, and other budget-implementing legislation... . Congress should complete action on the first resolution by April 15 of each year."

Students, the House—especially through its Veterans' Affairs and Rules Committees—discusses the budget resolution and paying for a New GI Bill entitlement in Chapter 6, and the Senate through its Veterans' Affairs and Budget Committees, in Chapters 8 and 9.

"Mandatory spending" means "amounts that Congress must appropriate because it has no discretion over it... ."[6] Entitlements such as Social Security benefits, veterans' benefits, military and federal civilian retirement benefits, and Medicare are good examples of mandatory spending.[7] Entitlements are drafted through committees. Chapters 8 and 9, too, discuss budget implications of mandatory spending.

Budget reconciliation is a "procedure for changing existing revenue and spending laws to bring total federal revenues and spending within the limits established in a budget resolution."[8] We give reconciliation lots of discussion in Chapter 15.

The visual on this page—*How Does A Bill Become A Law*—shows the basic role committees play in the larger context of how a bill travels the legislative road.[9]

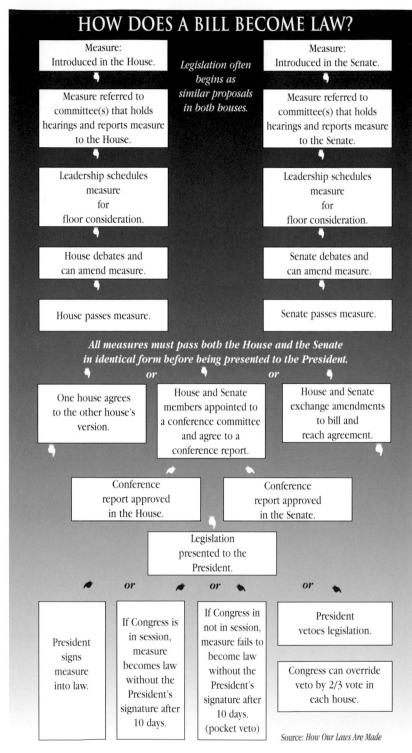

HOW DOES A BILL BECOME LAW?

Measure: Introduced in the House.		Measure: Introduced in the Senate.

Legislation often begins as similar proposals in both houses.

Measure referred to committee(s) that holds hearings and reports measure to the House.	Measure referred to committee(s) that holds hearings and reports measure to the Senate.

Leadership schedules measure for floor consideration.	Leadership schedules measure for floor consideration.

House debates and can amend measure.	Senate debates and can amend measure.

House passes measure.	Senate passes measure.

All measures must pass both the House and the Senate in identical form before being presented to the President.

or ... or

One house agrees to the other house's version.	House and Senate members appointed to a conference committee and agree to a conference report.	House and Senate exchange amendments to bill and reach agreement.

Conference report approved in the House.	Conference report approved in the Senate.

Legislation presented to the President.

or ... or ... or

President signs measure into law.	If Congress is in session, measure becomes law without the President's signature after 10 days.	If Congress in not in session, measure fails to become law without the President's signature after 10 days. (pocket veto)	President vetoes legislation.
			Congress can override veto by 2/3 vote in each house.

Source: *How Our Laws Are Made*

As you can see from the preceding visual, bills are introduced in the House or Senate. The Parliamentarian then refers the bill to a committee (or committees) that holds hearings on it. A bill is also sometimes known as a legislative "measure."

Any member of the House or Senate can introduce a bill on any topic. But I think it's accurate to say that bills introduced by a member of the committee of jurisdiction often receive the more favorable consideration. Why so? It's because expertise on an issue tends to reside within the committee that has jurisdiction over it. (The Parliamentarian, among other duties, has the responsibility of assigning—or "referring"—bills to committees, based on the bill's subject matter.)

The bill itself—and the introductory statement that accompanies it—represents the first of many "legislative widgets" that Congress produces to write laws. As I see it, a "legislative widget" is any written work product associated with a writing law.[10]

Why do I call them "widgets?"

All the widgets fit together to form the legislative product, which is a law. The widgets collectively create the "legislative history" of the law, meaning all the legislative events, debates, and analyses that led to enacting it.

This collection of legislative history—including the body of stakeholder testimony from public hearings—is largely the basis for determining legislative "intent."

To me, Congressional "intent" is what Congress had in mind when writing a law —what Congress wanted to achieve. The federal agency responsible for administering a given law—or the courts in the event that a dispute arises concerning the law's meaning or intent—often consult this history.

Committees often "amend," meaning revise a bill prior to "reporting" the bill. "Reporting" means voting on the bill and writing a report on it to send it for a vote to the full House or Senate. "Committee mark-up" means a committee meets on a bill and votes on it prior to "reporting" it to the full House or Senate.

> **"'REPORTING' A BILL MEANS VOTING ON THE BILL AND WRITING A REPORT ON IT TO SEND IT FOR A VOTE TO THE FULL HOUSE OR SENATE."**
> —*G.V. "Sonny" Montgomery*

In reporting a bill to the House or Senate so that the body can vote, the committee authoring it first must publish and file a committee report that it makes available electronically (or in hard copy) to every member of the House or Senate. Would a committee report be a "legislative widget?" Yes indeed!

In general, a committee report will include a bill summary; background on the bill; explanation of the provisions in the bill and the basis for them; cost estimates;

and the views of the federal agency or department that would carry out the legislation. The views of external organizations that have testified on the bill generally are not included in the committee report but appear verbatim in the committee's published record of the hearing. However, in some cases, a committee report on a bill will cite the verbatim testimony of external "stakeholders" in the report, especially when the testimony supports the committee's proposed legislation.

Next, the House (or Senate) leadership schedules the bill for "floor consideration," including debate, possible amendments, and voting. The person who mobilizes members to cast votes consistent with legislative priorities for the majority and minority parties is the Senator or Representative who is the legislative "whip." Whips are elected by the members of their party. The whip also helps decide which bill is brought to the floor for a vote, and when.[11] This occurs through a "whip notice."[12]

> **"'FLOOR CONSIDERATION' MEANS DEBATE, POSSIBLE AMENDMENTS, AND VOTING."**
> —*G.V. "Sonny" Montgomery*

To arrange "floor consideration," the chairman and ranking member of the authoring committee separately consult with House leadership of their respective parties, through the whip's office. Party leadership then schedules a date to bring the bill to the floor for a vote. The committee chairman and ranking member usually serve as the bill's "floor managers" for their respective parties.

The Speaker's Rostrum, U.S. House of Representatives, as it appeared in 2007.

The respective floor managers serve as chief spokespersons for the bill and decide who will speak on the bill during floor consideration/debate prior to the vote. (In the House of Representatives, the member presiding over debate sits in the Speaker's chair and is addressed as "Mr. or Madam Speaker." In the Senate, he or she is addressed as "Mr. President or Madam President.")

The bill may be amended on the floor with a two-thirds vote. But I preferred to work with the minority side of our committee to agree to the parliamentary option of "suspending" the operation of the regular rules regarding floor debate. By doing so, the House simply could debate and vote on the bill itself—with no amendments. In other words, no amendments would be permitted during floor consideration, and the bill would either pass or fail, exactly as it emerged from the committee.

Under "suspension," the idea was simply to vote on and pass the bill because the majority and minority sides of the committee bringing the bill to the floor wrote it together and agreed to its contents. [13]

I respected the viewpoints of the speaker and the majority leader. But as a committee chairman, I didn't think it was helpful for a Veterans' Affairs Committee bill to have floor amendments added to it when we had worked in such a bipartisan way in committee to get the bill right the first time.

With 435 members of the House, how do members vote on the House floor? There are many ways, but the booklet *How Our Laws Are Made* tells us that under modern practices that went into effect on January 23, 1973, recorded and roll call votes are usually taken by an electronic device.

VOTING BY "CREDIT CARD"

In the House, members use an electronic voting "station." Let's have my good friend Charles W. Johnson, who served with distinction for 40 years in the office of Parliamentarian, U.S. House of Representatives, explain: [14]

Mr. Johnson

A typical electronic voting station as used in the House.

"A number of 'vote stations' are attached to selected chairs in the [House] chamber. Each station is equipped with a vote-card slot and four indicators, marked 'yea,' 'nay,' 'present,' and 'open' that are lit when a vote is in progress and the system is ready to accept votes.

Charles W. Johnson

"Each member is provided with an encrypted vote-ID card. A member votes by inserting the voting card into any one of the

vote stations and depressing the appropriate button to indicate the member's choice….The machine records the votes and reports the result when the vote is completed. In the Senate, votes are taken by roll call."

Mr. Montgomery

Let's assume now the House and Senate have passed separate bills addressing the same issue; examples could include Social Security reform, minimum wage increase, immigration policy reform, or student financial aid policy. What happens now?

> "CONFEREES MEET FOR THE PURPOSE OF RECONCILING DIFFERENCES IN LEGISLATION THAT HAS PASSED BOTH CHAMBERS."
> —*G.V. "Sonny" Montgomery*

As our earlier visual illustrates, either (1) the House or the Senate can agree to the other body's version or (2) House and Senate members are appointed to a "conference committee," a temporary committee made up of House and Senate members who are known as "conferees." Conferees meet "for the purpose of reconciling differences in legislation that has passed both chambers." [15]

When the conference committee comes to agreement, it issues a "conference report" that reflects the negotiated agreement or "compromise" on the bill. Is a conference report a "legislative widget?" Sure, because it explains the outcome of the House-Senate conference toward writing a law.

There can also be a House-Senate "joint explanatory statement" that describes in detail the respective House- and Senate-passed provisions and the compromise agreement on each. An explanatory statement is another "widget" that helps complete the legislative picture.

In some respects, the Veterans' Affairs Committees of the House and Senate, members of the staff of the majority and minority side of both committees used procedures that were somewhat different than those used by others. They often negotiated a "compromise agreement," in lieu of a formal conference committee.

Some observers view the compromise agreement approved as a "phantom conference" [16] because committee professional staff—not members—negotiate based on member guidance so as to ultimately bring a proposed compromise to members for a vote.

Indeed, the role of Mr. Mack Fleming, our highly effective House Veterans' Affairs Committee Chief Counsel and Staff Director, is discussed in compromise agreement negotiation in the book *Unelected Representatives: Congressional Staff and the Future of Representative Government*, by author Michael Malbin.

House Veterans' Affairs Committee Chairman Olin Teague of Texas and then-Chairman Ray Roberts, both of Texas, preferred that staff directors and other professional staff of the House and Senate committees resolve legislative differences.[17]

Noted Chief Counsel Fleming, "I can't remember but one formal conference being held since 1973, when I came here."[18]

Observed Chairman Teague, "[I]t's just quicker and easier without a whole lot of people."[19]

Usually after multiple staff negotiating sessions, committee staff would submit the proposed compromise agreement—including the associated legislative language—to each of the chairmen and ranking members of the House and Senate Veterans' Affairs Committees. If the four parties agreed with the proposed compromise, each body would vote on the written compromise agreement, as expressed in the form of a joint explanatory statement, known as a "JES"[20]—rather than convening a formal conference committee. The JES is another "widget" that helps produce a law. It's "joint" because both the House and the Senate issue the official statement, as drafted by committee staff.[21]

"FOUR CORNERS"

In the Veterans' Affairs Committee, we sometimes call this negotiating process the "four corners" because the majority and minority sides of both the House and Senate Veterans' Affairs Committee participate. Each side has one vote.

Though not a formal rule but more an informal agreement, if any one of the "four corners" objects to a provision, it will not be part of the negotiated agreement—period. Writing public policy for the United States is important business. Three of four "corners" supporting a provision are insufficient to write it into the proposed compromise. It has to be unanimous. Four out of four sends the provision to the White House, assuming the full House and Senate pass the negotiated package crafted by the two Veterans' Affairs Committees.

Finally, the President receives the "enrolled bill" printed on parchment paper, as signed by the Speaker of the House and the President Pro Tempore of the Senate. As our earlier chart indicates, the President can then either sign or veto the bill.

As I mentioned, I felt it important that the Veterans' Affairs Committee operate in a bipartisan fashion.

It seems to me that being politically "partisan" is easy because the majority party has more members/votes on a committee and pretty much can push through whatever it wants.

> **"... I FELT IT IMPORTANT THAT THE VETERANS' AFFAIRS COMMITTEE OPERATE IN A BIPARTISAN FASHION."**
> —*G.V. "Sonny" Montgomery*

However, being "bipartisan" and truly listening to the views of the minority party takes work; work in the form of time, effort, and earnest commitment.

In my opinion, bipartisanship not only produces "ownership" of the legislation, but also often yields a more thoughtful product.

I believe, too, it is more important to be a powerful listener than a powerful speaker.

Each member of Congress today represents about 647,000 persons.[22] That's a crowd, isn't it? My biggest job as both a Representative from Mississippi's Third Congressional District and a Committee Chairman was to listen to both the descriptions of problems and the ideas for resolving them.

If one isn't willing to listen to the legislative views of others, it's hard to ask a constituent or a member of the committee to ultimately accept one's own legislative ideas. Beyond "hard," I'd also call it disrespectful.

A fair amount of the technical design of the Montgomery GI Bill, for example, emerged from others with technical knowledge and information that my elected colleagues and I did not possess.

These included ideas from professional staff of the Veterans' Affairs and Armed Services Committees, managers of veterans' educational assistance programs at the Departments of Veterans Affairs and Defense, and professional staff from national veterans, military personnel, and higher education organizations. Listening is learning. Without it, informed decision making is much harder.

LIKE MAKING SAUSAGE

Folks, there are many everyday phrases to describe the legislative process. Now is a good time for me to alert you to them because you'll see examples of them in the pages ahead.

One common metaphor regarding the legislative process goes something like this: "[W]riting a law is like making sausage: you'll like the end-product but you won't necessarily want to see how it's made (or what goes into making it!)."[23]

I think it is fair to say you'll see in our case study that writing the Montgomery GI Bill was at times a messy process. It was a process that contained a lot of different "ingredients" and involved a lot of different "cooks."

Those ingredients didn't always mix well. Finding the right legislative "recipe" can be challenging.

And the recipe all will find appetizing doesn't always emerge quickly! At times, the legislative process can be slower than a snail on crutches.[24]

> **"... SLOWER THAN A SNAIL ON CRUTCHES."**
> —*G.V. "Sonny" Montgomery*

Most laws do not take seven years to write like the Montgomery GI Bill did.

Getting a majority of 100 Senators and 435 Representatives to agree on something takes hard work. And it **should** take work. Ideally, only bills that are carefully thought through should receive majority support based on the bill's merit.

Folks, let's summarize a bit. In this chapter, we've talked about the importance of committees and the steps committees take to produce what I have referred to as "legislative widgets" to produce laws.

We've also talked about voting by "credit card," the "four corners," and the value of bipartisanship.

Before we move to 1980 when my colleagues and I began a legislative journey that led to Congress creating the Montgomery GI Bill in 1987, I want to talk about the concept of leadership.

Legislative leadership employed in writing laws is not different from leadership in other settings; one must develop a "followership" through one's depth of knowledge, one's character as a person, and one's professionalism in dealing with others, especially as a listener.

Momentarily, I'll share with you some words about leadership from Colin Powell, a soldier, statesman, and American icon.

Colin Powell visiting U.S. troops.

Colin Powell is a leader, having served as Secretary of State under President George W. Bush and as Chairman of the Joint Chiefs of Staff, under both President George H. W. Bush and President Bill Clinton.

Secretary Powell is one of the most respected persons in America and he's a person I admire.

Secretary Powell now serves as chairman of "America's Promise," an organization challenging Americans to scale up their investment in youth and commitment to making America's youth a national priority.

Secretary Powell wrote a masterful article in the February 2002 issue of *State Magazine* titled "What's the True Secret of Good Leadership? There is None." I've included this article in the appendix for you. I believe you can apply its lessons in every aspect of your life.

I am very honored to have Secretary Powell with us. I've asked the Secretary to share with you what I think is an important paragraph from his article.

COLIN POWELL ON LEADERSHIP

Mr. Powell

"Thank you, Mr. Chairman.

"Dare to be the skunk at the picnic. Every organization should tolerate rebels who tell the emperor he has no clothes. This is not a license to be mean or rude. But make the tough decisions, confront people who need it, reward those who perform best. Speak your mind. Work toward consensus building but don't hide from reality."[25]

Mr. Montgomery

Thank you, Mr. Secretary.

In a sense, at times my colleagues and I were "the skunks at the picnic," because I believe we spoke with candor regarding the need for a new, "non-contributory" GI Bill.

In 1980, we had to emphatically suggest to the Congress something much more than the lone fact that our post-Vietnam, all-volunteer military concept wasn't working.

We suggested that spending additional money on military hardware wasn't necessarily the sole answer. We felt the answer was spending more money on people to operate that sophisticated hardware[26] because education is an incentive to which Americans respond.

And that's essentially what we proposed to Congress in our New GI Bill legislation to help our all-volunteer force work.

Sonny's Lessons Learned

Folks, I think this chapter's lesson learned is what Secretary Powell just said: "Dare to be the skunk at the picnic."

If you want to be a leader, sometimes you have to politely and respectfully tell your peers and superiors what they may not wish to hear. And when you do, make sure you have the facts on your side.

We didn't have the soldiers, sailors, airmen, Marines, and Coast Guardsmen we needed to operate sophisticated military technology. In our view, a New GI Bill would help fix that problem and also help America's youth access post-military education and training.

Worth Repeating

"When one's job is to eat the elephant, we divide him up into steak-sized portions."
—*G. V. "Sonny" Montgomery*

"Committees and subcommittees are like little legislatures…"
—*G. V. "Sonny" Montgomery*

"The legislative process can be slower than a snail on crutches."
—*G. V. "Sonny" Montgomery*

"Dare to be the skunk at the picnic."
—*Secretary of State Colin Powell*

WHAT'S NEXT

Now let's start the first leg of the long legislative journey of the Montgomery GI Bill.

5

Throughout the text, the only committee assignments we list for members of Congress are for membership on the Veterans' Affairs, Armed Services, Budget, or Rules committees.

Charles Moskos, Professor and Military Sociologist, Northwestern University

Senator Bill Cohen (R-ME), Member, Committee on Armed Services

Darryl Kehrer, 1992 Woodrow Wilson Public Service Fellow, Representing U.S. Dept. of Veterans Affairs

General William Westmoreland, Chief of Staff of the Army

Representative Mike Simpson (R-ID), Chairman, Subcommittee on Benefits, Committee on Veterans' Affairs

General Edward "Shy" Meyer, Chief of Staff of the Army

Representative William F. Nichols (D-AL), Chairman, Military Personnel and Compensation Subcommittee, Committee on Armed Services

Senator Bill Armstrong (R-CO)

Senator Alan Cranston (D-CA), Chairman, Committee on Veterans' Affairs

Representative Bob Edgar (D-PA), Chairman, Subcommittee on Education, Training and Employment, Committee on Veterans' Affairs

1980-1983—Road to Enactment: How to Fix a "Hollow" Army

SONNY'S SUMMARY

*When both the drafting of 19-year-old males and the Vietnam Conflict ended in early 1973, our military had great difficulty persuading young people to enlist. Congress ended the **non-contributory** Vietnam-era GI Bill for new enlistees as of December 31, 1975, and created a new, **contributory**, but ineffective Veterans' Educational Assistance Program (VEAP) effective January 1, 1977.*

In fiscal year 1979, the four service branches failed to meet their recruiting objectives; and by 1980, only 54 percent of Army enlistees had a high school diploma. My colleagues and I realized our new, all-volunteer military concept would likely fail unless we created a solid, post-service educational incentive to encourage our youth to enlist and give them an earned opportunity for post-service education and training—what we called a New GI Bill. A handful of individuals in the House and Senate pressed forward with such legislation.

The Senate Veterans' Affairs Committee, chaired by Alan Cranston, received testimony in July 1980 on S. 2020 and S. 2596, introduced by Senators Bill Cohen and Bill Armstrong, respectively. Chairman Cranston introduced his bill, S. 3263, that December. On the House side, my few cosponsors and I—including Representative John Paul Hammerschmidt—introduced H.R. 1400 in 1981, which the Veterans' Affairs Committee approved on May 19. On the Senate side, absent a Senate Armed Services Committee hearing on their bills, Senators Armstrong and Cohen were unsuccessful on the Senate floor in adding an amendment to create a New GI Bill, as part of the FY 1984 DoD Authorization Act in the summer of 1983.

Sonny's Scene Setter & Journey Guide

Introducing and holding hearings on a New GI Bill in the House and Senate Committees on Veterans' Affairs.

On the Legislative Journey chart on pages 10 and 11, we'll travel from consultations we had with stakeholders in 1980 ("departure" box) through the May 16, 1983, House Veterans' Affairs Committee mark-up of H.R. 1400 (box H-5).

And we'll also visit the introduction of various Senate bills from 1979 to 1983 (boxes S-1 to S-3) and the Senate's disapproval of a New GI Bill amendment on July 13, 1983 (box S-4).

THE VIETNAM CONFLICT ENDS IN 1973

Mr. Montgomery

It's difficult to talk about the enactment of the Montgomery GI Bill in 1987 without discussing the Vietnam Conflict and the divisiveness of our Vietnam-era military draft policy.

A soldier in action during the Vietnam Conflict.

During the Vietnam era (from roughly 1964 through 1973),[1] United States draft policy generally permitted young men enrolled in college to receive a deferment from serving in our military. Women were not drafted.

Males not in college and who had not already enlisted in one of the service branches were subject to being drafted into the Army or Marine Corps. This policy tore at our social fabric, as some of our youth served, while others did not; more than 58,000 Americans died in the Vietnam Conflict.

"Uncle Sam" drafted young men into our military during World War II and the Korean Conflict as well. But there were no deferments allowing those enrolled in college not to serve.

Looking back, the Army and Marine Corps received these numbers of young American men during the peak years of the Vietnam Conflict: 299,000 in 1968; 289,900 in 1969; 163,500 in 1970; 98,000 in 1971; and 50,000 in 1972.[2] Many of these were 19-year-olds.[3]

The United States' involvement in hostilities in the Vietnam Conflict ended with the U.S. and Vietnam signing the cease-fire agreement of January 27, 1973.[4]

When the Vietnam Conflict ended in 1973, the military had great difficulty persuading young people to sign up, even though it was peacetime. "[O]nly 54 percent of Army recruits in fiscal year 1980 were high school diploma graduates, compared with 74 percent in FY 1978."[5]

High spirits as former American POWs return from Vietnam.

Renowned military sociologist Charles Moskos notes one of the consequences of relying on military volunteers and not drafting youth into our military, with additional data furnished by Senator Bill Cohen:

Dr. Moskos

Charles Moskos

"… In 1979, all four services did not meet their recruitment goals. Enlistment shortfalls are particularly severe among those who will serve in the ground combat arms and aboard ships. Along with enlistment shortfalls, educational levels of new recruits continue to drop. More than one-in-three service members fail to complete their initial enlistments. Desertion rates are double that of pre-Vietnam levels. The growing number of skilled technicians and career personnel leaving the military threatens to undermine the capability of our military forces. Army reserves are in a perilous state."[6]

Mr. Cohen

"Only 38 percent of male Army recruits in this fiscal year [1981] are high school graduates. This fact is evidence enough that we need a better program.[7]"

Bill Cohen

Mr. Montgomery

Data like these are why I think Chief of Staff of the Army—General Edward C. "Shy" Meyer—painfully declared our once-proud U.S. Army to be a "hollow" one.[8]

ORIGINS OF THE MONTGOMERY GI BILL

Darryl Kehrer, retrospectively in 1992, took Dr. Moskos's views one step further in suggesting the origins of the Montgomery GI Bill.

Mr. Kehrer

Darryl Kehrer

These key forces propelled enactment of the Montgomery GI Bill:[9]

1. **Memories of the draft.** Unpleasant recollections of the social divisiveness of the Vietnam-era draft policy ultimately led to the creation of a non-conscripted, All-Volunteer Force.

2. **Recruiting woes.** Major degradation emerged in the educational level of enlistees in the All-Volunteer Force after the Vietnam Conflict.

3. **Indefatigable leadership.** The tenacity of House Committee on Veterans' Affairs Chairman G.V. Montgomery in having convinced Congress that the success of the All-Volunteer Force was inextricably linked to the creation of a continuous, permanent GI Bill for recruiting and post-service educational purposes.

4. **Selected use of political capital.** Primarily the Non Commissioned Officers Association of the U.S., the American Association of Community and Junior Colleges, and the Fleet Reserve Association all lobbied heavily for the bill's enactment in the U.S. Senate during spring 1987.

DRAFT ENDS JANUARY 1, 1973; ALL-VOLUNTEER FORCE BEGINS

Mr. Montgomery

"… In January 1969, President Richard M. Nixon had announced the formation of a Commission on an All-Volunteer Armed Force, headed by former Secretary of

Defense Thomas S. Gates, Jr. The Commission, charged with investigating the possibility of a volunteer force, reported to the President in February 1970. It [the Commission] found that a volunteer force was feasible, but that a standby draft and a strong reserve would be necessary to meet unforeseen emergencies."[10]

"In his April 23, 1970, message to Congress, President Nixon established attainment of a volunteer armed force as a national objective and gave June 30, 1973, as the target date for reaching the goal of zero draft."[11]

Here's a statement from Army Chief of Staff General William Westmoreland[12] in October 1970 regarding the forthcoming transition from a military draft to an All-Volunteer Force. General Westmoreland noted four areas in which a concerted effort had to be made if the "Modern Volunteer Army" were to be a success:[13]

Gen. Westmoreland

William Westmoreland

"First, those of us in uniform in positions of high responsibility in the Army must attack this problem with all the vigor, imagination, and dedication we can muster and we must apply ourselves intensively to the task.

"Second, we must eliminate unnecessary irritants and unattractive features of Army life where they exist. But we will hold to those immutable principles of dedicated professionalism, loyalty, integrity of character, and sacrifice. They are the hallmarks of a disciplined, responsible Army. Young Americans thrive on challenges and high standards… .

"Third, we will not achieve our goal without the application of resources, and I mean money. We will need to increase pay. And we will probably find that we must put our money primarily in those jobs which are most arduous and have the least application to civilian pursuits[14]—the infantry, artillery, and armor.

"We will need money for housing our people—an item for which we have deferred expenditures throughout the Vietnam War. We will need money to maintain those houses. We will need modern barracks… .

"Fourth, we will need the support of the American people and their leaders in business, industry, the church, education, and the news media… ."

Mr. Montgomery

Knowingly or not, in creating the All-Volunteer Force, I think President Nixon took a step toward a permanent GI Bill.

For example, the American Council on Education observed the following in 1994:

> "The seeds of the first peacetime GI Bill, which became effective on July 1, 1985, were planted in 1969 [during the height of the Vietnam Conflict] when President Richard Nixon appointed a Commission to examine the subject of abolishing the draft and establishing an All-Volunteer Force (AVF).

> "In 1970, the Commission recommended that the country complete the transition to the AVF, and inductions of men into the armed forces ended on December 31, 1972.[15]"

> "During fiscal years 1976 and 1977, however, recruiting problems increased, and by fiscal year 1979, all **four** services [emphasis added] failed to meet their recruitment objectives—the first such across-the-board shortfall since the beginning of the AVF."[16]

Here's the general timeline regarding the conclusion of the Vietnam era and the creation of the post-Vietnam era GI Bill educational assistance program, as quoted from the 1981 Committee report that we filed on H.R. 1400:

> "Although the draft ended on December 31, 1972, entitlement to the Vietnam-era GI Bill continued to be extended to those joining the All-Volunteer Force. On May 7, 1975, President Gerald R. Ford issued a proclamation terminating the Vietnam wartime period. On the same day he issued the proclamation, the President transmitted to the Congress a proposed bill to set a termination date for veterans' educational benefits under Chapters 34 [Vietnam-era GI Bill] and 36 of Title 38, United States Code.[17]

> "Among other things, the legislation submitted by the President would have **terminated** [emphasis added] the eligibility period for [Vietnam-era] GI education and training benefits for persons entering military service on or after July 1, 1975.

> "On October 15, 1976, President Ford signed Public Law 94-502, which established December 31, 1976, as the termination date for accrual of eligibility for veterans' educational assistance benefits under Chapter 34 [Vietnam-era GI Bill] of Title 38, United States Code, and December 31, 1989, as the date when the program will end."[18]

Students, I'd add for you, as well, that as the text above suggests, the President may submit legislation to Congress to be introduced "by request." Generally, the chairman of the committee having jurisdiction on the President's proposed bill introduces the legislation, as a professional courtesy.

VIETNAM-ERA GI BILL ENDS DECEMBER 31, 1976, AND VEAP BEGINS JANUARY 1, 1977

Here is more historical background for you from our 1981 committee report on H.R. 1400:

> "Public Law 94-502, which established December 31, 1976, as the termination date for accrual of entitlement to veterans' educational assistance benefits under Chapter 34 [Vietnam-era GI Bill] of Title 38, also established a post-Vietnam era contributory veterans' educational assistance program [known in short, as VEAP] for those entering the Armed Forces on or after January 1, 1977."

The Senate Committee on Veterans' Affairs said the following in its report on S. 969, 94th Congress [1975 and 1976]:

> "As the Committee examined the future of the GI Bill, it was most concerned with the effect of termination upon the ability of the military to recruit and retain qualified young men and women. The Committee expects that the Chapter 32 [VEAP] program will be used by the Armed Forces to promote and assist them in attracting qualified men and women into the Armed Forces.

> "… A five-year test program, VEAP will terminate on December 31, 1981, unless the President recommends that the program be continued and neither House of Congress disagrees.

> "… Service members choosing to participate in VEAP may contribute from $25 to $100 monthly toward their post-service education fund… For each $1 contributed by the participant, up to a maximum of $2,700, the Veterans' Administration contributes $2, up to a maximum of $5,400.

> "… Participants receive monthly benefits for the same number of months they contributed to the VEAP fund, up to a maximum of 36 months for full-time training. Full-time students contributing the maximum of $2,700, for example, receive 36 payments of $225, ($75 contributed by the participant and $150 contributed by the Veterans' Administration)."[19]

Folks, VEAP was different from the Vietnam-era, Korean-era and WW II-era GI Bill programs because service members had to financially **contribute** to VEAP to be eligible for it.

So how did the first two years of the VEAP test go? Not so good. Here's more from my committee's 1981 report on H.R. 1400:

> "Persons entering military service on or after January 1, 1977, currently have the right to enroll in VEAP at any time during their active duty. The Department of Defense reports that 201,734 enlistees (about 23.3 percent)[20] and 2,099 officers enrolled in VEAP between 1977 and December 31, 1979.[21]

> "... The services struggled to meet qualitative and quantitative [recruiting] goals during FY 78 through FY 79, the first such across-the-board shortfall since the All-Volunteer Force began on January 1, 1973.[22]

> "... [T]he Veterans Administration believes that early indicators lead to a less than optimistic view as to the program's viability."[23]

1980

For my part, the seven-year legislative journey begins here.[24] In mid-1980, my Veterans' Affairs Committee staff held informal meetings over eight months with representatives of the Army, Navy, Air Force, and Marine Corps regarding the content of H.R. 1400 that we'd introduce[25] in early 1981.[26]

The purpose of these meetings was two-fold: first, to design an educational assistance program for the All-Volunteer Force that truly would help our service members in their transition back to civilian life; and second, to enhance the ability of the armed forces to recruit and retain high-quality young people.

We didn't introduce the bill and then get opinions and suggestions on the bill from interested parties—often known as "stakeholders." We got informal views and suggestions **before** introducing a draft bill.

Mack Fleming, Jill Cochran, and Richard Fuller of my committee staff learned that the service branches legitimately wanted different features in a New GI Bill regarding recruitment and retention of soldiers, sailors, airmen, and Marines. Recruiting **interests** were different because recruiting **needs** were different.

> "RECRUITING <u>INTERESTS</u> WERE DIFFERENT BECAUSE RECRUITING <u>NEEDS</u> WERE DIFFERENT."
> —G.V. "Sonny" Montgomery

I'd note the early 1981 letters each service branch sent to Alan Cranston, chairman of the Senate Veterans' Affairs Committee, regarding the Chairman's S. 3263, the proposed "All-Volunteer Force Educational Assistance Program Act of 1980." These letters expressed generally similar observations to those made to my staff during the meetings with each service branch. I greatly appreciated Senator Cranston's early leadership and vision on this issue. I felt we were on the same team.[27]

WHAT OUR TEAM LEARNED FROM THE SERVICE BRANCHES

Let's spend some time now on what we learned in mid-1980 by talking directly and informally with the military service branches about what a New GI Bill should entail. We absolutely needed to establish credibility with the service branches—and later with the veterans' organizations, military personnel organizations, and the higher education organizations—as to the merits of the bill we'd introduce in early 1981. Each of these groups had a different view point.

UNITED STATES ARMY

THE CHIEF OF STAFF

15 JAN 1981

Dear Senator Cranston:

I appreciate the opportunity to provide my views on the proposed "All-Volunteer Force Educational Assistance Program Act of 1980." Your bill embodies many features I support, especially cost-free educational assistance and a provision for eligible servicemembers to transfer unused benefits to their dependents. I do, however, suggest some additional features including benefits at a reduced rate for service in the Reserve Components, eligibility based on an honorable discharge, an increase in the monthly entitlement and a capability to supplement it.

Increasing the entitlement will assist in meeting today's high cost of education and make us more competitive with other federally funded programs which do not have a national service obligation. Allowing the Service Secretaries to selectively supplement the monthly entitlement will permit us flexibility in enlisting personnel into difficult-to-fill skill positions, especially in the combat arms.

I have enclosed a chart comparing your Bill provisions with the Army's initial position, its revised position developed in an attempt to reach Service unanimity and supporting rationale. I believe that a Bill containing these features will assist in solving many of our manpower needs. Thank you for your interest and support in this matter. Please do not hesitate to contact me if there is any other information you need.

Sincerely,

E. C. MEYER
General, United States Army
Chief of Staff

1 Incl
As stated

First, the Army. Mack Fleming, Jill Cochran, and Richard Fuller learned informally in 1980 that the Army, under the leadership of General "Shy" Meyer, Chief of Staff of the Army, wanted the New GI Bill to:[28]

• Attract college-oriented enlistees (more so than the existing VEAP);

• Yield high-quality recruits;

• Reduce disciplinary issues—such as drug problems and AWOLs [absent without leave]—in the enlisted ranks; and

• Grant selective authority to supplement the benefit with "kickers" paid for by the Army in hard-to-fill positions, especially in the combat arms.

Second, the Navy under the leadership of Admiral Tom Hayward,[29] Chief of Naval Operations, wanted graduated increases in the benefits based on longer periods of service. In fact, the Navy wanted sailors to serve eight years to qualify for full benefits. This approach would allow the Navy to get greater, longer-term returns from its skilled sailors in whom it invested so heavily in high-technology training.

Folks, I show the service branch letters here because the letters present, in a formal way, what I think Mr. Fleming, et al., basically learned in information discussions with the branches in mid-1980.

CHIEF OF NAVAL OPERATIONS

21 February 1981

Dear Mr. Chairman,

Thank you for allowing me to comment on your proposed "All-Volunteer Force Educational Assistance Program Act of 1980." As you know, the Services are vitally interested in legislation of this nature which includes incentives for reenlistment as well as enlistment. Your proposal certainly addresses this concept.

Specifically, I agree wholeheartedly in the following features of your proposed bill:

- Noncontributory program

- Administered by the Veterans' Administration

- Benefits accrue 1 month for 1 month up to 36 months

There are other provisions with which I agree in principle and offer the following comments:

- Same general benefits for all. Although the Services' needs vary, we must be careful not to develop a program which would favor one Service over the other. For example, the Army needs a program to encourage short-term enlistment in the regular Army and later service in the Army Reserve or National Guard. The Navy, on the other hand, seeks a program which would offer benefits for initial service, with benefits increasing for longer periods of service.

- Graduated benefits related to length of service. For the Navy to maximize retention at the most critical point, a minimum of eight years should be required for receipt of full benefits. Any new bill should meticulously avoid features which might unwittingly create an incentive to leave active duty in order to capitalize on the benefit.

- Eligibility for use of accrued benefits. Make eligibility for total benefits contingent upon receipt of an honorable discharge or medical discharge for a Service-connected disability, with authorization for inservice use of benefits following one year of honorable service.

- Entitlement for Reserves. This is an important feature, particularly for the Army, and I strongly support the Reserve Forces being included in this program.

- Transfer of unused benefits to spouse or children. This incentive will encourage a Service career commitment.

Of particular concern to me is the delimiting date of Title 38 Chapter 34. Many of our career personnel are leaving the Navy in order to take advantage of the educational benefits Chapter 34 makes available. The new educational assistance program should extend the delimiting date for up to ten years following separation

I hope the foregoing will be helpful to you and that the proposal being developed by the Services will meet with your approval and gain your support.

Sincerely,

T. B. HAYWARD
Admiral, U.S. Navy

The Honorable Alan Cranston
Chairman, Committee on Veterans' Affairs
United States Senate
Washington, DC 20510

DEPARTMENT OF THE AIR FORCE
OFFICE OF THE CHIEF OF STAFF
UNITED STATES AIR FORCE
WASHINGTON, D.C. 20330

19 JAN 1981

Honorable Alan Cranston
Committee on Veterans' Affairs
United States Senate
Washington, DC 20510

Dear Senator Cranston

This is in response to your letter of 19 December 1980, in which you ask for our comments on S3263, "The All Volunteer Force Educational Assistance Program Act of 1980." I very much appreciate your concern for enhancing the capability of the services to both attract well qualified men and women into the armed forces and to assist in their retention. A program such as that described in your Bill could well mean the difference between continuance of the All Volunteer Force concept and return to some form of conscription.

The major features of S3263 parallel quite closely those of proposed legislation under development by an inter-service working group. This group has achieved consensus on eight of ten provisions targeted at achieving the very purpose of your Bill. The inter-service proposal envisages a two-tiered approach as does yours--with a slightly higher initial amount-- as well as a transferability feature, so long as the military member agrees to career status. The inter-service proposal also contains a provision for a basic educational entitlement at a reduced rate for entry into the ready reserve (Guard or Reserve).

I have asked my staff experts to contact Ms Polzer and provide her with greater detail regarding the differences that exist between S3263, the inter-service proposal and the Air Force position in this latter regard. Thank you for the opportunity to comment on this important legislation.

Sincerely

LEW ALLEN JR., General, USAF
Chief of Staff

JAN 23 REC'D

Third, the Air Force, under the leadership of General Lew Allen, Jr., Chief of Staff of the Air Force,[30] wanted emphasis on retaining enlisted personnel it had trained to operate sophisticated instrumentation and technology. In this regard, it wanted "transferability" of the benefit to a spouse or child of the service member, as long as the service member agreed to serve a 20-year career.

Fourth, the Marine Corps, under the leadership of Bob Barrow, Commandant,[31] wanted to ensure the Marines could use a New GI Bill while on active duty rather than waiting until separation from the military.

DEPARTMENT OF THE NAVY
HEADQUARTERS UNITED STATES MARINE CORPS
WASHINGTON, D.C. 20380

IN REPLY REFER TO
MPP-39-msh
5800
13 JAN 1981

The Honorable Alan Cranston
United States Senate
Washington, D.C. 20510

Dear Senator Cranston:

I appreciate the opportunity to provide my views on the proposed "All Volunteer Force Educational Assistance Program Act of 1980."

The bill you have proposed has a number of features that I strongly support: cost-free educational assistance to members of the Armed Forces, incrementally higher benefits for continued service beyond three years, and provision for eligible service members to transfer unused benefits to their dependents. The following modifications would, in my judgment, provide an educational assistance program that most effectively meets our needs.

a. Entitlements tied to length of enlistment, by providing one month of benefit for one month of service through the third year (at which time full entitlements would be earned), would enhance educational opportunities for in-service use by the service member. Honorable service concluded prior to the end of the third year would entitle the service member to that portion of the benefits earned.

b. All funding and administration accomplished by the Veterans Administration would clearly establish responsibility for the educational assistance program in one agency, leaving other direct methods of encouraging enlistment and retention a responsibility of the Department of Defense.

c. A right of transferability of unused benefits, made to dependents after appropriate service, would provide a strong incentive to continue active service. Rather than the procedure proposed in the "All Volunteer Force Educational Assistance Program Act of 1980," we would prefer that after ten years' active service, the service member would have the right of transferability of unused benefits to dependents, if the service member remains on active duty, or until the service member enters retirement status at which time the service member or dependents have ten years to use the benefit.

d. An entitlement for Selected Reserves of up to one-half of the active duty benefit would improve manning of reserve forces.

e. A change to Chapter 34 of Title 38 United States Code providing for benefits up to ten years after separation would provide a necessary incentive for the group of service members eligible for educational assistance under that Act.

f. Requiring honorable service as a prerequisite to educational assistance would complement many other programs and efforts designed to encourage individual responsibility.

Along with pay comparability, an effective educational assistance program would return great dividends in gaining and keeping men and women who have characteristics that we need in the Marine Corps. Its additional long-term impact on our society in bringing out the abilities of individuals who otherwise might not have the advantage of other opportunities makes the investment doubly attractive.

I trust that the foregoing information will be of use to you. If I may be of assistance to you in the future, please do not hesitate to call on me.

Sincerely,

R.H. Barrow

R. H. BARROW
General, U.S. Marine Corps
Commandant of the Marine Corps

CHAIRMAN OF THE JOINT CHIEFS OF STAFF
WASHINGTON

10 January 1981

Honorable Alan Cranston
United States Senate
Washington, D.C. 20510

Dear Senator Cranston

I appreciate the opportunity to provide my views on the proposed "All-Volunteer Force Educational Assistance Program Act of 1980."

The details of S. 3263 and other similar proposals have not yet been carefully analyzed by the Joint Chiefs of Staff. However, the Chiefs are on record in support of a noncontributory education program for members of the Armed Forces as a means to assist in meeting manpower requirements.

The bill you have proposed has a number of features which I personally support: cost-free educational assistance to members of the Armed Forces, supplemental assistance for continued service, and provision for eligible Service members to transfer unused benefits to their dependents. The following additional features are offered for your consideration:

a. Provide benefits (at a reduced level) for service in the Reserve Components.

b. Increase the basic monthly stipend to more accurately reflect basic educational programs. As an example, the monthly stipend for a single veteran under the Vietnam-era GI Bill is $342.

c. Make eligibility conditional upon receipt of an honorable discharge or medical discharge for a Service-connected disability.

Your efforts on educational assistance are greatly appreciated. I look forward to a successful program that will fill a variety of needs and be an important recruiting and retention incentive.

Sincerely

David Jones

DAVID C. JONES
General, USAF

Finally, the Chairman of the Joint Chiefs of Staff, General David Jones, U.S. Air Force[32] wanted:

- Benefits—at a reduced level—for service in the Reserve components; and

- Eligibility conditioned upon receipt of an honorable discharge or medical discharge for a service-connected disability.

Each service branch organizationally, of course, was part of the Department of Defense. Students, do you think the policy position of the Department of Defense itself and its individual service branches would be the same?

No, they were different. Robert B. Pirie, Jr., Assistant Secretary of Defense for Manpower, Reserve Affairs, and Logistics:[33]

• Expressed concern about cost, given the $10 billion already available in federal education loan and grant programs for any citizen; and

• Questioned whether a transferability program like the Air Force wanted, in particular, would be a strong enough incentive to retain a service member past the 12-year point.

ASSISTANT SECRETARY OF DEFENSE
WASHINGTON D.C. 20301

MANPOWER
RESERVE AFFAIRS
AND LOGISTICS

JAN 1 5 1981

Honorable Alan Cranston
Committee on Veterans' Affairs
United States Senate
Washington, D.C. 20510

Dear Senator Cranston:

This is in response to your letter of 19 December 1980 concerning your legislation, S. 3263, the "All-Volunteer Force Educational Assistance Program Act of 1980."

In general, I believe that educational incentives can play a valuable role as a recruitment and retention tool for the Armed Services. But designers of new education programs for the military must in their planning take into account those education programs which are already available to both the civilian and military populations. The drawing power of generalized military educational assistance today is much different from what it was even five years ago because of the rapid growth in other education programs. Consequently, any new military educational benefit package must recognize the interests of both military and education constituencies and the full spectrum of federal programs in this area, as well as the realities of the federal budget.

As you know, the Department of Defense is currently testing several educational benefit proposals mandated by the Congress. We hope to answer several important questions about educational assistance: What is the proper benefit level? What retention provisions would prove attractive? Should the program be contributory or noncontributory? I believe it is premature to design any new program before our test results are complete. We plan a final report to the Congress in about one year's time.

Regarding your specific legislation, S. 3263, I have several comments.

a. Outlay level: An estimated 300,000 new enlistees receiving a $9000 educational entitlement means a potential $2.7 billion annual outlay. This price tag would not include the supplemental educational benefit to be funded by the Department of Defense. I question the merit of adding such large outlays in addition to the $10 billion currently authorized for federal loan/grant programs.

b. Retention: I support the efforts in the bill to provide retention incentives. The transfer provision is similar to one that we will test in the FY 81 test program, to learn whether it is truly a retention incentive. My presumption is that people will use the transfer provision, but there is as yet no data to support such a notion. And I am uncertain whether the transfer provision is a strong enough incentive to retain a member past the twelve year point.

c. Benefit Value: At this time there are differing views on what should be the proper benefit level and the value of specific educational incentives, e.g., transferability, in-service use, cash-out. Some favor a general entitlement; others believe educational benefits should be targeted, as in the FY 81 test package. Such questions are being addressed in our current test.

I hope that these comments are helpful. I appreciate your continued support of and concern for the All-Volunteer Force, and I believe we are in agreement that educational benefits for the military might indeed improve the quality and attractiveness of the AVF.

Sincerely,

Robert B. Pirie, Jr.
Assistant Secretary of Defense (MRA&L)

Folks, the view of each service branch's "stakeholders" indeed was legitimate. Our team's job, led by Chief Counsel Mack Fleming and Jill Cochran, was to constructively blend the service branch views into a coherent bill, with respect to recruitment (given that these particular stakeholders' primary interest was recruitment).

But at this point we had not yet solicited and factored in the external views of the military personnel, veterans, and higher education organizations. We'd learn their views were both the **same** as, and **different** from those of the service branches. So my staff talked with them and factored their interests into our draft bill, too. Let's hear some of their views.

First, the Air Force Sergeant's Association (AFSA) and the Non Commissioned Officers Association (NCOA)[34] both opposed a "transferability" provision. Most commissioned officers already had college degrees and most enlistees did not, for example. The organizations believed spouses and children of officers would have a disproportionately greater benefit from this proposed provision than would those of enlisted persons themselves.

Second, The American Legion and the Veterans of Foreign Wars of the United States[35] wanted the Department of Defense—rather than the Veterans Administration—to pay for a new GI Bill because of the strong emphasis on military recruiting and also because VA funding was already inadequate to carry out certain functions[36] mandated by Congress.

Third, the American Association of State Colleges and Universities proposed:[37]

• Monthly educational benefits to be more than $250[38] per month to keep up with the escalating costs of higher education; and

• That service members could use the benefits while still serving in the military.

I'm sure you see how the various concerns of these three different types of groups represented considerations in how we shaped H.R. 1400 in 1981. Did we listen to groups like The American Legion and Veterans of Foreign Wars of the United States with hundreds of thousands of members between them, for example?

Here's a lighthearted answer to my question of whether we listened.

Congressman Mike Simpson, former Speaker of the House in Idaho and later Chairman of the Subcommittee on Benefits, House Veterans' Affairs Committee,[39] humorously answered this question at a June 20, 2002, ceremony in which he and I participated at the Mayflower Hotel in Washington, D.C. The event marked the 58th anniversary of the World War II GI Bill.[40] Said Chairman Simpson—again lightheartedly—to the many veterans organizations attending:

Mr. Simpson

Mike Simpson

"We read all of your position papers—we're afraid **not** to!"[41]

Mr. Montgomery

Well said, Congressman!

Our new paradigm entailed having an ongoing GI Bill program that would always exist. In the past, Congress would create a GI Bill educational assistance program only when the U.S. was

> MANY CHAMPIONED THE ALL-VOLUNTEER FORCE, EITHER IN CONCEPT OR IMPLEMENTATION.
> —G.V. "Sonny" Montgomery

involved in a war, such as WW II, or military conflict, such as Korea or Vietnam. Veterans used the GI Bill as a tool for transitioning from military to civilian life, as they lagged many years behind their non-veteran peers[42] in the civilian job market.

Ours was a different paradigm because we designed this New GI Bill largely to help encourage youth to volunteer for the military instead of being drafted. Many championed the All-Volunteer Force, either in concept or implementation. These included Congressman Bill Steiger of Wisconsin, Congressman Spark Matsunaga[43] of Hawaii, former Secretary of Defense Thomas Gates, Lt. General George Forsyth, Secretary of the Army Bo Calloway, and others.[44]

MORE FROM 1980

I'd like to focus on some of the individuals I worked with directly who helped make the All-Volunteer Force work, especially regarding educational incentives. You'll hear more about them later as well.

First, Army General and Vice Chief of Staff Maxwell Thurman, *Maxwell Thurman* "one of the fathers of our All-Volunteer military. Brilliant and hard charging, the 'Be All You Can Be' marketing campaign was one of his creations."[45] Max was indefatigable. He was visionary and his leadership was unparalleled.

Second, Army Chief of Staff General "Shy" Meyer. General Meyer testified in 1981:[46]

Gen. Meyer

"The biggest single deterrent, despite all you've heard, to the current readiness of the Army, is turbulence... the principal contribution is the fact that the **non**-high school graduates [emphasis added] that we bring in stay at the rate of only 56 percent...

"... [T]hat means that 44 percent of them do not complete *Edward "Shy" Meyer* their initial tour of duty, and that just means that down in the companies we have this continuing turbulence of people in and people out, and

we are unable to train them to the level of readiness that we need...

"... In my personal judgment, all of these concerns will be ameliorated by educational benefits for high school graduates."

Mr. Montgomery

Third, General John Wickham was a key supporter of our vision as Chief of Staff of the Army from 1983 to 1987. His early 1983 internal Army "Project 14" study, headed by Colin Powell, looked at policies to support, change, and initiate so as to recruit quality enlistees and focus on the importance of educational opportunities. General Wickham's May 1985 *John Wickham* article in *Soldier Magazine* helped make the New GI Bill a household phrase and an understandable benefit for the Army.[47] And General Wickham also understood that we "enlist soldiers and reenlist families to sustain the Army."[48]

John Wickham

Bob Elton

Fourth, the Army's Lt. General Bob Elton played a leadership role, especially in the Senate Veterans' Affairs Committee in 1987, which we'll discuss in Chapter 12.

SENATOR COHEN'S AND ARMSTRONG'S BILLS

In the Senate, Armed Services Committee members Bill Cohen and Bill Armstrong were on the case, having introduced S. 2020, the proposed "Armed Forces Earned Educational Assistance Act," in 1979 and S. 2596, the proposed "Veterans' Educational Assistance Act of 1980," in 1980, respectively; each would create a new and better educational assistance program.

So we had two bills from two "Bills!"

A common feature of the two bills was not requiring a financial contribution from the service member, as was the case with the $2 government payment for $1 service member match of VEAP we discussed earlier. This was a major change. Ten senators cosponsored the Armstrong bill.

As you recall, under VEAP, the service member could contribute as much as $2,700, and the U.S. government would match it at double that amount for a total of up to $8,100. It drew little interest from service members.[49]

Do you know that members of Congress may testify on their own bills? Testifying on S. 2596 on June 19, 1980, in the Senate Committee on Veterans' Affairs, Senator Armstrong observed the following:[50]

Mr. Armstrong

"When the Army announced on October 20, 1976, that [Vietnam-era] GI Bill benefits would be terminated, they experienced the greatest surge[51] of volunteer enlistments for that time period than we have seen at any time during peacetime."

Bill Armstrong

Mr. Montgomery

Also testifying at the same hearing was Dr. Charles Moskos:[52]

Mr. Moskos

"The All-Volunteer Force is on the edge of survival… .

"Difficulties in recruiting an All-Volunteer Force have led to renewed talk of restoring conscription. But a return to the draft would pose a new question of who serves when most do not.

> **"THE ALL-VOLUNTEER FORCE IS ON THE EDGE OF SURVIVAL… ."**
> —*Dr. Charles Moskos*

"The major barriers to more effective recruitment have been the elimination of the GI Bill in 1976 and concurrent expansion of federal assistance to college students. Congress has created a system of educational benefits that offers more to those who do **not** serve [emphasis added] their country than to those who **do** [emphasis added]. This is perverse… .

"With the passage of the Middle Income Students Assistance Act [of 1978][53] … [I]n effect, we have created a GI Bill without the GI… .

"Proposals to have a 'test program' of post-service educational benefits are ill-considered. It makes no sense to handicap with constraints what may be the last chance to make the All-Volunteer Force work.

"… A "little GI Bill" for Reserve duty ought also be considered. Under such a program, budgetary costs could easily be contained within present limits, and over the long term, most likely, even reduced."

Mr. Montgomery

Folks, Senator Cohen also testified regarding his bill. I'll ask him to restate part of his oral testimony from the June 19, 1980, hearing and his statement when he introduced S. 2020 on November 16, 1979: [54]

Mr. Cohen

"… The bill that I have introduced was really, the work, background… [as] provided by the Non Commissioned Officers Association. They developed it. Dick Johnson, particularly, was outstanding in helping me with this… and the National Association of State Approving Agencies… Don Sweeney."

Mr. Montgomery

With the exception of Administration witnesses (including VA) at the June 19, 1980, hearing, all witnesses expressed support for the New GI Bill.[55]

On December 12, 1980, Alan Cranston, then-chairman of the Senate Veterans' Affairs Committee, introduced S. 3263, the proposed "All-Volunteer Force Educational Assistance Act of 1980."[56]

Senator Cranston's legislation, too, was designed to replace the unsuccessful VEAP program. VEAP would expire on December 31, 1981, unless the President would make a recommendation that the program should be continued.

In his introductory statement, Chairman Cranston said:[57]

Mr. Cranston

"… Mr. President, I remain deeply committed to and strongly supportive of the all-volunteer military force. But there is widespread recognition that the all-volunteer military faces a major challenge as the recruitment-age population continues to decrease… .

Alan Cranston

"… Major pay increases were enacted this year by Congress—both across-the-board increases and special pay increases for those with skills in acute, short supply. The military compensation system, however, has always been made up of both pay and benefits, and I believe that educational benefits have a special, very significant role to play in increasing the numbers and quality of the people we attract to—and retain in—the armed services… ."

Mr. Montgomery

What does "Administration" mean? Administration means the sitting president and his political party. In this case, the Reagan Administration.

Although candidate Ronald Reagan specifically expressed support for the notion of a New GI Bill during the 1980 campaign, once he was inaugurated, the President's Office of Management and Budget repudiated the idea.[58]

What is the Office of Management and Budget (OMB)?

OMB articulates administration policy on all manner of federal budget, public policy, legislative, regulatory, procurement, e-gov, and management issues.[59] Currently, about 550 employees work at OMB—most of whom are part of the career civil service.[60]

John Paul Hammerschmidt   *Richard White*   *Marjorie Holt*   *Les Au Coin*   *Thomas Hartnett*

On January 28, 1981, five of my House colleagues and I introduced H.R. 1400, the "Veterans' Educational Assistance Act of 1981," referred to as the New GI Bill. My five colleagues were Representatives John Paul Hammerschmidt (R-AR), Richard White (D-TX), Marjorie Holt (R-MD), Les Au Coin (D-OR) and Thomas F. Hartnett (R-SC)

On February 5, 1981, Senator Cranston introduced S. 417,[61] the proposed "All-Volunteer Force Educational Assistance Act," but there were no hearings on it.

One of the five original cosponsors of H.R. 1400 was my friend John Paul. John Paul and I spoke with one voice on this issue. John Paul was a B-17 pilot during World War II. I think I can say with accuracy that John Paul understood from personal experience the importance of having a strong military force.

No person consistently supported our efforts like Rep. Hammerschmidt. John Paul's leadership over the seven years proved truly invaluable.

In the spring of 1981, under the leadership of Subcommittee Chairman Bob Edgar of Pennsylvania and Ranking Member Margaret Heckler of Massachusetts, the Subcommittee on Education, Training, and Employment held six hearings—both in Washington, D.C., and across the country.[62] The subcommittee received testimony from nearly 100 witnesses, including representatives from the active-duty military, the Veterans Administration, military personnel associations, and veterans' organizations. I join Bob in commending his subcommittee staff director at that time, Mr. Richard Fuller, and staff assistant, Ms. Beth Kilker, for organizing such comprehensive hearings.

On May 19, 1981, the House Veterans' Affairs Committee unanimously marked-up H.R. 1400. Jointly referred by the House Parliamentarian, H.R. 1400 then went to the House Armed Services Committee for consideration. Why two committees?

The Parliamentarian referred the bill to the Veterans' Affairs Committee—because the bill was a transition tool to civilian life for veterans—and to the Armed Services Committee because it contained "kickers" to help fill critical military occupational specialties.

On June 24, 1981, I accompanied Subcommittee Chairman Bob Edgar when he testified on H.R. 1400 before the Subcommittee on Military Personnel and Compensation of the House Armed Services Committee.[63] Earlier that year, Representatives Duncan Hunter (R-CA) and Bill Whitehurst (R-VA) of the Armed Services Committee[64] testified before the Edgar/Heckler subcommittee in support of H.R. 1400.[65]

1981

I'd like to call on Chairman Edgar now to share with us six short paragraphs from his June 24 testimony:[66]

Union Calendar No. 348

97TH CONGRESS
2d SESSION

H. R. 1400

[Report No. 97–80, Parts I and II]

To amend title 38, United States Code, to establish new educational assistance programs for veterans and for members of the Armed Forces.

IN THE HOUSE OF REPRESENTATIVES

JANUARY 28, 1981

Mr. MONTGOMERY (for himself, Mr. HAMMERSCHMIDT, Mr. WHITE, Mrs. HOLT, Mr. AUCOIN, and Mr. HARTNETT) introduced the following bill; which was referred jointly to the Committees on Veterans' Affairs and Armed Services

MAY 19, 1981

Reported from the Committee on Veterans' Affairs with an amendment
[Strike out all after the enacting clause and insert the part printed in italic]

MAY 17, 1982

Additional sponsors: Mr. SPENCE, Mr. HEFNER, Mr. STUMP, Mr. EMERY, Mr. DICKS, Mr. SUNIA, Mr. EDGAR, Mr. MAZZOLI, Mr. BRINKLEY, Mr. LEHMAN, Mr. EVANS of Indiana, Mr. McCLOSKEY, Mr. HUTTO, Mr. DeNARDIS, Mr. COELHO, Mr. SIMON, Mr. SAM B. HALL, JR., Mr. FITH-IAN, Mr. ATKINSON, Mr. LONG of Maryland, Mr. EDWARDS of California, Mr. DANIELSON, Mr. MOTTL, Mr. APPLEGATE, Mr. BONER of Tennessee, Mr. SHELBY, Mr. MICA, Mr. DASCHLE, Mr. DORGAN of North Dakota, Mr. WON PAT, Mrs. HECKLER, Mr. WYLIE, Mr. SAWYER, Mr. SOLOMON, Mr. JEFFRIES, Mr. McEWEN, Mr. DUNN, Mr. SMITH of New Jersey, Mr. SIL-JANDER, Mr. LEATH of Texas, Mr. CONTE, Mr. WORTLEY, Mr. FORSYTHE, Mr. ENGLISH, Mr. OBERSTAR, Mr. PEPPER, Mr. de la GARZA, Mr. WHITEHURST, Mr. DERRICK, Mr. HORTON, Mrs. BYRON, Mr. HERTEL, Mr. FOGLIETTA, Mr. TRIBLE, Mr. BURGENER, Mr. IRELAND, Mr. LAGOMAR-SINO, Mr. PARRIS, Mr. ESTEL, Mr. KAZEN, Mr. MITCHELL of Maryland, Mr. BAILEY of Pennsylvania, Mr. FORD of Michigan, Mr. DELLUMS, Mr. HYDE, Mr. RAHALL, Mr. DYMALLY, Mr. ZEFERETTI, Mr. RICHMOND, Mr. GONZALEZ, Mr. DOUGHETY, Mr. STARK, Mr. CLAUSEN, Mr. BROWN of California, Mr. BEDELL, Mr. BEVILL, Mr. WEBER of Minnesota, Mr. DUNCAN, Mr. JONES of North Carolina, Mr. EDWARDS of Oklahoma, Mr.

H.R. 1400, the reported bill.

Mr. Edgar

Bob Edgar

"The Congress has voted in recent weeks, at the request of the President, the greatest budget reduction in recent history. At the same time it has mightily increased defense spending. Many decisions will be made in the months ahead on how best to utilize those funds. Certainly there will be arguments over weapons systems, technology and military hardware. But no matter how advanced the hardware, the effectiveness of our defense force rests in the quality of those who will man those weapons.

"As the President [Reagan] said recently at West Point, 'Weaponry alone does not mean security.' Quoting General George Patton, he said 'Wars may be fought with weapons, but they are won by men.' And as he added, won by women as well. 'It is the spirit of the men (and women) who follow and the men (and women) who lead that will gain the victory.'

"… Patriotism cannot be bought, but it should be rewarded.

"The drawing power of the GI Bill was clearly demonstrated in the closing months of 1975 when recruiting offices around the country were swamped with potential enlistees trying to take advantage of the last days of eligibility for the Vietnam-era education program. From that point on, we have been trying to operate an All-Volunteer Force and encourage recruitment with education benefits **far below** [emphasis added] those offered to military personnel under draft conditions.[67] Many of our witnesses agreed that the drastic reduction in the quality and quantity of recruits from 1976 to 1980 is directly attributable to that loss in education benefits. While at the same time, billions of dollars were authorized for federal education grants to students who had no obligation for national service.

"Both the Veterans Administration and the troops in the field have called the contributory Veterans' Educational Assistance Program (VEAP), which replaced the Vietnam-era GI Bill, an abysmal failure. Participation rates for training within the VEAP program have consistently fallen below projected levels. Out of approximately 350,000 service personnel who have entered into the program since 1976, nearly half (157,000) have either stopped making contributions (59,000) or have cashed out of the program entirely by requesting refunds out of the program (98,000), according to the Veterans Administration."

Mr. Montgomery

I'd like Chairman Edgar to close by citing from his testimony his observation with regard to our transferability provision, as well as numbers regarding attrition and quality of enlistees.[68]

COLD, WET, AND MISERABLE

With regard to the provision in H.R. 1400 allowing the service member to transfer his or her educational benefits to a spouse or child… .[69]

Mr. Edgar

"A first lieutenant asked: How can you ask someone to be cold, wet and miserable in the combat arms if that soldier was denied transferability while others [in other military occupational specialties] were granted it?

"In 1979, the General Accounting Office reported that 444,000 first-term volunteers had left the service between 1974 and 1977 before completing their initial enlistments. The cost to the federal government for this loss was $5.2 billion.[70]

"At the same time, the Department of Defense projected that up to an estimated one-third of active duty male first term enlistees from FY 1976 to FY 1978 failed to complete three years of initial service, 'mostly because of lack of aptitude or motivation.'

"Current DoD data estimates that high school graduates are twice as likely to complete their full enlistments as are high school dropouts. H.R. 1400 would attract only high school graduates.

"Thank you, Mr. Montgomery."

Mr. Montgomery

Last, during June, September, October, and November of 1981—and also March of 1982—the Military Personnel and Compensation Subcommittee of the House Armed Services Committee conducted 12 field hearings on "New Educational Incentives for Recruiting at Military Installations Across the Country."[71] A great way to learn is to go beyond the beltway of Washington![72] In this case, both the Veterans' Affairs and Armed Services committees had done so. I'd like to point out, as Michael Ballard and Craig Piper noted in a book they wrote about me called *Sonny Montgomery: The Veteran's Champion*, the House Parliamentarian referred to H.R. 1400 jointly to the Committee on Veterans' Affairs and the Committee on Armed Services. H.R. 1400 originated in the Committee on Veterans' Affairs because it would provide a permanent, new VA educational assistance program to help military veterans transition to civilian life.

H.R. 1400 assigned the Defense Department responsibility for paying "kickers" to New GI Bill benefits for skills critically needed. In a secondary way, H.R. 1400 was also designed to help the service branches in recruiting and retention of service members for both active-duty service and the Guard and the Reserve. So understandably, the bill had to be considered by the Armed Services Committee.

1982

On May 11, 1982, the Armed Services Committee marked-up H.R. 1400 with minor amendments.[73] Remember that in Congressional parlance, "reported" means approved and referred to the full House for a vote.

The vote in the Military Personnel and Compensation Subcommittee of the House Armed Services Committee, chaired so ably by Representative Bill Nichols (D-AL), with excellent leadership, as well, from Ranking Member Don Mitchell (R-NY), was 12 to 1 in favor of the proposed New GI Bill. The vote in the full House Armed Services Committee was 40 to 1.[74]

After we won the vote, there was not strong support for the proposed New GI Bill from the House Armed Services Committee (HASC) leadership. As you'll read in a page or so, the HASC leadership let 1982 pass by without taking H.R. 1400 to the House floor for a vote.

Nevertheless, here are some of Representative Nichols' observations during discussion of the bill at the May 11, 1982, full committee mark-up.[75]

Mr. Nichols

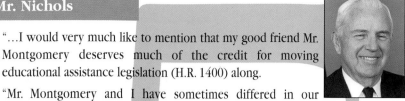

"…I would very much like to mention that my good friend Mr. Montgomery deserves much of the credit for moving educational assistance legislation (H.R. 1400) along.

"Mr. Montgomery and I have sometimes differed in our philosophy, as to what the program should look like, but he has my congratulations for his perseverance and skill during consideration of this very important [proposed] new program.

William F. Nichols

"As all of you know, the Vietnam-era educational assistance program was terminated for new enlistees on January 1, 1977. A new program involving contributions from enlistees was substituted in its place. This current program is called VEAP, standing for Veterans' Educational Assistance Program. There seems to be unanimous agreement that this new program has not been effective.

"… The Defense Department has been all over the map on this bill. They have come to us repeatedly—and I am speaking of every branch of the service—and indicated to us that the GI Bill was the finest thing that had come along since indoor plumbing."[76]

Mr. Montgomery

Representatives Nichols and Mitchell's leadership was crucial because in Secretary of Defense Caspar Weinberger's April 27, 1982, official comment on the H.R. 1400, the proposed New GI Bill, the Defense Department opposed the legislation. Noted Mr. Weinberger: "We favor a continuation of the VEAP program with supplemental kickers; a continuation of the Selected Reserve educational benefits; and an extension of the 1989 delimiting date on the current GI Bill."[77]

As I mentioned above, the committee was unconvinced regarding the Department of Defense argument and supported a New GI Bill in H.R. 1400, amended, by a vote of 40 to 1. I was a member of the subcommittee chaired by Mr. Nichols. Here are excerpts from my statement during the committee's debate, prior to the 40 to 1 vote.[78]

"Mr. Chairman [Les Aspin, (D-WI)], there are several things I like about the bill that is being recommended by our subcommittee.

"First, it will improve the quality of recruitment and retention for all branches of the military service.

"Second, the cost of the bill will be shared by the Veterans' Administration and the Department of Defense.

"Third, the ability to recruit and retain quality individuals in the Selected Reserve will be greatly enhanced.

"Fourth, the Individual Ready Reserve will be strengthened.

"Fifth, enactment of a new GI education bill will also solve a major problem that the Navy and Air Force now face in that it will provide education benefits for those currently serving on active duty who would otherwise be leaving the service in order to take advantage of the Vietnam-era GI Bill. As many of you know, the current Vietnam-era GI Bill will expire on December 31, 1989. Testimony has revealed that many individuals are currently leaving the service in order to take advantage of that program. If this bill is enacted, they will remain on active duty because benefits will be available for those who continue to serve beyond the 1989 date.

"When compared with the Vietnam-era GI Bill's $1.3 billion [cost] in fiscal year 1983, the subcommittee bill is not a costly measure. According to CBO, the maximum annual cost of this bill would only be $762 million in 1995 (VA cost $403 million and DoD cost $359 million). The net cost will be even less because a large part of the cost of the bill will be offset by the following:

(1) A reduction in DoD's annual billion-dollar recruiting and advertising budget;

(2) Reduced retraining costs;

(3) Termination of the existing Veterans' Educational Assistance Program (VEAP), a program that is quite expensive yet has not worked very well at all; and

(4) Curtailment in the postsecondary education [pilot] program now being conducted by the Department of Defense."

BUT NO HOUSE VOTE

For unknown reasons, the House took no vote on the legislation, so it died in committee.[79] Also, for unknown reasons, the leadership of the Armed Services Committee elected not to bring the bill to the floor for a vote.

1983

On February 20, 1983, we reintroduced H.R. 1400.

You'll recall that we introduced our original bill H.R. 1400 in 1981 during the 97th Congress. The year 1983 began the 98th Congress. Bills do not "carry over" from one Congress to next. Members have to reintroduce them.

Following hearings held by the Subcommittee on Education, Training, and Employment, during which nearly all witnesses expressed substantial support for the program, the full Committee on Veterans' Affairs reported H.R. 1400 on May 16, 1983.

Do you see how we waited until H.R. 1400 became available as a bill number? We wanted to establish an "identity" for our bill by using the same bill number from the previous Congress. Bill numbers are assigned chronologically as they are introduced. So one has to a make special effort to "reserve" a number with the Bill Clerk's office, which is part of the House Office of Legislative Operations.[80]

However, the House Armed Services Committee would take no action on H.R. 1400 until 1984, doing so as part of the FY 1985 DoD Authorization Act instead of bringing H.R. 1400 to the House floor for a vote as a separate, "clean" bill.

The Senate reintroduced bills as well.[81] Senator Cranston introduced S. 8, the proposed "All-Volunteer Force Educational Assistance Act," on January 8, 1983; Senator Armstrong introduced S. 691, the proposed "Veterans' Education Assistance Act of 1983" on March 7, 1983; and Senator Cranston, et al., introduced S. 1747, the proposed "Peacetime Veterans' Educational Assistance Act" on August 3, 1983.

But the big policy push in 1983 was on the Senate floor rather than in committee. Senator Bill Armstrong, on behalf of himself and Senators Cohen, Hollings, Matsunaga, Cranston, Boschwitz, DeConcini, Hart, Dole, Kasten, Kennedy, Pressler, Hawkins, Bradley, Mitchell, and D'Amato[82]—offered an amendment during the Senate's 1983 debate on S. 675, the FY 1984 DoD Authorization Act… an amendment that failed by a vote of 52 to 46.[83]

This amendment essentially took the form of S. 691,[84] discussed above.[85]

The debate on Senator Armstrong's amendment formed around the following five[86] issues:

- Legislative procedure associated with the amendment itself;[87]
- Need for a New GI Bill;[88]
- Substantive purpose of a New GI Bill;[89]
- Cost of a New GI Bill;[90] and
- "Politics" of a New GI Bill.[91]

Senator Armstrong would offer a similar floor amendment in 1984 that we'll discuss in detail in Chapters 7, 8, and 9. Senator John Glenn would offer a floor amendment in 1984, too.

So for the 1980-1983 period, what GI Bill legislation did we achieve? None! Because neither the House nor the Senate passed a bill. But it did allow us to bring attention to our legislation and foster support for the bill.

WHAT'S NEXT

Instead of continuing to push solely for a "stand-alone" bill, we'll make our New GI Bill legislation part of an omnibus funding bill called the fiscal year 1985 Department of Defense Authorization Act.

Sonny's Lessons Learned

Do your legislative homework before you introduce your bill.

Examples in this chapter include the following:

*(1) Our consulting with the service branches **before** introducing H.R. 1400;*

*(2) Senator Cranston having a public hearing on possible bill components **before** introducing S. 3263; and*

*(3) Senator Cohen consulting extensively with the Non Commissioned Officers Association and National Association of State Approving Agencies **before** developing S. 2020.*

Worth Repeating

"When the Vietnam War ended in 1975, the military had great difficulty persuading young people to sign up, even though it was peacetime… and in 1980 only 54 percent of Army recruits had a high school diploma."
—*Professor Charles Moskos*

"As the President [Reagan] said recently at West Point, 'Weaponry alone does not mean security.'"
—*Bob Edgar*

"The drawing power of the GI Bill was clearly demonstrated in the closing months of 1975 when recruiting offices around the country were swamped with potential enlistees trying to take advantage of the last days of eligibility for the Vietnam-era education program."
—*Bob Edgar*

6

SONNY'S
CAST OF
CHARACTERS

Representative Bob Edgar (D-PA), Chairman, Subcommittee on Education, Training, and Employment

Representative David Bonior (D-MI), Member, Committee on Rules

Representative Del Latta (R-OH), Member, Committee on Rules

Late Spring 1984—
Road to Enactment:
House Passes a New GI Bill Unopposed

SONNY'S SUMMARY

Under Title VII of H.R. 5167, the proposed Department of Defense Authorization Act for 1985, the House Committee on Armed Services, of which I was a member, approved on April 19, 1984, a new GI Bill educational assistance program for military personnel effective October 1, 1984. The full House approved this provision on May 31, which was derived from our bill H.R. 1400, the Veterans' Educational Assistance Act of 1983. As proponents of the bill reiterated many times, we designed the new program to attract and retain high-quality young men and women in both the active and reserve forces of our military and then entitle them to four years of postsecondary education after their service. As a matter of legislative history, the House Veterans' Affairs Committee also had approved H.R. 1400 on May 16, 1983, and had approved an earlier version on May 19, 1981, which the House did not vote on.

Sonny's Scene Setter & Journey Guide

**Committee on Armed Services
of the U.S. House of Representatives and later
the House floor during deliberation on the
FY 1985 DoD Authorization Act.**

On the Legislative Journey chart on page 11,
we are at boxes H-6, H-7 and H-8 with respect to
H.R. 5167, The DoD Authorization Act of 1985,
of which a New GI Bill was a very small part.

1984—BUT FIRST, A LOOK BACK

Mr. Montgomery

> "TWENTY HEARINGS—
> 1981 TO 1983—
> TO ACHIEVE 1984
> HOUSE PASSAGE…"
> —*G.V. "Sonny" Montgomery*

Prior to discussing the House's May 31, 1984, passage of a New GI Bill as part of the 1985 DoD Authorization Act, here are a couple of morsels to remember from the earlier stages of our journey and the initial May 19, 1981, House Veterans' Affairs Committee approval of H.R. 1400:

- First, as we learned in the last chapter, the Military Personnel and Compensation Subcommittee of the House Armed Services Committee (HASC) held 12 hearings at military installations across the country from June 24, 1981, to March 11, 1982, on "New Educational Assistance Program for the Military to Assist Recruiting." Representatives Bill Nichols (D-AL) and Don Mitchell (R-NY) convened the hearings.[1]

- Second, the Subcommittee on Education, Training, and Employment of the House Veterans' Affairs Committee held six hearings in Washington, D.C., and across the country from March 17 to April 23, 1981, on the Veterans' Educational Assistance Act of 1981 and two more such hearings on March 31, 1982, and April 12, 1983. Subcommittee Chairman Bob Edgar (D-PA) and ranking member Margaret Heckler (R-MA) convened those hearings.[2]

- Third, on May 11, 1982, the HASC marked-up H.R. 1400 with amendments.

- Fourth, the House Veterans' Affairs Committee marked-up H.R. 1400, the Veterans' Educational Assistance Act of 1983, on May 12, 1983.

- Fifth, the HASC marked-up a New GI Bill-type educational assistance program very similar to H.R. 1400 on April 19, 1984.

Students, Title VII: Educational Assistance Programs, of the 399-page report filed by

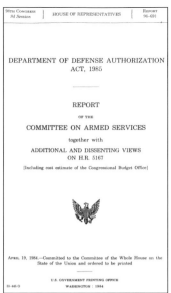

the Armed Services Committee on H.R. 5167, the Department of Defense Authorization Act of 1985, speaks to the specifics of the New GI Bill provision that the House would pass on May 31, 1984.

Let's look at the wording in the Committee Report on H.R. 5167[3] filed by the Armed Services Committee.

The words we'll quote verbatim are important because they convey information about the "why" and "how" of the bill—more specifically, why the House Armed Services Committee crafted a New GI Bill, and how it was structured.

FIRST, THE "WHY"

The findings of the Armed Services Committee generally were similar to those of the Veterans' Affairs Committee.[4]

- "The purpose of Title VII is to establish a new educational assistance program for military personnel effective October 1, 1984… designed to attract and retain high-quality young men and women in both the active and Reserve forces by offering them financial assistance for obtaining a college education.

- "… The Committee is concerned that the services' recent recruiting and retention success may not continue if the national economy continues to improve or if one of a number of other factors currently favorable to recruiting and retention changes adversely… .

- "As the number of 18- and 19-year-olds declines over the remainder of the decade, the

> "… THE COMPETITION FROM COLLEGES AND UNIVERSITIES AND FROM PRIVATE INDUSTRY FOR THE SHRINKING POOL OF HIGH-QUALITY YOUNG PEOPLE WILL INTENSIFY."
> —*1984 House Armed Services Committee Report*

competition from colleges and universities and from private industry for the shrinking pool of high-quality young people will intensify. At the same time, the services will require an increasing number of high-quality personnel to operate and maintain the sophisticated weapon systems coming on line in the late 1980s and 1990s… .

- "Of particular concern as well is the recent downturn in recruiting experienced personnel by the Army National Guard and the Army Reserve during the first quarter of fiscal year 1984. Army National Guard accessions [enlistments] were down 34 percent from a year earlier; Army Reserve accessions were off by 11 percent from the same period in fiscal year 1983. With the growing reliance on the reserve components envisioned by the committee, a special enlistment and reenlistment incentive for the Reserve and Guard is vital.

- "… A number of witnesses, including recruiters and military personnel chiefs, have testified in public hearings that educational incentives are one of the best recruitment and retention tools. Regardless of the recruiting situation that may exist in the future, the military services will never be faced with too many applications for enlistment of high-quality personnel."

NOW, THE "HOW"

The Armed Services Committee derived the educational benefits in H.R. 5167 from H.R. 1400, including the following:[5]

Basic Educational Assistance

- "Basic monthly educational assistance allowance of $300 per month, with a maximum of 36 months [four academic years] of entitlement for military personnel who served for three years on active duty or two years on active duty and four years in the Selected Reserve [a generic term for both the Guard and Reserve forces of each service branch]… .

Kicker to the Basic Benefit

- "The Committee recommends authority for the Secretary of Defense, at his discretion, to increase the amount of the basic benefit by up to an additional $400 per month for individuals in critical or difficult-to-recruit-for skills… .

Supplemental Benefit

- "In addition, the committee recommends a supplemental benefit of $300 per month to service members who complete the initial period of service required for the basic benefit and serve an additional five years on active duty or an additional two years on active duty and four years in the Selected Reserve. This provision is intended to provide the Secretary of Defense with additional discretionary authority to target additional benefits toward critical or difficult-to-retain skills… .

Transferability to Spouse or Children

- "The Committee recommends a provision that would authorize the Secretary of Defense, at his discretion, to permit a service member to transfer the earned educational entitlement to the service member's dependents for their use… .

Educational Assistance for the Selected Reserve

- "Title VII would also establish an educational assistance benefit specifically for members of the Selected Reserve. Selected Reservists would receive $140 per month entitlement for up to 36 months paid by the Department of Defense… .

Termination of Other Educational Programs

- "The bill would terminate the existing Veterans' Educational Assistance Program (VEAP) and [a very small DoD-funded test under Title 10 U.S.C.] Selected Reserve educational benefits program. Individuals currently participating in these programs would be covered under the new

U.S. House of Representatives Chamber as it appeared in 1995.

program…" I'd add that new enlistees would have to have a high school diploma or equivalency to qualify for these post-service education benefits.

The House debated H.R. 5167—a $208-billion authorization bill—on seven different days between May 15 and May 31 and then sent it to the Senate.[6] There were on the order of 50 proposed floor amendments.[7] The debate was highly-contentious at times because of issues of military technology and weapons systems, including thermonuclear ones.

None of the debate or amendments involved opposition to a New GI Bill.[8]

Let me highlight my statements and those of Subcommittee Chairman Bob Edgar during the spirited debate on May 15 and May 16. As we saw it, it was hard to discuss cold-war, high-technology military weapons systems without discussing having skilled people to operate them. Noted Mr. Edgar:[9]

Mr. Edgar

Bob Edgar

"… I rise in support of Title VII of H.R. 5167, the Department of Defense Authorization Act for fiscal year 1985.

"As we expand our military forces in hardware and technology, we must be prepared to act now to provide the incentives to meet these challenges in the coming years.

"[I quote] Maj. Gen. Kenneth Peek, Deputy Chief of Staff for Manpower and Personnel, U.S. Air Force:

'A New GI Bill would help us attract and retain the kinds of people we need in the increasingly complex and high technology Air Force that we have today.'"

Mr. Montgomery

I added the following during the debate:[10]

"While procurement of weapon systems is necessary, Congress must also [ensure] recruitment and retention of sufficient numbers of quality personnel to operate and maintain these sophisticated weapons. The required weapons systems are expensive, but we must not let their cost have an adverse effect on personnel expenditures or readiness. We must give first priority to our military people. The educational assistance program contained in Title VII reflects that priority."

Plus, there was discussion regarding how to pay for a New GI Bill that I think students would benefit from hearing.

In a nutshell, the Rules Committee waived section 303(a)(4) of the Congressional Budget and Impoundment Control Act of 1974 (also known as "Budget Act" and "Congressional Budget Act") with respect to our veterans' education provisions.

Representative David Bonior explained this matter on the House floor on May 15, 1984, just prior to commencing debate.[11]

Mr. Bonior

David Bonior

"The rule provides a waiver of section 303(a)(4) of the Congressional Budget Act of 1974 against consideration of the committee substitute [meaning H.R. 5167, the committee bill]. This section of the Budget Act prohibits the consideration of measures containing new spending authority, which would become effective in a fiscal year.

"Several sections of the committee substitute provide new spending authority for fiscal year 1985 and as members well know, the first concurrent budget resolution for fiscal year 1985 has not yet been adopted.[12]

"Section 601 of the committee substitute provides a 3.5-percent increase in basic pay for nearly all military personnel to take effect on January 1, 1985, and Title VII of the substitute authorizes new spending authority through an education assistance program [for military recruitment and veterans' transition].

"However, the fiscal impact of the education assistance program in 1985 is negligible and

> "SEVERAL SECTIONS OF THE COMMITTEE SUBSTITUTE PROVIDE NEW SPENDING AUTHORITY FOR FISCAL YEAR 1985..."
> —*Representative David Bonior, Michigan*

the pay increase is assumed in the House-passed budget resolution.

"In order to provide for consideration of the committee amendment, the Committee on Rules waived that section of the Budget Act."

Mr. Montgomery

Representative Del Latta of the Rules Committee spoke to this matter, as well:[13]

Mr. Latta

Del Latta

"Mr. Speaker, while the provisions of the rule have been described in detail, there is a waiver which should be [further] noted.

"There is a waiver of section 303(a)(4) of the Budget Act. This section was waived in order to allow consideration of new entitlement authority before final action in the first budget resolution.

"Mr. Speaker, one of the new entitlements in this bill would provide education benefits payable to certain veterans. The bulk of the entitlement under this program would be for individuals who serve in the Armed Forces after September 30, 1984, for at least three years from that date and meet other eligibility requirements.

> "THERE IS A WAIVER OF SECTION 303(A)(4) OF THE BUDGET ACT."
> —*Representative Del Latta, Ohio*

"The cost of the program, while small in the near term, would balloon in the outyears, as is typical of entitlement programs. The Congressional Budget Office estimates that this provision of the bill would cost $106 million in fiscal year 1985, $305 million in fiscal year 1986, and $369 million in fiscal year 1987. But the fiscal year 1995 cost would soar to $778 million.

"Mr. Speaker, the Defense Department authorization is one of the most important bills we consider during the course of each year. In this case, the Armed Services Committee has cut the authorization level far below the administration's original request, which was for a 13-percent real growth rate after inflation. According to testimony presented in the Rules Committee, this bill provides [meaning it "assumes"] for approximately a 16-percent, real growth rate after inflation.

"The authorizations for appropriations for fiscal year 1985 recommended for procurement, research and development, operations and maintenance, working capital funds, and civil defense, total $208.1 billion. This amount is

$16.4 billion **below** [emphasis added] the total of $224 billion requested by the President... .

"Mr. Speaker, under this open rule,[14] the House will be able to consider each item in this bill on its own merits.

"I support the rule so that the House may begin its consideration of this major legislation."

Mr. Montgomery

Getting the waiver was very important. Absent getting it, any member and especially a member of the Budget Committee or Rules Committee could have called for a violation of the Budget Act, and the New GI Bill provision likely would have been struck from the bill.

Sonny's Lessons Learned

Cooperation between committees is essential.

If you have cooperation, you can get things done. If you don't, you can't.

Many of us were members of both the Armed Services and Veterans' Affairs Committee. Who had the job to strike a chord of harmony and cooperation between these two committees that had jurisdiction over the New GI Bill provision? Those of us who sat on both.

Worth Repeating

"The Military Personnel and Compensation Subcommittee of the House Armed Services Committee held 12 hearings at military installations across the country from June 24, 1981, to March 11, 1982... "
—*G.V. "Sonny" Montgomery*

"A new GI Bill would help us attract and retain the kinds of people we need in the increasingly complex and high technology Air Force that we have today."
—*Major General Kenneth Peek, Deputy Chief of Staff, U.S. Air Force*

"There is a waiver of section 303(a)(4) of the Budget Act. This section was waived in order to allow consideration of new entitlement authority before final action in the first budget resolution."
—*Representative Del Latta*

WHAT'S NEXT

Let's move to the Senate floor for debate on its version of a new education incentive for our All-Volunteer military.

7

SONNY'S
CAST OF
CHARACTERS

Senator Nancy Kassebaum
(R-KS), Presiding Officer
(presiding over the debate)

Senator Bob Kasten (R-WI),
Presiding Officer

Senator Howard Baker
(R-TN), Majority Leader

Senator Bill Armstrong
(R-CO)

Senator John Tower (R-TX),
Chairman, Committee
on Armed Services

Senator John Glenn (D-OH)[1]

Senator James Abdnor (R-SD),
Presiding Officer

Senator Bill Cohen (R-ME),
Member, Committee on Armed
Services

Senator Alan Simpson
(R-WY), Chairman,
Committee on
Veterans' Affairs

Senator Alan Cranston
(D-CA), Ranking Member,
Committee on
Veterans' Affairs

Senator Spark Matsunaga
(D-CA), Member,
Committee on
Veterans' Affairs

Senator Sam Nunn (D-GA),
Ranking Member,
Committee on
Armed Services

Summer 1984—Road to Enactment: Senate Passes Glenn Test Citizen-Soldier Education Program 96 to 1—First Vote

SONNY'S SUMMARY

In this chapter, on June 11, we'll see the Senate debate extensively the test Citizen-Soldier Education Program, proposed by Senator John Glenn, as an amendment to The Omnibus Defense Authorization Act of 1985 (S. 2723). Also in this chapter, on June 13. in the first of six votes on the Glenn amendment that day, the Senate approves the Glenn Test Citizen-Soldier Education Assistance Program, 96 to 1. The next five substantive and procedural GI Bill votes are debated in Chapters 8 and 9.

Principals in the debate throughout were Senators Glenn (D-OH), John Tower (R-TX), Alan Simpson (R-WY), and Sam Nunn (D-GA), all of whom advocated the proposed test Citizen-Soldier Program. The Glenn group preferred what broadly may be described as a lower-cost, four-year test program in which service members would serve for two years and financially contribute to their GI Bill benefits— legislation the Senate approves in this chapter.

Senators Bill Armstrong (R-CO), Bill Cohen (R-ME), Alan Cranston (D-CA), and Spark Matsunaga (D-HI) advocated the proposed Peacetime Veterans' Educational Assistance Act. The Armstrong group wanted what broadly may be described as a higher-cost, permanent GI Bill program in which service members would serve generally for four years and not require them to contribute financially to their benefits (as a condition of program participation), legislation that we'll see voted down in Chapters 8 and 9.

Mr. Montgomery

This chapter—and the next two chapters—contain some of the richest debate of the seven-year legislative history of the Montgomery GI Bill.

By my count, 21 Senators spoke during about nine hours of debate on different amendments proposed principally by Senators Glenn and Armstrong to create new GI Bill-type programs for our all-volunteer military as part of the Fiscal Year 1985 Omnibus Department of Defense (DoD) Authorization Act. The Senate Armed Services Committee had both introduced and marked-up the bill on the same day (May 31, 1984).[2]

> **"... SOME OF THE RICHEST DEBATE OF THE SEVEN-YEAR LEGISLATIVE HISTORY OF THE MONTGOMERY GI BILL."**
> —*G.V. "Sonny" Montgomery*

Each year a defense authorization act furnishes authority for hundreds of billions of dollars in funding for the military services to fulfill their missions the following fiscal year.[3]

How many billions of dollars is the Senate talking about? For example, Senator Dixon of Illinois unsuccessfully moved to send the proposed DoD Authorization Act for FY 1985 back to the Senate Armed Services Committee to mark-up at a figure of $293.7 billion, which would have been 5 percent real growth for FY 1985 for the DoD Authorization bill.[4]

Students, this is an excellent chapter to use the interactive role-play approach embodied in our text. Just assign a student to play the role of each speaker listed in *Sonny's Cast of Characters* at the beginning of this chapter.

I've done my best to reflect in our text the Senate debate of June 11 and June 13 that expresses the various viewpoints—and captures the debate's overall flow—as recorded in the *Congressional Record*.[5]

The *Congressional Record* is the substantive, verbatim account of daily proceedings—especially debate and votes on the House and Senate floor. "At the back of each daily issue is the 'Daily Digest,' which summarizes the day's floor and committee activities."[6]

Said another way, I've tried my best to show the arguments—both for and against—the Glenn and Armstrong amendments, as Senators stated them. The two amendments had the same underlying objective: achieving a better GI Bill to recruit high-quality individuals into our all-volunteer military and furnishing a quality post-military service education benefit. But the approaches were very different.

> **"... NINE HOURS OF DEBATE OVER TWO DAYS..."**
> —*G.V. "Sonny" Montgomery*

I have divided the nine hours of debate over two days according to the debates and six votes:

FIRST VOTE—THIS CHAPTER—JUNE 11 AND 13, 1984

- The debate (June 11); and
- Glenn amendment passes 96 to 1 on a roll-call vote (June 13).

SECOND VOTE—CHAPTER 8—JUNE 13, 1984

- Tower motion to table the Armstrong amendment defeated 51 to 46 on a roll-call vote.

THIRD, FOURTH, FIFTH, AND SIXTH VOTES—CHAPTER 9—JUNE 13, 1984

- Armstrong motion to waive relevant portions of the Budget Act defeated 48-44 on a roll-call vote (third);
- Glenn motion to make his amendment subject to an annual appropriation, approved by unanimous consent with no roll-call vote (fourth);
- Tower second motion to table the Armstrong amendment passes 47-45 on a roll-call vote (fifth); and
- Glenn amendment, as modified by annual appropriation language, approved by a roll-call vote of 72-20 (sixth).

Students, Chapters 7, 8, and 9 reflect the Senate floor debate closely, so I am involving myself generally only to open and close each of the chapters and offer occasional clarifying comments.

One of you please assume the role of the Senate's Presiding Officer as well. That's the Senator who presides over the debate, a sort of parliamentary "referee." If the majority party in the Senate is the same party as the party occupying the White House, the Vice President sometimes presides over debate to be positioned to cast a tie-breaking vote.

For this chapter, and Chapters 8 and 9, I am not providing endnotes for the italicized words spoken during the debate because the only source is the *Congressional Record* for that day.

Except to open the floor debate/Senate session, I also do not include Senator's requests to the Presiding Officer seeking permission to be recognized to speak. And since the Presiding Officer essentially facilitates the debate, I do not necessarily show his or her picture in the text each time a new presiding officer assumes the chair.

Lastly, the format in this chapter and Chapters 8 and 9 reflects the debate/format as it appears in the *Congressional Record*.

We start with the debate on June 11, 1984, at page 15,628 of the *Congressional Record*. On June 11, the Senate will discuss the pros and cons of Senator Glenn's amendment but not vote on it. Senator Armstrong is not present that day, although he had a longstanding interest in this issue.[7]

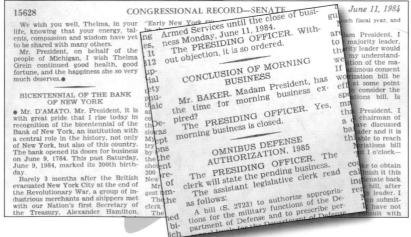

The U.S. Senate Chamber

FIRST VOTE: THE DEBATE (JUNE 11)

Conclusion of morning business:[8] Senator Howard Baker addresses the Presiding Officer, Senator Nancy Kassebaum.

Mr. Baker

"Madam President, has the time for morning business expired?"

Presiding Officer

Nancy Kassebaum, Presiding Officer

"Yes, morning business is closed.

OMNIBUS DEFENSE AUTHORIZATION ACT, 1985

"The clerk will state the pending business:"

"A bill (S. 2723) to authorize appropriations for the military functions of the Department of Defense and to prescribe personnel levels for the Department of Defense for fiscal year 1985, to authorize certain construction at military installations for such fiscal year, to authorize appropriations for the Department of Energy for national security programs for such fiscal year; and for other purposes."

Mr. Tower

John Tower

"Madam President, I note that there are not many amendments currently filed at the desk to the DoD Authorization Act. I hope Senators will file their amendments and be prepared to offer them.⁹"

AMENDMENT NO. 3179 ¹⁰

Purpose: To provide a new GI educational assistance program.

Mr. Glenn

John Glenn

"Madam President, I send an amendment [currently filed] to the desk and ask for its immediate consideration."

> **"... I SEND AN AMENDMENT TO THE DESK AND ASK FOR ITS IMMEDIATE CONSIDERATION."**
> —*Senator John Glenn, Ohio*

Presiding Officer

"The amendment will be stated. On page 54 [of S. 2723], between the lines 14 and 15, insert the following new section:

New GI Educational Assistance Program

Chapter 29—Citizen-Soldier Educational Assistance Program."

Mr. Montgomery

Students, I'll jump in here just to tell you the legislative language of the amendment continues for two-plus pages in the *Congressional Record*.¹¹ Note that Chairman Tower amended the Glenn amendment with a "perfecting" amendment to make it a pilot (as in "test") program; however, we'll skip that part of the discussion since Senator Glenn didn't oppose the Tower amendment.

Mr. Glenn

"Mr. President [Senator Abdnor has assumed the Chair],¹² this amendment which I have termed the Citizen-Soldier GI Bill,¹³ will establish a means by which young people who desire to serve their country in the military will have an option to serve for two years at reduced pay and, in return, receive substantial post-secondary education benefits upon their departure from the service.

> **"... THIS AMENDMENT, WHICH I HAVE TERMED THE CITIZEN-SOLDIER GI BILL... WOULD HARNESS THE DRIVE OF OUR YOUNG PEOPLE..."**
> —*Senator John Glenn, Ohio*

"I believe an enlistment category of this nature [most enlistments in the mid-1980s were for three, four or six years] would harness the drive of our young people who want to serve their country in a rewarding and significant manner; it would reinforce the concept of societal responsibility and national community by encouraging military service among the widest spectrum of our youth; it would assist the military in achieving recruitment goals with high-quality recruits; and it would enhance educational opportunities by expanding post-service education assistance at a reasonable cost to the federal government... .

"There is yet another and overarching concern about the military and its relationship to our society that I know is shared by many. Since the Gates Commission Report of 1970 introduced the All-Volunteer Force, the concept of enlisting in the military as a patriotic and public service has been reduced to it being widely viewed as a mere compensated occupation, as only a job rather than as a service to our country. This has led

> **"THE BETTER EDUCATED, BETTER CONNECTED, MORE AFFLUENT YOUNG MEN AND WOMEN FREQUENTLY CONSIDER MILITARY SERVICE AS SOMETHING TO AVOID..."**
> —*Senator John Glenn, Ohio*

to a disproportionate share of our military services being manned by disadvantaged segments of our society.

"The better educated, better connected, more affluent young men and women frequently consider military service as something to avoid rather than as a golden opportunity to serve their country directly in partial compensation for all the rights and benefits they enjoy as citizens.

COMMON HERITAGE... SIMILAR ASPIRATIONS

"The maturing process that takes place for our young men and women in the military as they mix on common ground with others of widely different economic, racial, ethnic, and regional backgrounds cannot be achieved comparably in any other process of which I am aware. The reinforcement of their jointly held values as American citizens, sharing a common heritage and often similar aspirations, has a cohesive effect that cannot be matched anywhere else in our society. The whole nation is stronger for it.

"For all of these reasons I feel that the All-Volunteer Force must become more representative of our society as a whole.

"Like most Senators, I prefer not to see us go back to a compulsory draft. But neither do I want to see a future in which America's military consists only of soldiers of misfortune. Instead, we want a military that is truly representative of our society, and I believe that the program I am proposing will help us to achieve it.

> " ... THE ALL-VOLUNTEER FORCE MUST BECOME MORE REPRESENTATIVE OF OUR SOCIETY AS A WHOLE."
> —*Senator John Glenn, Ohio*

"The Citizen-Soldier GI Bill is designed to make short-term service an attractive alternative for highly motivated high school graduates. Young people who choose to join the military for two years under this option would receive lower active duty pay than career soldiers of the same rank, but, upon completing their service, would receive substantial benefits for college or vocational training.

"In other words, they contribute while in the service, but receive more than favorable compensation that makes up for that loss once they leave the service.

"The general outline of the bill includes:

- Two years of active duty;
- A reduction of active pay by $250 per month;
- No cash payments for subsistence or quarters, unless specifically authorized by their service;
- Duty in military occupational specialties selected by the military service;
- Post-service education benefits of $500 per month for 36 months (four school years); and
- Benefits can be used for any approved program of post-secondary education, including technical schooling."

JUNE 11—DEBATE BEFORE THE VOTE CONTINUES

Mr. Tower

"Mr. President, I commend the Senator from Ohio in offering this very thoughtful amendment. Some of us do not feel that now we should go into a full-scale GI Bill program. This program outlined by Senator Glenn[14] is a targeted program and, if the [perfecting] amendment offered by Senator Nunn and myself to the amendment of the Senator from Ohio is adopted, it would make this a test program for four years and provide [that] not more than 12,500 personnel may elect to participate in the program... and we will be able to learn if additional educational benefits will have the favorable effect on recruiting as is predicted by the proponents."

> "SOME OF US DO NOT FEEL... WE SHOULD GO INTO A FULL-SCALE GI BILL PROGRAM."
> —*Senator John Tower, Texas*

Mr. Cohen

Bill Cohen

"Mr. President, I rise in opposition both to the amendment offered by the Senator from Ohio, Senator Glenn, and the perfecting amendment, as such, offered by the Chairman of the Armed Services Committee, Senator Tower... .

> "I RISE IN OPPOSITION... TO THE AMENDMENT..."
> —*Senator Bill Cohen, Maine*

"Mr. President, the reason I rise in opposition is because I think the amendment pending before the Senate this afternoon is not much of an improvement over the program [VEAP] we currently have. In fact, it may even be less attractive, particularly to those enlisted personnel at the lower end of the pay scale.

"I am going to speak principally, not so much in opposition to the proposal of the Senator from Ohio, but rather in favor of a measure that Senator Armstrong, Senator Cranston, Senator Matsunaga, Senator Hollings, and I joined in an effort a year ago on the Senate floor. The approval of our amendment would have called for a return of GI Bill education benefits for

> "WE WERE DEFEATED LAST YEAR ON A PROCEDURAL MOTION RATHER THAN AN UP OR DOWN VOTE ON THE MERITS OF OUR PROPOSAL."
> —*Senator Bill Cohen, Maine*

those serving in our Armed Forces. We were defeated last year on a procedural motion rather than an up or down vote on the merits of our proposal. But I believe that the argument we made over a year ago would have even greater validity today.

"… There are warning signs on the horizon—warning signs that cannot be ignored. Even the [Senate] Armed Services Committee, which capped pay and froze it for the most junior personnel, took note in its report[15] of the increasing challenge facing military recruiters. I would like to quote from the report itself:

> … [I]t is not clear how long the military services will be able to sustain the current recruiting momentum. As the economy improves and the unemployment rate drops, the services will face increasing competition for 18- to 21-year-olds. The services also must deal with the demographic reality that the size of the 18- to 21-year-old youth population will decrease by approximately 15 percent between fiscal year 1983 and fiscal year 1992. Earlier this year, General John Wickham, the Army Chief of Staff, testified that the Army had experienced a 22-percent decline in the first quarter of fiscal year 1984 compared to last year in the number of young people coming into Army recruiting stations to take the military entrance exams. General Wickham suggested that this 22-percent reduction 'may be a harbinger of an upturn in the [private sector] employment opportunities' for young people… .

"The Armed Services Committee, in this paragraph [stated above], has made an excellent case for reinstitution of GI Bill education benefits. The GI Bill, after all, has consistently been named by recruiters as the recurring tool they most like to have.

SOME ACCOMMODATING AMNESIA

"There are those in the administration perhaps, who suffer from some accommodating amnesia. I recall when President Reagan was running, he made a commitment to reinstitute the GI Bill. I recall Cap Weinberger coming up to his confirmation hearings to be Secretary of Defense and saying, 'We have to have a GI Bill.' Now we are saying, let us postpone it a little bit longer, let us make some sort of makeshift amendment to the VEAP program, which has proved to be disastrous.

"Let me quote what [Army] General Thurman said in answering questions for the record by my distinguished colleague and cosponsor, Senator Matsunaga. He [Thurman] made a powerful case for a New[16] GI Bill.

"The general pointed to the Army's problems in the late 1970s after Congress terminated the [Vietnam-era] GI Bill [on January 1, 1977]. He noted that between 1977 and 1979, the Army failed to meet its recruiting objective. In addition, quality dropped precipitously. The percentage of high school graduates enlisting was [just] 54.3 percent in 1980, and 52 percent non-prior service accessions [first-term enlistees] were in category IV [the next to lowest intelligence category].

> "… THE PERCENTAGE OF HIGH SCHOOL GRADUATES ENLISTING WAS 54.3 PERCENT IN 1980…"
> —*Senator Bill Cohen, Maine*

"General Thurman attributed this decline in quality accessions to the end of the GI Bill, coupled with erosion of pay comparability, the decline in unemployment, and the reduction in recruiting resources. What is troubling me is that many of the three elements are with me today.

"In its 1983 recruit survey, the Army Research Institute found that over 32 percent of category I and II [the highest intelligence categories] enlistees placed college money as the most important reason for enlisting. Over 23 percent of those people in those categories said they would not have enlisted without money for college.

"'Clearly, these individuals are influenced by education benefits more than by bonuses,' General Thurman told the Veterans' Affairs Committee. 'Clearly, education benefits expand the market by attracting bright young men and women intent on a college education.'

"[Mr. President,] we intend to see to it, to the best of our ability, that we have a chance to vote on a GI Bill and not on an amendment that would deal with a proposed VEAP program—one that would fail to achieve the kind of fundamental reform that is necessary by reinstating the GI Bill."

Mr. Glenn

"Mr. President, I will respond briefly to the distinguished Senator from Maine… This amendment was not submitted as a modified VEAP program in any way. It is a program that would stand on its own.

"I suppose that my strongest area of contention with the Senator from Maine would be that he places the GI Bill in the forefront as being practically the only reason why we are not getting more intelligent soldiers. I disagree with that as a basic premise.

"A number of things occurred in the past that were societal, that were economic, that tended to make some of our best young people look elsewhere for their livelihood, and they were enticed into the military only when things become tough economically in the country, and we started to get higher-quality recruits. Not that they are not all good and patriotic young people; but with respect to the ones with the higher education level, the percentage of high school graduates, and so forth, the numbers coming into the military were definitely affected by economic conditions, the ability to get jobs on the outside, and so forth. So it was a wholly different situation.

"Mr. President, what we are up against with the present situation is that we do have economic problems in this country. We are running debts and budget deficits beyond any conception of just a few years ago, beyond any possible acceptability into the long-term future. We cannot go on seeing $200-billion-a-year deficits, and going up.

> **"WE CANNOT GO ON SEEING $200 BILLION-A-YEAR DEFICITS, AND GOING UP."**
> *—Senator John Glenn, Ohio*

"The figures put out by the Congressional Budget Office regarding the cost of the GI Bill, as the Senator from Maine discussed, go up in rather staggering proportions, to add to that deficit, and eventually, that national debt. The first year, according to the CBO estimates, it is $7 million; the second year, $261 million; the third year, $341 million; and by the tenth year it is $775 million a year—three quarters of $1 billion.

"Much as I would like to agree with the Senator from Maine, I cannot do so…. So it [our amendment] is a compromise, I admit that, going in. But it tries to be very realistic about the situation in which we find ourselves budget-wise now and to address the need for high-quality recruits in the military at the same time."

> **"SO IT [OUR AMENDMENT] IS A COMPROMISE, I ADMIT THAT GOING IN."**
> *—Senator John Glenn, Ohio*

Mr. Simpson

Alan Simpson

"Mr. President, as chairman of the Veterans' Affairs Committee, we have been dealing with the GI Bill for some time. Senator Cranston, Senator Armstrong, and Senator Cohen have a proposal which I have not agreed with…. The GI Bill, of which I was a recipient and beneficiary, enabled me to obtain a law degree at the University of Wyoming and go to law school; it was a marvelous project, but it was an act of gratitude for those who served. It was never intended to be an inducement or recruitment tool,

> **"THE GI BILL… WAS NEVER INTENDED TO BE AN INDUCEMENT OR RECRUITMENT TOOL…"**
> *—Senator Alan Simpson, Wyoming*

and that is what we have here. And that is why I have a great deal of difficulty with the original proposal of Senator Armstrong.

"The reason that I opposed that and still oppose it is that here we have a new noncontributory GI Bill. We never had that before [in times in which we were not at war]. It is too costly at a time of extraordinary deficits that we have talked about and will continue to talk about here.

"Senator Glenn has always been very thoughtful, and I have watched him with some admiration and awe in my five years here of how thoughtful he is, and Senator Cohen, and Senator Tower, all of them deeply involved, and, of course, Senator Cranston who has followed the issue so ably…"

Mr. Cranston

Alan Cranston

"Will the Senator yield for a question?"

A typical Senate chamber desk.

Mr. Simpson

"Yes, I yield."

Mr. Cranston

"I would like to ask the distinguished chairman of the committee if it is not true that when the amendment that Senators Armstrong, Cohen, Hollings, Matsunaga, and I will be offering shortly was offered in substantially the same form, although with one difference, one year ago, the distinguished Chairman objected to our considering it on the [Senate] floor because we had not had hearings on it at that time [in the Committee on Veterans' Affairs]."

Mr. Simpson

"Mr. President, the Senator from California is correct in his review. It was a procedural motion to strike at the heart of the Armstrong-Cranston proposal and that carried by 6-10 votes, as I recall.[17] So I was indeed

> **"IT WAS A PROCEDURAL MOTION TO STRIKE AT THE HEART OF THE ARMSTRONG-CRANSTON PROPOSAL…"**
> *—Senator Alan Simpson, Wyoming*

involved in an effort to put aside the Armstrong-Cranston-Cohen GI Bill. That is correct."

Mr. Cranston

"Part of your reasons for objecting to the consideration at that time, as I recall, were that we had not had a hearing on it in the [Veterans' Affairs] Committee."

Mr. Simpson

"And then, Mr. President, we did have hearings [in the Veterans' Affairs Committee]. I kept that commitment that I made at that time."

Mr. Cranston

"Indeed, you did, and that was very much appreciated. Have there been hearings on the pending Glenn amendment in the [Veterans' Affairs] Committee?"

Mr. Simpson

"Mr. President, there have been no hearings before the Veterans' Affairs Committee on the Glenn proposal. There have been hearings since the point of order was upheld on the Cranston-Cohen-Armstrong proposal, plus the Simpson proposal,[18] and we did hold hearings on that, on GI Bill

> "MR. PRESIDENT, THERE HAVE BEEN NO HEARINGS BEFORE THE VETERANS' AFFAIRS COMMITTEE ON THE GLENN PROPOSAL."
> —*Senator Alan Simpson, Wyoming*

benefits in general. That has been held since that last vote, in line with my commitment to do so."

Mr. Cranston

"I thank the Chairman."

Mr. Simpson

"I thank the Senator from California and always enjoy working with him."

Mr. Cranston

"May I ask the distinguished Chairman of the Armed Services Committee [Mr. Tower], have there been any hearings in the Armed Services Committee on this [Glenn] proposal?"

NOT COST EFFECTIVE

Mr. Tower

"Mr. President, I say to the distinguished Senator from California, there have not been hearings in the Armed Services Committee on this matter, which is one of the reasons I felt constrained to offer an amendment to make this a test program.... The distinguished ranking member [Mr. Nunn] and I have joined in my committee with making it a test program. We have looked into the matter of the GI Bill quite a bit. It is our view that it is not cost effective at this time.

"But I also have the very pragmatic view that something is likely to pass and I want to minimize the budget impact. I do not believe that a general, comprehensive GI Bill is warranted at this time based on the testimony that has been given in the Veterans' Affairs

> "... SOMETHING IS LIKELY TO PASS AND I WANT TO MINIMIZE THE BUDGET IMPACT."
> —*Senator John Tower, Texas*

Committee and based on all the staff work the various Senators on the Armed Services Committee have done."

Mr. Cranston

"I thank the Chairman....

"Mr. President, I have grave questions about the workability of the pending amendment offered by Senator Glenn with the modification to it proposed by Senator Tower....

"Mr. President, at this time, however, I join with my colleagues—Senators Armstrong, Cohen, Hollings, and Matsunaga, as well as Senators Boschwitz, DeConcini, Hart, Kasten, and Kennedy—in urging the Senate to approve our legislation to establish a new peacetime GI Bill....

"I have long believed very strongly that educational incentives, if properly designed and implemented, can aid significantly in helping to ensure the success of the All-Volunteer Force.

"... I first introduced in December 1980 a measure designed to establish such a program of benefits. That was S. 3263,[19] the proposed 'All-Volunteer Force Educational Assistance Act of 1980,' in the 96th Congress.[20] I

> "... I FIRST INTRODUCED IN DECEMBER 1980 A MEASURE DESIGNED TO ESTABLISH SUCH A PROGRAM OF BENEFITS."
> —*Senator Alan Cranston, California*

reintroduced modified versions of that legislation in the 97th Congress as S. 417 on February 5, 1981, and as S. 8 in this Congress."

Mr. Montgomery

Folks, allow me to step in here for just a moment to describe in brief the bill Senators Cranston, Armstrong, Cohen, et al., were advocating. Senator Cranston's very detailed description of his bill appears at pages 15,640 and 15,641 of the June, 1984, *Congressional Record*.

I'd add, too, that with the exception of Administration witnesses [including VA] at the June 19, 1980, Senate Committee on Veterans' Affairs hearing, all witnesses expressed support for the New GI Bill.[21]

The general outline of the Cranston-Armstrong-Cohen et al., peacetime veterans' educational assistance program legislation includes:

- Permanent program whether America is at peace or at war;
- No pilot test period;
- No service member monthly pay reduction to become eligible;
- Serve at least two years to receive $300 per month in post-service educational benefits for 36 months (four academic years);
- Reservists would be eligible to receive GI Bill benefits for the first time, but in a lesser amount;
- "Kickers" of $300 per month in additional post-service education benefits in specific military occupations; and
- "Supplemental" benefits of $300 per month in additional post-service education benefits for service in the combat arms or other critical specialty areas for those who reenlist for three years.

The bill's estimated cost was $806 million over 10 years, not indexed for inflation. As you can see, the Cranston bill is very similar to what we marked-up in the House Armed Services Committee on April 19 and which the House passed, as part of the FY 1985 DoD Authorization Act on May 31, 1984—as we learned in Chapter 5.

Folks, now back to the debate before the vote on the Senate floor! We'll soon conclude this section. We're picking up at page 15,641 of the *Congressional Record*, June 11, 1984:

Mr. Matsunaga

"Mr. President, will the Senator yield for a question?"

Spark Matsunaga

Mr. Cranston

"I am delighted to yield."

JUNE 11 DEBATE CONTINUES

Mr. Matsunaga

"As a cosponsor of the Armstrong-Cranston-Cohen-Hollings-Matsunaga amendment, we have fully expected that Senator Armstrong would be here to offer the amendment regarding the GI Bill. I am truly disappointed that this matter has come up in the absence of Senator Armstrong. My question to the Senator from California is that since we have not had real time to study the proposal now being considered on the floor,

> "... THIS MATTER SHOULD BE PUT OVER UNTIL TOMORROW WHEN SENATOR ARMSTRONG WILL BE HERE WITH HIS AMENDMENT..."
> —*Senator Spark Matsunaga, California*

does not the Senator from California feel this matter should be put over until tomorrow when Senator Armstrong will be here with his amendment, of which we are cosponsors, so that the Senate can weigh the differences between our proposal and the proposal now being considered on the floor?"

Mr. Cranston

"I thank my friend from Hawaii for that question. The answer is yes. I believe that we should not proceed to a vote today for two reasons: one, out of fairness to Senator Armstrong who has had no opportunity, nor advance notice that could have caused him to be with us today, to speak to the Glenn amendment or our amendment. Second, many, many Senators are very interested in this issue, and they have had no time to study the proposed 15-page amendment by Senator Glenn and others—in order to analyze its virtues or non-virtues... ."

Mr. Nunn

"Mr. President, would the Senator from California yield?"

Mr. Cranston

"Certainly."

Sam Nunn

Mr. Nunn

"Speaking for myself, I certainly agree that a person such as Senator Armstrong should be present. I certainly have no intention of trying to push for a vote before they have a chance to debate. On the other hand, Senator Tower made a point a little while ago which I concur in. We have been basically on this bill [the Fiscal Year 1985 DoD Authorization Act] for three days waiting for people to come forward with amendments. Senator Glenn was ready and prepared. His amendment was going to come up with some opportunity. We need to get amendments up. I would hope that Senators would cooperate… ."[22]

> ## "I CERTAINLY HAVE NO INTENTION OF TRYING TO PUSH FOR A VOTE BEFORE THEY HAVE A CHANCE TO DEBATE."
> —*Senator Sam Nunn, Georgia*

Mr. Tower

"Will the Senator yield? I am perfectly prepared to ask unanimous consent that this amendment be temporarily set aside if someone else is prepared to offer an amendment. I have no desire to force this to a vote, certainly in the absence of others. They are necessarily absent today. I feel that it is incumbent on me to attempt to have this bill [the Fiscal Year 1985 Omnibus DoD Authorization Act] become law. We have a very short period of time in which to try to pass this bill in the Senate, go to conference, complete a conference report and get it to the President by the time we break for the Fourth of July.

"Otherwise, the appropriations process is going to overtake us… .

"Mr. President, I ask unanimous consent that the amendment of the Senator from Ohio (Mr. Glenn) be laid aside. I further ask unanimous consent that it be made the pending business when the Senate turns to the consideration of the DoD Authorization [Act], S. 2723, on Wednesday [June 13]."

Presiding Officer

"Is there objection?… ."

James Abdnor, Presiding Officer

Mr. Nunn

"In fairness to Senator Glenn, he is not here [at this moment], but to protect his interest, he would certainly want a firm understanding of the parties that on this subject, his amendment will be the first one pending on Wednesday morning, and we will not take up any other amendment on this in the interim."

Mr. Cranston

"The Tower amendment will be the subject on Wednesday."

Mr. Nunn

"The Tower amendment to the Glenn amendment; that is correct."

Presiding Officer

"Is there objection? The Chair hears none, and it is so ordered."

Mr. Montgomery

Students, as you can see the vote is postponed until Wednesday, June 13.

READY FOR VOTE ONE ON GLENN AMENDMENT, JUNE 13

Folks, this first vote on the Glenn amendment gets the legislative ball rolling. It will still be rolling about seven hours—and five more votes—from now.

We now are operating from the June 13, 1984 *Congressional Record-Senate*, at page 16,058. And Senator Bob Kasten is the Presiding Officer.

16058	CONGRESSIONAL RECORD—SENATE	June 13, 1984
Charging and punishment In 1975, The Association adopted the position that "the several jurisdictional bases should be removed from the definitions of the substantive crimes, where they are now found in Title 18." The Criminal Code Reform Act of 1978 legislation (S. 1437) that passed the Senate in January, 1978, which would have separated the jurisdictional	lishing the standardization of the computer and the integrity of the data input before the printout will be accepted into evidence as an exception to the hearsay rule. Case law has been concerned with the "mystique" of the computer and its evidentiary output. See *U.S. v. DeGeorgia*, 420 F 2d 889 (9th Cir. 1969); *U.S. v. Russo*, 480 F.2d 1228 (6th Cir. 1973) cert. den. 414 U.S. 1157	The PRESIDING OFFICER. The pending question is amendment No. 3180, offered by the Senator from Texas, to amendment No. 3179, offered by the Senator from Ohio. Mr. TOWER. Mr. President, we debated this matter at some length last Monday. I do not know that there is

OMNIBUS DEFENSE AUTHORIZATION ACT, 1985

Presiding Officer

"The clerk will report the pending business: 'A bill (S. 2723) to authorize appropriations for the military functions of the Department of Defense and to prescribe personnel levels for the Department of Defense for fiscal year 1985… .'"

The Senate resumed consideration of the bill. Pending:

Bob Kasten, Presiding Officer

(1) Glenn amendment No. 3179, to provide a new GI educational assistance program; and

(2) Tower-Nunn amendment No. 3180 (to Glenn amendment No. 3179), of a perfecting nature.

AMENDMENT NO. 3180

Mr. Tower

"Mr. President, what is the pending business?"

Presiding Officer

"The pending question on amendment No. 3180 offered by the Senator from Texas, to amendment No. 3179, offered by the Senator from Ohio."

Mr. Tower

"Mr. President, we debated this matter at some length last Monday [June 11, 1984]. I do not know that there is much in addition I can say about my amendment, which is designed to make the proposal of the Senator from Ohio a test program. I am prepared to get a vote on that rather soon… I ask for the yeas and nays on my amendment." [It was a Glenn amendment, then perfected by Tower and Nunn.]

> "… I ASK FOR THE YEAS AND NAYS…"
> —*Senator John Tower, Texas*

Presiding Officer

"Is there a sufficient second? The yeas and nays were ordered."

Mr. Glenn

"Monday, after some rather spirited discussion and opposition by Senators Cohen, Cranston, and Matsunaga, who argued that the Armstrong GI Bill was preferable, we achieved an agreement that the citizen-soldier bill amendment should be laid aside until this morning when we would take it up first thing, and that is where we are now.

"On the desk of each Senator is a second 'Dear Colleague' letter on the citizen-soldier bill, to bring them up to date.

"This new 'Dear Colleague' is cosigned by the amendment's cosponsors, Senators Jepsen [Iowa], Thurman [South Carolina], Warner [Virginia], and myself. It incorporates the provision of the Tower-Nunn amendment and reiterates the major attributes of the program. I commend it to you as a reference point in our discussion this morning.

"I feel that this citizen-soldier bill will do precisely what it is designed to do; that is, induce high-quality recruits to join the military from a wide spectrum of American society. This will have the concurrent effect of enhancing a national attitude of societal responsibility and boosting our post-secondary educational system at the same time. All this can be achieved at less cost than comparable plans, though it would not conflict or prevent utilization of plans already in place.

"… I yield the floor."

> "… JOIN THE MILITARY FROM A WIDE SPECTRUM OF AMERICAN SOCIETY."
> —*Senator John Glenn, Ohio*

Mr. Armstrong

Bill Armstrong

"[I] express my appreciation to the Senator from Ohio, the Senator from Texas, the Senator from California, the Senator from Wyoming, and others who were kind enough when this issue arose and I was away from the chamber to arrange it to recur at a moment I could be here.

"As Senators know, I have long been a champion of the GI Bill. I believe it to be one of the most successful of all the programs which have been undertaken in the entire history of our country.

"For several years, I have been urging my colleagues to consider bringing back the GI Bill, which in my opinion, was unwisely terminated in 1976.[23]

"The pending question, as I understand it, is the Tower amendment. Now I happen to believe for reasons I will explain a little later that the Glenn amendment really does not address itself to the needs of this country, neither from a national defense standpoint nor from an educational standpoint.

"Now, I do not wish at this time to discuss either the Glenn amendment nor the alternative proposal which I will shortly introduce, which is a full-blown GI Bill education program.

"So, Mr. President, I have nothing to add at this point. We are sort of jockeying for position to get the various proposals on the table as fairly and as cleanly as we can so that everyone can reflect and make up his own mind, and I am certainly going to vote for the Tower amendment."

Presiding Officer

"Mr. President, the yeas and nays have already been ordered on my amendment, and I think it is fitting we have a roll-call vote on it.

"The clerk will call the roll."[24]

> "THE YEAS AND NAYS HAVE BEEN ORDERED … THE CLERK WILL CALL THE ROLL."
> —*The Presiding Officer*

"Without objection, it is so ordered."

"Is there further debate? If not, the question is on agreeing to the amendment of the Senator from Texas [Mr. Tower]. The yeas and nays have been ordered and the clerk will call the roll."

[And the legislative clerk called the roll...]

FIRST VOTE: GLENN AMENDMENT
PASSES 96 TO 1

Presiding Officer

"Are there any other Senators in the Chamber wishing to vote?[25]

"The result was announced—yeas 96, nays 1... .

"Mr. Tower's amendment was agreed to [meaning approved]."[26]

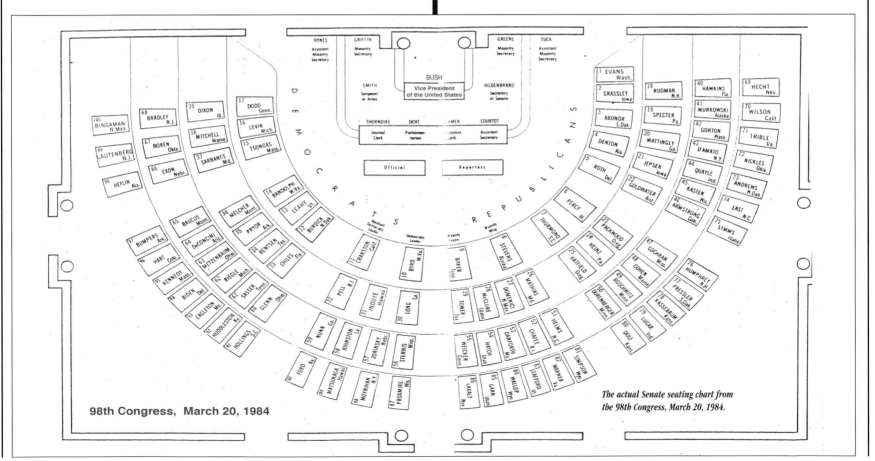

98th Congress, March 20, 1984

The actual Senate seating chart from the 98th Congress, March 20, 1984.

Sonny's Lessons Learned

The lesson is what I call legislative discretion. Did you see how Senators Armstrong, Cohen, and Cranston voted for the Glenn amendment, even though they had their own amendment? Senator Armstrong and company knew they'd have the opportunity to offer their own amendment to the Senate, too. There was no reason to be perceived as overly rigid, especially since Senator Glenn had the support of the chairman and ranking member of the Armed Services Committee (Mr. Tower and Mr. Nunn). Sometimes the best course is to strategically yield and prepare for a later opportunity to make your case.[26]

Worth Repeating

"Since the Gates Commission Report of 1970 introduced the All-Volunteer Force, the concept of enlisting in the military as a patriotic and public service has been reduced to it being widely viewed as a mere compensated occupation, as only a job rather than as a service to our country."
—*Senator John Glenn*

"Like most Senators, I prefer not to see us go back to a compulsory draft. But neither do I want to see a future in which America's military consists only of soldiers of misfortune. Instead, we want a military that is truly representative of our society, and I believe that the program I am proposing will help us to achieve it."
—*Senator John Glenn*

"Some of us do not feel that now we should go into a full-scale GI Bill program."
—*Senator John Tower*

"There are those in the administration perhaps, who suffer from some accommodating amnesia."
—*Senator Bill Cohen*

"I suppose that my strongest area of contention with the Senator from Maine would be that he places the GI Bill in the forefront as being practically the only reason why we are not getting more intelligent soldiers. I disagree with that as a basic premise."
—*Senator John Glenn*

"The GI Bill, of which I was a recipient and beneficiary, enabled me to obtain a law degree at the University of Wyoming and go to law school; it was a marvelous project, but it was an act of gratitude for those who served. It was never intended to be an inducement or recruitment tool, and that is what we have here."

—*Senator Alan Simpson*

"Mr. President, I have grave questions about the workability of the pending amendment offered by Senator Glenn..."

—*Senator Alan Cranston*

"... I happen to believe... that the Glenn amendment really does not address itself to the needs of this country neither from a national defense standpoint nor from an educational standpoint."

—*Senator Bill Armstrong*

WHAT'S NEXT

About seven more hours of Senate debate on the Glenn and Armstrong proposals and five more votes appear in the next two of our chapters.

8

SONNY'S
CAST OF
CHARACTERS

Senators participating in the debate are the same as Chapter 7 with the addition of:

Senator Daniel Evans (D-WA)

Senator Ernest "Fritz" Hollings (R-SC)

Senator Rudy Boschwitz (D-MN)

Senator David Boren (R-OK)

*Senator Edward Kennedy (D-MA),
Member, Committee on Armed Services*

Senator Larry Pressler (R-SD)

Senator Arlen Specter (R-PA), Presiding Officer

***Also featured in this chapter as Presiding Officers:
Senator Nancy Kassebaum (R-KS)
Senator Gordon Humphrey (R-NH)
Senator Warren Rudman (R-NH)***

Summer 1984—Road to Enactment: Senate Fails to Table Armstrong Peacetime Veterans' Educational Assistance Act 51 to 46—Second Vote

SONNY'S SUMMARY

Following robust debate by both sides, Senators Armstrong, Cohen, Cranston, Hollings, and Matsunaga prevailed in the second vote. They overcame efforts by Senators Glenn, Tower, Simpson, and Nunn to have the Senate table the Armstrong bill, which was conceptually similar to H.R. 1400, as passed by the House. The Armstrong group argued on the grounds that an educational incentive was essential to save the All-Volunteer Force and cure recruiting woes. The Glenn group argued that the Armstrong bill would inflate the already high federal deficit, due to a new entitlement, and that the recruiting picture was not as bleak as some suggested. At various times, each side became both animated by and frustrated with the other's views. The debate indeed proved frank and direct.

UNITED STATES, OF AMERICA

Congressional Record

PROCEEDINGS AND DEBATES OF THE 98th CONGRESS

SECOND SESSION

June 13, 1984 — CONGRESSIONAL RECORD—SENATE

SENATE—Wednesday, June 13, 1984

(Legislative day of Monday, June 11, 1984)

Mr. Montgomery

We now join the debate at page 16,060 of the June 13, 1984, *Congressional Record*. Senator Bill Armstrong addressed the Chair (meaning the Presiding Officer).[1]

Presiding Officer

(Mrs. Kassebaum) "The Senator from Colorado."[2, 3]

AMENDMENT NO. 3189

Purpose: To establish two new programs of educational assistance for veterans of peacetime service, and for other purposes.

Nancy Kassebaum

Mr. Armstrong

"Madam President, I send an amendment to the desk and ask for its immediate consideration."

Presiding Officer

"The amendment will be stated."

[The assistant legislative clerk read as follows:]

"The Senator from Colorado (Mr. Armstrong) proposes an amendment numbered 3189 to amendment 3179, as amended [by the Tower amendment]."

"The amendment of Mr. Glenn (Amendment 3179) is amended by striking out all after 'NEW' on page 1, line 3, through the end of such amendment and inserting in lieu thereof the following:

"Title IV: Veterans' Educational Assistance Amendments (Short Title)

SEC. 401. This title may be cited as 'Peacetime Veterans' Educational Assistance Act.'

NEW EDUCATIONAL ASSISTANCE PROGRAMS

"SEC 402. (a) Title 38, United States Code, is amended by inserting before Chapter 31 the following new chapters:

"Chapter 29: Peacetime Veterans' Educational Assistance Program... ."

Mr. Montgomery

Students, the extensive legislative language of the amendment continues in the June 13, 1984, *Congressional Record* pages 16,060 to 16,065.

Following the clerk's reading of the Armstrong amendment language, the Presiding Officer will now move the debate along.

Presiding Officer

"The Senate will be in order. The Senator from Colorado."

A portion of the Armstrong amendment.

Mr. Armstrong

"Madam President.... I ask for the yeas and nays [meaning requesting a vote] on the amendment."

Presiding Officer

"Is there a sufficient second? There is a sufficient second."[4]

[The yeas and nays were ordered.]

Mr. Armstrong

"Madam President, Congress is caught between a rock and a hard place. We are facing large and mounting budget deficits that demand that we hold spending down. At the same time, every member of this body wants and, indeed, insists upon providing the level of national defense which is needed to assure the security and safety of this country. As we try to stretch too few dollars to cover too many needs, I believe it is particularly appropriate that we are now considering reinstating a program which now not only strengthens this nation's defense but will save us money in the process—the GI Bill.

> "MADAM PRESIDENT, CONGRESS IS BETWEEN A ROCK AND A HARD PLACE."
> —*Senator Bill Armstrong, Colorado*

"Madam President, Congress passes hundreds of bills every session. Some of this legislation has done a great deal of good; some of it has proven to be mediocre. Some of it, of course, has proven to be positively harmful and counterproductive. But as we look back over the whole history of this country, over 200 years of legislation and federal action in various aspects of American life, I believe there are only a handful of programs that stand out—indeed, that tower above the legislative landscape as the most outstanding and successful programs of all time.

"I think, for example, of the great land grant university program—that is certainly a towering success of the federal government; the great hydroelectric projects of the 1930s; and the interstate highway programs of the 1950s, 1960s, and 1970s. Programs like these have succeeded not only in their fulfilling their intended purpose, but indeed have conferred benefits generation after generation as an investment in the future of this country.

"The decision of Congress to terminate the GI Bill in December of 1976, in my judgment, has proven to be one of the worst decisions ever made by the Congress of the United States. The Army warned us in advance what was likely to happen. In September of 1974, the Army conducted a survey of 11,336 recruits at armed forces examining stations throughout the United States. Twenty-four percent of those who were interviewed said flatly they would not have enlisted in the service if it were not for the GI Bill. An additional 36 percent said they were not sure whether they would have enlisted if they had not been made eligible for education benefits.... .

"That was not all. In its report to the Secretary of Defense, the Army said that terminating the GI Bill would require a 17-percent increase in annual accessions just to offset increased losses due to attrition; that is, service members administratively discharged prior to completing their term of obligated service.

"... I say to my friends, the actual result of terminating the GI Bill program has been even worse than was feared by the Army in 1976. By the 1980 fiscal year, the number of Army recruits scoring in the highest mental category had dropped by more than half. The attrition rate had climbed to nearly 40 percent, more than double the 18-percent rate the Army predicted would be totally acceptable by Congress.

"... In the Air Force, the proportion of recruits scoring in the two highest categories on the armed forces Qualification Test dropped from 53.8 percent in fiscal year 1997 to 40.2 percent by fiscal year 1979, nearly a 25-percent drop in high-aptitude recruits in just two years.

"A Center for Naval Analysis study indicated that cancellation of the GI Bill reduced the pool of recruits willing to enlist in the Marine Corps by 17 percent and reduced the number of high school graduates willing to become Marines by 24 percent. In the Navy, the percentage of recruits scoring in the two highest mental categories declined from 43 percent in fiscal year 1976 to 35 percent in 1979 and the percentage of recruits in the lowest category quadrupled from 5 percent to 21 percent.

"In 1979 and 1980, we reached a point where the Army Chief of Staff, General Meyer, said his was a 'hollow Army... .'

"Well, that has turned around to some extent, thanks in part to long overdue increases in military compensation voted by members of the Congress in 1980 and 1981 and also in part to a severe recession which sent unemployment into the double-digit range, the highest since the Great Depression, I might note.

> "... GOOD ECONOMIC TIMES HAVE TRADITIONALLY MEANT HARD TIMES FOR MILITARY RECRUITERS."
> —*Senator Bill Armstrong, Colorado*

"My friends, we do not need a crystal ball to see what is looming in the future. All we have to do is project the demographic trends which are already evident to see what disaster is ahead. We are in the midst of a recovery, and good economic times have traditionally meant hard times for military recruiters. The recovery, moreover, is coinciding with a period in the life of our country when there will be and is a sharp decline in the number of young people in the military age-brackets.

"The 18-year-old population will decline a full 20 percent—by 1.3 million—between fiscal year 1982 and 1987. Let me say that again. There is going to be a 20 percent decline in the number of young people in the age group from which we expect to draw most of our new recruits and that will occur in just five years, between 1982 and 1987, and will decline still further in the 1990s.

"If we make no serious effort to recruit the upwardly mobile, college-bound young people who are so much needed in the armed services today, we are going to face a problem of gradually mounting proportions which again will reach the crisis point.

> **"THE 18-YEAR-OLD POPULATION WILL DECLINE A FULL 20 PERCENT, BY 1.3 MILLION, BETWEEN FISCAL YEAR 1982 AND 1987."**
> *—Senator Bill Armstrong, Colorado*

"… Survey after survey has made it plain that educational incentives are the only effective means of recruiting voluntarily the high aptitude young people the armed forces need the most. Typical are the findings of the most recent comprehensive study conducted by the Army Research Institute at Army reception centers throughout the country from May through August 1982. Overall, money for college ranked second of the 11 reasons cited as the most important considerations for enlisting, trailing behind, and this is significant—the category labeled 'To get trained for a skill.' 'Money for college' ranked far ahead of such categories as 'Earning more money' or 'I was unemployed.' Among recruits in the two highest mental categories, however, money for college ranked far ahead of such categories as 'Earning more money' or 'I was unemployed.'

"Among recruits in the two highest mental categories, however, money for college was the most important reason cited for enlistment, being mentioned by 36.3 percent of the recruits interviewed in this period. This compared with just 7.8 percent who said they joined the Army because they could not find a job elsewhere and 3.3 percent who said they joined the Army to obtain higher pay…

"Gen. Maxwell Thurman, the Vice Chief of Staff and formerly the Army's top recruiter, has told Congress flatly:

> 'The Army must have an educational pull mechanism permanently authorized in law which is not subject to the vagaries of year-to-year change. The education benefits about which we are speaking do two

things at once. They are recruiting incentives for us and they are rewards for service to the nation.'

"This legislation, Madam President, is supported not only by recruiters, but by distinguished, thoughtful military sociologists from the academic sector, and by [the military] service chiefs. It is also backed by the Non Commissioned Officers Association [of the United States]; National Association of Uniformed Services; Reserve Officers Association; Association of the U.S. Army; National Guard Association; Fleet Reserve Association; Naval Reserve Association; and Air Force Sergeants Association.

"Mr. President [Senator Humphrey had assumed the Chair], I want to turn from the general to the specific, and outline with precision exactly what is in the amendment I have sent to the desk which is now pending as an amendment to the Glenn amendment. It is a perfecting amendment of course, but it is in spirit, if not in a parliamentary form, a substitute. It is an alternative. I want to tell you what is in our amendment and  *Gordon Humphrey* why it is preferable to the proposal which has been brought forward by the Senator from Ohio.

"Our proposal will establish two new programs of educational assistance to veterans of peacetime service…. It would close the post-Vietnam era educational assistance program to new participants. That is the so-called VEAP program—I am going to come back to that in a moment—and would repeal the termination date of the Vietnam-era GI Bill. Our proposal provides a basic benefit of $300 a month to be funded by the Defense Department to service members who complete two or more years of honorable service starting September 30, 1985…. Benefits vest at the rate of one month of benefits for each month of service to a maximum of 36 months.

"… For Reserves, or the National Guard, benefits would vest at the rate of one month of benefits for every three months of service. The Service [S]ecretaries would be permitted to supplement the [$300 per month] basic benefits to encourage enlistment in the combat arms, and in military occupational specialties —where critical skills are required.

"Our bill would also establish a career-member supplementary educational assistance program through which service members with 10 or more years of honorable service would be permitted to contribute from $25 to $100 a month, to a maximum of $6,000, to a special fund. After a two-year vesting period the service member's contribution would be matched two-for-one by the Defense Department. These funds could be used either by the service member, or by his spouse or dependent child.

"A third provision of our bill would permit career service members to utilize their

GI Bill benefits full time without interrupting or abandoning their military careers. In their discretion, the Service Secretaries would be permitted to offer an educational leave of absence of up to 12 months.

"… Let me make it plain that the VEAP program, which we replace and phase out, is not gaining large participation. Even among those who contribute to it initially, and get into it, most end up cashing out their benefits. They do not end up using it for educational purposes."

Mr. Cohen

"Mr. President, will the Senator yield?"

Mr. Armstrong

"Yes, I would be happy to yield."

VEAP—A PROGRAM OF REFUNDS, NOT EDUCATION

Mr. Cohen

"I would point out that last year the VA paid out almost two times as much in VEAP refunds as it did in VEAP benefits. If that is any indication of what is happening to those going in and getting out, it seems to me the statistics of our two-times more in refunds than benefits is a story of the lack of success of the VEAP program."

Mr. Armstrong

"I thank the Senator for pointing that out. I hope every one of our colleagues will listen closely to what he said because it not only bears on the VEAP program, but in a moment I will turn my attention to the alternative GI Bill proposal suggested by the Senator from Ohio which is a form of a super-VEAP, I guess you would have to call it. And, in view of the real failure of the existing VEAP program, it is difficult for me to see why we would want to now saddle ourselves with something which combines the worst features of the prepayment with some new idea which I think puts it greatly at hazard for its success.

"So it just seems to me that the evidence is overwhelming. In fact, I cannot help [state] what Victor Hugo said about an idea whose time has come. Greater than the threat of a mighty army is an idea whose time has come,

> "GREATER THAN THE THREAT OF A MIGHTY ARMY IS AN IDEA WHOSE TIME HAS COME… ."
> —Senator Bill Armstrong, Colorado

and I think the GI Bill idea has come again, and so do quite a number of my colleagues.

"When I sent this [amendment] to the desk a few moments ago, I did so with the co-sponsorship of Senator Cohen, Senator Matsunaga, Senator Hollings, and Senator Cranston. I now ask unanimous consent that the following Senators be added as cosponsors of this amendment: The Senator from Massachusetts,[5] Senator Huddleston, Senator Pressler, Senator Inouye, Senator Ford, Senator Kasten, Senator Bradley, Senator Hawkins, Senator Hart, Senator Trible, Senator DeConcini, Senator Boschwitz, Senator Baucus, Senator Mitchell, Senator Evans, Senator Lautenburg, Senator Boren, Senator Johnston, Senator Specter, and Senator Durenberger.

"Mr. President, I yield at this time to the Senator from Hawaii [Mr. Matsunaga]."

Mr. Matsunaga

"… As a cosponsor of the original bill, with Representative Steiger, who is now deceased, to create a voluntary military force, I feel privileged to work with the Senator from Colorado in cosponsoring his amendment.

> "…BECAUSE OF [VEAP'S] EXTREMELY LOW PARTICIPATION AND HIGH DROP-OUT RATE, [IT] HAS BEEN CONSIDERED A DISASTER."
> —Senator Spark Matsunaga, Hawaii

"Mr. President, I rise to voice my opposition to the amendment offered by the Senator from Ohio [Mr. Glenn]. And my strong support for the Armstrong-Cohen-Matsunaga-Cranston-Hollings GI Bill amendment.

"At the outset, I want to say to the Senator from Ohio that after reading his 'Dear Colleague' letter on his amendment, I believe that we, the sponsors of the GI Bill amendment, share his basic objective…

"Unfortunately, where we do not agree with the Senator from Ohio is in what fashion these educational benefits should be offered by the military. We are very concerned, frankly, that the program which would be established by the Senator's amendment would not be much more than a modification of the current Veterans' Educational Assistance Program, better known as VEAP. That program, because of its extremely low participation rate and high drop-out rate, has been considered a disaster… . Only when the Congress authorized the military to augment the basic VEAP program with so-called 'kickers' did the program begin to attract greater numbers of high-scoring graduate recruits. It is important to note that it took 'kickers' of $8,000 to $12,000 to actually make a significant difference in high-quality recruiting. The point is that solid educational benefits are necessary to attract the highly intelligent high school graduate that the military services need. Anything else will not do the job, and the program that is being proposed in the Glenn amendment would, by any measure, provide far less than a GI Bill.

"Under the Glenn amendment, service members electing to participate in the program would make a contribution of $250 per month to an educational benefits fund, which would come out of his or her active pay, and forego cash payments for subsistence or quarters. Based on the low participation rate of the VEAP program, under which service members may contribute from as low as $25 to as high as $120, I cannot see how a program which requires an even greater contribution and, at the same time, takes away cash for quarters or subsistence, will be any greater attraction to high-quality recruits. The success of the Army College Fund,[6] under which service members are provided the basic VEAP plus $8,000 to

> "... THE MORE NONCONTRIBUTORY THE EDUCATIONAL PROGRAM IS, THE GREATER ITS ATTRACTIVENESS TO THE HIGH-QUALITY RECRUIT."
> —*Senator Spark Matsunaga, Hawaii*

$12,000 for which they have to make no contribution, proves very conclusively that the more noncontributory the educational program is, the greater its attractiveness to the high-quality recruit.

"Mr. President, the fact of the matter is that there is simply no evidence to suggest that the program created by the Glenn amendment will encourage any more high-quality young people to join the military.

"The main point of [Vice Chief of Staff of the Army] General Maxwell Thurman's testimony [before the Senate Veterans' Affairs Committee earlier this year] was that the military's high-quality recruiting market must be viewed as a dual-track affair—the first track being high school graduates that are 'employment-oriented,' that is, those who have a propensity to go directly to work after school, and the second track being high school graduates who are 'college-oriented,' that is, those who have a propensity to go directly to college after high school. According to General Thurman, the military services have been recruiting heavily from the 'employment-oriented' group for a number of years. Indications are that recruiting from that group, which responds primarily to cash bonuses for enlistment, cannot be expanded to any further degree. 'There is not much more we can get from the employment-oriented group,' General Thurman said 'especially in an improving economy.'

"On the other hand, the college-oriented group responds primarily to money for college and, according to General Thurman, 'the market can still be expanded for the college-oriented group by a well-designed, non-contributory GI Bill program.'"

Mr. Cohen

"In 1979, I believe, when the first effort was made to reestablish the GI Bill, Senator Armstrong was, in fact, the first to offer this measure. I was pleased to join him then in 1979 and am pleased to do so now.

> "... SENATOR ARMSTRONG WAS, IN FACT, THE FIRST TO OFFER THIS MEASURE."
> —*Senator Bill Cohen, Maine*

"Let me also say I rise with some regret today in opposition to the amendment of the Senator from Ohio [Mr. Glenn], though his amendment was, in fact, amended by the Senator from Texas [Senator Tower]. I admire Senator Glenn a great deal... .

"I continue to admire Senator Glenn for his contribution to the committees on which I serve with him.

"Mr. President, I pass over for the moment my admiration for Senator Tower, which I could take perhaps the next two or three hours to talk about, the role he has had in shaping our defense forces for the past 20 years or so that he has served in this body.

"The Citizen-Soldier GI Bill, as the Glenn amendment is called, in my judgment is anything but a GI Bill. Those who wish for a GI Bill should not vote for the Glenn amendment, but should vote for the Armstrong-Cohen-Matsunaga, et. al., amendment with the 25 cosponsors that we now have. That, in fact, is the only true GI Bill that will be on the floor today.

> "THE CITIZEN-SOLDIER GI BILL, AS THE GLENN AMENDMENT IS CALLED, IN MY JUDGMENT IS ANYTHING BUT A GI BILL."
> —*Senator Bill Cohen, Maine*

"If they should support the Glenn approach, what they will be supporting is an unattractive version of one of the least effective and most unpopular programs ever established, the Veterans' Educational Assistance Program, otherwise known as VEAP.

"If the Glenn amendment is approved today, we will be doing a great disservice to potential recruits, to the military services, and to the nation. Calling something a GI Bill does not make it one.

"Our amendment, which lost narrowly last year on a procedural motion, has been the subject of hearings in the Veterans' Affairs Committee, and it has received the endorsement of such recognized manpower experts as former Chief of Staff of the Army Edward "Shy" Meyer and the Army's present Vice Chief of Staff, General Maxwell Thurman.

"General Meyer, in a letter to my colleague [Mr. Armstrong] pointed out, I thought rather forcefully:

"'… In my view, a GI Bill containing the features (contained in the Armstrong proposal) would be an extremely critical piece of legislation the Congress could enact in the interest of promoting the long term readiness of the military services.'

"I mentioned this [GI Bill as a recruiting device] on Monday. We hear a lot about campaign promises. President Reagan made a very strong campaign promise. He said he was going to call for the reintroduction of the GI Bill.

EVERYBODY'S TRYING TO PICK UP SOME VOTES

Mr. Cohen

"Cap Weinberger, during his first year as Secretary of Defense, said he wanted a GI Bill.[7] Unfortunately, every time we would come to a GI Bill proposal, they would say, 'Well, not right now, we cannot really afford it right now; let us try again maybe next year.' So every time, we have waited until next year. We waited from 1979 to 1980, we waited 1980 to 1981 and from 1981 to 1982, and then we waited until 1983. Then last year we took this measure up. I think we were even accused at that time of acting politically. The statement was made, I know you people are all concerned about something that is politically attractive, as I recall those words; that is why it is being introduced during an election year—everybody's trying to pick up some votes.

"I do not know what we do in this body. We listen to our professional military witnesses, the Chiefs of Staff, the Vice Chiefs of Staff; we listen to retired admirals, who can speak even more freely than when they were in the service themselves. Every one of them to a person says we need the GI Bill. They are not looking for votes; they are looking out for the best interests of this country. They want to make sure we do not repeat the mistakes of the past, as we did back in the seventies."

Mr. Tower

"Will the Senator yield for a question?"

Mr. Cohen

"Certainly, Mr. President."

Mr. Tower

California Senator George Murphy started the tradition of the "candy desk" at his seat in 1968; today, whoever is assigned to the desk keeps the tradition going.

"According to the CBO estimates, what we are paying is about $200,000 for each additional high-quality recruit. It gets to be a very expensive program. We would be better advised to give them bonuses for signing up.

"That is a pretty high premium to pay for whatever we would get in the way of additional high-quality recruits."

Mr. Cohen

"I submit to my friend from Texas in terms of the high price that has to be paid for high-quality personnel, we get a pretty good deal. If you want to ask the members of this body to start supporting procurement requests, M-1 tanks, if you want to ask the members to start supporting requests for all of these very exotic, new, complicated weapons systems, you better have the kind of people who are going to be attracted to come in to man those systems."

Mr. Tower

"… Let me say to the Senator from Maine that I know that people who advocate this program feel it is a good way to hedge against the possibility we may have to have a draft. What I am telling the Senator is with restraints on military spending and with annual assaults being made on the presidential spending requests for defense, personnel costs are at a very high percentage for military spending. With the GI Bill, I think you are going to add more to personnel costs than what you are going to realize in the way of additional recruitment, and the more costly you make personnel the more likely you are to hasten the day when the Congress may give some serious consideration to going back to a draft.

"Now I think there are a lot of things worse than a draft. When I think of the generation of Americans who were drafted in the service, it turned out pretty good. John Glenn was not drafted; he volunteered but he would have been drafted if he had not volunteered. I volunteered, but I know I would have been drafted if I had not volunteered. There is probably no greater incentive for people volunteering for the service than the draft. Let me just warn the Senator from Maine that he is initiating a costly program."

> **"NOW I THINK THERE ARE A LOT OF THINGS WORSE THAN A DRAFT."**
> *—Senator John Tower, Texas*

> **"… MORE MONEY FOR SHIPS OR MORE MONEY FOR QUALITY PERSONNEL… ."**
> *—Senator Bill Cohen, Maine*

Mr. Cohen

"… Let me cite the Secretary of the Navy, who when faced with a choice of whether or not he would rather have more money for ships or more money for quality personnel, came out in favor of the manpower. I do not know that anyone has disputed that in the Senate Armed Services Committee, including the chairman himself.

"Second, let me read what General Thurman has said in response to the kind of objection that the Senator has offered. He said:

'… Provisions can be made to aid retention of soldiers who want to stay in the military and who want to be the leaders of today and tomorrow. Foremost among the possibilities is transferability. If a soldier sees that the education of his children is provided for, he and his spouse are more likely to stay, accepting often arduous assignments but gratified by the service they perform.'

"So here we have one of the leading spokespersons within the Army itself giving two very good reasons as to why we should support the GI Bill."

Mr. Evans

"Mr. President, I rise to join the Senator from Colorado and my other colleagues as a supporter of this [Armstrong] GI Bill amendment.

"I suppose one of the fundamental questions that could be asked is, 'Why vote for this relatively large expenditure just after we have concluded five weeks of debate and a vote on a deficit reduction package?' We make expenditures in Congress and we

Daniel Evans

make expenditures in this country. We make them because we want to or because we have to. But we also make investments. There is sometimes a considerable difference between an expenditure and an investment.

"Here is where my responsibility and experience as Governor, I think, bear on this GI Bill. To the degree that, through education, we can reduce future failures, we have a chance to reduce the governmental costs which are associated with those failures."

Mr. Hollings

"The Reagan administration promises an economic revival while our young people grow desperate for work.

"But the DoD incredibly boasts that it is successful in personnel goals.

"They hide the truth that their success comes only from the pains of idleness and unemployment resulting from callous policies that favor the wealthy at the deprivation of all others.

Ernest "Fritz" Hollings

"And now we are confronted with the prospect of thousands of college graduates unable to find employment in the Reagan depression.

"Their only hope lies in our armed forces.

"This is not the commitment for national duty—but the path of last resort.

"… More than a demonstration of military power, we need a demonstration of will power. Everyone needs to be committed to our national defense. But since we do not have a cross section of the population in the services, we lack a cross section of support."

"… By the year 2000, it [the Armstrong amendment] will be $877 million. That is a nominal cost when one considers the costs of weapons systems in the multi-billions and billions of dollars. When you consider in 1980 we had a $145 billion defense bill and by next year we are going to have to double that to almost $300 billion. Fifty percent of that, of course, is going to equipment procurement, R&D, and the other 50 percent has gone to our manpower needs and these continue to go up in order to maintain the numbers, much less the quality that has been lacking."

Mr. Boschwitz

"It is interesting to note, Mr. President, that for each defense dollar we spend, about 55 percent is spent for pay, housing, clothing, and feeding of the young men and women who serve in the armed forces of the United States. Considering that such a large portion of our defense spending is for personnel, it seems most appropriate to take a step that would increase the intellectual caliber of those people and

Rudy Boschwitz

that would draw to the active services the most qualified people we can possibly find."

Mr. Glenn

"… Not much has been said yet this afternoon about the cost of the two programs. The costs of the program that is being proposed this afternoon by the GI Bill advocates, Senator Armstrong's bill, the CBO estimates would go up steadily until, when it was in full blossom after about a 10-year period, it would cost $775 million a year, three quarters of a billion a year. It goes up to that over a 10-year period.

"But the amendment that I have this afternoon would cost nothing in the first year and second year, and the third year cost would be $80 million maximum and the fourth year $160 million maximum, and the cost would remain not above that level just by the way we designed this amendment. So that is the major consideration.

"I do not argue with anyone about the advantages of the GI Bill… . But the facts are we would break the bank right now and we have very serious, tremendously serious economic problems in this country.

"... Much comparison was made here earlier this morning about the amendment I proposed, and comparing it with the VEAP program. But I do not think it compares at all with the VEAP program or the ultra-VEAP program [meaning VEAP with 'kickers' for critical military specialties]. There has been very little participation in that program. It is not similar to the one that I am proposing because the benefits that I propose on this are considerably greater than either VEAP or ultra-VEAP because the Glenn monthly benefit would be $500 per month and the VEAP benefit [is] about $200 per month."

Mr. Cranston

[Senator Rudman had assumed the Chair.] "Mr. President, I rise to speak in very strong support of the pending amendment that I join in offering with the distinguished Senator from Colorado [Mr. Armstrong], and Senators Cohen, Matsunaga, and Hollings... .

Warren Rudman

"This amendment, which is essentially identical to S. 1747, [a bill Mr. Cranston introduced on March 7, 1983] is designed to establish two new programs of educational assistance in order to assist the armed forces in recruiting and retaining highly qualified men and women.

"Let me begin by assuring the Senate that I, too, am deeply concerned about rising budget deficits and the need to control government spending. However, I believe that, when viewed in a real-world context, the costs of this measure are reasonable and prudent and that it is a cost-effective measure. Above and beyond that, these costs and the dollars invested in a GI Bill are dollars invested in people —dollars invested in human futures, for individuals and their families... .

"Mr. President, the President's budget for defense in fiscal year 1985 estimates outlays of $272 billion. The average cost per year in the first 10 years of spending —fiscal years 1988 through 1997—in which our amendment could be effective, is $507.5 million. That is less than two-tenths of one percent of the amount of the President's projected outlays in the upcoming fiscal year—two-tenths of one percent.

"To me, that is a small—very small—price to pay to ensure that this nation's All-Volunteer Force remains effective, efficient, and strong.

"From a slightly different perspective, Mr. President, in fiscal year 1985, the Department of Defense will pay out more than $760 million in enlistment, reenlistment, and anniversary benefits. These are benefits—cold cash—paid out to get people in the service and to keep them there. How much of that $760 million, when

> " ... WHAT WE DO NOT NEED IS ANOTHER TEST... "
> —*Senator Alan Cranston, California*

in the hands of an 18-year-old-enlistee, goes to pay for a car or an expensive vacation and how much is invested in a quality education? I think the answer is clear.

"...What we do not need is another test—especially a test as ill-designed and hastily conceived as the underlying amendment by Senator Glenn represents. At best, as Senator Cohen and I noted in our 'Dear Colleague' letter to Senators yesterday, the underlying Glenn amendment is a poor cousin to the existing program that attempts to meet the needs of the armed forces today."

> "WE HAVE NEVER HAD ONE OF THESE [PEACE-TIME GI BILLS] BEFORE, EVER."
> —*Senator Alan Simpson, Wyoming*

Mr. Simpson

"... It [the proposed Armstrong amendment] is the first peace-time GI Bill we have ever had. We have never had one of these before, ever.[8] This has always been for readjustment for veterans for after a conflict. We have never ventured into this area. So I can tell Senators that I would certainly be agreeable to any kind of joint referral [of the Glenn amendment to the Committee on Veterans' Affairs and the Committee on Armed Services].

"... If you walked up to a guy on the street and said, 'What should we do for the veterans of this country?' He would say, 'Anything it takes.' And yet there are millions of veterans who have never served more than six months, never left the United States and have never been involved in any kind of combat activity who draw every single benefit that a combat veteran draws. There are hundreds of thousands who mashed their toe in the turret at Newport during their summer cruise who have been drawing a green check. There are hundreds of thousands who may have been looking for a case of lemon extract in the mess tent to finish off a three-day pass who mashed their big toe and have been drawing a green check for 30 years. That is the kind of arena in which I get to play [as Chairman of the Veterans' Affairs Committee].

"... I went to school on the GI Bill, thank heaven. There were times when they nearly took the check back. Those were the days when I thought beer was food and it was very difficult to go to school under those circumstances.

"... But the issue is that this is an entitlement program. You can call it anything you want. It really startles me to

> " ... I WENT TO SCHOOL ON THE GI BILL, THANK HEAVEN... THOSE WERE THE DAYS WHEN I THOUGHT BEER WAS FOOD..."
> —*Senator Alan Simpson, Wyoming*

see some of my colleagues who voted for freezes, and budget this and budget that, and who are probably the most responsible people in the chamber, coming up with really what is in effect an entitlement program. And not only that, you have not just $300 a month but with the kickers that are in this proposal, it comes to $900 per month and it starts in 1985.

"… As I mentioned the other day, if anybody really believes that the Department of Defense is going to keep this in their budget, they are really wrong because this is going to end up in the Veterans' Administration budget and it is going to come out of some existing veterans' benefit.

"… No one is going to stay in the service if they are going to receive something in the form of $900 a month with the various benefits…"

Mr. Tower

"Mr. President, I ask unanimous consent to have printed in the Record a letter from the Executive Office of the President, Office of Management and Budget, signed by Mr. David Stockman, dated June 6, in strong opposition to the measure offered by the distinguished Senator from Colorado.

> "IT IS AN ELECTION YEAR. YOU [CAN] GET 30 COSPONSORS ANY DAY."
> —*Senator John Tower, Texas*

"Recruitment and retention are good now, and 'if it ain't broke, don't fix it.'

"I think there are some very serious implications in this bill for retention. This is an attractive bill. It is an election year. You [can] get 30 cosponsors any day.

Mr. Cohen

"There you go, again."

Mr. Tower

"I am not saying that is your motivation. I am saying it is attractive in an election year."

Mr. Cohen

"The Senator has been saying that since 1979."

Mr. Tower

"I know the Senator from Maine is honestly motivated. Anyone who sits under the lovely trees and on the seashores in Maine, who writes the beautiful poetry the Senator from Maine does, cannot ever be accused of being dishonestly motivated. He is a man of spirit, heart, and deep conviction. I know him to be that. I would never impugn his motives, nor those of the distinguished Senator from Colorado who is well known for his public-spirited, charitable work.

"But the fact is this is an election year, and that is why a lot of people will not vote on this bill on the merits. It is that simple."

Mr. Cohen

"I thank the Senator for his comments.

"Let me just read from a letter [on this issue as] addressed by the former Chief of Staff, General Meyer… .

"Here are the key words: 'Unfortunately,

> "BUT I SIMPLY SUGGEST THAT THIS BILL IS NOT, AS WAS IMPLIED, POLITICALLY MOTIVATED."
> —*Senator Bill Cohen, Maine*

the future does not look as promising as the past years and the return to a non-contributory GI Bill is imperative. This program should contain the following features:

- Basic benefits adequate enough to compete equally with non-military federal loans and grants;
- Supplementary benefits for us in targeting selected recruits and skills;
- Transferability of benefits to dependents to act as a retention incentive; and
- Inclusion of the Selected Reserve to compensate the 'Total Army.'

"These are precisely the elements that are currently in the amendment the Senator from Colorado and I have offered.

"Let me conclude in not so poetic terms. My friend from Texas seems to diminish the significance of a phrase, be it lyrical or prosaic. But I simply suggest that this bill is not, as was implied, politically motivated.

"I heard that charge last year and the year before. Frankly, I resent it. I resent it because it flies in the face of the experience of this particular bill, the legislative history or non-history, I should say, of this particular measure. It was introduced in 1979 when this Senator certainly was not facing reelection, in 1980, 1981, 1982, 1983, and now in 1984… .'

> "ONE MIGHT BE HONESTLY MOTIVATED IN OFFERING AN AMENDMENT ENDORSING REGULAR ATTENDANCE AT SUNDAY SCHOOL."
> —*Senator John Tower, Texas*

Mr. Tower

"One might be honestly motivated in offering an amendment endorsing regular attendance at Sunday School. Now, despite the motivation, it is a politically attractive idea that I doubt if anyone would vote against... ."

Mr. Simpson

"Mr. President, having known the two who have just participated here in this particular dialogue, and knowing them quite well, they are enjoying this down deep. I see that. And I hope people realize that their friendship is one of the richest in this body... .

"So here we are. The maximum cost of Senator John Glenn's proposal is $12,000 per recruit. The cost of Senator Armstrong's proposal is approximately $200,000 per recruit. And that is the issue... .

"Plus, as I say, [the Armstrong proposal is] a most extraordinary adventure into benefit land, which is benefits for the survivors of children—the children [of service members] not survivors [of deceased or disabled service members]. The phrase is for the benefit of dependents; the benefit could be transferred to them. We have never done that before... .

"... It is essential to point out that recruitment and retention difficulties in the past have varied from service-to-service, grade-to-grade, and occupation-to-occupation, and there has never been an 'across-the-board' problem—one that might call for an across-the-board solution such as the one proposed by this amendment. What clearly is needed, as the amended Glenn proposal recognizes, is:

- First, identification of specific manpower problems or needs;
- Second, a solution that is applied only to the problem and not to areas where there is no problem; and
- Third, a solution that is the most cost-effective one available.

"This simply cannot be done in advance by enactment of this untargeted educational assistance amendment offered by my good colleagues, Senators Armstrong, Cohen, Cranston, Matsunaga, and Hollings... .

"Mr. President, I am disturbed by the notion that when we are routinely dealing with deficits in the neighborhood of $200 billion a year, we would consider enacting two new uncontrollable programs which have a potential for awesome expense, are virtually unrestricted in scope and are wholly lacking in any present justification whatsoever.

"... It cannot be emphasized strongly enough that this is not a GI Bill like any previous GI Bills. The goal in the past has always been to readjust to civilian life after service in a period of war. No GI Bill has ever been enacted solely in order to assist the armed forces in recruitment and retention... ."

Mr. Matsunaga

"Would the Senator from Wyoming yield?"

Mr. Simpson

"Yes."

Mr. Matsunaga

"The Senator has made much of the fact that the proposal will not go into effect immediately but a few years hence. The Senator was, I believe, in the hearing when General Wickham testified before the Senate Veterans Affairs' Committee. He indicated this, and I remind the Chairman of the Veterans' Affairs Committee of what he said: 'The Army has recently experienced a 22-percent decline in the number of young people coming into the Army recruiting stations to take the military entrance exam.' General Wickham suggested that this 22-percent reduction 'may be a harbinger of an upturn in employment opportunities for young people.' The fact of the matter is that many top military officials believe that we are seeing the first signs of recruiting difficulties that they ran into in the 70s, and that this will continue in months ahead and in the immediate years ahead... .

"We must not be shortsighted where our military manpower is concerned. We did that during the 1970s. We found ourselves faced with a manpower readiness crisis that caused the then-Chief of Staff of the Army, Gen. Edward C. Meyer, to call his force 'a hollow Army.' If Congress fails to learn the lessons of just a few short years ago, and allows the services to once again experience recruiting shortfalls, I doubt that we will ever be able to stop the momentum toward the abandonment of the volunteer system, and a return to the peacetime draft that would be inevitable."

Mr. Glenn

"If the Senator [Mr. Armstrong] will yield, I want to make a comment about the statement of the Senator from Hawaii.

"He started off commenting about the Army's getting people interested these days. That is exactly what my amendment approaches. It exactly approaches that Army problem. It is not a basic problem of the Navy, Air Force or Marines. It is an Army problem.

"When we have the option of going from what is an approach of about a $1-billion-a-year program when it is fully in place as opposed to the program that is guaranteed not to go over $160 million per year, if we specifically address the problem the Army has, and if we can get high-quality recruits in, then it seems to me that is the most cost-effective way to go. That is the reason I proposed this.

"So we are addressing specifically the problem you addressed your remarks to."

Mr. Nunn

"Mr. President, I will make just a few brief comments because I know the debate has gone on for quite a while and I am sure that there may be other remarks... .

"... The amendment the Senator from Ohio has offered is a much more carefully targeted program [than that of the Senator from Colorado]. It is designed to hold down costs and to a specific segment of the youth population. That segment would be the high school graduates, people who have the ambition to go to college, people who are willing to sacrifice at the front end of their career so they can get a larger benefit, people who are willing to go on a low-cost track in terms of pay and benefits so they can go forward with their education...

"Let me mention one other point that I believe needs to be emphasized.

"The Armstrong approach is a broad-based benefit. That across-the-board benefit way of proceeding is the least effective recruiting tool because it gives benefits to so many people who would come into the military services even if this program did not exist.

"There are some who would not come in without this Armstrong amendment. I recognize that. I concede that point. But there are huge numbers—I do not know whether it will be 75, 85, or 95 percent—who would come in without this, and we are paying everybody across the board... .

TAKES AWAY ARMY'S COMPETITIVE EDGE

"... Offering the same benefits to all the services and to all recruits in the Army, Navy, Air Force and Marine Corps, takes away from the Army the competitive edge they now have because they now have the most lucrative educational benefit program of any of the services.[9]

"This program will inevitably draw more recruits into the Air Force, Navy and Marine Corps; it will have a relatively detrimental effect on the Army, in my view. It will draw recruits away from the services and skills which involve the greatest risks and are not readily transferable to the civilian economy; in other words, the Army combat arms.

"... So I urge my colleagues to vote against the Armstrong-Cohen-Matsunaga-Cranston proposal.

"... It seems to me everyone who votes today should ask himself the question: Is this the time to create a new major entitlement program before we do what we are supposed to do about getting budget reduction this year?

"... I yield the floor."

Mr. Boren

David Boren

"Mr. President, each year when the Senate struggles with the defense authorization bill and later the appropriations bill, the headlines are made by what we accept or reject in weapons systems—the MX, the B-IB, strategic defense initiative, ASAT,[10] and others.

"Too little attention, if any, is paid to the one element of our defense without which all others fail. That is, the people who make these sophisticated systems work. The men and women who operate the tanks, fly the planes, fire the artillery, supply the ammunition, cook the food, wash the clothes, repair the equipment, lead the troops, the men and women who have chosen to enter the service of their country, and have expressed the willingness to defend the rest of us with their lives if necessary... .

"I am proud to join the Senator from Colorado and others as a cosponsor of this amendment which provides for a GI Bill as an expression of commitment made by this nation to the maintenance of the quality and caliber of people required by today's armed forces.

"... I have been consistent in my call for equal sacrifice by all to address the horrendous budgetary imbalances we face year after year. In this case, the cost of this program is, on balance, well within the limits of prudence and priorities. If we must forgo a weapons system to fund this program within budgetary limits, Mr. President, we will have made the wiser choice. This program is cost effective."

Mr. Armstrong

"Someone has asserted, 'Well, this is something we have never done before; it [a non-contributory GI Bill] has never happened in peacetime.' But I want to note we had it in peacetime. We had it up until December 1976. It was working well.[11] The predictions for what would happen when we eliminated this successful program were dire and catastrophic, and even they proved to underestimate the severe effects of terminating this program."

Mr. Kennedy

Edward Kennedy

"Mr. President, I am pleased to join my colleagues in the Senate as cosponsor of this important amendment which will help to ensure that our armed forces are staffed with qualified men and women. I commend Senators Armstrong, Cohen, Cranston, Hollings, and Matsunaga for their hard work in developing this GI Bill. I am aware of their continued interest in this area and the amendment we have put before us represents a well thought out compromise."

Mr. Pressler

Larry Pressler

"Mr. President, I rise today to support the amendment offered by my distinguished colleague from Colorado, Senator Armstrong. I am a cosponsor of this amendment and cosponsored this legislation in its [freestanding] bill form, as S. 1747.[12]

"… The increased earning power of former service men and their contributions to our economy are usually overlooked by those who question the necessity of the proposed New GI Bill.

"… It is clear to me that the New GI Bill, as proposed by Senator Armstrong, is a much more effective educational package than the often unused VEAP Program or that proposed by Senator Glenn."

> "IT IS A NEW ENTITLEMENT PROGRAM, AND ONCE YOU GET THEM ON THE BOOKS THEY ARE AWFULLY HARD TO TAKE OFF."
> —*Senator John Tower, Texas*

Mr. Tower

"Mr. President, the impact of this proposal on retention is enormously uncertain. In my view, it could very well be adverse. It is far too costly. And even though it might achieve in a limited way its purpose, $200,000 per recruit is much too high. It is a new entitlement program, and once you get them on the books they are awfully hard to take off.

"We have had some four hours of debate [today]. Therefore, Mr. President, I conclude that it is time for me to move, and I do move, to table the amendment of the Senator from Colorado."

Mr. Armstrong

"I ask for the yeas and nays."

Presiding Officer

Arlen Specter, Presiding Officer

"The yeas and nays have been requested. Is there a sufficient second? There is a sufficient second."

[The yeas and nays were ordered.]

"The clerk will call the roll."

[The Legislative Clerk called the roll. Senator Specter had assumed the Chair].

"Are there any other Senators in the chamber who desire to vote?"

SECOND VOTE: TOWER MOTION TO TABLE ARMSTRONG AMENDMENT FAILS 46 TO 51

The result was announced—yeas 46, nays 51… [13]

Mr. Montgomery

So, the Tower amendment to table the Armstrong proposal failed (in other words, it failed to cut off debate on it).

Sonny's Lessons Learned

I think the lesson is in Senator Towers' request to table the Armstrong amendment on procedural grounds rather than substantive grounds. Instead of asking for a vote on the substance of the Armstrong amendment, Senator Tower asked for a vote to table it. And the Senate voted NOT to table it, 51 to 46. Mr. Armstrong then immediately asked the Chair for a vote on the substance of his amendment. It appears the procedural vote gave Senator Tower a preview of how close a vote on the substance of the Armstrong amendment might be.

WHAT'S NEXT

Three more votes are ahead in the Senate Chamber.

Worth Repeating

"The decision of Congress to terminate the GI Bill in December of 1976, in my judgment, has proven to be one of the worst decisions ever made by the Congress of the United States."
—Senator Bill Armstrong

"... As a cosponsor of the original bill, with Representative Steiger, who is now deceased, to create a voluntary military force, I feel privileged to work with the Senator from Colorado in cosponsoring this amendment."
—Senator Spark Matsunaga

"... More than a demonstration of military power, we need a demonstration of will power."
—Senator Fritz Hollings

"... For each defense dollar we spend, about 55 percent is spent for pay, housing, clothing, and feeding, of the young men and women who serve in the armed forces of the United States."
—Senator Rudy Boschwitz

"Senator Armstrong's bill... when it was in full blossom after about a 10-year period, would cost $775 million per year."
—Senator John Glenn

"Now I think there are a lot of things worse than a draft."
—Senator John Tower

9

SONNY'S
CAST OF
CHARACTERS

Senators participating in the debate are the same as Chapters 7 and 8 with the addition of:

*Senator Lawton Chiles (R-FL),
Chairman, Committee on the Budget*

*Senator Pete Domenici (D-NM),
Ranking Member, Committee on the Budget*

*Senator John Stennis (D-MS),
Chairman, Committee on Appropriations*

*Senator Barry Goldwater (R-AZ),
Immediate Past Chairman,
Committee on Armed Services*

*George H.W. Bush, Vice President
of the United States, Presiding Officer*

*Also featured in this chapter as Presiding Officer:
Senator Arlen Specter (R-PA)*

Summer 1984—Road to Enactment: Senate Passes Amended Glenn Test Citizen-Soldier Education Program 72 to 20—After Third, Fourth, Fifth, and Sixth Votes

SONNY'S SUMMARY

After two earlier New GI Bill votes on June 13, the Senate debate continued with four additional votes in this chapter, for a total of six in all.

In the third vote, the Senate voted down 48 to 44 Senator Armstrong's motion to waive Budget Act requirements[1] (associated with creating a new entitlement for a year for which the budget resolution had not been adopted to pay for it) for his Peacetime Veterans' Educational Assistance Act legislation.

In the fourth vote, the Senate approved by unanimous consent (meaning without a roll-call vote) Senator Glenn's motion to make his test Citizen-Soldier Education Program subject to the Congress having to appropriate funds for it each year.

In the fifth vote, the Senate voted for a second time 47 to 45 to table Senator Armstrong's proposed program.

In the sixth vote, the Senate approved—this time by a 72 to 20 roll-call vote—the Glenn amendment, requiring an annual appropriation to pay for his proposed program.

So now the Senate has established what will be its official position in the forthcoming conference with the House: a four-year pilot program for up to 12,500 new service members per year, who would serve on active duty for two years and contribute $250 per month in order to receive 36 months (four academic years) of post-service education benefits of $500 per month, subject to Congress annually appropriating the money for same.

Arlen Specter

Sonny's Scene Setter & Journey Guide

The Senate floor, as a flurry of votes concludes about nine hours of debate on the Glenn and Armstrong amendments.

On the Legislative Journey chart on page 11, we're still at box S-7 with respect to debate on S. 2723. Are we stuck? At the moment it seems like it, doesn't it? But we'll find our way along by and by—but with *déjà vu* not too far down the road.

Mr. Montgomery

Folks, let's review the four amendments the Senate will debate and vote on June 13 in **this** chapter:

- In the third vote, the Senate will defeat 48-44 Senator Armstrong's motion to waive pay-go portions of the Budget Act regarding his Peacetime Veterans' Educational Assistance Act amendment;

- In the fourth vote, the Senate will approve, by unanimous consent (no roll-call vote), Senator Glenn's motion to make his test Citizen-Soldier Education Program amendment subject to an annual appropriation;

- In the fifth vote, the Senate will approve 47-45 (and thus table), Senator Tower's motion to table the Senator Armstrong Peacetime Veterans' Educational Assistance Act amendment; and

- In the sixth vote, the Senate will approve 72-20 on a roll-call vote, the Glenn test Citizen-Soldier Education Program amendment, as modified by annual appropriation language.

June 13, 1984	CONGRESSIONAL RECORD—SENATE	16095

ARMSTRONG, is a much more effective educational package than the often unused VEAP Program or that proposed by Senator GLENN.

One other item is the extension of the 1989 cutoff date for the Vietnam-era GI bill. Originally, this extension was a part of S. 1747. However, it was not necessary to include it in this amendment before us because it was included in the fiscal year 1985 DOD authorization bill. This extension is essential for many Vietnam veterans who wish to complete their military careers before utilizing the benefits to

serves or the National Guard. The Reserve and National Guard constitute an important component of our military forces. This type of national service should qualify reservists and guardsmen for eligibility for benefits under this program.

The Armstrong-Cohen-Cranston amendment would also recognize the contribution of career military men and women, those who have served over 10 years, and provide them with the opportunity to contribute to an educational assistance fund and have their contributions matched on a 2-

Delaware [Mr. ROTH] are necessarily absent.

I further announce that, if present and voting, the Senator from Wisconsin [Mr. KASTEN], would vote "nay".

The PRESIDING OFFICER (Mr. SPECTER). Are there any other Senators in the Chamber who desire to vote?

The result was announced—yeas 46, nays 51, as follows:

[Rollcall Vote No. 123 Leg.]

YEAS—46

| Abdnor | Grassley | Percy |
| Baker | Hatfield | Proxmire |

We pick up the debate at page 16,095 of the *Congressional Record* (above). I'll see you at the end of this chapter, which concludes the almost nine hours of debate on the issue of a proposed New GI Bill.

Now let's go back to the Senate Chamber. Senator Tower addressed the Chair.[2]

Presiding Officer

[Mr. Specter] "The Senator from Texas."

Mr. Tower

"Mr. President, I want to tell the Senate what we have done. We have agreed to a brand new entitlement program on the floor of the Senate and the cost is going to grow annually. I am hopeful, since this is not needed as a recruiting tool and perhaps may have an adverse effect on retention, that we can perhaps consider an amendment that would take this out of the [budget] function 050[3] and put it in the veterans' function so that the Department of Defense, which has opposed this measure, will not have to bear the expense of it."

Mr. Baker

"Mr. President, after consulting with the distinguished chairman of the [budget] committee, and other Senators, it appears to me appropriate at this point to suggest that a point of order does lie against this amendment.

"At this time, Mr. President, I make the point of order that the amendment violates section 303 of the Budget Act by creating a new entitlement program for a year for which a first budget resolution has not been adopted."[4]

> "... THE AMENDMENT VIOLATES SECTION 303 OF THE BUDGET ACT ..."
> —*Senator Howard Baker, Tennessee*

Mr. Armstrong

"I move to waive various sections of the Budget Act,[5] and I understand that is a debatable motion. I do not intend to debate it at great length but I think the Senate should understand why we are in this situation.

"... The reason why a waiver is necessary, and why the majority leader's point lies [against it], is not because of something that is wrong with the amendment, or because there is something wrong with the procedure for bringing the amendment to the floor, but because we have not yet passed a budget resolution in due course. In other words, if we had completed work on the budget resolution, in the normal timetable, this amendment would in fact be in order, and would not be violative of the Budget Act."

Mr. Chiles

Lawton Chiles

"If I may answer that [as to when a new entitlement program of this type would be considered in order], it would be after the Budget Committee would decide to embark on this program. The purpose of the [Budget] act is to try to keep us from passing entitlement programs binding out-year [meaning "future"] appropriations without being considered by the Budget Act and by this body without a deliberate decision of the body that we are ready to create new entitlement programs."

Mr. Baker

"Mr. President, I do not know a single person more concerned about the state of the budget, the deficit, and the question of entitlements than the Senator from Colorado. What I am about to say is not critical of him. But if we are going to hatch new entitlement programs that begin two or three years in the future, and do so with a general waiver of the Budget Act, then we might as well throw away the Budget Act."

Mr. Armstrong

"I have been a member of the Budget Committee for five years, and the Budget Committee does not consider the individual components except in arriving at their totals. When the Senate votes on a budget resolution, it is not whether we need a new Food Stamp Program or a New GI Bill or a new airplane. It votes only on budget totals.... It is perfectly possible for the Budget Committee to send forth a resolution in which one Senator says, 'I am putting in extra money for a new bomber,' and another one says, 'I am putting it in for the New GI Bill.' But that really is not the issue."

Mr. Baker

"Mr. President, I do not wish to pursue it further.... Had this proposal been to enact a GI Bill but subject to appropriation, you would have an entirely different situation. But that is not what it is. We are committing funds without going through the authorizing process, without going through the appropriating process, and it does require a waiver of the act to do that. I oppose it."

Mr. Cranston

"... The budget resolution, when it has been approved, would not be affected by one penny of what we are talking about, because there is no money to be spent in 1985 and no money to be spent in 1986 under the amendment we have approved in the Senate just now.

"I would also like to add that if this point of order holds against the amendment the Senator from Colorado offered, it would hold against the amendment offered by the Senator from Ohio. The same logic would knock it down. I do not think we want to knock down a program that is designed to help us meet our military manpower needs."

> "... THE BUDGET RESOLUTION, WHEN IT HAS BEEN APPROVED, WOULD NOT BE AFFECTED BY ONE PENNY OF WHAT WE ARE TALKING ABOUT..."
> —*Senator Alan Cranston, California*

Mr. Domenici

Pete Domenici

"Mr. President, I think this is a very important issue. I do not believe it is a casual point of order. I did not think the Budget Act was cavalier at all about it....

"I can remember, Mr. President, for those who wonder how entitlements got to where they are, an entitlement program that was described on the Senate floor as costing only $700 million per year. I just refreshed my memory by reading the *Congressional Record*.

"Let me tell you about that program: That program [which is operating] this year, which was voted into existence on the floor, because it did not go through any committees, is [now] costing the American government... $21 billion and is [now] costing the various states of the United States $23 billion a year.[6] That is how things happen around here.

"Frankly, I think if we are going to decide that a Budget Act which says you cannot create new entitlements in the out-years in this manner, if we are going to say it does not really mean anything, then we may just as well decide that committees mean nothing, that estimates mean nothing, that we are just going to come to the Senate floor and create new entitlements when we please; appropriations mean nothing; and having some way to control these things means nothing.

"Out in the country, people ask us why we cannot get the budget under control. There is a word we keep giving them. We say because 65 percent of the budget is uncontrollable— "uncontrollable" in quotation marks.

> "... 65 PERCENT OF THE [FEDERAL] BUDGET IS UNCONTROLLABLE..."
> —*Senator Pete Domenici, New Mexico*

They end up looking back at us and saying 'What do you mean, uncontrollable [budget]? Do you not run the country?' We end up trying to explain to them that every year, the appropriators pass a bill.

"They say, 'That is what we spent for our country. Why not take that appropriations bill and cut it?'"

Mr. Stennis

John Stennis

"Mr. President, … I have supported [military] pay increases over the years, but I have restrained myself today. I have not said anything. I have voted the other way because I have said, as have many others, we absolutely must take care of the budget deficit and these entitlements… ."

Mr. Domenici

"… I just refer the Senators to the Congressional Budget and Impoundment Control Act of 1974, as amended, page 18, section 303, subsection (c).

There is a very detailed procedure for waiver, and there is a process for doing it without waiver. It can be done. It is not being done that way in this case and maybe it is because committees are not prone to do it the way it is prescribed in this amendment because they do not think we ought to be doing this kind of thing. I think that is a pretty good sign to us that we ought not be doing it, either."

Mr. Cohen

"Mr. President, earlier this afternoon, or just a few moments ago actually, reference was made to our 'hatching' an entitlement program. 'Hatching' to me sounds like something you do in secret, like a covert action. Maybe we hatch a Stealth bomber program.

"This particular amendment has been offered in public session, not closed session. It has been the subject of debate since 1979 and the subject of debate at length this afternoon. The message to me from what is taking place this afternoon is that if we cannot win on the merits; we will beat you to death on procedure. This issue is no longer being discussed on the merits but, rather, placed on the altar of Budget Committee sanctity.

"We keep hearing the issue about costs.

> "… ON THE ALTAR OF BUDGET COMMITTEE SANCTITY."
> —*Senator Bill Cohen, Maine*

The Tomahawk missile is going to come up later tonight or tomorrow. I recall being told that missile programs had a $250 million cost overrun. I tried to find out why, and they said, 'Well, it was mismanagement… .'

"No big deal, just a little mismanagement on the part of the Navy and the contractor at that time. But in the GI Bill, we are talking about putting in a program which we know has worked in the past in substitute for a program, VEAP, that is not working today. What we are getting is a lot of legislative razzle-dazzle… .

"Let me address one more subject. Do you really believe, Mr. President, we are going to create a GI Bill that is subject to annual appropriations? Are we going to tell the young recruits, 'By the way, we have this good program for you. If you will give us two years, three years, maybe four years, five years or six years, you will have the following educational benefits that will have accrued to you in terms of money, subject, of course, to the whims and caprice of Congress, assuming they will appropriate the money for that given year.'"

Mr. Baker

"…We have been an hour or more on this. I would recommend that we do one of several things since time is moving on. We either have a vote on the waiver, which I am prepared to do; or, I will move to table the waiver, if necessary. Or the waiver will be withdrawn… .

"Mr. President, there are all sorts of variations on this. There is no doubt in my mind that one way or the other you can probably fit this thing together. But it

> "… WHEN YOU TRY TO CUT, FIT, AND PASTE ON THE [SENATE] FLOOR YOU END UP NOT REALLY KNOWING WHAT YOU ARE DOING."
> —*Senator Howard Baker, Tennessee*

has been my experience also that when you try to cut, fit, and paste on the [Senate] floor you end up not really knowing what you are doing. At least I do not know what I am doing… .

"… I would ask the Senator from Colorado if he is prepared to go forward with a vote on the waiver, or to withdraw the waiver and let the point of order be ruled upon."

Mr. Armstrong

"…Aside from the fact that I would like to pass this amendment, which despite what the majority leader and others have said has not been cut and pasted on the floor, the fact is it has been under development, and is the work of quite a large number of Senators and staffers here, in the Pentagon, and elsewhere. This is not something that has been thrown together in a slap-dash way. In fact, it has been rather carefully developed after extensive hearings."

Mr. Tower

"Mr. President, it is my intention to object to the consent request to amend the amendment offered by the Senator from Colorado. I suggest that the best way to proceed is to go ahead and vote on the motion of the Senator from Colorado to waive the rule, then go from there and let us get this thing moving.

"We are going to be in all night now I think, Mr. President. We have spent six- and one-half hours [so far today] on this measure, an inordinate amount of time.[7] We have some big ticket items in this bill… . We have all these fancy social and economic programs in defense. Nobody ever wants to cut those out of defense. Now they want to lard this [peace-time GI Bill] on it."

Mr. Goldwater

"I am inclined to agree with the Senator [Armstrong] that sometime this will pass. What would be wrong with introducing it as a piece of legislation and having it pass as a bill?"[8]

Barry Goldwater

Mr. Armstrong

"Mr. President, let me say to my friend from Arizona, that is what I did five years ago; that is what I did four years ago; that is what I did three years ago; that is what I did two years ago; that is what I did last year… .

"Frankly, we have just been stiff-armed at every occasion in Armed Services. The Veterans' Affairs Committee has had extensive hearings on it. And the hearing record not only this year but the year before, not only in the Senate but in the Armed Services Committee of the House and the Veterans' Affairs Committee of the House, just bolster the case. In fact, of the members of the committee which has jurisdiction over this matter, eight of the 12 members of the committee, are cosponsors of the amendment. So the Senator's suggestion is a valid one."

> "FRANKLY, WE HAVE JUST BEEN STIFF-ARMED AT EVERY OCCASION IN ARMED SERVICES."
> —*Senator Bill Armstrong, Colorado*

Mr. Goldwater

"Eight out of 12 could not get it out of committee?"

Mr. Armstrong

"Well, they have not been able to do so yet, I say to the Senator.

"Mr. President, all I can tell you is that we are offering it as a floor amendment again, as we did before. All I want to do at this point is expedite the process, and so I am going to reluctantly suggest that the best way to do that is to first have a vote on the motion to waive. That is part of the Budget Act process. Even though I do not think it is the most orderly and best way, it seems to be the best approach… ."

Mr. Cranston

"I ask for the yeas and nays."

Presiding Officer

"Is there a sufficient second? There is a sufficient second." [The yeas and nays were ordered.]

THIRD VOTE—SENATOR ARMSTRONG'S MOTION TO WAIVE PAY-GO PORTIONS OF THE BUDGET ACT IS DEFEATED 48-44

Presiding Officer

"The clerk will call the roll." [The assistant legislative clerk called the roll.

[The Vice President of the United States, George H.W. Bush, had assumed the Chair, as Presiding Officer.] "Are there any other Senators in the chamber who wish to vote?"

Vice President George H.W. Bush

Mr. Montgomery

The result was announced—yeas 44, nays 48.[9]

So the motion to waive portions of the Budget Act was rejected.

Presiding Officer

"On a point of order an identical amendment was ruled out of order one year ago. This amendment fails."

AMENDMENT NO. 3179, AS MODIFIED

Mr. Glenn

"Mr. President, my intentions are to ask unanimous consent that I may be able to modify my amendment, which is at the desk, if I get the floor to do that.

"May I do that at this time?"

Presiding Officer

"Is there objection to the request from the Senator from Ohio?"

Mr. Armstrong

"Mr. President, reserving the right to object, could we understand the nature of the modification?"

Mr. Glenn

"Yes. It makes the amendment subject to an annual appropriation."

Mr. Armstrong

"Mr. President, I am disposed not to object to this amendment offered by the Senator from Ohio even though at one level it might be natural if I would do so because a similar request was objected to when I offered to do that. It would be my intention not to object, but then immediately if the Chair will recognize me to offer my amendment again in a slightly modified form so that both are before us and we get a fair up-or-down choice between the two proposals.... .

"Some of those who have voted against us on the last vote have said they would like to vote with us the next time around, that they have scruples against voting against the budget waiver even though we have done it hundreds of times."

Mr. Domenici

"... The Senator from Colorado makes a point that we waive the Budget Act all the time. Let me make one point: we do not waive the Budget Act all the time under section 303, which prohibits the creation of new entitlements in this manner.

"In fact, section 303 is waived very rarely.

"What we do is waive the whole act from time to time. But I remind you that for good reason the Congress of the United States prescribed a very excellent process for new entitlements.

"We are supposed to introduce a resolution saying that we want to waive section 303, pursuant to the Budget Act and have a new entitlement."

FOURTH VOTE—SENATOR GLENN'S MOTION TO MAKE A PILOT CITIZEN-SOLDIER EDUCATION PROGRAM SUBJECT TO AN ANNUAL APPROPRIATION APPROVED BY UNANIMOUS CONSENT

Presiding Officer

"Is there objection to the unanimous consent request [to make the Glenn amendment subject to an annual appropriation]? Without objection, it is so ordered. The amendment is so modified.[10]

"The Senator from Texas."

Mr. Tower

"Mr. President, I just want to suggest that the Senator from Colorado go ahead and offer his amendment, and let us get on with this."

> " ... LET US GET ON WITH THIS."
> —*Senator John Tower, Texas*

AMENDMENT NO. 3191

Purpose: To establish two new programs for educational assistance for veterans of peacetime service, and for other purposes.

Mr. Armstrong

"Mr. President, I send an amendment to the desk and ask for its immediate consideration.

"... Since we were not successful in the budget waiver and since some members who voted against the GI Bill concept on the waiver motion issue expressed to me privately their willingness and desire to vote squarely on the issue if I could get it before the body in a form that we were just voting on that and not some procedural question, I have felt constrained to offer this.

Ordinarily, I would not come back a third time. But I do think we understand the issue.

"It is not my desire to drag it out. I just ask the 51 who voted with us an hour or two ago [in opposition to Mr. Tower's proposal to table my amendment to create a permanent peacetime GI Bill] to do so again, and let us get on with the task."

Mr. Tower

"Mr. President, I would simply ask the 49 Senators that voted with us on the last vote to vote with us again. I think that the Senator's views on the issue to create a new entitlement are clear.

"I move [again] to table the amendment of the Senator from Colorado."

Mr. Armstrong

"Will the Senator withhold for just a moment?"

Mr. Tower

"I will withhold for a moment but we have been debating this issue for over seven hours today, and I do not think we could get anymore enlightenment on it. Senators are going to be here all night voting on amendments that are germain to this bill."

> "... WE HAVE BEEN DEBATING THIS ISSUE FOR OVER SEVEN HOURS TODAY."
> —*Senator John Tower, Texas*

Mr. Armstrong

"Since there was a tabling motion previously, I wonder if the Senator would now not be willing to have an up-or-down vote on the issue itself, rather than a tabling motion. We had this tabling motion earlier, I would just appeal to the Senator that we have been through that, and could we not now just vote on the pending question?"

Mr. Tower

"Without the tabling motion the matter is still debatable. Therefore, Mr. President, I move to table the amendment of the Senator from Colorado."

Mr. Armstrong

"I reluctantly ask for the yeas and nays."

Presiding Officer

"Is there a sufficient second? There is a sufficient second."

[The yeas and nays were ordered.]

"The question is on agreeing to the motion of the Senator from Texas [Mr. Tower] to table the amendment of the Senator from Colorado [Mr. Armstrong]. The yeas and nays have been ordered and the clerk will call the roll."

[The bill clerk called the roll.]

FIFTH VOTE—SENATOR TOWER'S MOTION TO TABLE THE SENATOR ARMSTRONG PEACETIME VETERANS' EDUCATIONAL ASSISTANCE ACT APPROVED 47-45

Presiding Officer

"Are there any other Senators in the Chamber wishing to vote?"[11]

[The result was announced—yeas 47, nays 45[12]... so the motion to lay on the table amendment No. 3191 was agreed to.]

> "ARE THERE ANY OTHER SENATORS IN THE CHAMBER WISHING TO VOTE?"
> —*Vice President George H.W. Bush*

Mr. Armstrong

"...When we last visited this issue about six months ago, we failed by four or five votes. I guess today, after three roll calls, they finally got us by a vote or two.[13] I expect that some of us will want to make this effort again. In fact, I think the clear sentiment which has been expressed is increasing support for the concept of a GI Bill. There are parliamentary questions to be answered; there are details that need to be reconciled."

> "... AFTER THREE ROLL-CALL VOTES, THEY FINALLY GOT US BY A VOTE OR TWO."
> —*Senator Bill Armstrong, Colorado*

AMENDMENT NO. 3179, AS MODIFIED

Mr. Glenn

"Mr. President, I would like to have a recorded vote on this [rather than by unanimous consent]. I ask for the yeas and nays."

Presiding Officer

"Is there a sufficient second? There is a sufficient second."

[The yeas and nays were ordered.]

Mr. Glenn

"Mr. President, as I explained before, this amendment is a targeted effort to assist the services in acquiring high-quality recruits for two-year enlistments from a wide cross section of American society and at a limited cost.

"It does not conflict with, or change, any existing programs.

"It is a contributory program; the recruit forgoes $250 per month on pay for the full 24 months... .

"Mr. President, with the absence of a draft and the high pay given recruits, it is unfair to ask the taxpayers to wholly subsidize service-connected educational benefits. Therefore, I believe this amendment, which requires the government to match a serviceman's funds at a rate of about 2 to 1, is equitable and fair to the soldier and the taxpayer. I urge my colleagues to vote for its adoption."

Mr. Cohen

"Mr. President, before we vote, I would like to call to the attention of my colleagues on the floor that in the Glenn proposal, there have been no hearings held whatsoever. The basic objection we have heard here on our proposal is that we have not had hearings again. The record is voluminous, yet not quite enough hearings have been held. On the proposal of the Senator from Ohio, there have not been any hearings held, to my knowledge.

> "... IN THE GLENN PROPOSAL, THERE HAVE BEEN NO HEARINGS HELD WHATSOEVER."
> —*Senator Bill Cohen, Maine*

$25 PER MONTH CONTRIBUTION VS. $250 PER MONTH CONTRIBUTION

Mr. Cohen

"Also, I point out if my colleagues think VEAP is a failure, then this, it seems to me, is also going to be doomed to failure. We have a system in which there is a $25 per month contribution on the part of the service personnel and the program is, in fact, failing. Now we are going to have a $250 a month contributory program. If that is not doomed to failure, I do not know what is."

Mr. Glenn

"Mr. President, the VEAP program the Senator from Maine refers to certainly was not successful. I hope ultra-VEAP can be considered a success. I think the amendment I am proposing will be a response to that."

Presiding Officer

"Is there further debate? If not, the question is on agreeing to the amendment of the Senator from Ohio. The yeas and nays have been ordered. The clerk will call the roll."

[The legislative clerk called the roll.]

SIXTH VOTE—SENATOR GLENN'S PILOT CITIZEN-SOLDIER EDUCATION PROGRAM AMENDMENT AS MODIFIED BY REQUIRED ANNUAL APPROPRIATION APPROVED 72-20

"Are there any other Senators in the Chamber wishing to vote?"

Mr. Montgomery

The result was announced—yeas 72, nays 20...[14]

So the amendment No. 3179, as modified, was agreed to.

The Senate now had a "New GI Bill" position, as the full Senate approved S. 2723 on June 20, 1984: A four-year pilot program for 12,500 new service members per year, who would serve on active duty for two years and contribute $250 per month in order to receive 36 months of post-service educational assistance at $500 per month, but only if Congress annually appropriates the funds.

UNITED STATES SENATE

Sonny's Lessons Learned

Know the meaning of votes beyond the numbers. Vote tallies— like 72 to 20—sometimes tell only part of the story, whether it's a House vote or a Senate vote. In this case, do you think the Senate's position was a strong and unified one? I heard some pretty strong dissent. This included dissent from many of the 25 Senators cosponsoring the Armstrong amendment, including eight of the 12 members of the Senate Armed Services Committee. The House conferees respectfully would factor in this lack of consensus in putting together the House's approach to negotiating with the Senate conferees in the House-Senate conference committee.[15]

Worth Repeating

"But if we are going to hatch new entitlement programs that begin two or three years in the future, and do so with a general waiver of the Budget Act, then we might as well throw away the Budget Act."
—*Majority Leader Howard Baker*

"I would also like to add that if this point of order holds against the amendment the Senator from Colorado offered, it would hold against the amendment offered by the Senator from Ohio. The same logic would knock it down."
—*Senator Alan Cranston*

"... If we are going to say the Budget Act does not really mean anything, then we may just as well decide that committees mean nothing, that estimates mean nothing, that we are just going to come to the Senate floor and create new entitlements when we please... ."
—*Senator Pete Domenici*

"What we are getting is a lot of legislative razzle dazzle... "
—*Senator Bill Cohen*

WHAT'S NEXT

It's now time for the House and Senate to go to conference on the FY 1985 DoD Authorization Act, of which a New GI Bill is a very small provision, though those working on the provision didn't think so.

10

SONNY'S
CAST OF
CHARACTERS

G. Kim Wincup, Staff Director,
Committee on Armed Services,
House of Representatives

Senator John Tower (R-TX),
Chairman, Senate Armed Services Committee

Mack Fleming,
Staff Director and Chief Counsel,
Committee on Veterans' Affairs,
House of Representatives

Representative Ron Dellums (D-CA),
Member, House Armed Services Committee

Representative Melvin Price (D-IL), Chairman,
House Armed Services Committee

Senator Sam Nunn, (D-GA), Ranking Member,
Senate Armed Services Committee

Senator Alan Cranston (D-CA),
Ranking Member,
Senate Veterans' Affairs Committee

Fall 1984—Road to Enactment: House-Senate Conference on the FY 1985 DoD Authorization Act

SONNY'S SUMMARY

The 31 House-Senate conferees accepted neither the New GI Bill provisions of H.R. 1400 approved by the House in its version of the DoD Authorization Act nor the version approved by the Senate in the New GI Bill Program amendment. The wee-hours Conference Committee produced a compromise three-year, statutory test program in which service members would contribute $100 per month for 12 months so as to become eligible for 36 months (four academic years) of post-service education benefits at $300 per month. Eligibility for the New GI Bill was limited to service members entering the military between July 1, 1985, and June 30, 1988.

Highly fatigued conferees ate readily available M&M's® daily to augment their energy levels. Conference Chairman John Tower scheduled the conference's vote on a GI Bill provision last, following weeks of hard negotiating over the $211 billion defense authorization bill. The bill included provisions for the MX missile, the B-1B bomber, the Pershing missile, the Trident submarine, the Strategic Defense Initiative (known pejoratively as "Star Wars" in some quarters), and anti-satellite weaponry.

At the conclusion of the conference, professional staff of the House and Senate Veterans' Affairs and Armed Services Committees even found themselves in disagreement about what they had agreed to regarding a New GI Bill— prolonging the strained relationship on this issue.

BACKGROUND TO THE HOUSE-SENATE CONFERENCE COMMITTEE

Mr. Montgomery

I'll ask Mr. Kim Wincup, who served on the staff, including as majority staff director of the Committee on Armed Services, U.S. House of Representatives, from 1974 through 1984, to comment further on setting the scene for you, our students.[1]

Then I'll ask Mr. Mack Fleming to help describe the conference. Mack served on the staff of the House Committee on Veterans' Affairs from 1974 to 1994, including 14 years as majority staff director and chief counsel.[2]

Mr. Wincup

Kim Wincup

"Thank you, Mr. Chairman.

"First, by way of background, the annual DoD Authorization Act is one of the most important bills Congress considers each year. The House-Senate conferees authorized funds of $211.7 billion for fiscal year 1985; $12.8 billion below the President's budget request.[3]

"House conferees are known as 'Managers on the Part of the House' and Senate conferees as 'Managers on the Part of the Senate.'

"It was a big bill. The report on H.R. 5167—the House's version of the FY 1985 DoD Authorization Act—filed by the House Armed Services Committee on April 19, consumed 399 pages.[4] The May 31 report filed by the Senate Armed Services Committee on its version—S. 2723—filled 527 pages.[5]

"Second, before we got to the House-Senate Conference, the full House had debated H.R. 5167, on May 15, 16, 17, 23, 24, 30, and 31.[6] It was unusually contentious, with members at times shouting at one another during the debate on thermonuclear weapons systems, for example.[7]

"Students, during tense times on the House floor, I can say to you that Representative Sonny Montgomery was often a calming force because—based on what I saw—both sides of the aisle respected him.[8] He typically was like an island of reason in a sea of dispute when things boiled over.[9]

"By the time of the House-Senate Conference, we on the House side had already expended considerable energy and emotion on this $211 billion bill just to formulate a House position. I suspect a similar dynamic existed in the Senate as the Senate debated its bill, S. 2723, on June 7, 8, 11, 12, 13, 14, 15, 18, 19, and 20.[10] As you know, the Senate debated the Glenn and Armstrong New GI Bill amendment on June 11 and 13 for about nine hours.

98TH CONGRESS | HOUSE OF REPRESENTATIVES | REPORT
2d Session | | No. 98-691

DEPARTMENT OF DEFENSE AUTHORIZATION ACT, 1985

APRIL 19, 1984.—Committed to the Committee of the Whole House on the State of the Union and ordered to be printed

Mr. PRICE, from the Committee on Armed Services, submitted the following

REPORT

together with

ADDITIONAL AND DISSENTING VIEWS

[To accompany H.R. 5167]

[Including cost estimate of the Congressional Budget Office]

The Committee on Armed Services, to whom was referred the bill (H.R. 5167) to authorize appropriations for fiscal year 1985 for the Armed Forces for procurement, for research, development, test, and evaluation, for operation and maintenance, and for working capital funds, to prescribe personnel strengths for such fiscal year for the Armed Forces and for civilian employees of the Department of Defense, and for other purposes, having considered the same, report favorably thereon with amendments and recommend that the bill as amended do pass.

The amendment to the text of the bill is a complete substitute therefor and appears in italic type in the reported bill.

The title of the bill is amended to reflect the amendment to the text of the bill.

EXPLANATION OF THE COMMITTEE AMENDMENT

The committee adopted an amendment in the nature of a substitute during its consideration of H.R. 5167. The bill, as amended, is discussed in detail in the remainder of the report.

The House Report

OMNIBUS DEFENSE AUTHORIZATION ACT, 1985

REPORT

[To accompany S. 2723]

ON

AUTHORIZING APPROPRIATIONS FOR FISCAL YEAR 1985 FOR THE ARMED FORCES FOR PROCUREMENT, FOR RESEARCH, DEVELOPMENT, TEST, AND EVALUATION, AND FOR OPERATION AND MAINTENANCE, TO PRESCRIBE PERSONNEL STRENGTHS FOR SUCH FISCAL YEAR FOR THE ARMED FORCES AND FOR CIVILIAN EMPLOYEES OF THE DEPARTMENT OF DEFENSE, TO AUTHORIZE APPROPRIATIONS FOR SUCH FISCAL YEAR FOR CIVIL DEFENSE, TO AUTHORIZE CERTAIN CONSTRUCTION AT MILITARY INSTALLATIONS FOR SUCH FISCAL YEAR, TO AUTHORIZE APPROPRIATIONS FOR THE DEPARTMENT OF ENERGY FOR NATIONAL SECURITY PROGRAMS FOR SUCH FISCAL YEAR, AND FOR OTHER PURPOSES

together with

ADDITIONAL VIEWS

COMMITTEE ON ARMED SERVICES
UNITED STATES SENATE

MAY 31, 1984—Ordered to be printed

U.S. GOVERNMENT PRINTING OFFICE
WASHINGTON : 1984

The Senate Report

"Third, the Democratic party was in the majority in the House, and the Republican party was in the majority in the Senate during this period of the Ronald Reagan presidency. Our work was challenging because not only the two political parties—but also the two chambers of Congress themselves—had very different philosophies on how best to use funds for our national defense. It seemed as if even the smallest difference of opinion could magnify itself into something larger.

"Fourth, members were worn out. The 31 members of the House-Senate Conference Committee on the FY 1985 DoD Authorization Act[11] had been working daily for about two weeks on resolving major differences between the House- and Senate-passed bills.

"Conferees and staff painfully worked through heavy-duty issues to authorize funds in the tens of billions of dollars for programs such as the MX advanced intercontinental ballistic missile system, the B-1B bomber program, the Pershing II missile program, the Trident ballistic missile submarine program, various cruise missile programs, the space-based Strategic Defense Initiative, and anti-satellite weaponry, to name just a few.[12]

"The compromise legislation that the House and Senate ultimately approved and sent to the White House consumed 176 pages and the report issued by the conference managers 354 pages.[13]

"Fifth, we had been living on M&M's® much of the time. Can you believe it?

"The Mars Corporation, producers of M&M's®, was located in the rural Virginia Congressional district of Representative Dan Daniels. Mr.

Late-night energy food for the conferees.

Daniels was a member of the Conference Committee and kept conferees and staff alike supplied with the M&M's® to sustain us the many times we worked late into the evening or early-morning hours.

"Sixth, as Chairman of the Conference Committee, Senator Tower scheduled discussion of a New GI Bill last, because he was unconvinced the legislation was necessary.[14] But he knew he'd probably have to accede to the House's wishes in some way.[15]

"Seventh, because there were 42 conferees during discussion of the New GI Bill provision,[16] we met in room S. 407 of the main Capitol.

> **"THERE WERE 42 [HOUSE-SENATE] CONFEREES DURING DISCUSSION OF THE NEW GI BILL PROVISION..."**
>
> —G. Kim Wincup,
> *Staff Director, Committee on Armed Services, House of Representatives*

"Last, with respect to substantive policy, there was no real voter constituency for the New GI Bill issue. Does this surprise you?

Across the country, Americans understandably were focused on the business of going to work every day, raising families, and participating in their local communities. The military budget was not necessarily an issue they followed closely. And if they did follow it, it often was because of the high-technology weapons systems that made the newspaper headlines.

"So Mr. Montgomery and a handful of his colleagues in the House and Senate—with help from the civilian and military leadership of the Army, the Non Commissioned Officers Association, the Fleet Reserve Association, and others—had to make the case for spending money, however little, on a New GI Bill that represented a paradigm shift from previous GI Bill programs. Senator Simpson talked of this paradigm shift extensively in the Senate debate in Chapter 8.[17]

"That's the dynamic I saw at work as we entered the House-Senate Conference.

MORE BACKGROUND

Mr. Montgomery

Thank you, Kim.[18]

What we see depends on where we sit. So I'd just add four small points to Kim's good observations, as background to the conference.

First, as I mentioned at the end of Chapter 5, the House Armed Services Committee (HASC) could have brought H.R. 1400—designed to create a New GI Bill—to the House floor in 1982 for a vote as a stand-alone, "clean" bill. Instead, in 1984, HASC leadership elected to include the provisions of H.R. 1400 in the massive Fiscal Year 1985 DoD Authorization Act—again, instead of as a stand-alone bill.

Second, when Mack Fleming saw the conferee list furnished by Speaker Tip O'Neill's office on about June 23,[19] he noticed the Armed Services Committee had 13 conferees—seven Democrats and six Republicans—and the Veterans' Affairs Committee had none.[20] So he immediately informed me.

I went directly to Speaker O'Neill and asked him to appoint a more equal number of conferees from the two committees.[21] On June 25, the House concurred without objection that the Speaker add nine conferees from the Veterans' Affairs Committee for the discussion on the New GI Bill part of

> **"... IF YOU DON'T ASK, THE ANSWER IS NO!"**
>
> —G.V. "Sonny" Montgomery

the conference.[22] So students, if you don't **ask**, the answer is no!

These conferees are informally known as "outside conferees," meaning they come from a committee other than the committee having primary jurisdiction on a bill. Five new conferees were Democrats and four were Republicans.[23]

I never hesitated on requesting conferees be appointed from the Veterans' Affairs Committee because the New GI Bill provisions in H.R. 5167 were derived from H.R. 1400 that the Veterans' Affairs Committee had approved in 1983. The Parliamentarian of the House indeed had referred H.R. 1400 jointly to both committees.[24]

Third, I obtained proxies[25] signed by House Veterans' Affairs Committee conferees from both sides of the aisle who could not be present at the final late-night session.

Fourth, House Armed Services Committee Chairman Melvin Price asked me to manage the negotiations for the House on the New GI Bill aspect.[26]

I knew the negotiation with the Senate would be a challenging one, and he wanted to be able to lead the discussion on behalf of the House team, just as Chairman Tower would lead the negotiation on behalf of the Senate team.

Proxies were obtained for those who could not be present at the final, late-night session. This sample is from another conference.

WEE HOURS CONFERENCE COMMITTEE

Mr. Montgomery

None of us had eaten supper and I was so hungry I felt I could eat a folded tarp![27] So the Pentagon sent in boxes of "meals-ready-to-eat" for the hungry conferees.[28] Known as "MREs," these are the meals soldiers eat when they are deployed in the field.

I did not want conferees to leave the conference for supper because I didn't want to give Chairman Tower time to round up more votes in support of his position.[29]

As Kim Wincup said a minute ago, Chairman Tower scheduled consideration on the House and Senate provision relating to a New GI Bill as the very last item to be negotiated. At various times during that final evening of the conference, I asked Chairman Tower when he thought the conference would discuss this issue. As I remember it, at one point our brief exchange went like this:

Sonny brought in MREs to feed the conferees so they wouldn't break for supper and allow Chairman Tower to potentially round up more votes. This is a current-day version of a MRE.

Mr. Tower

"We'll get to it. You'll be all right on this. You don't need to worry."[30]

John Tower

Mr. Montgomery

"Oh, I know I'll be all right, Mr. Chairman (as I patted an envelope in my breast pocket of signed proxies from House conferees who had to depart due to the lateness of the hour)."[31] All present in the room knew I had a sufficient number of signed proxies to control the issue on the House side.

So how did it play out? Let me turn to Staff Director and Chief Counsel Fleming.

Mr. Fleming

"When John Tower and Sam Nunn would make a proposal, at times our own House conferees would huddle around Chairman Montgomery as we caucused privately and would say, 'Take it, Sonny, take it!' I think some of our folks were concerned we'd end up with nothing at all."[32]

Mack Fleming

"And then the passionate Representative Ron Dellums[33] would say to our House conferees, who were still huddling, something like the following:"

Mr. Dellums

"Just make the House proposal to Chairman Tower on our behalf, because if **you** propose it, Chairman Montgomery, we'll win."[34]

Ron Dellums

Mr. Fleming

"Chairman Tower understandably called for votes of the conferees on the [House-passed New GI Bill proposal] with hopes of defeating it because he earnestly felt it unnecessary for the reasons he articulated in opposition to the Armstrong amendment.[35]

"And then, still in the huddle, Mr. Dellums repeatedly would exhort our House conferees with something like the following:

"'Let's just have Chairman Montgomery handle this directly and we'll prevail.'"[36]

Mr. Montgomery

I was confident. For each vote, I would take the proxies given to me [by House conferees who were not present] and vote them. Each time the House would insist on its position.[37] Mr. Tower said to me more than once during the negotiations words something like these, followed with the one-time response from Mr. Dellums:

Mr. Tower

"Congressman, I am prepared to go back to my colleagues in the Senate telling them the House and Senate have no deal on the DoD Authorization Act because the House insists on a New GI Bill. Chairman Montgomery is holding up the entire bill because of his insistence on this one provision."[38]

Mr. Dellums

[Pointing his index finger toward Chairman Tower].

"Help the brother out here, Senator, help the brother out!"[39]

> "HELP THE BROTHER OUT, SENATOR, HELP THE BROTHER OUT."
> —*Representative Ron Dellums, California*

Mr. Montgomery

After many votes, I suggested the following to Chairman Tower:

"Maybe I had made a mistake in the logo we designed for the GI Bill we [the House] supported. Rather than a logo consisting of a cap and gown, I should have placed the education provisions in a cylinder with a nose cone at the front and a fuse in the back so that it looked like a missile that would destroy a convoy of ammo trucks, and then it would pass."[40]

I also reminded everyone that education benefits for military personnel would enhance lives upon leaving service. Further, I noted that GI Bill benefits had been carefully analyzed and shown to be the very best incentive for recruiting and retaining quality personnel.[41]

The Senate conferees from the Armed Services Committee were not willing to agree with the position of the House —and vice versa.

Before we could get a positive move by Senator Tower, we had to accept his very strong view (by Senators Nunn, Glenn and others) that any service member who participated in the New GI Bill could do so only by agreeing to have $100 per month for 12 months deducted from his or her pay. No such requirement appeared in the legislation passed by the House.[42]

As you remember, the Glenn amendment that passed the Senate in Title VII of the FY 1985 DoD Authorization Act had a $250-per-month service-member contribution.

And I was thinking to myself, "That dog won't hunt!"[43] We couldn't accept a pay reduction, including $200 per month.

In any case, with the strong support of Senators Bill Cohen of Maine and Alan Cranston of California and my fellow conferees from both the Armed Services and Veterans' Affairs Committees of the House, we prevailed in conference. Senator Tower relented, and we all thought we had reached full agreement on the new, permanent GI Bill for the All-Volunteer Force.[44]

AN AGREEMENT THAT WAS NOT AN AGREEMENT

At about 2 a.m.[45] on September 25,[46] the staff from the House and Senate Armed Services and Veterans' Affairs Committees met with the legislative counsels of the House and Senate in the basement of the Cannon House Office Building to work out all technical aspects of the bill.[47] The basement of the Cannon building is where the House Office of Legislative Counsel is located.

U.S. Capitol

Legislative counsels are the attorneys who draft legislation. They work for the Office of Legislative Counsel in both bodies and not for the individual committees or individual members of Congress. They are invaluable.[48] They draft into legislation the language that conferees agree to.

LEGISLATIVE COUNSEL

Sonny and Bob Cover after the enactment of the New GI Bill provisions (H.R. 1400).

Karen Heath of the Democratic side of the House Armed Services Committee and Patrick Tucker of the Republican side of the Senate Armed Services Committee looked over Assistant Legislative Counsel Bob Cover's shoulder as he drafted into legislative language that Ms. Heath and Mr. Tucker told him the conference agreed to.[49]

Mr. Cover diligently completed the legislative drafting at about 3:30 a.m.[50]

However, to the surprise of the majority and minority staffs of both the House Veterans' Affairs and Armed Services Committees, and Senator Cranston, the ranking member of the Senate Veterans' Affairs Committee,[51] something changed. Now the staff was told their members had only agreed to accept the New GI Bill as a three-year "test" program.

That was news to me when my chief counsel and staff director, Mack Fleming, awakened me at home with this information. At that hour, with the conference agreement going to the floor for a vote that morning, there was little chance of calling the members back to resolve the issue.[52]

I asked Mr. Fleming to meet with the House Armed Services Committee staff that morning so we could be assured the three-year "test" position taken by the Senate Armed Services Committee staff was not what we had agreed to and that the House Armed Services Committee would continue to support us in making the GI Bill permanent.[53] We learned that House Armed Services Committee staff's recollection was the same as our staff's, but there was no time to have the Conference Committee re-visit the issue.

Plus, on a smaller issue, House staff thought that we had agreed to repeal VEAP, but the Senate conferees thought we hadn't.[54]

As I recall, Mack informed the Senate staff that "tonight you may have won the battle on this issue, but you will lose the war when Chairman Montgomery moves to correct it."[55] And it would take us until 1987 to make the New GI Bill

98TH CONGRESS
2d Session | HOUSE OF REPRESENTATIVES | REPORT
98-1080

DEPARTMENT OF DEFENSE AUTHORIZATION ACT, 1985

SEPTEMBER 26, 1984.—Ordered to be printed

Mr. PRICE, from the committee of conference, submitted the following

CONFERENCE REPORT

[To accompany H.R. 5167]

The committee of conference on the disagreeing votes of the two Houses on the amendments of the Senate to the bill (H.R. 5167) to authorize appropriations for fiscal year 1985 for the military functions of the Department of Defense, to prescribe military personnel levels for that fiscal year for the Department of Defense, and for other purposes, having met, after full and free conference, have agreed to recommend and do recommend to their respective Houses as follows:

That the House recede from its disagreement to the amendment of the Senate to the text of the bill and agree to the same with an amendment as follows:

In lieu of the matter proposed to be inserted by the Senate amendment insert the following:

SHORT TITLE; TABLE OF CONTENTS

SECTION 1. (a) This Act may be cited as the "Department of Defense Authorization Act, 1985".

(b) The table of contents for this Act is as follows:
Sec. 1. Short title; table of contents.

TITLE I—PROCUREMENT

Sec. 101. Authorization of appropriations, Army.
Sec. 102. Authorization of appropriations, Navy and Marine Corps.
Sec. 103. Authorization of appropriations, Air Force.
Sec. 104. Authorization of appropriations, Defense Agencies.
Sec. 105. Authorization of appropriations for certain NATO cooperative programs.
Sec. 106. Extension of authority provided Secretary of Defense in connection with the NATO Airborne Warning and Control System (AWACS) program.
Sec. 107. Limitation on waivers of cost-recovery requirements under Arms Export Control Act.
Sec. 108. Waiver of limitation on foreign military sales program.
Sec. 109. Transfer of certain military equipment or data to foreign countries.

38-729 O

The Conference Report

Mr. Price

Melvin Price

"The conference on this bill has been the most difficult one I have ever experienced. The conferees struggled with resolution of the two sides' positions with respect to the MX missile, as well as testing of the anti-satellite weapon and other important defense questions and, in addition, a large number of general provisions…. .

"The conference broke up in late July when no agreement could be reached on resolution of the MX missile issue and overall funding levels. The House conferees felt they could not accept the uncompromising position offered by the Senate. The conference was in recess for almost a month and a half

permanent public policy.

The House adopted, in Conference, the 354-page **Conference Manager's Report on H.R. 5167** on September 26, 1984,[56] and the Senate on September 27, 1984.[57]

In bringing the manager's report to the House floor, Armed Services Committee Chairman Price observed the following:[58]

FY 1985 DOD AUTHORIZATION ACT

> "THE CONFERENCE ON THIS BILL HAS BEEN THE MOST DIFFICULT ONE I HAVE EVER EXPERIENCED."
> —*Representative Melvin Price, Illinois*

before negotiations between the Speaker and the majority leader of the Senate produced an agreement on these issues. When this agreement was reached, the conference was reconvened, and this Conference Report is consistent with the agreement negotiated by the Speaker and the majority leader of the Senate with respect to MX and overall funding.

"For the MX, funds are authorized at a level of $2.5 billion for fiscal year 1985. However, only $1 billion of those funds may be spent for deployment of the missiles authorized in fiscal year 1984 and for certain long-lead requirements and spare parts for the fiscal year 1985 program. The remaining $1.5 billion is fenced until the Congress approves, through a joint resolution, expenditure of the funds for the procurement of 21 MX missiles in fiscal year 1985 in a vote to occur in March."

Mr. Montgomery

I, too, had not experienced a conference as difficult as this one.[59]

In the Senate, John Tower, Sam Nunn, and Alan Cranston spoke when the conference report came to the floor for a vote.

First, Senator Tower spoke regarding the entire DoD authorization bill, as Representative Price had done on the House side:[60]

Mr. Tower

"We started conference on this bill with the House on Friday, June 22, in the absence of a first concurrent resolution on the budget. In effect, we were working with different budget figures on how much should be spent for defense. The conferees worked diligently through several sessions to complete their work prior to the August recess.

"However, it became obvious that without a resolution of the budget figures for national defense and without some resolution of the issue of how to proceed with the MX missile system, it would be impossible for the conferees to complete work on this important defense bill.

"As a result of this impasse, leadership from the Senate and the House of Representatives undertook a series of negotiations which were finally completed on Thursday, September 20. Since that time, we have been able to complete Conference action on the defense bill."

Mr. Montgomery

Then Mr. Nunn spoke:[61]

Mr. Nunn

Sam Nunn

"Mr. President, one of the toughest issues facing the conference was the question of a new program of educational incentives for military service.

"The House contained a new GI entitlement program for everyone entering military service sponsored by Congressman Montgomery. The Senate bill contained a much more limited program of educational benefits, introduced by Senator Glenn, designed to appeal to high-quality, motivated recruits who would come into service for one enlistment in return for a college education.

> "... ONE OF THE TOUGHEST ISSUES FACING THE CONFERENCE WAS THE QUESTION OF A NEW PROGRAM OF EDUCATIONAL INCENTIVES FOR MILITARY SERVICE."
> —*Senator Sam Nunn, Georgia*

"The conferees agreed to a three-year test program in which all members entering active service for three years beginning July 1, 1985, will be eligible to receive post-service educational benefits in return for a reduction in pay of $100 per month for the first 12 months of active duty... .

"I stress my belief that the conferees intend this strictly as a test-program, although it is far too large a test for my own appetite.

> "... IT IS FAR TOO LARGE A TEST FOR MY APPETITE."
> —*Senator Sam Nunn, Georgia*

"Notwithstanding my opposition to this particular provision, I want to pay special tribute to the hard work and effective leadership in this area by Congressman Montgomery, Senator Cohen, and Senator Armstrong, who are committed to ensuring we obtain the high quality of recruits we need today. They have spearheaded the effort for a peacetime GI Bill. While we do disagree on the approach, I think we all agree on the final goal."

Mr. Montgomery

Then Senator Tower, again:[62]

Mr. Tower

"Mr. President, I am bound to say that I am very much in sympathy with what the Senator from Georgia said, and I share his concerns and would have preferred to see nothing of this type in the bill.

> "... I ... WOULD HAVE PREFERRED TO SEE NOTHING OF THIS TYPE IN THE BILL."
> —*Senator John Tower, Texas*

"I felt it was necessary to try to effect some sort of compromise with the House of Representatives in the interests of getting out a Conference Report, and it was under that kind of situation that I did agree to a somewhat more limited GI Bill than what was originally proposed in the House bill, but I must say I do share the concerns of the Senator from Georgia."

Mr. Montgomery

Finally, Senator Cranston: [63]

Mr. Cranston

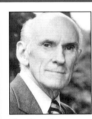

Alan Cranston

"... I am pleased that the Conference Report that is now pending before the Senate contains provisions—Title VII—that would establish a new All-Volunteer Force Educational Assistance Program.

"Regrettably, there is one element of the package with which I am particularly unhappy and that is the status of the current VEAP program. Under the provision in the Conference Report, that contributory-matching program would not be repealed—as had been proposed in the House-passed legislation and in the amendment I had joined in offering in the Senate—but rather, it would be, in essence, 'suspended' for new entrants during the period July 1, 1985, through June 30, 1988.

"Madam President, I am aware of the great concern expressed on the floor of the other body by my friend from Mississippi [Mr. Montgomery] about the insistence of the Senate Armed Services Committee that the VEAP program be suspended for three years rather than terminated, as the House bill provided.

> "MR. MONTGOMERY HAD GOOD REASON TO BELIEVE THAT THE SENATE HAD AGREED TO TERMINATE VEAP."
> —*Senator Alan Cranston, California*

"Mr. Montgomery had good reason to believe that the Senate had agreed to terminate VEAP, and I regret very much the way that this matter was handled and the outcome that Mr. Montgomery had to accept at the 11th hour in order to salvage the entire Conference Report... he was not treated properly on this issue."

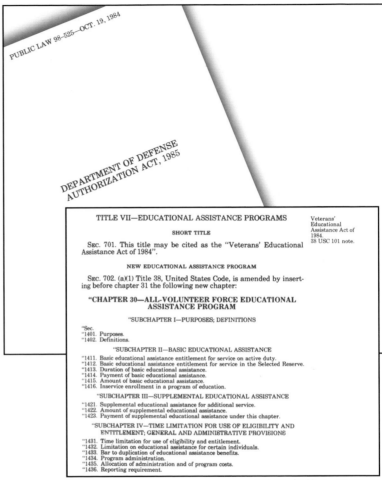

Title VII of Public Law 98-525

Mr. Montgomery

So the All-Volunteer Force GI Bill became law but was limited to a three-year test program and a $100-per-month pay reduction for 12 months. Nonetheless, I was confident the New GI Bill would eventually be made permanent within the so-called three-year test period. It would stand or fall on its own merits. [64]

President Reagan signed the DoD Authorization Act into law on October 19, 1984, enacted as Public Law 98-525. [65]

Let me reiterate that the three-year test New GI Bill we had to accept from the Senate in 1984 was quite different from H.R.1400, approved by the House Veterans' Affairs Committee in 1981:

- First, as introduced and approved by my five House colleagues and me in 1981, we structured the program as an entitlement and required **no** reduction of basic pay of $100 per month for 12 months for service members to become eligible for the New GI Bill.

- Second, under H.R.1400, a service member on active duty at the time of enactment of the bill would have had the option of switching to the New GI Bill if he or she was eligible under earlier programs, such as the Vietnam-era GI Bill or VEAP;

- Third, the New GI Bill proposed in H.R. 1400 would have been established as a permanent program, not as a **test** program;

- Fourth, H.R. 1400, as introduced, would have permitted—under certain circumstances—service members to transfer their education benefits to their dependent children or spouses; and

- Fifth, H.R. 1400 would have terminated the VEAP program for new participants rather than suspended it.

My colleagues and I wanted the "full loaf" in the form of sending the substance of H.R.1400 to the President's desk. But often we have to compromise in the short term in order to prevail in the long term.

As of July 1, 1985, the service branches began testing the New GI Bill. On June 24, 1985, I wrote a personal letter to each member of the House of Representatives telling them about it.[66]

After completing a three-year enlistment, the former service member would receive $10,800 in education benefits—$300 per month for 36 months—from the VA.[67] Remember, this is 1985, when the average annual tuition for a commuter student at a four-year public college was $1,318.[68]

AMENDMENTS BEFORE THE INK WAS DRY

Folks, let me add a postscript to this chapter regarding proposed **additional** legislative amendments to the three-year GI Bill test program that I'd like you to know about.

It's not something we'll spend much time on, because Congress did not enact into law the provisions of either H.R. 752, the proposed Veterans' Educational Assistance Eligibility Amendments of 1984; or section 522 of S. 1160, the proposed National Defense Authorization Act for Fiscal Year 1986.[69]

Both bills proposed amendments to the New GI Bill test program that Congress had just enacted into law a few months earlier on October 19, 1984.

Our H.R. 752 passed the House March 28, 1985.[70]

H.R. 752's main provision (among three in all) would have extended New GI Bill eligibility to individuals with prior military service who return to active duty.[71]

A four-provision bill passed by the Senate Veterans' Affairs Committee[72] was generally the same as H.R. 752. But it included a slightly different provision regarding New GI Bill eligibility for service members with prior service who returned to active duty. The Senate Veterans' Affairs Committee met in open session on April 18, 1985, and approved its bill.

The Senate Armed Services Committee[73] sought and received a limited-time sequential referral of H.R. 752, as amended by the Senate Committee on Veterans' Affairs.[74] The Senate Armed Services Committee did not support any of the provisions of H.R. 752 in its report on S. 1160 filed August 1.[75]

The Senate Armed Services Committee amendments to the New GI Bill test program, as included in section 522 of S. 1160, contained provisions that would:

- Require a service member to have to opt-in to the New GI Bill test program instead of having to opt-out;

- Give a service member up to two years after signing up for the New GI Bill test program to withdraw his $1,200 to establish eligibility for the program, so as to gain $10,800 in educational benefits (for those who changed their minds about participating); and

- Make certain changes to New GI Bill eligibility for service members already on active duty who reenlist.[76]

The full House and the Senate Committee on Veterans' Affairs Committee did not support any of the Senate Armed Services Committee-passed provisions.[77]

So Congress enacted the provision of **neither** of those two bills into law.[78]

CELEBRATING A TEAM EFFORT

Though the House preferred a permanent New GI Bill rather than the three-year test program, when an informal team of legislators and persons/organizations external to the legislative branch work on legislation for about four years,[79] it's important to pause and celebrate the team's efforts.

One of the more selfless acts I saw continually during some 40 years of public service was how organizations such as the Disabled American Veterans (DAV), Paralyzed Veterans of America (PVA), and Blinded Veterans Association (BVA) earnestly supported legislative proposals benefiting non-disabled Americans.

I found such support rather extraordinary because disabled veterans had their own version of the GI Bill through VA's rehabilitation program.

In any case, working alone, I suspect none of us could have made even a New GI Bill test program happen because of the increased cost of the entitlement benefit. Elected Representatives and Senators, veterans' service organizations, aspects of the higher education community, military personnel groups, selected executive branch officials, and reportorial interest of the *Army Times* all contributed in unique ways.

Here are just a few photos from our end-of-session gathering.[80]

With Rep. Marcy Kaptur (D-OH)…

Sonny with House Armed Services Committee staff members Karen Heath (center), and Kim Wincup as they celebrate H.R. 1400.

With HVAC staff member Mack Fleming…

With NCOA Government Relations Director Dick Johnson…

With Rep. Bob Edgar (D-PA)…

Lt. General Emmett "Mickey" Walker…

With Rep. Bob Stump (R-AZ)…

Sonny and House Committee on Veterans' Affairs staff: from left, Jill Cochran stands next to LTC Joe Selman; then Mack Fleming and Frank Stover.

With House committee staffer Candace Sniffen...

With Julie Susman of the Senate Committee on Veterans' Affairs...

Sonny with Rep. Ron Dellums (D-CA).

With House committee staffer Beth Kilker...

General Max Thurman signs the H.R. 1400 replica.

Back row, from left, Betty Ann Colley, Sonny and Rep. John Paul Hammerschmidt (R-AK); in front, Chad Colley of the DAV.

From left, Bob Moran of the PVA; (unidentified) and Frank DeGeorge of the PVA.

Sonny's Lessons Learned

Folks, go for the full loaf in your ideas. But if you don't get it, don't go away mad. Take half a loaf—as we did in the three-year New GI Bill test program. Come back the next time, and get the other half. We often have to compromise in the short term in order to prevail in the long term.

WHAT'S NEXT

In the next chapter we'll discuss the departments of Veterans Affairs and Defense implementing the test program.[81]

Worth Repeating

"Just make the House proposal to Chairman Tower on our behalf, because if you propose it, Chairman Montgomery, we'll win."

—*Representative Ron Dellums, Armed Services Committee*

"I am prepared to go back to my colleagues in the Senate telling them… Chairman Montgomery is holding up this entire bill because of his insistence on this one provision."

—*Chairman John Tower, Senate Armed Services Committee*

"I regret very much the way that this matter was handled and the outcome that Mr. Montgomery had to accept at the 11th hour in order to salvage the entire Conference Report… he was not treated properly on this issue."

—*Ranking Member Alan Cranston, Senate Veterans' Affairs Committee*

11

SONNY'S
CAST OF
CHARACTERS

Robert C. DeCamara, Reporter

Adell Crowe, Reporter, USA Today

Richard Halloran, Reporter, New York Times

Lieutenant General Robert Elton, U.S. Army

George C. Wilson, Reporter, Washington Post

P.J. Budahn, Reporter, Army Times

Otto Kreisher, Reporter, Copley News Service

Tim Carrington, Reporter, Wall Street Journal

*Honorable Bob Stump (R-AZ),
Committee on Armed Services, 2001*

**Also featured in this chapter:
Paul Smith, Reporter, Army Times**

1985-1986—Road to Enactment: Implementing the Three-Year New GI Bill Program

SONNY'S SUMMARY

Just six months into the three-year test of the New GI Bill, limited to service members entering military service between July 1, 1985, and June 30, 1988, 70 percent of Army enlistees signed up for this new education benefit. Almost four times as many enlistees signed up for the New GI Bill in its first year than for VEAP in its first year. We also won two hard-fought battles we didn't expect to fight, especially with the test program going so well: (1) an OMB-proposed economic measure to repeal the statutory test program and return to the inferior VEAP program, and (2) a proposal from within my own party to reinstate the draft and discontinue our All-Volunteer Force.

Mr. Montgomery

President Reagan signed the three-year New GI Bill program into law (Public Law 98-525) on October 19, 1984, and it took effect July 1, 1985. On June 24, 1985, I sent a letter to each of the 435 members of the House of Representatives describing the program and its many advantages for the nation.[1]

During the ramp-up period in early 1985 when the service branches began developing information and brochures to publicize and explain the New GI Bill, we learned of a small issue. Some of the information packets the service branches produced referred to "veterans' education benefits" rather than the "New GI Bill."[2] Some argued the differences in the words produced a distinction without a difference. But we saw a big difference.[3]

My colleagues and I felt the words "GI Bill" promoted a well-known, powerful image and represented a program revered by many Americans due to its unqualified earlier successes.[4]

So, we simply worked informally—over many months—with officials of the Department of Defense and each service branch.[5] Each ultimately adopted the words "New GI Bill."

Folks, let me make two observations about the way we resolved this matter.

The **first** is that if we take care of the little things, the big things tend to take care of themselves.

I believe resolving the small semantic issue about what to call the program made a difference in how youth, parents, guidance counselors, and media received the New GI Bill. The GI Bill already had name recognition in America's heritage.

Ask an adult in America to name one government program that has worked and I suspect many will mention the World War II GI Bill.

The **second** observation is that most problems are more easily resolved with honey rather than vinegar. I'd say the vinegar approach is represented in a nutshell by the wry Washington phrase some of you may have heard: "Grab them by their budgets; their hearts and minds will follow!"

> " ... HONEY RATHER THAN VINEGAR."
> —*G.V. "Sonny" Montgomery*

In my experience, this saying generally refers to Legislative Branch oversight of the Executive Branch and the inherent power of Congress in deciding the dollar amounts to be appropriated to federal departments and agencies. Only Congress can appropriate money.

There was no reason to beat up the service branches by formally directing them, for example, through Appropriations Committee "report language"[6] accompanying an annual DoD spending bill to use the words "New GI Bill" rather than "veterans' education benefits" in recruiting literature. Instead, we resolved this small matter informally through direct, non-threatening discussion.

Another saying I think works to describe an approach to problem solving is "use a scalpel, not a meat ax." I've found this approach helpful. Isolate the problem, then fix it!

The three-year New GI Bill program went forward as planned on July 1, 1985, but it was difficult to get the media to focus on it. Notes reporter Robert C. DeCamara:[7]

Mr. DeCamara

Robert DeCamara

"Young people can obtain all the money they require for college.

"Uncle Sam will give it to them—tens of thousand of dollars per individual. It isn't a loan, it doesn't have to be repaid, and it isn't based on need.

ROBERT C. DECAMARA

Military college remedy

The great anguish and writhings among a knot of educators and student activists earlier this year over President Reagan's attempt to cut higher education subsidies have obscured one small fact:

Young people can readily obtain all the money they require for college.

Uncle Sam will give it to them—tens of thousands of dollars per individual. It isn't a loan, it doesn't have to be repaid, and it isn't based on need.

Last fall without fanfare, Con-

"Last fall without fanfare, Congress established a generous student-aid program along those lines, effective the beginning of this month.

"If you're unfamiliar with it, that's understandable. The media have ignored it. In all the debate over federal grants and loans for students in post secondary schools, it's never mentioned. It's the mystery education subsidy, a darker secret (what is not?) than a CIA covert operation.

"It's called *The New GI Bill and the Army College Fund*.[8]

"All the military branches got the improved version of the GI Bill on July 1, but only the Army has a college fund, too, which makes its aid package easily the most lucrative. The sums involved are substantial—$10,800 from the GI Bill and $14,400 from the Army College Fund—for a combined pay-out of $25,200 for a four-year enlistment.

"That kind of money will buy a bachelor's degree at many institutions, according to *The Chronicle of Higher Education*. The authoritative trade journal puts the average annual cost of tuition, room, and board at a bargain at $3,381 at public universities, a steeper $7,635 at private schools.

"… No youngster willing to serve his country for two to four years need go without a college education for lack of money. That's a quiet achievement of which Americans can be proud."

Mr. Montgomery

Here's how Adell Crowe of *USA Today* reported service member interest during the New GI Bill initial implementation:

Ms. Crowe

"Just six months into the New GI Bill, the program was doing better than we ever thought it would. Seventy percent of Army enlistees, 55 percent of Air Force enlistees, 38 percent

of Marine Corps enlistees, and 35 percent of Navy recruits have signed up for the program."[9]

Mr. Montgomery

The New GI Bill proved financially more attractive than the post-Vietnam era Veterans' Educational Assistance Program, known as VEAP, that Congress initiated in 1977. We designed the New GI Bill that way. We **intended** it to be more financially attractive.

Under VEAP, the service member could contribute up to $2,700 and the VA would match it at $5,400, for a total of $8,100—a ratio of three-to-one.

Under the New GI Bill, the service member would put in $1,200 (the House-passed bill did not contain this provision) and would receive $10,800,[10] a ratio of nine-to-one.

By percentage, almost four times as many enlistees signed up for the New GI Bill in its first year than did so for VEAP in its first year.[11] For the Air Force and Marine Corps, the sign-up rate was even greater. Plus, VEAP was not easy to administer, given the process of service members putting money into the account and then taking it out, thus changing the government's contributory match.

As I see it, those of us in Congress did not do a good job designing VEAP. Noted former Secretary of the Army John Marsh, "VEAP was like the Articles of Confederation. It wasn't the answer."[12]

> "VEAP WAS LIKE THE ARTICLES OF CONFEDERATION. IT WASN'T THE ANSWER."
> —*Sec. of the Army John Marsh*

We did our best to make the New GI Bill both easy to use and easy to understand.

1986

During January 13-15, 1986, I headed a delegation of the House Veterans' Affairs Committee to visit basic training sites for each service branch.[13] With the three-year New GI Bill program now under way, the delegation wanted to learn what enlistees had to say about it.

We visited the Basic Training Center, Lackland Air Force Base, San Antonio, TX; Naval Training Center, San Diego, CA; Marine Corps Recruit Depot, San Diego,

CA; and Army Air Defense Artillery Center, Ft. Bliss, TX.

We attended the orientation each service branch gave to new enlistees on the New GI Bill program. Based on this orientation, recruits would then decide whether to have $100 per month deducted from their pay for 12 months in order to receive $10,800 in New GI Bill benefits.

I found talking directly with new soldiers, sailors, airmen, and Marines gratifying and informative. We designed the New GI Bill specifically for them. It was important to get away from Washington and learn from the service members themselves how we were doing.

By this time, some six years after our informal team in 1980 first got a gleam in our eye about a permanent GI Bill to encourage quality men and women to enlist—instead of drafting them—journalists started taking an interest in our vision.

Noted writer Richard Halloran of the *New York Times*:

Pentagon

G.I. Bill, Once a Reward, Is Now a Lure to Sign Up

By RICHARD HALLORAN
Special to The New York Times

WASHINGTON, Dec. 4 — At the end of World War II, Congress voted the first G.I. Bill of educational benefits to help transition back to civilian life for those who had served. Later the bill was extended to those who served in Korea and Vietnam.

Since the end of the draft and the advent of all-volunteer services in 1973, however, the purpose of the G.I. Bill has fundamentally changed. It has become become less a reward and more an incentive to attract young recruits to all the services.

Today, halfway through a three-year test of a new version of the G.I. Bill, the Army has found in a survey that the prospect of money for college is now the leading reason young men and women enlist, replacing a negative motivation: inability to get a civilian job. The next reason given is to learn a skill.

Big Rise in Participation

fits. For this fiscal year, the outlay will be only $400,000. By 1993, according to Army projections, it will have jumped to $400 million a year.

Less Than Civilian Grants

As against Government aid to education for civilians, however, that is a relatively small sum. The Department of Education's budget last year for Pell Grants cost the taxpayers $3.9 billion.

Another cost of the G.I. Bill over the long run is that it does not help, and many hinder, efforts to retain experienced soldiers. The prospect of a large sum of money to help pay for college gives bright young people an incentive to leave.

But Army officers argue that their service, unlike the Navy and Air Force, which need many technicians, wants large numbers of ''grunts,'' or combat soldiers, for a relatively short period. Only a small portion need be retained as sergeants. In addition, the Army offers bonuses for young men

Mr. Halloran

"Today [December 5, 1986], halfway through a three-year test of a new version of the GI Bill, the Army has found in a survey that the prospect of money for college is now the leading reason young men and women enlist, replacing a negative motivation: inability to get a civilian job. The next reason given is to learn a skill."[14]

Richard Halloran

Mr. Montgomery

One factor in our vision for a strong educational incentive for three or four years of service was the objective fact that the supply of potential recruits was dwindling, but the need or demand for such enlistees was undiminished.

As I've noted, many of my Veterans' Affairs Committee colleagues and I also served on the Armed Services Committee.

So we knew the pool of young men and women from which our service branches would have to recruit would decline by 20 percent between 1982 and 1987.[15]

By 1991, there would be just over 12 million young adults in the relevant age group, down from 17.5 million in 1980.[16] This meant the service branches would have to draw a higher percentage of the available pool. According to economist Sharon Cohany writing in the Bureau of Labor Statistics *Monthly Labor Review* in October 1986, in an article titled "What Happened to the High School Class of 1985," "the proportion of high school seniors going on to college... reached a record 58 percent in 1985."

To cope with the decline in eligible recruits, the Army planned to contact more prospects between the ages of 20 and 26. One group to focus on was college drop-outs. Noted Lieutenant General Bob Elton, deputy chief of staff of the Army:

Lt. Gen. Elton

"Forty percent of Americans drop out of college the first year; maybe we ought to be there for them."[17]

Bob Elton

> **"FORTY PERCENT OF AMERICANS DROP OUT OF COLLEGE THE FIRST YEAR; MAYBE WE OUGHT TO BE THERE FOR THEM."**
> —*Lt. General Bob Elton*

Mr. Montgomery

As you learned earlier, by law the New GI Bill test program ran from July 1, 1985, to July 1, 1988, to see if it would help with recruiting. Two separate problems emerged almost immediately.

PROBLEM: ABANDON THE TEST PROGRAM

In early 1986 the **first** problem emerged.

The ink was barely dry on the New GI Bill program when the Defense Department officially notified Congress that, as an economic measure, it would propose legislation to abandon the test program and return to VEAP.[18]

I had both an analysis and public testimony from the General Accounting Office concluding "the New GI Bill has strengthened Army recruiting" and "recruits were signing up for the New GI Bill at a far greater rate than they did for VEAP."[19]

GENERAL COUNSEL OF THE DEPARTMENT OF DEFENSE

WASHINGTON, D.C. 20301

March 28, 1986

Honorable Thomas P. O'Neill
Speaker of the House of Representatives
Washington, D.C. 20515

Dear Mr. Speaker:

Enclosed is a draft of legislation "To repeal the Veterans'
Educational Assistance Act of 1984 and for other purposes." The
Office of Management and Budget advises that there is no objection to the presentation of this proposal for the consideration
of the Congress. Enactment of this draft bill would be in
accord with the program of the President.

Purpose of the Legislation

I also obtained a pile of Pentagon documents that buttressed my argument. George C. Wilson quoted some of these documents in the March 21, 1986, *Washington Post*.[20]

Here is what each service branch said in internal documents, as reported by Mr. Wilson:[21]

Mr. Wilson

George C. Wilson

Army: "Switching back to VEAP after completing the costly conversion to and implementation of the New GI Bill will… cause damage to the recruiting program in general and to the Army's educational incentive programs in particular."

Navy: "Secretary John F. Lehman, Jr., in recent testimony before the House Armed Services Committee, said of the New GI Bill, 'it is a great program, and you are to be congratulated on it.'"

Air Force: "An internal memo said suspension of the New GI Bill would have 'serious impact' on recruiting quality people and 'would send a clear signal to the youth population that [the military] services do not care about their educational development.[22] Request that the New GI Bill be permitted to continue though the life of its originally legislated three-year period.'"

March 21, 1986

Lawmaker Goes to War To Preserve GI Benefits

Captured Papers Gainsay Budget-Cutters

By George C. Wilson

Mr. Montgomery

By June 1986 we had won the skirmish. Here's what two *Army Times* reporters wrote—Paul Smith on April 7, and P. J. Budahn on June 9:

Mr. Smith

OMB to Review Plan To Kill New GI Bill

By PAUL SMITH — April 7, 1986
Times Staff Writer

WASHINGTON — The Reagan administration may be backing away from its proposal to kill the New GI Bill on Capitol Hill...

Auditors found evidence that the New GI Bill has strengthened Army recruiting. They reported that top military recruiting officials believe returning to VEAP "could have a negative effect on the serv..."

"The Reagan Administration may be backing away from its proposal to kill the New GI Bill, Capitol Hill sources say.

"Although the Administration announced plans earlier in the year to cancel the three-year test program, no request for legislation to do so has been sent to Congress, a staff member said.

"James Miller, director of the White House's Office of Management and Budget, whose office first proposed the cancellation, had promised to review the proposal."[23]

Mr. Budahn

P.J. Budahn

"The Reagan Administration has abandoned for this year its fight to kill the New GI Bill."[24]

Army Times

An Independent Newspaper Serving Army People

NO. 44   JUNE 9, 1986 $1.75

OMB Defers Effort To Kill New GI Bill

By P.J. BUDAHN
Times Staff Writer

WASHINGTON — The Reagan administration has abandoned for this year its fight to kill the New GI Bill.

Mr. Montgomery

Ladies and gentlemen, my colleagues and I won the March to June 1986[25] scrap to keep the New GI Bill moving forward.

I'd like to tell you why I believe the service branches and I were correct on this issue. Here's part of what I said in a letter to Barry Goldwater of Arizona, then-chairman of the Senate Armed Services Committee:[26]

"The National Guard and Reserves are already offsetting the cost of the [New GI Bill] program through increased retention. Re-enlistments for our Reserve components have increased 20 percent over the last year through the GI Bill. That amounts to savings of $50,000 per individual in reduced training costs in the Air Guard.

"Also, in the Reserves, the sign-up is now for six years instead of three years, which will produce great savings in the training cycle.

"… Recruits are signing up in great numbers for the educational benefits offered by the GI Bill. As a result, I think we can reduce the large bonuses now being paid to recruit young men and women into the service… ."

PROBLEM: REVIVE THE DRAFT

The **second** problem emerged in November of 1986 when we had to debate with some of my fellow Democrats who wanted to revive the draft. In fact, I, too, had sponsored a bill for several years that would have reinstated the draft.

But I dropped it because the country had no appetite for it. I believe military service of two or three years is an obligation of citizenship. But Congress would not support the bill to reinstate the draft unless the Soviets were landing on the eastern shore of Maryland![27]

Nevertheless, back in February 1985, Senator Fritz Hollings (D-NC)—an advocate going back to 1979 for a New GI Bill—and Senator Steve Simms (R-ID), introduced a bill to revive the draft.[28] Further, in October 1984, our Army General Bernard Rogers, commander of the North American Treaty Organization forces in Europe, also called for a universal draft.[29]

Let's hear some of the highlights from reports by Otto Kreisher, Copley News Service,[30] and Tim Carrington of the *Wall Street Journal*.[31]

Mr. Kreisher

"As the bitter memory of Vietnam fades, some Democratic members of Congress and even a few military leaders[32] are beginning to talk about a subject long considered politically unmentionable—restoration of the draft."

Otto Kreisher

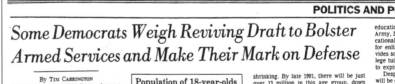

Military Draft Is Not Unmentionable Any More
Democrats in Congress Weigh Alternatives

BY OTTO KREISHER   Dec. 17, 1986
Copley News Service

WASHINGTON — As the bitter memory of Vietnam fades, some Democratic

among senior military leaders in expressing that view.

Defense Secretary Caspar Weinberger, Army Chief of Staff Gen. John Wickham and Adm. Carlisle Trost, the

manpower subcommittee in the new Democrat-controlled Senate.

Glenn's program would encourage high school graduates to volunteer for either military or civilian public service

"… faced with population projections showing a sharp decline in military age males over the next decade and with prospects that continuing budget deficits will force constraints on military pay and other compensation, [some Democratic] officials are searching for an alternative to the current All-Volunteer Force (AVF)."

Mr. Carrington

Tim Carrington

"The once unthinkable notion of reviving the draft is gaining ground, despite bitter memories of military conscription and [Reagan] administration support for the current All-Volunteer Force.

"Some Democrats [Senators Sam Nunn and Gary Hart] are looking to put their imprint on the national security policy. But that is only one reason why some form of national conscription is again being talked about. A combination of demographics and economics—fewer young people and skimpier federal budgets to support current bonus and recruitment programs—may create a shortage of soldiers by the 1990s. And some critics of the all-volunteer armed forces say a draft would be more equitable."

70 THE WALL STREET JOURNAL MONDAY, NOVEMBER 17, 1986

POLITICS AND P[...]

Some Democrats Weigh Reviving Draft to Bolster Armed Services and Make Their Mark on Defense

By TIM CARRINGTON
Staff Reporter of THE WALL STREET JOURNAL

WASHINGTON — The once-unthinkable notion of reviving the draft is gaining ground, despite bitter memories of military conscription and strong administration support for the current all-volunteer

Population of 18-year-olds
(In millions)

4.2

4.0

shrinking. By late 1991, there will be just over 13 million in this age group, down from 17.5 million in 1980. That means the services will have to draw a higher percentage from the available pool.

Meanwhile, budget pressures are eroding many of the bonuses and financial in-

Mr. Montgomery

Indeed, in the Carrington article Senator Nunn said, "It was a mistake to abolish the draft."[33]

But Congress did not reinstate the draft, even though military service is the most fundamental and longstanding form of service to the nation. Years later,

STEVEN WALDMAN

THE BILL

How the Adventures of Clinton's National Service Bill Reveal What Is Corrupt, Comic, Cynical — and Noble — About Washington

however, Congress created a voluntary program of civilian—not military—national service called AmeriCorps, which President Clinton signed into law in 1993.[34]

Steven Waldman wrote a book about how AmeriCorps became law. He called it *The Bill: How the Adventures of Clinton's National Service Bill Reveal What Is Corrupt, Comic, Cynical—And Noble—About Washington.*[35]

Folks, Mr. Waldman's book reveals how one of my best friends, Representative Bob Stump (R-AZ), and I joined forces to ensure that the post-service educational benefit of AmeriCorps volunteers did not exceed the educational benefit paid to the men and women serving in our all-volunteer military. We both believed our service members incur greater personal risks.

That said, persons who serve America through AmeriCorps and similar programs earn their post-service education benefit, too. I respect that. Conversely, we provide billions in financial aid for other deserving individuals who nevertheless do not serve their nation.

Why serve when financial aid abounds for those who do not serve?[36]

As I see it, military service goes back to colonial America.[37] The National Guard, for example, conducted its first training drill on the village green in Salem, MA, in 1636.[38]

In any case, I considered it a personal honor that Rep. Stump succeeded me as chairman of the Veterans' Affairs Committee for six years when the Republican Party won a majority in the November 1994 Congressional elections.

Bob then went on to chair the Armed Services Committee prior to his retirement in 2002. Bob passed away in June 2003.

Like so many young Americans during World War II, Bob Stump was unabashedly less than fully open about his age when he enlisted in our military.

Bob served near Iwo Jima as a Navy corpsman/combat medic at age 16. In Iwo Jima, our Marines suffered 26,000 casualties,[39] including 6,800 who died fighting the Japanese Army in taking the island. As Americans, if we ever wondered about the price our fellow citizens have paid for our every day freedoms, Iwo Jima provides one of the answers.

However flattering, I don't think Bob would say he was part of the "greatest generation," a term first coined by Tom Brokaw.

I think he'd say that as a teen he was proud to do his part to serve America. And I think he'd also say we should not assume the world is a safe place.

On September 11, 2001, when we learned that extremists were commandeering U.S. commercial airliners to harm us, one member of Congress refused to evacuate his office in the Capitol complex when the Capitol Police came to get him. That was Bob Stump of the House Armed Services Committee.

Noted Chairman Stump at the time:

Mr. Stump

Bob Stump

"Hell's fire, I'm staying here. This is my duty station. Whoever is responsible for these bombings can't make me leave."[40]

Mr. Montgomery

And he didn't.[41]

In closing this chapter, I'd note that we nevertheless achieved a major legislative victory in 1986 working principally with the National Association of State Approving Agencies and Alan Cranston and Bill Cohen in the U.S. Senate. In Public Law 99-576, enacted on October 28, Congress made on-job training and apprenticeship an eligible program for usage under the 1985-1988 New GI Bill program that, at this point, had become know unofficially as the three-year test program.[42]

Sonny was recognized by many organizations and received many special awards, including this unique lobster from the National Association of State Approving Agencies.

Sonny's Lessons Learned

Congressional oversight of executive branch implementation of law is both legitimate and important.

An oversight example from this chapter is the initial service branch brochures to publicize and explain the New GI Bill using the words "veteran's education benefits" rather than "New GI Bill." The words "GI Bill" historically have promoted a powerful image with parents, guidance counselors, and the American public. So we asked the service branches to use "New GI Bill" in their promotional materials. They agreed to do so. I believe it made a positive difference in how the test program was received.

WHAT'S NEXT

Let's travel the legislative road in the House and Senate Veterans' Affairs Committees that leads to enactment of the Montgomery GI Bill in 1987. At times it was a bumpy one.

Worth Repeating

"Today, halfway through a three-year test of a new version of the GI Bill, the Army has found in a survey that the prospect of money for college is now the leading reason young men and women enlist, replacing a negative motivation: inability to get a civilian job. The next reason given is to learn a skill."
—*Richard Halloran, New York Times*

"The once unthinkable notion of reviving the draft is gaining ground, despite bitter memories of military conscription and administration support for the current all-volunteer armed forces."
—*Tim Carrington, Wall Street Journal*

"Congress would not implement a draft unless the Soviets were landing on the eastern shore of Maryland!"
—*G.V. "Sonny" Montgomery*

"Hell's fire, I'm staying here! This is my duty station. Whoever is responsible for these bombings can't make me leave!"
—*Bob Stump, House Armed Services Committee, 9/11/01*

12

SONNY'S
CAST OF
CHARACTERS

*Jill Cochran, Staff Director,
Subcommittee on Education,
Training, and Employment,
Committee on Veterans' Affairs,
U.S. House of Representatives*

*Senator Alan Cranston (D-CA),
Chairman, Committee on Veterans' Affairs*

*Senator Frank Murkowski (R-AK),
Ranking Member, Committee on Veterans' Affairs*

*Senator Spark Matsunaga (D-HI),
Member, Committee on Veterans' Affairs*

*Lieutenant General
Earnest Cheatham,
U.S. Marine Corps*

Lieutenant General Bob Elton, U.S. Army

*Dennis Shaw,
Deputy Assistant
Secretary
of Defense
for Reserve Affairs*

Vice Admiral Dudley Carlson, U.S. Navy

*Allan Ostar, President,
American Assn. of
State Colleges and
Universities*

*Chris Yoder,
Republican Professional
Staff Member,
Committee on
Veterans' Affairs*

*Lieutenant General Thomas Hickey,
U.S. Air Force*

*Representative
Lane Evans (D-IL)*

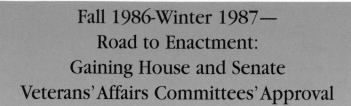

Fall 1986-Winter 1987—
Road to Enactment:
Gaining House and Senate
Veterans' Affairs Committees' Approval

SONNY'S SUMMARY

When we introduced H.R. 1400 in 1981, we had just five original cosponsors. When we introduced H.R. 1085 in 1987, we had 174 original cosponsors. From its beginnings on July 1, 1985, through early 1987, the New GI Bill test program showed recruiters could penetrate the college-oriented population of young Americans. Without it, they were generally restricted to employment-oriented young people. The Veterans' Affairs Committee leadership, especially that of Senators Alan Cranston and Frank Murkowski, introduced S. 12 to make the New GI Bill permanent. Their leadership largely neutralized OMB's initial opposition to S. 12 and helped engender support from the three-star personnel chiefs of each service branch testifying at the February 2, 1987, committee hearing. The committee approved S. 12 on February 26. We now had real Senate energy on this issue. The House Committees on Veterans' Affairs and Armed Services marked up H.R. 1085 unanimously on March 4 and March 11, respectively.

1986

Mr. Montgomery

As you recall, from March to about October 1986, our team prevailed over both a proposed return to VEAP—the less financially attractive Veterans' Educational Assistance Program—and a proposed return to a military draft.

Before we proceed to 1987, the seventh and final year my colleagues and I worked on creating a permanent New GI Bill,[1] I'd like to share with you some data on the three-year New GI Bill program initiated July 1, 1985, that shows how it fared as a recruiting tool. The November 14, 1986, briefing paper crafted from various sources by Ms. Jill Cochran, staff director, Subcommittee on Education, Training, and Employment, is instructive. I'll ask Ms. Cochran to paraphrase from the summary:[2]

Ms. Cochran

"Thank you, Mr. Chairman.

• "According to the Army, 35 percent of today's recruits cite the educational benefits as their principal reason for enlisting.

Staff Director Jill Cochran with Sonny at subcommittee hearing.

Upper mental category recruits, the high-quality individuals the services increasingly need, are attracted by education benefits, not bonuses.

• "The Army estimates that the loss of the New GI Bill would result in an annual reduction of 6,000 upper-half high school graduates. This would, in turn, increase attrition by 1,400 losses at a cost of $25+ million. The Army expects a 10-percent lower job performance from those who replace the high-quality personnel.

• "The New GI Bill has already improved the Reserve components' recruiting effort. High-quality recruits in the Army Reserve components increased 24 percent the first 12 months of the New GI Bill. High school graduate recruits increased 9 percent and six-year enlistments increased 28 percent.

• "The Army estimates the loss of the New GI Bill would result in a loss of 6,300 high school graduates, 6,100 upper-half TSC [test score category] recruits, and 9,500 six-year enlistments.

• "The New GI Bill allows recruiters to penetrate the 'college-oriented' population of young people. Without it, they are restricted to 'employment-oriented' young people.

• "There is currently in the Department of Education a 'GI Bill without a GI;' $3.82 billion in Pell grants are available with no requirement for service.[3]

• "As a readjustment mechanism for veterans returning to civilian life, an incentive to attract high-quality young people into military service, and a prudent investment in our nation's human resources, it would be difficult to design a better program than the New GI Bill. The size of this program in dollars in return for service to the nation pales in significance to the massive Pell educational grant program of close to $4 billion annually, which is provided with no expectation of service to the nation whatsoever. The Army and the nation can't afford to have the New GI Bill killed."

> "THEY ARE SELLING THE NEW GI BILL AS THE BEST AMERICAN INVENTION[S] SINCE PEANUT BUTTER AND LIPSTICK."
> —*Frank Mensel*

Mr. Montgomery

Generally, the Army signs up almost as many recruits as the Air Force, Marine Corps, and Coast Guard put together.[4] By the end of 1986, my colleagues and I felt the Army and National Guard units were clearly furnishing potential recruits something they wanted to buy—post-service educational opportunities.

Frank Mensel, vice president for Federal Relations, American Association of Community and Junior Colleges, observed to me in a November 12, 1986, letter:[5] "The presentations that the National Guard is now making at conventions and other meetings around the country are superbly supportive. They are selling the New GI Bill as the best American invention[s] since peanut butter and lipstick."

The historic 100th Congress meets in January of 1987.

1987—NINE SENATORS INTRODUCE S. 12

It's now January 1987, the opening of the historic 100th Congress. Every two years we have a new, numbered Congress. After the founding fathers created the Congress in Article I, Section 1, of the Constitution, adopted by the Constitutional Convention on September 17, 1787, the first Congress met in 1789 in Federal Hall in New York City.[6] Each Congress has two sessions—one for each of the two years of that numbered Congress.

The service branches had been using the New GI Bill as a recruiting tool since July 1, 1985, and data has become available.

Knowing that the three-year New GI Bill test program would expire in one year and likely revert to the ineffective VEAP program, Senate Veterans' Affairs Committee[7] Chairman Alan Cranston of California introduces legislation to convert the New GI Bill test program to what my colleagues and I viewed as a permanent, peacetime GI Bill.

Senator Cranston has been on the case for about seven years now.[8]

Following a month of informal discussions between committee staff and representatives of the service branches as to how best to shape the bill,[9] Chairman Cranston introduced S. 12 on January 6, 1987:[10]

Mr. Cranston

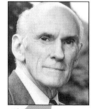

Alan Cranston

"Mr. President, I rise today to introduce the proposed 'New GI Bill Continuation Act.' The New GI Bill now allows recruiters, for the first time, to penetrate the college-oriented market of young people that we need to operate our sophisticated weaponry… to enhance our preparedness for the complexities of modern warfare.

"It is vital that we do everything necessary to make the All-Volunteer Force work and to avoid returning to conscription to meet our uniformed services personnel needs.

"The last thing our nation needs at this point—especially for its young people—is a return to the divisiveness that inevitably accompanies a military draft."[11]

Mr. Montgomery

Eight other Senators cosponsored the legislation, including the committee's ranking minority member, Senator Frank Murkowski of Alaska.

Mr. Murkowski

Frank Murkowski

"I am proud to be an original cosponsor of S. 12, which will make this important and necessary veterans' education program a permanent part of the benefits programs we rely upon to reward our veterans for their service and to assist them in their readjustment to civilian life… .

"Balancing the **obligation of the nation to individual citizens against the obligations of individual citizens to their nation** [emphasis added] is one of this body's most important functions.[12] This interlocking tapestry of duty and responsibility is perhaps nowhere more vivid than in the protection of our independence and liberty… .

"… [A] service member who knows that an honorable discharge will create an opportunity for education is more likely to provide enthusiastic and honorable service than one whose enlistment was motivated by the prospect of immediate gratification from a bonus or high rate of pay… .

"… [I]n addition, the service member is more likely to derive long-term advantage from an investment in education than from the pleasures and objects which can be purchased with ready cash. This advantage, like the advantage to the nation of skilled, knowledgeable citizens, will last throughout the individual's lifetime… .

"… [T]he New GI Bill is an important step in the necessary process of ensuring

> "… OBLIGATION OF THE NATION TO INDIVIDUAL CITIZENS… OBLIGATION OF INDIVIDUAL CITIZENS TO THEIR NATION."
> —*Senator Frank Murkowski, Alaska*

By Mr. CRANSTON (for himself, Mr. MURKOWSKI, Mr. MATSUNAGA, Mr. DeCONCINI, Mr. MITCHELL, Mr. ROCKEFELLER, Mr. GRAHAM, Mr. COHEN, and Mr. HOLLINGS):

S. 12. A bill to amend title 38, United States Code, to remove the expiration date for eligibility for the educational assistance programs for veterans of the All-Volunteer Force; and for other purposes; to the Committee on Veterans' Affairs.

NEW GI BILL CONTINUATION ACT

Mr. CRANSTON. Mr. President, as the chairman of the Committee on Veterans' Affairs, I am today introducing S. 12, the proposed "New GI Bill Continuation Act." Joining with me as original cosponsors of this measure are the former chairman and now ranking minority member of the committee, the Senator from Alaska [Mr. MURthat those who have served in our armed forces will be able to obtain the education necessary to participate in the decisions that shape American life; not just at the highest levels of national power but also on the shop floor, in small businesses, in school, church, labor and fraternal organizations, in the media, and on the street.

"It is critical for the nation—that understands the capabilities and limits of military power—that the graduates of America's higher education include those who have served in the armed forces."[13]

Mr. Montgomery

Also cosponsoring S. 12 was Republican Whip Alan Simpson. When Mr. Simpson was Speaker of the Wyoming legislature, he was known as the "fastest gavel in the West!"[14]

Alan Simpson

As we discussed in Chapter 4, a "whip" mobilizes the vote within his or her political party based on legislative priorities and policy positions and decides when bills are scheduled for a floor vote.

S. 12 proved unique because Alan Cranston was the Democratic Whip and Alan Simpson was the Republican Whip. Both sat on the Veterans' Affairs Committee. How about that?

An original S. 12 cosponsor was Senator Spark Matsunaga of Hawaii, a decorated Army combat infantryman who graduated from Harvard Law School on the World War II GI Bill. "Sparky" earlier led Hawaii's quest to become a state.[15] And he was an original cosponsor of the All-Volunteer Force Educational Assistance Act of 1980 (S. 3263) with Senator Cranston and others.

One of the best-liked members of the Senate, Mr. Matsunaga offered some humor at the February 4, 1987, Senate Veterans' Affairs Committee hearing on S. 12 by telling the witnesses how traveling from Washington, D.C., to Hawaii messed up his body clock…

Mr. Matsunaga

Spark Matsunaga

"Ladies and gentlemen, I can live with the six-hour time change, but the only problem is, I get sexy at meal time and hungry at bed time."[16]

> "… I CAN LIVE WITH THE SIX-HOUR TIME CHANGE, BUT… I GET SEXY AT MEAL TIME AND HUNGRY AT BED TIME."
> —*Senator Spark Matsunaga, Hawaii*

House Veterans' Affairs Committee, 1987.

174 MEMBERS INTRODUCE H.R. 1085

Mr. Montgomery

Back on the House side, on February 11, 1987, 174 members of the House (out of 435) joined me in introducing H.R. 1085, legislation comparable to S. 12.

This time we didn't wait for our familiar H.R. 1400 bill number to become available because of good energy in the Senate with its introduction of S. 12!

When we first introduced H.R. 1400 in 1981, we had only five original cosponsors,[17] a far cry from the 174 who joined us in 1987![18]

Were we pleased that the Senate had a bill very similar to ours? Heck, we were happier than lost kittens in a creamery![19]

> "… HAPPIER THAN LOST KITTENS IN A CREAMERY!"
> —*G.V. "Sonny" Montgomery*

100TH CONGRESS
1ST SESSION

H. R. 1085

To amend title 38, United States Code, to make permanent the new GI bill educational assistance programs established by chapter 30 of such title, and for other purposes.

IN THE HOUSE OF REPRESENTATIVES

FEBRUARY 11, 1987

Mr. MONTGOMERY (for himself, Mr. SOLOMON, Mr. DOWDY of Mississippi, Mr. SMITH of New Jersey, Mrs. PATTERSON, Mr. WYLIE, Mr. JONTZ, Mr. RIDGE, Mr. EVANS, Mr. DORNAN of California, Ms. KAPTUR, Mr. STENHOLM, Mr. KENNEDY, Mr. EDWARDS of California, Mr. HAMMERSCHMIDT, Mr. APPLEGATE, Mr. STUMP, Mr. MICA, Mr. McEWEN, Mr. PENNY, Mr. BURTON of Indiana, Mr. STAGGERS, Mr. BILIRAKIS, Mr. ROWLAND of Georgia, Mr. ROWLAND of Connecticut, Mr. BRYANT, Mr. SMITH of New Hampshire, Mr. FLORIO, Mr. DAVIS of Illinois, Mr. GRAY of Illinois, Mr. KANJORSKI, Mr. ROBINSON, Mr. HARRIS, Mr. JOHNSON of South Dakota, Mr. PRICE of Illinois, Mr. DICKINSON, Mr. BENNETT, Mr. SPENCE, Mr. STRATTON, Mr. BADHAM, Mr. NICHOLS, Mr. HOPKINS, Mr. DANIEL, Mr. DAVIS of Michigan, Mr. DELLUMS, Mr. HUNTER, Mrs. SCHROEDER, Mr. MARTIN of New York, Mrs. BYRON, Mr. KASICH, Mr. MAVROULES, Mr. BATEMAN, Mr. HUTTO, Mr. SWEENEY, Mr. SKELTON, Mr. BLAZ, Mr. LEATH of Texas, Mr. IRELAND, Mr. McCURDY, Mr. HANSEN, Mr. FOGLIETTA, Mr. WELDON, Mr. DYSON, Mr. KYL, Mr. HERTEL of Michigan, Mr. RAVENEL, Mrs. LLOYD, Mr. SISISKY, Mr. RAY, Mr. SPRATT, Mr. MCKEY, Mr. ORTIZ, Mr. DARDEN, Mr. BUSTAMANTE, Mrs. BOXER, Mr. BRUECKNER, Mr. BRENNAN, Mr. PICKETT, Mr. QUILLEN, Mr. JE... Mr. HEFNER, Mr. LANCASTER, Mr. RAHALL, Mr. PERKINS, Mr. HU... Mr. VALENTINE, Mr. HUBBARD, Mr. ROEMER, Mr. HALL of Tex... RODINO, Mr. BONER of Tennessee, Mr. LENT, Mr. LAGOMARSIN... LUJAN, Mrs. SMITH of Nebraska, Mr. COLEMAN of Texas, Mrs. CO... Mr. DE LA GARZA, Mr. STANGELAND, Mr. JACOBS, Mr. GAYDOS, M... ZALEZ, Mr. MOLLOHAN, Mr. DERRICK, Mr. LIPINSKI, Mr. PEPPE... NOWAK, Mr. ATKINS, Mr. MORRISON of Connecticut, Mr. MAC... BAKER, Mr. BOUCHER, Mr. OXLEY, Mr. MYERS of Indiana, Mr. MA... Mr. LOWERY of California, Mr. WOLF, Mr. YOUNG of Florida, Mr... ARDSON, Mr. KOSTMAYER, Mr. GRANDY, Mr. SENSENBRENNER, M... FRANK, Mr. DOWNEY of New York, Mrs. BOGGS, Mr. BEVILL, Mr. WORTLEY, Mr. MANTON, Mr. DAUB, Mr. HUGHES, Mr. TRAXLER, Mr. COELHO, Mrs. KENNELLY, Mr. McGRATH, Mr. FISH, Mr. ROSE, Mr. PARRIS, Mr.

PUBLIC HEARINGS ON S. 12

As I mentioned, on February 4, 1987, the Senate Veterans' Affairs Committee held its public hearing on S. 12.

The Committee took testimony from 22 witnesses,[20] including the Chief Benefits Director of the Veterans Administration,[21] Assistant Secretary of Defense for Force Management and Personnel,[22] and the three-star personnel chiefs from the four service branches. (The committee inadvertently neglected to invite the Coast Guard, as it was under the jurisdiction of the Transportation Department.)

The witnesses—including the four personnel chiefs led by the Army's Lieutenant General Bob Elton, a West Point graduate who had a master's degree in physics—all supported a permanent New GI Bill. General Elton was the first witness and told the committee:[23]

Lt. Gen. Elton

Lt. Gen. Bob Elton

"Mr. Chairman, we strongly support this valuable recruiting incentive. We have managed to save about a division's worth of manpower each year. We save between $200 million and $250 million per year in the way of recruiting costs and additional training because these recruits [who respond to an educational incentive] just stay around longer."

Vice Admiral Carlson testified:[24]

Vice Admiral Carlson

Vice Admiral Dudley Carlson

"We in the Navy totally endorse the New GI Bill.... We have seen our percentage of those signing up for the GI Bill in our new recruits increase dramatically over time; and in December [1986], we were having new recruits signing up for the GI Bill at 58 percent of those coming on board... ."

Air Force Lieutenant General Hickey told the Committee:[25]

Lt. Gen. Hickey

Lt. Gen. Thomas Hickey

"We do, in fact, see the New GI Bill as a very potent recruiting tool... . Not only have we had a significant increase in participation of our new recruits, we have found that the vast majority of those who do participate are in the top two mental categories. So, we are getting the kinds of quality that we are interested in."

Lieutenant General Earnest Cheatham, U.S. Marine Corps, observed:[26]

Lt. Gen. Cheatham

Lt. Gen. Earnest Cheatham

"In excess of 65 percent of the people that come in now—and are talking to us—are talking about the GI Bill. It brings people to us—good quality people. We support it, and we love it. It is a No. 1 priority for our young people."

In his testimony, Principal Deputy Assistant Secretary of Defense for Reserve Affairs Dennis Shaw said:[27]

Mr. Shaw

Dennis Shaw

"... During FY 1986, 34,500 more Selected Reserve recruits were high school graduates than in FY 1984, the last full year preceding the effective date of the New GI Bill."

Mr. Montgomery

OMB supported making the program permanent,[28] as stated in the February 4, 1987, testimony of the Assistant Secretary of Defense (Force Management and Personnel) and Chief Benefits Director of the Veterans Administration, but it proposed a major revision.

The OMB-directed testimony proposed that the Defense Department, rather than the Veterans Administration, fund the New GI Bill program.[29] For some 40 years of previous GI Bill educational assistance programs, Congress funded such programs through the VA's budget.

Neither the House nor Senate Veterans' Affairs Committees supported this approach because the New GI Bill continued to serve as a tool for ex-GIs to transition from military to civilian life. Like all previous GI Bill programs, the Veterans Administration funds transition assistance programs for former service members—not the Department of Defense.[30]

EXECUTIVE OFFICE OF THE PRESIDENT
OFFICE OF MANAGEMENT AND BUDGET
WASHINGTON, D.C. 20503

JAN 21 1987

Honorable G.V. Montgomery
Chairman, Committee on
 Veterans' Affairs
U.S. House of Representatives
Washington, DC 20515

Dear Mr. Chairman:

　　Thank you for your letter and the Washington Reporter article on the All-volunteer educational assistance test program (New GI Bill).

What does it say on the top of the letter?

The Office of Management and Budget indeed is part of the Executive Office of the President—no matter who the President is. As we learned earlier, the OMB articulates the President's position, which is known as "administration policy."

A key witness for the higher education community was Allan Ostar, then-serving in his 21st year as president, American Association of State Colleges and Universities. Mr. Ostar enlisted in the Army in 1942 and served in Europe from 1944-46 with the 42nd Rainbow Infantry Division. His awards include the Combat Infantryman's Badge and two Bronze Star Medals for valor. After World War II, he was a beneficiary of the GI Bill at Pennsylvania State University and the University of Wisconsin, Madison.[31]

Here are some highlights of Mr. Ostar's testimony:[32]

Mr. Ostar

"... America's state colleges and universities grant more than 31 percent of bachelor's degrees each year in the United States... . The GI Bill is an important aid to the quality of American education in general in that it provides confident, motivated students... who bring a sense of responsibility to our nation's college classrooms... .The strength of our society is based on a strong

Allan Ostar

and balanced relationship between three major elements of American life: the national defense, a productive healthy economy, and an effective system of education. America cannot be strong if any one leg of the three-legged stool is weak. In effect, the GI Bill is a model program for this triad. It strengthens all three. This program uses a military/higher education partnership which strengthens both partners, and our economy and society as well."

> " ... THREE MAJOR ELEMENTS OF AMERICAN LIFE: THE NATIONAL DEFENSE, A PRODUCTIVE HEALTHY ECONOMY, AND AN EFFECTIVE SYSTEM OF EDUCATION.
> —*Allan Ostar*

REFLECTIONS ON LAWMAKING

Mr. Montgomery

Folks, let's pause and reflect a bit.

HOW A BILL BECOMES LAW

As introduced

As amended in committee

As amended on second reading

As enacted

As funded by joint budget committee

As implemented by the state agency

As reported by the media

As understood by the public

As amended on second reading

I never served in the U.S. Senate, but let me offer **three** thoughts on what I consider some everyday realities of policy making that emerged in the Senate.

"APPEAR AND RESPOND"

"THE 48-HOUR PEEK"

"GET SOME REALITY"

The **first** thought is that the chairman and ranking member of the Senate Veterans' Affairs Committee asked the general-officer personnel chiefs representing the service branches simply to appear before the committee to respond to questions.[33]

To their delight,[34] the generals were **not** required to submit to the committee an official written testimony that would have to be cleared with OMB first.[35]

This proved an unexpected opportunity because the general officers could state the view of their service branch rather than the executive branch/DoD view.

The **second** observation is that the Senate Veterans' Affairs Committee's official rules of procedure require witnesses to submit their written testimony to the committee 48 hours in advance of the public hearing.

Practically speaking, this procedure gives Senators and committee staff an opportunity to get a good preview of what witnesses will say.

Further, the written testimony submitted by subject-matter experts representing higher education, veterans, and military personnel groups often contains information/data to help make a persuasive case for the bill in the committee report. Plus, committee staff often used this information in drafting proposed hearing questions for the members they served.

And the **third** observation is to get away from Washington and talk to the folks on the business end of your proposed policy.

As we discussed in Chapter 11, as I also was the No. 2 ranking member on the House Armed Services Committee, I led a delegation of eight Congressmen and representatives from 30 military personnel and veterans' organizations to recruit training bases of the Army, Navy, Marine Corps, and Air Force.[36] The 30 organizations were very important members of the informal team we formed.

The purpose of the visits was to learn from the recruits themselves whether the New GI Bill "test" program served as an incentive for them to enlist. And if so, to what extent?

The Congressional delegation (known as a CODEL) filed a detailed trip report with the House Veterans' Affairs Committee, citing evidence to support its conclusion that the New GI Bill was bringing quality recruits into the military, rather than doing so through a military draft. The delegation's report quoted the Adjutant General of Kentucky, General Billy Wellman:

"You give a recruit a dollar today and it's gone. You give a recruit an education,

In February 1987, Sonny led a Congressional delegation (CODEL) on a series of visits to learn from the recruits themselves whether the New GI "test" program served as an incentive to enlist.

and the recruit will have it the rest of his or her life. The New GI Bill is a No. 1 priority because of what it offers long range, to the service member, his family, and the service."[37]

Further, the report concluded:

"The delegation believes that the New GI Bill is accomplishing those purposes for which it was created. Recruits entering the armed forces have available to them an excellent educational assistance benefit which will facilitate their readjustment to civilian life following military service. The military services have a powerful, cost-effective tool which is aiding in the recruitment and retention of high-quality young people. New GI Bill implementation, as observed by the delegation, is being carried out effectively by all services."[38]

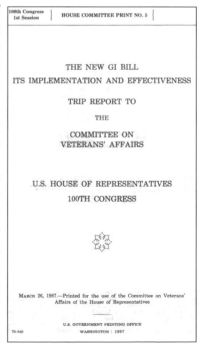

100th Congress
1st Session

HOUSE COMMITTEE PRINT NO. 5

THE NEW GI BILL
ITS IMPLEMENTATION AND EFFECTIVENESS

TRIP REPORT TO

THE

COMMITTEE ON
VETERANS' AFFAIRS

U.S. HOUSE OF REPRESENTATIVES
100TH CONGRESS

MARCH 26, 1987.—Printed for the use of the Committee on Veterans'
Affairs of the House of Representatives

U.S. GOVERNMENT PRINTING OFFICE
WASHINGTON : 1987

My colleagues and I advanced the notion that a permanent, peacetime GI Bill and the All-Volunteer Force concept were directly linked.[39]

We used the word "peacetime"[40] because the New GI Bill would exist for our veterans whether we were at war or not. The New GI Bill wouldn't "come and go," as wars came and went. It would be there permanently, including in peacetime.

SENATE COMMITTEE MARK-UP

The Senate Veterans' Affairs Committee also met in open session on February 26, 1987, and unanimously reported the Cranston/Murkowski bill with certain amendments.[41] Through the amendments, the committee added new "purpose clauses" to the New GI Bill.[42]

What would you think is meant by a "purpose clause" in a law—in this case for the New GI Bill?

Charles "Chris" Yoder served as a professional staff member on the Republican staff of the Committee on Veterans' Affairs.

A big part of Mr. Yoder's job was to advise the committee conceptually as to what legislation both should say and do.[43]

I'll ask Chris to talk with you about a declared purpose clause in a law.

REPORT

OF THE

COMMITTEE ON VETERANS' AFFAIRS

UNITED STATES SENATE

TO ACCOMPANY

S. 12

MARCH 17, 1987.—Ordered to be printed

U.S. GOVERNMENT PRINTING OFFICE
WASHINGTON : 1987

Mr. Yoder

"Thank you, Mr. Chairman.

"A purpose clause describes a law's objectives—what Congress wants a law to do. In effect, objectives in a law reflect the objectives of United States policy, as stated through an act of

Chris Yoder (far right) with Chairman Montgomery (center) and, left to right, staffers Deborah Lee, Darryl Kebrer, Jill Cochran and Karen Heath after the signing of the Montgomery GI Bill enrolled bill (H.R. 1085, as amended) in Statuary Hall.

Congress. These objectives should be clear and, to the greatest extent possible, they should be measurable—quantifiable—if you will.

"Senator Murkowski asked Veterans' Affairs Committee Republican Chief Counsel

Anthony Principi and me whether Congress should create additional purpose clauses for a New GI Bill. After reviewing the body of testimony from the February 4 hearing, we suggested that Mr. Murkowski do so in an amendment to S. 12 during committee mark-up—preferably on behalf of himself and Chairman Cranston.

"Congress had designed the various GI Bill education programs over the decades for a 'different era, a different economy, a different society, a different technology, and in fact, a different (non-conscripted) veteran.'[44] But the obligation of the nation to those who serve has remained the same.

"So Senator Murkowski proposed three additional purpose clauses during mark-up of S. 12 for the New GI Bill, the first two of which Congress had enacted as part of the Vietnam-era GI Bill education program:[45]

- Extending the benefits of a higher education to those who might not otherwise be able to obtain such benefits;

- Providing vocational readjustment and restoring lost educational opportunities; and

- Enhancing our nation's competitiveness through the development of a more highly educated and productive workforce.

"With respect to the first two new purpose clauses above, the House Veterans' Affairs and Armed Services Committees, too, would add such clauses at mark-up a few weeks later. And the full House would embrace the third one in May.

"With respect to the third new purpose clause, a banker and businessman by education, Mr. Murkowski held the view that 'the challenge to American economic world leadership has never been greater. Our competitive edge depends upon a skilled labor force. Critical, sophisticated, new-growth industries—computers, robotics, and biotechnology to name a few—demand workers skilled in technology and a populace conversant with the rudiments of science…. Our nearest world competitor, Japan, recognized the importance of education for its own future 25 years ago [1962], when its Economic Council declared, 'Economic competition among nations is a technical competition that has become an educational competition.'[46]

"Workforce development was an important issue. Our ability to compete internationally in the new, emerging world economy very much was a topic of Congressional debate in 1987.[47]

"Senator Murkowski viewed those who serve in our military as engaging leaders and as a competitive business asset due to their discipline, energy, and reliability. Add in their ability to gain civilian skills under a New GI Bill and indeed they would become a unique national resource for America.

"Appropriately, Congress ultimately added these three purpose clauses to the Montgomery GI Bill, as signed into law by President Reagan."[48]

HOUSE SUB-AND FULL COMMITTEE MARK-UP

Mr. Montgomery

The House Veterans' Affairs Subcommittee on Education, Training, and Employment held its public hearing on February 18, 1987,[49] one week after the trip to the recruit training sites.

On March 4, 1987, the subcommittee voted in open session unanimously to report a permanent New GI Bill to the full House Veterans' Affairs Committee.

I must say, the full committee's work on the bill brought an un-expected surprise and high honor for me, as its chairman.

Before reporting H.R. 1085 on March 4, the full Committee unanimously approved Congressman Lane Evans' amendment to name the GI Bill the Montgomery GI Bill Act of 1984. In offering his amendment at the full committee mark-up, Mr. Evans commented on my role in the proposed legislation:

100TH CONGRESS 1st Session	HOUSE OF REPRESENTATIVES	REPT. 100-22 Part 1

MONTGOMERY GI BILL

MARCH 11, 1987.—Ordered to be printed

Mr. MONTGOMERY, from the Committee on Veterans' Affairs, submitted the following

REPORT

[To accompany H.R. 1085, which on February 11, 1987, was referred jointly to the Committees on Veterans' Affairs and Armed Services]

[Including cost estimate of the Congressional Budget Office]

The Committee on Veterans' Affairs, to whom was referred the bill (H.R. 1085) to amend title 38, United States Code, to make permanent the new GI bill educational assistance programs established by chapter 30 of such title, and for other purposes, having considered the same, reports favorably thereon with an amendment, by unanimous vote, and recommends that the bill as amended do pass.

The amendment is as follows:

Add the following at the end of the bill:

SEC. 2. NEW SHORT TITLE.

Section 701 of the Department of Defense Authorization Act, 1985 (Public Law 98-525; 38 U.S.C. 101 note) is amended to read as follows:

"SHORT TITLE

"SEC. 701. This title may be cited as the 'Montgomery GI Bill Act of 1984'.".

INTRODUCTION

On February 11, 1987, the Honorable G. V. (Sonny) Montgomery, Chairman of the Committee on Veterans' Affairs, introduced H.R. 1085, a bill to make permanent the New GI Bill educational assistance programs established by chapter 30, title 38, United States Code and chapter 106, title 10, United States Code, for himself and 174 original cosponsors.

69-957 O

Mr. Evans

Lane Evans

"You had the vision to conceive the New GI Bill. You had the courage to fight for it against strong and committed opposition. You had the leadership needed to succeed. It has done what you said it would and even more."[50]

Mr. Montgomery

Lastly, the House Armed Services Committee also marked-up H.R. 1085 on March 11.[51] In so doing, the committee rejected a proposal included in President Reagan's FY 1988 Budget to shift funding for the New GI Bill benefit from the VA to DoD.[52]

Here is some of the language from the report the House Armed Services Committee filed following the committee's March 11, 1987, vote in favor of H.R. 1085.[53]

"Based on the information available to date, the committee is convinced the New GI Bill is a highly successful program. The committee will not restate the wealth of backup data provided in Part I of the report on H.R. 1085 filed by the Committee on Veterans' Affairs. Participation rates by service members have far exceeded even the most optimistic predictions when the legislation was formulated two- and a-half-years ago. Witnesses before the committee have uniformly endorsed the continuation of the New GI Bill as a vital tool to maintaining the outstanding recruiting and retention results currently experienced by the services.

"The Army's success during fiscal year 1986, the first year of experience under the New GI Bill, illustrates the importance of a viable educational assistance program. In fiscal year 1986, the active Army—the service that traditionally has experienced the greatest difficulty in recruiting goals—recruited 91 percent high school graduates, with only 4 percent in Mental Category IV, the lowest Mental Category eligible for enlistment. In the Army Reserve, Mental Category I-IIIA, the cream of the crop in recruiting, increased 24 percent and six-year enlistments increased 28 percent during the first year of the New GI Bill in comparison to the previous year.

"The committee believes the test program has been an unqualified success and, therefore, recommends that the June 30, 1988, expiration date for the New GI Bill be eliminated, thus making the program permanent."

So we were positioned to take the bill to the House floor.

Worth Repeating

"There is currently in the Department of Education a 'GI Bill without a GI;' $3.82 billion in Pell grants are available with no requirement for service."
—Dr. Charles Moskos (as quoted by Jill Cochran)

"Mr. President, I rise today to introduce the proposed 'New GI Bill Continuation Act.' The New GI Bill now allows recruiters, for the first time, to penetrate the college-oriented market of young people that we need to operate our sophisticated weaponry...
to enhance our preparedness for the complexities of modern warfare."
—Chairman Alan Cranston

"Balancing the <u>obligation</u> of <u>the nation to individual citizens</u> [emphasis added] against the <u>obligations of individual citizens to their nation</u> [emphasis added] is one of this body's most important functions."
—Ranking Member Frank Murkowski

"... [T]he New GI Bill is an important step in the necessary process of ensuring that those who have served in our armed forces will be able to obtain the education necessary to participate in the decisions that shape American life; not just at the highest levels of national power but also on the shop floor, in small businesses, in school, church, labor and fraternal organizations, in the media, and on the street."
—Ranking Member Frank Murkowski

"You give a recruit a dollar today and it's gone. You give a recruit an education, and the recruit will have it the rest of his or her life."
—General Billy Wellman

"Ladies and gentlemen, I can live with the six-hour time change, but the only problem is, I get sexy at meal time and hungry at bedtime!"
—Senator Spark Matsunaga

"Heck, we were happier than lost kittens in a creamery!"
—G.V. "Sonny" Montgomery

Sonny's Lessons Learned

Finding common ground pays dividends. Chairman Cranston and ranking member Murkowski jointly introduced S. 12. Their doing so proved a bipartisan advantage. They were together on the issue, sharing the same view as to an educational assistance policy for our All-Volunteer Force. And seven other Senators of both political parties joined them as original cosponsors of the bill. These included the Senate Majority Leader George Mitchell of Maine, Senate Minority Whip Al Simpson of Wyoming, and the venerable Strom Thurmond of South Carolina. All served on the Veterans' Affairs Committee.

WHAT'S NEXT

Let's move to the final few months—April, May, June 1987—that put the New GI Bill on the President's desk.

13

SONNY'S
CAST OF
CHARACTERS

Jill Cochran, Staff Director,
Subcommittee on Education,
Training, and Employment,
Committee on Veterans' Affairs,
U.S. House of Representatives

Representative Wayne Dowdy (D-MS),
Chairman, Subcommittee on Education,
Training, and Employment,
Committee on Veterans' Affairs

Representative Tim Penny (D-MN),
Member, Committee on Veterans' Affairs

Representative
John Paul Hammerschmidt (R-AR),
Ranking Member,
Committee on Veterans' Affairs

Representative Lane Evans (D-IL),
Member, Committee on Veterans' Affairs

Representative Christopher Smith (R-NJ),
Ranking Minority Member,
Subcommittee on Education,
Training, and Employment,
Committee on Veterans' Affairs

Representative Beverly Byron
(D-MD), Chairman, Military
Personnel and Compensation
Subcommittee, Committee
on Armed Services

Representative Bill Gray (D-PA)
Chairman, Budget Committee

Representative
Leon Panetta (D-CA)

Representative
Thomas Coleman,
(R-MO)

Darryl Kehrer,
1992 Woodrow Wilson
Public Service Fellow,
Representing U.S. Dept.
of Veterans Affairs

Senator John Glenn,
(D-OH), Chairman,
Subcommittee
on Manpower and
Personnel, Committee
on Armed Services

John Marsh,
Secretary of the Army,
1981-1989

Spring 1987—Road to Enactment: House Passage and Senate Armed Services Committee Approval

SONNY'S SUMMARY

The House's 401-2 passage of H.R. 1085 on March 17, 1987, and the Senate Veterans' Affairs Committee's February 26, 1987, 11-0 mark-up of S. 12 serve as backdrops to the Senate Armed Services Committee hearing held on S. 12 March 24, 1987.

At the hearing, Senators John Glenn of Ohio and Pete Wilson of California, Dr. Neil Singer of the Congressional Budget Office's National Security Division, and the Reagan Administration continued to express various concerns about S. 12. Conversely, the veterans, higher education, and military personnel organizations supported it.

We'll review several events that would lead to the full Senate Armed Services Committee's April 30, 1987, 12-0 vote favorably reporting S. 12 to the full Senate.

These events included elements of the House lobbying the Senate, the Executive Branch lobbying the Legislative Branch, and one Senate committee lobbying another Senate committee. I use the term "lobbying" in this sense because each party aggressively attempted to persuade the other party toward its point of view, in support or opposition to S. 12.

1987

Mr. Montgomery

March 24, 1987, marked an important fork in the long legislative road traveled by the Cranston/Murkowski S. 12 legislation that would create a permanent New GI Bill.[1]

That's the day the Subcommittee on Manpower and Personnel, Senate Armed Services Committee, under the leadership of Chairman John Glenn and Ranking Member Pete Wilson of California, held a public hearing on S. 12.[2]

Senators John McCain of Arizona, Richard Shelby of Alabama, and Jim Exon of Nebraska served on the subcommittee and participated in the hearing. Senators Glenn and Wilson asked most of the questions.[3]

Ladies and gentlemen, please remember the Senate Committee on Veterans' Affairs approved S. 12 on February 26, 1987, with minor amendments and filed its report on March 17.

But under Senate rules (the House has similar rules), the full Senate cannot consider the bill until Senator Glenn's subcommittee and the full Senate Armed Services Committee mark it up (a phrase we learned earlier for approving it) and reports it to the full Senate.[4] This is because the Parliamentarian referred S. 12 to both the Veterans' Affairs and Armed Services Committees. Both committees had jurisdiction: Veterans' Affairs regarding the GI Bill as a tool for transition from military to civilian life and Armed Services regarding it as a tool for recruitment/retention.

Let's see what happened at the Subcommittee on Manpower and Personnel hearing. We'll start with the views of Chairman Glenn.

Ms. Jill Cochran, staff director of my Subcommittee on Education, Training, and Employment, attended the hearing and prepared an informal summary for me.

I can tell you that working with my outstanding team of Veterans' Affairs Committee Chief Counsel Mack Fleming and Deputy Chief Counsel Patrick Ryan, Communications Director Jim Holley, and staff assistant Beth Kilker and legislative assistant Candis Sniffen, Jill was my "eyes and ears" and sometimes even my "voice" for some five years on this bill. Richard Fuller was subcommittee staff director in that first year or two with Congressman Bob Edgar. They all labored on H.R. 1400 in the early years, carrying out a lot of research, analysis, staff negotiation, and plain hard work![5]

I say Ms. Cochran was my "voice" because she drafted almost everything I would say on this issue for hearings, committee mark-ups, floor debate, letters, media interviews, and a lot more. That's what staff do!

Ms. Cochran did it well. And with real commitment.[6]

Let's ask Ms. Cochran to summarize.

SENATE ARMED SERVICES SUBCOMMITTEE

Ms. Cochran

Jill Cochran

"Thank you, Mr. Chairman. At the hearing Chairman Glenn:[7]

- "Observed if we are going to have a New GI Bill, it should be structured at a benefit level that means something;

- "Expressed appreciation of former GI Bills and their contribution to society as a whole;

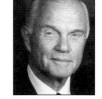
John Glenn

- "Said empirical data regarding increases in quality, longer enlistments in Reserve components, etc., cannot be specifically attributed to the New GI Bill;

- "Said he did not support the Department of Defense funding the New GI Bill instead of the Veterans Administration, which has done so since 1944; and

- "Said he didn't think it necessary to reduce benefits for lesser terms of service.

"Ranking Member Wilson:[8]

- "Assumed the New GI Bill would have a negative effect on retaining quality service members; and

- "Seemed inclined to want to continue the New GI Bill test program rather than make the bill permanent."

Pete Wilson

Mr. Montgomery

Assistant Secretary of Defense for Reserve Affairs Dennis Shaw testified on behalf of the Reserve components of the four services branches:[9]

"…We have compared the number of high school graduates we recruited in 1984 before the enactment of the New GI Bill for the Selected Reserve and the number we recruited in 1986. The difference was an increase of 34,500 high school graduates between those two years.

"So I think we can conclude that the GI Bill is having an impact for the Selected Reserve on the number of high school graduates, which is a quality indicator for that segment of our force."

Here is a summary of the testimony of the Army, Navy, Air Force and Marine Corps witnesses. Go ahead Jill, please.

Ms. Cochran

"Regarding the service branches: [10]

- "Each service branch testified in support of S. 12;
- "Each service branch agreed the VA should continue to pay for the education benefit and administer it; and
- "Lt. General Cheatham (Marine Corps) and Lt. General Hickey (Air Force) testified saying: 'if it's [New GI Bill] not broken, don't fix it!'"

Mr. Montgomery

Dr. Neil M. Singer testified on behalf of the national security division of the Congressional Budget Office, known as CBO.

Dr. Singer focused mostly on cost projections.

Ms. Cochran

"Dr. Singer:[11]

- "Testified that the number of service members signing up for the New GI Bill was far higher than CBO anticipated;

- "Said cost of the benefit will be correspondingly higher, as well;
- "Preferred to continue the 'test program' so as to get more data; and
- "Felt the New GI Bill would have a negative effect on retaining service members beyond an initial term of service."

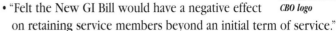

CBO logo

Mr. Montgomery

Now you've heard the highlights from the body of testimony at the March 24, 1987, Senate Armed Services Subcommittee hearing.[12]

COMMITTEE ON ARMED SERVICES

UNITED STATES SENATE

Again, I have such a high regard for Chairman Glenn I regret that—even though we reviewed and analyzed pretty much the same data—we evidently drew different conclusions from it.

Chairman Glenn expressed concern that increases in recruiting numbers and in the quality of new enlistees could not specifically be attributed to the New GI Bill, in terms of empirical data.

As I saw it, the data cannot be sorted so specifically as to attribute behaviors with regard to joining the military to one factor alone. But the New GI Bill was the centerpiece of a recruiting package that needed to be held together.[13]

In February 1987, when our Veterans Affairs' Committee Congressional Delegation visited the individual basic training sites of the four service branches, the recruits told us unequivocally getting money for college was a major factor—if not their main reason—in joining the military for two, three or four years.[14]

THE HOUSE VOTE

The full House overwhelmingly passed our bill containing 195 cosponsors by a vote of 401 to 2 on March 17, 1987. A wonderful day![15] We now had 21 more cosponsors than when we introduced the bill February 11. Members certainly can sign on to cosponsor a bill after it's introduced.[16]

401 "AYES" AND 2 "NAYS"
—Vote on H.R. 1085 March 17, 1987

Here are some excerpts from the floor debate on the bill. We'll hear from five members of the House Veterans' Affairs Committee, including Representatives

Wayne Dowdy of Mississippi, Tim Penny of Minnesota, John Paul Hammerschmidt of Arkansas, Lane Evans of Illinois, and Christopher Smith of New Jersey.

We'll also hear comments of Armed Services Committee Subcommittee Chairman Beverly Byron of Maryland; as well as Representative Bill Gray of Pennsylvania, chairman of the Budget Committee; and Representative Tom Coleman of Missouri.[17]

As we learned in Chapter 4, in the House of Representatives, the presiding member sits in the Speaker's Chair and is addressed during debate as "Mr. or Madame Speaker." In the Senate, he or she is addressed as "Mr. or Madame President."

Mr. Dowdy

Wayne Dowdy

"Mr. Speaker, I rise in strong support of H.R. 1085, as amended, which is sponsored by 195 of our colleagues.

"Clearly, this program is doing what its supporters said it would do. The New GI Bill is providing additional educational opportunities for hundreds of thousands of young people. It is also bringing smart, eager men and women into the armed forces."[18]

Mr. Penny

Tim Penny

"Mr. Speaker, I rise in strong and enthusiastic support of H.R. 1085, the bill to make permanent the GI Bill. Our committee has watched the implementation of this program over the last couple of years and are tremendously excited about the success of the program.

"Mr. Speaker, I urge adoption of this legislation."[19]

Mr. Hammerschmidt

John Paul Hammerschmidt

"Mr. Speaker, after our hearings on the New GI Bill and our trip to military facilities to obtain first-hand information about how the New GI Bill is working, the arrival of this day for final House approval of H.R. 1085 is almost anticlimactic.

"… I would like to point out that during the 20 years I have been a member of this great body I have never witnessed an event as occurred recently before the Subcommittee on Education, Training, and Employment. A speaker of the House had never in anyone's memory come before our committee to testify on behalf of legislation.

"I was surprised and pleased when our friend and colleague, Speaker Jim Wright, made an appearance before us a few weeks ago to praise the GI Bill as 'the best investment this country has ever made.' His statement reflects his strong support for this legislation, and his unprecedented testimony reflects the great respect he and all of us have for our distinguished chairman, Mr. Montgomery."[20]

Mr. Evans

Lane Evans

> "…VISION, COURAGE AND LEADERSHIP…"
> —*Representative Lane Evans, Illinois*

"Mr. Speaker, the New GI Bill is an overwhelming success.

"The New GI Bill is in the best tradition of America.

"During full committee consideration of this bill, I offered an amendment to honor the distinguished chairman of our committee whose vision, courage, and leadership are responsible for the New GI Bill's success. My amendment was adopted, and the legislation which first established the New GI Bill is now [will be] known as the Montgomery GI Bill Act of 1984."[21]

Mr. Smith

Christopher Smith

"Mr. Speaker, as the ranking minority member of the Education, Training, and Employment Subcommittee, I am very pleased that H.R. 1085—to make the New GI Bill permanent—has had strong bipartisan support and I'm very proud to be an original cosponsor of this legislation… .The GI Bill to the veteran is both a reward for service and a vital tool to prepare him or her for the future.

"… The cost-effectiveness of the GI Bill as a readjustment benefit alone has been amply demonstrated over the years in terms of additional taxes resulting from increased earnings by veterans who otherwise would not have attended college."[22]

Ms. Byron

Beverly Byron

"Mr. Speaker, as the chairman of the Subcommittee on Military Personnel and Compensation of the Armed Services Committee, I rise in strong support of H.R. 1085 to make the New GI Bill permanent.

"There is no better investment in the future than education. America is what it is today because of the accomplishments of those World War II veterans who returned to college under the first GI Bill to become the scientists, engineers, doctors, teachers, and political leaders of their generation… .

"In Title VII of the FY 1985 Defense Authorization Act—Public Law 98-525—Congress approved a three-year test of a new educational assistance program for both the active and Reserve components, funded jointly by the Veterans Administration and the Department of Defense. The test was an unqualified success… .

"I urge my colleagues' whole-hearted support."[23]

Mr. Gray

Bill Gray

"Mr. Speaker, brain power is like a bank account. If you don't put it in, you can't draw it out. This legislation on the GI Bill will allow that brain power to come out for the betterment of our country and our service personnel."[24]

> "… BRAIN POWER IS LIKE A BANK ACCOUNT. IF YOU DON'T PUT IT IN, YOU CAN'T DRAW IT OUT."
> —*Representative Bill Gray, Pennsylvania*

Mr. Panetta

Leon Panetta

"… While expenditures on weapon systems are necessary to ensure our nation's security, I have always felt that we must give first priority to our military people. In my view, we ought to be providing benefits which not only ensure their recruitment and retention, but will also give them the means of improving their quality of life."[25]

Mr. Coleman

Thomas Coleman

"The New GI Bill program of educational assistance was established by the 1985 Defense Authorization Act to help service personnel readjust to civilian life and to help recruitment efforts and retention of personnel by the armed forces.

"It replaced the Veterans' Educational Assistance Program [VEAP], under which participants contributed up to $2,700 from their pay, which the Veterans Administration matched on a two-to-one basis. Unfortunately, the participation rate was less than 20 percent, taking into account those who requested refunds of their contributions."[26]

> "UNFORTUNATELY, THE [VEAP] PARTICIPATION RATE WAS LESS THAN 20 PERCENT…"
> —*Representative Thomas Coleman, Missouri*

Mr. Montgomery

"Mr. Speaker, I want to point out that I appreciate the kindness and the compliments accorded me in this debate. But I want to still say that there are many, many members of the House of Representatives and other laymen who have participated and made the bill possible. It is not one individual's efforts. As I keep repeating, it has been a team effort all the way."[27]

> "… IT HAS BEEN A TEAM EFFORT ALL THE WAY."
> —*G.V. "Sonny" Montgomery*

Ms. Byron

"Mr. Speaker, let me say in closing a debate that was supposed to be a very short and very quick one, but so many people wished to participate… it had to be extended… [that] I cannot really say that this has been a debate, because it really has not been. We are still waiting for those in opposition to show up and ask for time.

"I think I must say it has been more of a love-in. First, for a chance to talk about the Committee on Veterans' Affairs Chairman, the gentleman from Mississippi [Mr. Montgomery], who, I think we have to say, is the father of this New GI Bill, but more important, for the future of the next generation with educational opportunities.

> "… THE GENTLEMAN FROM MISSISSIPPI [MR. MONTGOMERY], WHO, I THINK WE WILL HAVE TO SAY, IS THE FATHER OF THE NEW GI BILL…"
> —*Representative Beverly Byron, Maryland*

"As a new chairman of the Subcommittee on Compensation, Pension, and Insurance of the Committee on Armed Services,[28] nothing has given me more pleasure than the first bill to come out of that subcommittee, to come out of the Committee on Armed Services this year, than the New GI Bill. I am glad to say it happened on my watch."[29]

THREE REALITIES OF LAWMAKING

Mr. Montgomery

I want to pause and share with you three more everyday "realities" of policy making that emerge in this specific case from Darryl Kehrer, a 1992 Woodrow Wilson Public Service Fellow, representing the U.S. Department of Veterans Affairs:[30]

Mr. Kehrer

EXECUTIVE "LOBBIES" LEGISLATIVE
HOUSE "LOBBIES" SENATE
COMMITTEES "LOBBY" COMMITTEES

Darryl Kehrer

"Congress [of course] writes laws.

"But the first reality is that the Executive Branch 'lobbies' the Legislative Branch.

"The second is House committees 'lobby' Senate committees.

"And third, Senate committees 'lobby' one another![31]

"Each entity—proponent and opponents—uses all of its persuasive power to 'lobby' the others, especially when enactment of legislation is imminent."[32]

Mr. Montgomery

Here are some examples.

Senator Glenn, distinguished chairman of the Senate Armed Services Subcommittee on Manpower and Personnel, largely agreed with the late Senator Tower. John Glenn is an American icon and was indeed a major player in successfully offering his Citizen-Soldier GI Bill amendment to the FY 1985 Omnibus DoD Authorization Act. Observes Senator Glenn:

Mr. Glenn

"The fact is that there is considerable 'economic rent' in this program—we are offering a very

As one of the original group of Mercury astronauts, Glenn piloted NASA's first U.S. manned orbital mission aboard Friendship 7 on February 20, 1962.

attractive benefit to many people in order to get a marginal return on high-quality recruits."[33]

> "THE FACT IS THAT THERE IS CONSIDERABLE 'ECONOMIC RENT' IN THIS PROGRAM— WE ARE OFFERING A VERY ATTRACTIVE BENEFIT TO MANY PEOPLE IN ORDER TO GET A MARGINAL RETURN ON HIGH-QUALITY RECRUITS."
> —*Senator John Glenn, Ohio*

Mr. Montgomery

σ: Army Times FEBRUARY 23, 1987

Army Leads Services In High Test Scores Of Recruits in 1987

By LARRY CARNEY
Times Staff Writer

WASHINGTON — The Army enlisted a higher percentage of high-quality recruits during the first three months of fiscal 1987 than the Air Force, Navy and Marine Corps, new enlistment statistics show.

The statistics show that 75.8 percent of the recruits who entered the Army between Oct. 1, 1986, and Jan. 12, 1987, scored 50 or higher

The Army, an official said, has been making a "tremendous effort" in recent years to recruit high-scoring recruits.

And the official said the effort appears to be paying off in improved readiness and reduced discipline problems.

The number of soldiers scoring above 50 on the AFQT has increased sharply since 1980 when Congress ordered the Army to improve the caliber of enlistments. The legislators established a ceiling on the number of recruits who

But the Army had the most challenging recruiting problem, and the Army respectfully did not share Senator Glenn's view. Did you know John Glenn served with great distinction in the U.S. Marine Corps, flying combat missions during the Korean Conflict—long before the national Aeronautics and Space Administration (NASA) selected him as an astronaut?[34]

So here's the **first** reality.

The Executive Branch—in the person of Secretary of the Army John Marsh—directly "lobbied" the Legislative Branch's Senator Glenn and every member of the Armed Services Subcommittee he chaired, saying:

Mr. Marsh

"The New GI Bill test program is a winner for the soldier, the Army, and the nation…. In recent years, the quality of Army recruits has improved in terms of education and armed forces qualification test scores….

John Marsh

"This is due, in part, to improved recruiting incentives. Today, over 90 percent of Army recruits are high school graduates, compared to 54 percent in 1980."[35]

Mr. Montgomery

And as we'll learn in an *Army Times* article by Rick Maze later in this chapter, Chapman B. Cox, DoD top manpower official, will tell "military legislative liaison officers to quietly let Senators know that the Pentagon supported making the New GI Bill permanent… ."[36]

And the **second** reality is the House "lobbied" the Senate—not as part of a formal conference committee but on its own initiative.

Strom Thurmond

I can tell you I was as nervous as a long-tailed cat in a room full of rocking chairs[37] regarding my friend, the venerable Strom Thurmond of South Carolina. I contacted the Senator, a former paratrooper with the 82nd Airborne who landed near Normandy on the eve of D-Day.[38]

He was (Spring 1987) now having second thoughts on S. 12 to make the New GI Bill permanent, perhaps due to the program's estimated cost.[39] But both H.R. 1085 and S. 12 made New GI Bill benefits permanently available for members of the Guard and Reserve. I had a hunch this provision would interest Senator Thurmond, given his 36 years of service in the Army and Army Reserves, where he reached the rank of Major General.[40]

I called Senator John McCain (R-AZ) as well to ask him to oppose in the Manpower Subcommittee of the Armed Services Committee any efforts to continue to test the three-year New GI Bill program, rather than making it permanent. I was delighted Senator McCain said he'd take the lead in this regard.[41] I used the word "test" because that's how the Senate Armed Services Committee, in particular, viewed the New GI Bill.

Representative Marcy Kaptur also "lobbied" the Senate. In the next column is the May 7, 1987, letter Ms. Kaptur wrote to fellow Ohioan, Chairman Glenn, making the case for our bill.

> "TODAY, OVER 90 PERCENT OF ARMY RECRUITS ARE HIGH SCHOOL GRADUATES COMPARED TO 54 PERCENT IN 1980."
> —*John Marsh, Secretary of the Army*

> "… I WAS AS NERVOUS AS A LONG-TAILED CAT IN A ROOM FULL OF ROCKING CHAIRS REGARDING MY FRIEND, THE VENERABLE STROM THURMOND OF SOUTH CAROLINA."
> —*G.V. "Sonny" Montgomery*

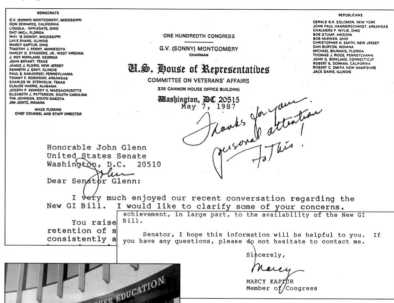

Marcy Kaptur

In the letter, Ms. Kaptur addressed issues of retention, cost, and Reserve enlistments, and recruiting/youth employment/unemployment issues.[42]

Ms. Kaptur served with distinction on the Education, Training, and Employment Subcommittee. She wrote one of her Senators!

Among many others, my colleagues and I worked with the AACJC and the NCOA, which put a "full-court press" on the Senate Armed Services Committee.[43]

And **third**, committees "lobby" one another.

The Veterans' Affairs Committee staffs of Senator Cranston "lobbied" the staff of Armed Services Subcommittee member Senator Edward Kennedy (D-MA), who had served as an Army enlistee in West Berlin… .[44]

And the Veterans' Affairs Committee "lobbied" the staff of Senator McCain,

Ted Kennedy

John McCain

providing them with various manpower and recruiting analyses, some of which originated in the Pentagon.[45]

Senators Kennedy, McCain, and Thurmond—a trio some staff light-heartedly referred to as the "unholy troika"[46]—helped shape the debate to allow the New GI Bill for the All-Volunteer Force to make it through the Armed Services Manpower/Personnel Subcommittee and the full committee, with continued leadership from committee member Senator Cohen.

"THE UNHOLY TROIKA"

Here are the vote tallies.

SENATE ARMED SERVICES COMMITTEE VOTES

In late April, by a vote of five ayes to two nays, Chairman Glenn's Manpower and Personnel Subcommittee approved S. 12.[47] And on April 30, the full Senate Armed Services Committee approved the bill 12-0.[48][49]

Let's review the press release issued by Murray Flander on behalf of the Chairman, Senate Veterans' Affairs Committee.[50]

```
Cranston-GIBILL-2
        Cranston said the 12-0 vote in the Senate Armed Services
Committee last Thursday, an earlier 11-0 vote by the Senate
Veterans' Affairs Committee, and the overwhelming 401-2 vote by
the full House in March "dramatically underscore the fact that a
vast majority of both Democrats and Republicans alike hold the
same view".
        He said he expects the full Senate to "follow suit in short
order". His bill is cosponso...
        Under current law, activ...
the military for the first t...
30, 1988, are entitled to ba...
$300 a month for 36 months. ...
three-year tour of duty.
        Personnel who complete t...
years in the Selected Reserv...
assistance of $250 a month for 36 months.
```

```
assistance of $250 a month for 36 months.
        The Cranston bill, entitled the "New GI Bill Continuation
Act", would eliminate the June 30, 1988, cut-off for new entrants
to be eligible for those benefits.
                              -0-

UNITED STATES SENATE
WASHINGTON, D.C. 20510-0601
PUBLIC DOCUMENT
OFFICIAL BUSINESS                        Alan Cranston
                                              U.S.S.

        10035-8  VZ
        MACK FLEMING
        COMMITTEE ON VETS AFFS
        335 CANNON HOB
        WASHINGTON, DC 20515
```

"Senator Alan Cranston (D-CA) predicted rapid Senate passage of his legislation making permanent the New GI Bill program of educational benefits following unanimous approval of the measure last week by the Senate Armed Services Committee.

"Cranston, the assistant Senate majority leader and chairman of the Veterans' Affairs Committee, said today that 'making the program permanent will enhance the ability of our armed forces to recruit, train, and retain the kind of top-quality people we need for a strong military defense.'

"He called the educational benefits provision in the New GI Bill 'a blue-chip investment in our nation's human resources.'

"Cranston's bill, S. 12, which he introduced Jan. 6, the first day of the new Congress, extends indefinitely educational benefits for veterans and members of the National Guard and the Reserve. Under current law, the benefits are scheduled to expire in 1988.

"'It is vital that we do everything necessary to make the All-Volunteer Force work and to avoid recourse to conscription to meet our military personnel needs,' Cranston said.

"'The last thing our nation needs—especially our young people—is a return to the divisiveness of the draft.

"'I have long been convinced that education assistance, along with readjustment benefits for military personnel when they return to civilian life, are recruitment and retention tools for the all-volunteer armed forces,' he said.

"Cranston said the 12-0 vote in the Senate Armed Services Committee last Thursday, an earlier 11-0 vote by the Senate Veterans' Affairs Committee, and the overwhelming 401-2 vote by the full House in March 'dramatically underscore' the fact that a vast majority of both Democrats and Republicans alike hold the same view."

> " ... A VAST MAJORITY OF BOTH DEMOCRATS AND REPUBLICANS ALIKE HOLD THE SAME VIEW."
> —*Senator Alan Cranston, California*

Mr. Montgomery

From my vantage point, I'd say Senators Kennedy, McCain, and Thurmond, respectively, ended up supporting the bill for completely different reasons.[51]

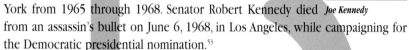

REASONS FOR TURNAROUND IN SUPPORT...

- HELPS DISADVANTAGED YOUNG PEOPLE
- HELPS ALL-VOLUNTEER FORCE RECRUITING
- HELPS MILITARY RESERVE RECRUITING

It appeared that Senator Kennedy provided important leadership in part at the behest of his nephew, Congressman Joe Kennedy of Massachusetts, a member of the House Veterans' Affairs Committee.[52]

Joe Kennedy

Joe is the son of the late Robert Kennedy, Attorney General of the U.S. from 1961 through 1964, and U.S. Senator from New York from 1965 through 1968. Senator Robert Kennedy died from an assassin's bullet on June 6, 1968, in Los Angeles, while campaigning for the Democratic presidential nomination.[53]

I valued both Joe's help and friendship.

Sonny's Lessons Learned

The Executive Branch, too, is involved in writing laws.

In this case, the Executive Branch played a role in "lobbying" the Senate long after its witnesses first testified at a committee hearing. In a sense, the Executive Branch has no choice but to stay actively involved. Here are three generalized scenarios as to why:

First, if Congress has gotten the public policy correct, as expressed in the proposed legislation, the Executive Branch has to reinforce that policy so it continues unchanged.

Second, if in the view of the Executive Branch the policy in the bill is not correct, the Executive Branch has to try to make it right, because the Executive Branch obviously implements bills once enacted into law—being stuck with a bad law is no fun!

Third, the policies in the bill may be correct, but the bill may be administratively too onerous, cumbersome, or costly to implement.

Worth Repeating

"If it's not broken, don't fix it."
—*Lieutenant General Earnest Cheatham, USMC*
—*Major General Thomas Hickey, USAF*

"Congress of course writes laws, but the Executive Branch 'lobbies' the Legislative Branch, House committees 'lobby' Senate committees, and in this case, Senate committees 'lobby' one another."
—*Darryl Kehrer, 1992 Woodrow Wilson Public Service Fellow Representing U.S. Department of Veterans Affairs*

"The fact is there is considerable 'economic rent' in this program. We are offering a very attractive benefit to many people in order to get a marginal return on high-quality recruits."
—*Chairman John Glenn*

"The New GI Bill test program is a winner for the soldier, the Army and the nation... today over 90 percent of the Army recruits are high school graduates compared to 54 percent in 1980."
—*John Marsh, Secretary of the Army*

"... I was as nervous as a long-tailed cat in a room full of rocking chairs regarding my friend, the venerable Strom Thurmond of South Carolina."
—*G.V. "Sonny" Montgomery*

WHAT'S NEXT

Let's move now to the Senate chamber for the vote on S. 12, as amended.

14

SONNY'S
CAST OF
CHARACTERS

Senator Edward Kennedy
(D-MA), Member, Committee
on Armed Services

Senator Alan Cranston (D-CA),
Chairman, Committee
on Veterans' Affairs

Senator Frank Murkowski (R-AK),
Ranking Member,
Committee on Veterans' Affairs

Senator John Glenn (D-OH),
Chairman, Subcommittee on
Force Management and Personnel,
Committee on Armed Services

Senator Bill Armstrong (R-CO)

Senator John McCain (R-AZ),
Member, Committee
on Armed Services

Senator Strom Thurmond (R-SC),
Member, Committees
on Veterans Affairs
and Armed Services

Senator Bill Cohen (R-ME),
Member,
Committee on Armed Services

Senator Spark Matsunaga (D-HI),
Member, Committee
on Veterans' Affairs

Senator Alan Simpson
(R-WY), Member,
Committee on
Veterans' Affairs

Senator Tom Daschle
(D-SD)

Rick Maze, Congressoinal
Editor, Army Times

Honorable
Thomas Turnage,
Administrator of
Veterans Affairs

Honorable Howard Baker,
Chief of Staff
to President Reagan

Honorable
George H. W. Bush,
Vice President
of the United States

Honorable
Ronald W. Reagan,
40th President
of the United States

John Marsh,
Secretary of the Army,
1981-1989

Col. Michael Meese,
U.S. Military Academy

Summer 1987—
Road to Enactment:
Senate Passage, Conference, and Rose Garden

SONNY'S SUMMARY

We conclude the almost seven-year journey with four culminating events: First, the Senate approving S. 12 as amended on May 8, 1987; second, the House and Senate resolving minor differences between S. 12 and H.R. 1085, as amended on May 13, 1987; third, the Speaker of the House and the President Pro Tempore of the Senate signing the enrolled bill on May 19; and fourth, the President signing H.R. 1085 into law (Public Law 100-48) on June 1, 1987, in a Rose Garden ceremony. Secretary of the Army John Marsh and Assistant Secretary of Defense Chapman Cox had quietly helped move the bill along.

Mr. Montgomery

S. 12, as amended, survived the vote in the Senate Armed Services Committee. Noted one observer speaking both seriously and humorously:

"The debate in the Armed Services Committee was sufficiently spirited at one point that the sometimes-used Washington saying of 'blood, hair, and eyeballs all over the floor' may very well have applied, as Senators debated the 'opportunity cost' of the program and whether it would bring in high-quality recruits."[1]

I wrote scores of thank you letters to persons and organizations that supported our legislation over the seven years.[2] It's important to thank people. In this letter, I offered my thanks to Congressman Joe Kennedy for his support and leadership.

"... BLOOD, HAIR, AND EYEBALLS ALL OVER THE FLOOR..."

And I offered my thanks to Senator Edward (Ted) Kennedy in this letter. Senator Kennedy consistently supported my efforts and those of Senators Armstrong, Cohen, and Cranston over the seven years.

The Senator sent me a letter, too.

Note Senator Kennedy's postscript at the bottom of his letter, in which he speaks of the significance of his nephew, Representative Joe Kennedy, serving on the House Veterans' Affairs Committee and in fact pushing for a New GI Bill.

Mr. Kennedy

"Now when they say 'who does that darn Kennedy think he is?'—there's a 50-50 chance they don't mean me!"

THE SENATE VOTE

Mr. Montgomery

It's now May 8, 1987, and the full Senate approves S. 12, as amended, 89 to zero![3]

The full Senate convenes.

Here's a sampling of what 11 Senators had to say during the debate on S. 12 in the Senate chamber prior to voting on it.

These are selected excerpts from each Senator's remarks, not the full statements.

We'll start with Senators Cranston and Murkowski, who were the Democratic and Republican floor managers, respectively, for the bill, and then we'll hear comments from nine other Senators who spoke on the bill.

Mr. Cranston

Alan Cranston

"The dividends our country has already reaped from past GI Bills [are] so vast as to be virtually incalculable. However, it is widely accepted that for every dollar spent in GI Bill benefits, the nation is returned $3 to $6 in increased tax revenues… .

"While there has been a major emphasis on building a 600-ship Navy, for developing and acquiring the very best and fastest planes for our Air Force, and for purchasing the latest in high technology and weapons for our troops, we must not overlook the fact that we will always need to recruit the very best young men and women for positions of leadership and responsibility in our military in order to guarantee that America's defense of today and tomorrow will remain strong. A New GI Bill will help us maintain this strength to defend our shores as well as those of our allies throughout the free world… .

> "THE DIVIDENDS OUR COUNTRY HAS ALREADY REAPED FROM PAST GI BILLS [ARE] SO VAST AS TO BE VIRTUALLY INCALCULABLE."
> —*Senator Alan Cranston, California*

"Finally, the young people going to school under the New GI Bill will pay more in taxes over their lifetimes because more education will increase their income. Veterans' Administration statistics show that in 1985, the median income for veterans with a high school diploma was $19,720. For veterans who were college graduates, the median income jumped to $35,800. This 83-percent increase in income associated with additional education results in significantly increased federal, state, and local income taxes flowing to government coffers."[4]

Mr. Murkowski

"The ability and wisdom to learn from experience are qualities that distinguish a wise and mature society. I believe they also distinguish this nation and this body. For over 40 years, we have been gaining experience in providing educational benefits to America's veterans… .

Frank Murkowski

"Mr. President, this legislation is evidence that the nation's commitment to veterans will continue. Our commitment is not just to those who served in the past, but also to those who will serve in the future. This legislation, and that commitment, have been brought to life by the perseverance and determination of the chairman of the House Committee on Veterans' Affairs, Mr. Sonny Montgomery, whose name has already been inscribed on the new bill through his indelible record of action, and with the input of many years by his colleague on the minority Republican side, John Paul Hammerschmidt, and with the input of now ranking member, Gerry Solomon."[5]

Mr. Montgomery

Jon Steinberg

Thank you, Alan and Frank. And Jon Steinberg, Ed Scott, Babette Polzer, Jennifer McCarthy, Tony Principi, and Chris Yoder of your staffs, who all furnished helpful policy guidance on this issue. Jon Steinberg, in particular, helped in the final language of H.R. 1085 in that service members automatially would be "enrolled" in the Montgomery GI Bill (meaning eligible to use it), unless they specifically elected to "disenroll."

Next, we'll hear from Senators Glenn, Armstrong, McCain, Thurmond, Cohen, and Kennedy, all members of the Armed Services Committee; Senators Matsunaga and Simpson of the Veterans' Affairs Committee; and then Senator Daschle.

Ed Scott

Mr. Glenn

John Glenn

"… Mr. President, there was no doubt about the merits of extending the expiration date of existing authority in the Committee on Armed Services. The only question that was raised was whether or not the extension should be for a specified period, such as three years. That is the only question I raised in the subcommittee. There was some sentiment, which I shared, that we should make sure we know the effect of the current test program regarding both retention and overall costs before we move to make the program permanent.

"That is a big move. When we move to make something like this permanent, it becomes another entitlement program and it goes on into the years ahead. We have all decried the growth of entitlement programs in the past. We wanted to make sure that any new entitlement program was worthy of being included permanently in the budget of the United States of America. So we wanted to get a little more experience with this. That was the only reason we questioned whether this should go through or not.

"I would like to take a few minutes to share with you our reservations because I believe it is important that we have all of the facts on the record. In testimony that we received from the Congressional Budget Office (CBO) and from the Department of Defense, it is clear that the effect of the GI Bill on the recruitment of high-quality personnel for the military is inconclusive, except for the Army, where the benefit is supplemented by so-called 'kickers,' which add as much as one-and-a-half times the value of the basic benefit for certain categories of skills, or up to $24,200 for a $1,200 investment. Given the results, it was not surprising that when I asked the service personnel chiefs whether or not they would support the programs if the paying for it had to come out of that service's budget and not the Veterans' Administration which administers the program now, whether or not they would support the program if they had to pay for all of it, only the Army replied in the affirmative. The other services—the Marine Corps, the Air Force, and the Navy—said if they had to take it out of their own service budget, they did not feel it was doing them much good. The fact is there is considerable 'economic rent' in this program—we are offering a very attractive benefit to many people in order to get a marginal return on high-quality recruits… .

> "… I AM HERE TO ENTHUSIASTICALLY SUPPORT PASSAGE OF THIS BILL TODAY, AND WOULD URGE ALL SENATORS TO VOTE FOR IT. I THINK ONE OF THE BEST THINGS WE CAN DO IS HAVE A UNANIMOUS VOTE ON THIS. FEW THINGS GET UNANIMOUS AROUND HERE. THIS IS ONE THAT DESERVES IT…"
> —*Senator John Glenn, Ohio*

"… So because of these uncertainties I was initially disposed in subcommittee toward putting a sunset on the extension of the current program so we could get a better handle on some of these concerns… . However, after weighing these concerns against the broader context of the benefit to our population of young people as a whole, the Committee on Armed Services and subcommittee I head decided to report out S. 12 without amendment… .

"… I think this nation became largely what it is through education and basic research. Education in this United States of America is not just for the kids from the castle or the politically advantaged or well connected or the economically well off. It was for every single young person… .

"… I do not know many who would argue against this, especially in light of what this administration has done to cut education. So it is on this basis that I was [the] one who proposed the amendment on the floor of the Senate in 1984 that became the basis for much of the current GI Bill that we are about to make permanent. It is the bill we worked on with Congressman Sonny Montgomery over in the House who has done yeoman's service in this area, has been a proponent for this for a long time. We want to give him due credit because he has done a masterful job in that area… .

"… Let me go through the procedures of what happened in the Senate Armed Services Committee because I think that was somewhat misunderstood by our colleagues over in the House side. We reported it out of our subcommittee with a recommendation, with a unanimous vote, of the Veterans' Affairs Committee in the Senate and a unanimous vote of the Veterans' Affairs Committee in the House, to approve this extension of the GI Bill. We approved it out of subcommittee with my vote in favor of it. When it got to the actual committee, one of our members objected basically on the grounds that maybe we needed more experience. That got some support. There was a considerable debate. We put off a final vote on that until another day. The objection that was raised in the first meeting was removed in the second meeting, and we voted out unanimously to approve this bill.

"… I am glad to be part of that support, the full support of the Committee on Armed Services for this bill on the floor today… .

"… I am here to enthusiastically support passage of this bill today, and would urge all Senators to vote for it. I think one of the best things we can do is have a unanimous vote on this. Few things get unanimous around here. This is one that deserves it… ."[6]

Mr. Armstrong

Bill Armstrong

"Mr. President, there is an old saying around Congress that bad legislation can become law in a day, but to get a good bill to become law takes years of hard work. That perfectly summarizes the legislative history of the GI Bill. It has taken four years[7] of tireless work to sell Congress, the administration, and the nation on the simple notion that restoring the GI Bill is good for America.

"Today that work pays off.[8] The Senate is about to pass legislation making the New GI Bill permanent.

"And well it should. The GI Bill pays educational benefits to those serving in the All-Volunteer Armed Forces. This is one of those rare pieces of legislation in which everybody wins—taxpayers, the military, and young service men and women, colleges, and the nation.

"In what may rank as one of the worst military decisions every made [by

Congress], the GI Bill was terminated in 1976. Killing the GI Bill created a mammoth manpower crisis… . At the beginning, there were just four Senators besides myself willing to step into the breach and fight for the All-Volunteer Army: Senator Cohen, Senator Hollings, Senator Matsunaga, and Senator Cranston.

"I cannot begin to tell the Senate all the machinations, the parliamentary maneuvers, the hearings, the debate, the acrimony involved in getting the GI Bill restored. Fortunately, the fact, the proven record and the inherent wisdom of the GI Bill prevailed. In 1984, the New GI Bill was restored [as a test program]. So it is with particular satisfaction that I applaud the Senate making permanent the GI Bill."[9]

> "THIS IS ONE OF THOSE RARE PIECES OF LEGISLATION IN WHICH EVERYONE WINS— TAXPAYERS, THE MILITARY, AND YOUNG SERVICE MEN AND WOMEN, COLLEGES, AND THE NATION."
> —*Senator Bill Armstrong, Colorado*

Mr. McCain

John McCain

"Mr. President, it is with great pride that I join my colleagues in supporting S. 12 and H.R. 1085, bills that would make permanent the New GI Bill. These bills are, in large measure, the work of my good friends, Senators Strom Thurmond, Ted Kennedy, Representative Sonny Montgomery, and many others to whom we owe a large debt of gratitude."[10]

> "MR. PRESIDENT, IT IS WITH GREAT PRIDE THAT I JOIN MY COLLEAGUES IN SUPPORTING S. 12 AND H.R. 1085, BILLS THAT WOULD MAKE PERMANENT THE NEW GI BILL."
> —*Senator John McCain, Arizona*

Mr. Thurmond

"Mr. President, in the Armed Services Committee, consideration was given to maybe continuing it [the New GI Bill test"program] for [another] three years and then taking a look. But since it has been so successful and has done so much for the armed services, and has done so much to help so many young people get an education, we think it is better to go ahead

Strom Thurmond

and approve the bill. That is the reason I made the motion in the Senate Armed Services Committee that it be approved.

"Mr. President, I think this is a good bill. I think it is very helpful. I believe it benefits all concerned. Therefore, I hope our colleagues will pass this bill as it is now written.

"Mr. President, I yield the floor."[11]

> "… I MADE THE MOTION IN THE SENATE ARMED SERVICES COMMITTEE THAT [S. 12] BE APPROVED."
> —*Senator Strom Thurmond, South Carolina*

Mr. Cohen

Bill Cohen

"Mr. President, the legislation we are considering today is one of the most significant measures the Senate will act on in the 100th Congress… .

"When I first introduced legislation in 1979 to restore [non-contributory GI Bill] benefits, our military services were facing serious problems, and both from the standpoint of quality and quantity, they were unable to recruit the people they needed… .

"Secretary of the Navy John Lehman testified [in the Senate Armed Services Committee] that if he had to choose between having new ships or having more and better qualified people, he would take the men and women each time. And the Army Chief of Staff, Gen. Edward "Shy" Meyer, told us of the 'hollow Army' which was desperately in need of GI Bill benefits to encourage educationally motivated men and women to consider Army service.

"Despite these calls for assistance, the fight to restore GI Bill benefits was not an easy one. In 1983, Bill Armstrong and I stood on the floor, making what we felt was a persuasive case for these benefits, only to be narrowly defeated on procedural grounds. We were joined by Alan Cranston, Spark Matsunaga, and Fritz Hollings, both in that floor battle and in other legislative efforts to bring these much deserved benefits to service personnel.

> "WE SHOULD REMEMBER THAT WHEN GI BILL BENEFITS WERE ESTABLISHED IN 1944, THEY WERE THE INITIAL STEP IN THE FEDERAL PROVISION OF EDUCATIONAL ASSISTANCE."
> —*Senator Bill Cohen, Maine*

"Finally, in 1984, there was a breakthrough. Sonny Montgomery, who has really been the spearhead in this effort, won approval of his bill on the House side. We were not quite as successful here, but in the House-Senate conference on the Defense Authorization Bill for Fiscal Year 1985, we were able to win approval of a test program of educational benefits.

"The battle was not an easy one. It came down to the wee hours of the morning on the last day of the conference, and there were those who said they would close down the conference before they would agree to a GI Bill provision. Sonny stood his ground and the test program was accepted.

"We should remember that when GI Bill benefits were established in 1944, they were the initial step in the federal provision of educational assistance. Until 1965, the GI Bill stood virtually alone as a source of aid to post-secondary students. And as late as 1975, the Vietnam-era GI Bill provided over 50 percent of all student aid to those in post-secondary schools.

"It gives me great pleasure to see this once seemingly unattainable goal achieved today. The young men and women serving in our armed forces will have this important benefit as a recognition of the great contributions they are making to their nation through that service."[12]

Mr. Matsunaga

Spark Matsunaga

"As the chairman of the Trade Subcommittee of the Senate Finance Committee, I have been involved in efforts to encourage and legislate such training programs [to promote America's role in a modern international economy] but for a variety of reasons there has been some reluctance to implement them. In the GI Bill however, we have a wildly successful training program already at hand which has almost 43 years of history behind it. It would not do to let it slip out of existence."[13]

> "IT WOULD NOT DO TO LET [THE GI BILL] SLIP OUT OF EXISTENCE."
> —*Senator Spark Matsunaga, Hawaii*

Mr. Kennedy

"It is not often that we have an opportunity to pass legislation that both assists directly in our national defense and increases our competitiveness in the world marketplace."[14]

Ted Kennedy

Mr. Simpson

Alan Simpson

"Mr. President, I am pleased to add my wholehearted support to that of my colleagues for the New GI Bill Continuation Act.

"As a veteran and former chairman of the Senate Committee on Veterans' Affairs, I appreciate the value of this measure to our nation and its veterans. I certainly appreciated being able to receive benefits under the original GI Bill, which enabled me to obtain my law degree at the University of Wyoming."[15]

> "I CERTAINLY APPRECIATED BEING ABLE TO RECEIVE BENEFITS UNDER THE ORIGINAL GI BILL, WHICH ENABLED ME TO OBTAIN MY LAW DEGREE AT THE UNIVERSITY OF WYOMING."
> —*Senator Alan Simpson, Wyoming*

Mr. Daschle

"Every year we spend approximately $7 billion dollars on no-obligation educational assistance for college students. This, of course, is a worthy expenditure and a prudent investment in the future of our country. But we should not forget that it is also important that educational assistance be provided to those patriotic young people who have agreed to delay their education so that they can serve their country in a tour of military service."[16]

Tom Daschle

Mr. Montgomery

Again, the final tally, 89 to 0 in favor of S. 12, as amended![17]

> "EVERY YEAR WE SPEND APPROXIMATELY $7 BILLION ON NO-OBLIGATION EDUCATIONAL ASSISTANCE FOR COLLEGE STUDENTS... WE SHOULD NOT FORGET... THOSE PATRIOTIC YOUNG PEOPLE WHO HAVE AGREED TO DELAY THEIR EDUCATION SO THAT THEY CAN SERVE THEIR COUNTRY..."
> —*Senator Tom Daschle, South Dakota*

HOW S. 12 HAPPENED

Army Times
An Independent Newspaper Serving Army People

| , NO. 40 | MAY 18, 1987 | ©1987 Times Journal Co. | $1.75 |

Senate Votes to Make New GI Bill Permanent

By RICK MAZE
Times Staff Writer

WASHINGTON — The Senate voted unanimously May 8 to make the New GI Bill a permanent educational benefit.

The House earlier overwhelmingly passed go along with the proposal.

Sen. John Glenn, D-Ohio, a long-time supporter of veterans' educational benefits, who wanted to extend the current test program rather than make it permanent to allow more time to study the plan, said, "It's a big move to make something like this permanent."

One method of modifying the program to prevent the manpower drain would be to allow service members to transfer the educational benefits to their children, Glenn said. The senator promised to study the idea next year.

The services support the idea of transferring they are getting in to use the benefits)," he said.

Let's reflect a little now. Here's what Mr. Rick Maze, congressional editor of the *Army Times,* wrote about the vote. It's a helpful 20-paragraph article because it summarizes the many competing policy views associated with the bill:[18]

Mr. Maze

Rick Maze

"The Senate voted unanimously May 8 to make the New GI Bill a permanent education benefit. The House earlier overwhelmingly passed similar legislation.

"A short House-Senate conference will be necessary before the legislation becomes final to work out the one small difference between the House and Senate bills: the House wants to rename the New GI Bill the 'Montgomery GI Bill' in recognition of the efforts of Rep. G.V. 'Sonny' Montgomery (D-MS), the Veterans' Affairs Committee chairman who has championed the educational benefits package. The Senate bill contains no such provision and is expected to go along with the proposal… .

"… Sen. John Glenn (D-OH), a long-time supporter of veterans' educational benefits, who wanted to extend the current test program rather than make it permanent to allow more time to study the plan, said, 'it's a big move to make something like this permanent.'

John Glenn

"Despite his doubts, Glenn said he based his final decision on the belief 'the program will undoubtedly help a lot of young people get an education they

> ## "IT CANNOT HELP BUT GET PEOPLE IN, BUT THEY ARE GETTING IN TO GET OUT [TO USE THE BENEFITS]."
> —*Senator John Glenn, Ohio*

would otherwise not get… whether it helps the services in recruiting or not, we ought to support this legislation,' he said… .

"… Glenn said he is concerned that the program may hurt the military in the long run by encouraging people to leave in order to use the benefits. 'It cannot help but get people in, but they are getting in to get out [to use the benefits],' he said.

"'One method of modifying the program to prevent the manpower drain would be to allow service members to transfer the educational benefits to their children,' Glenn said. The senator promised to study the idea next year… .

"… The services support the idea of transferring the benefits, believing that earning educational benefits that could later be given to children could also be a recruiting tool as well and keep members

from feeling compelled to leave the service to use the benefits.

"Sen. Alan Cranston (D-CA), the Senate Veterans' Affairs committee chairman, said making the bill permanent is an important symbol of support for people who volunteer for military service, and that offering the educational benefits will help the services 'meet the challenge' of continuing to operate without a military draft… .

"… Senate passage became assured after the legislation cleared what could have been a major stumbling block in the Armed Services Committee.

"The Armed Services Committee unanimously approved making the New GI Bill permanent only after a massive lobbying effort by military organizations, lawmakers who supported the bill, and even Pentagon officials who once opposed making the program permanent.

"… Chapman B. Cox, DoD's top military manpower official, told military legislative liaison officers to quietly let Senators know that the Pentagon supported making the current program permanent, even though the official administration position was to reduce program costs, military sources said.

"Key Senate aides said the Pentagon switch probably had little effect on the outcome or the vote because the private position of the services was already known. However, Cox's decision to lobby for the legislation did not escape notice at the White House Office of Management and Budget… .

"… OMB Director James Miller called Defense Secretary Caspar Weinberger to complain about Cox's failure to follow the Administration line, although Weinberger did not take the criticism very 'seriously,' said a key official involved in the last-minute lobbying effort.

"Most of the pressure was aimed at Sen. Strom Thurmond (R-SC), a senior Armed Services Committee member who shocked the bill's supporters by speaking against the measure in a closed-door session… .

"… Although other committee members, particularly Chairman Sen. Sam Nunn (D-GA), and Glenn, chairman of the Manpower and Personnel Subcommittee, also objected to making the program permanent, Thurmond's opposition seemed out of character to supporters

> **"NUNN DELAYED THE COMMITTEE VOTE ON THE MEASURE FOR FOUR DAYS AFTER THE SENATORS PRESENT APPEARED EVENLY DIVIDED…"**
> —*Rick Maze, Army Times, May 18, 1987*

and opponents because he was one of the bill's 58 cosponsors.

"Nunn delayed the committee vote on the measure for four days after the Senators present appeared evenly divided on the issue and key supporters, including Sen. Edward Kennedy (D-MA), were unable to attend the session, aides said.

"… The four-day delay allowed supporters to pressure Thurmond to switch his position, and the pressure worked. He dropped his opposition in the committee and spoke in favor of the measure on the Senate floor, expressing no reservations about indefinitely continuing the program.

"The New GI Bill took effect July 1, 1985, in what was to have been a three-year test period. Under the voluntary program, active-duty recruits who forfeit $100 a month in pay for one year are eligible for basic, post-service deduction benefits of $300 a month for three years of active service or a combination of two years' active and four years' inactive service. The basic benefit is $250 a month for three years for a two-year active-duty enlistment… .

"… In addition to the basic benefits, the Army and Navy offer supplemental benefits for those who enter critically needed skills. The maximum monthly post-service benefit legally can be as much as $1,300, although a $400-a-month supplement is the current limit [on the $1,300].

"For Reservists, no contribution is required. Those who enlist for six years can receive $140 a month in educational benefits without having to wait until the obligation is completed."

Mr. Montgomery

On May 13, the House and Senate resolved minor differences between H.R. 1085 and S. 12, both as amended.[19]

Th 89-0 Senate vote on May 8 mentioned earlier was anticlimactic. Any members who may initially have had reservations in the Armed Services Committee voted "aye."

> SENATE ACCEPTED HOUSE'S MGIB-NAMING PROVISION, IN H.R. 1085, AS AMENDED.
>
> HOUSE ACCEPTED SENATE'S ENHANCE-OUR-NATION'S COMPETITIVENESS PURPOSE CLAUSE IN S.12, AS AMENDED.

THE ENROLLED BILL

H.R. 1085—the enrolled bill—was signed on May 19, 1987,[20] by Speaker of the House Jim Wright of Texas and President Pro Tempore of the Senate John Stennis of my home state of Mississippi, which we'll see in a minute. Thirty-six House members and Alan Simpson attended the enrolled-bill signing ceremony in Statuary Hall at the Capitol.[21] In addition, some 40 representatives of military personnel associations, veterans' organizations, each service branch's leadership, service branch GI Bill program managers, the higher education community, and service members participating in the New GI Bill were present, as well.[22]

House Speaker Jim Wright, D-Texas, (center) appears at a rare congressional bill-signing ceremony to mark final passage of legislation making the New GI Bill a permanent education benefit. At left is G.V. "Sonny" Montgomery, D-Miss., author of the bill.

H.R. 1085—the enrolled bill—is signed on May 19, 1987, by Speaker of the House Jim Wright (D-TX).

How does the President know whether to sign a bill?

The Office of Management and Budget's Assistant Director for Legislative Reference sends the enrolled bill to the cabinet department (or departments) that would have responsibility for implementing the bill and who would be most affected by it.

In this case, OMB, housed at the New Executive Office Building, sent the enrolled bill (H.R. 1085, as amended) to the Veterans' Administration and Defense Department. VA and DoD had two days to comment on H.R. 1085 with the following OMB-furnished guidance: "Your cooperation in meeting this deadline is needed to provide maximum time for the Presidential action on the enrolled bill."[23]

HOW DOES THE PRESIDENT KNOW WHETHER TO SIGN A BILL?

4 PENTAGRAM — Thursday, May 21, 1987

Permanent GI Bill signed into law

House Speaker Rep. Jim Wright (D-Texas) signed a document making the New G.I. Bill a permanent measure Tuesday at the Capitol.

Without this provision, the New G.I. Bill would have expired in 1988.

Wright said that the country needs a bill like this. During an address in January he said the World War II G.I. Bill was a "very good investment" for the country. "It sent an entire generation of Americans to college, and our country has been reaping the dividends since."

Wright stressed that the New G.I. Bill has been instrumental in keeping the quality of recruits for all services at an all time high.

Since the Bill was adopted more than 293,000 active duty recruits have participated in the program. The Army has the highest percentage of recruits in the system with 81 percent enrolled. The Navy has 58 percent of the recruits in the system while the Marines have 76 percent. The Air Force has 45 percent of recruits taking advantage of the opportunity.

The bill, sponsored by Mississippi Congressman G.V. "Sonny" Montgomery in 1984, is limited to individuals who entered service after July 1, 1985. Unless recruits opt out of the system, they are automatically enrolled. Those who chose to participate have their pay reduced by $100 per month for 12 months. The money is not refundable to servicemembers. Once they take advantage of the system they are eligible for $300 per month for 36 months (based on three years of active service or two years of active duty and four years of Guard or Reserve duty) or $250 per month for 36 months (based on two years of active duty).

In addition to the New G.I. Bill, soldiers can receive a kicker from the Army College Fund which is paid by the Department of Defense to soldiers who enlist in critical jobs. This benefit can go as high as $400 per month. Supplemental benefits can raise the total to $1,300 per month.

The New G.I. Bill covers college education, on-the-job and apprentice training, correspondence courses and VA work-study programs. (MDW Public Affairs)

House Speaker Representative Jim Wright speaks to dignitaries assembled for the signing of the amended G.I. Bill at Statutary Hall in the Capitol. The signing officially made the G.I. Bill permanent. (Photo by Steve Baker)

Here is some paraphrased language from Administrator of Veterans Affairs Tom Turnage's May 20, 1987, letter to OMB director Jim Miller:[24]

Mr. Turnage

Tom Turnage

"We favor making the New GI Bill a permanent program... . We recommend that the President sign this enrolled bill... . We have prepared, for your consideration, a proposed signing statement which is enclosed."

> "WE RECOMMEND THAT THE PRESIDENT SIGN THIS ENROLLED BILL. WE HAVE PREPARED... A PROPOSED SIGNING STATEMENT..."
> —*Thomas Turnage, Administrator of Veterans Affairs*

Mr. Montgomery

Needless to say, President Reagan planned to sign the bill and Vice President George H.W. Bush recommended a signing ceremony in the Rose Garden.

Howard Baker, Chief of Staff to President Reagan, sent the following memorandum to Vice President George H.W. Bush on May 14, 1987—six days before Administrator Turnage had commented on the bill:[25]

Mr. Baker

Howard Baker

"I concur with your recommendation that there be a signing ceremony at the White House, and I have asked Will Ball to take the necessary steps to bring it about. I do not have the details yet as to timing and the size of the crowd that the President will invite, but we can work that out.

"You can be sure that Sonny will get a fair share of the credit for this hard-fought legislation. Thanks for the heads up."

THE WHITE HOUSE
WASHINGTON

May 14, 1987

MEMORANDUM FOR THE VICE PRESIDENT

FROM: HOWARD H. BAKER, JR.

SUBJECT: SIGNING CEREMONY FOR THE G.I. BILL

I concur with your recommendation that there be a signing ceremony at the White House, and I have asked Will Ball to take the necessary steps to bring it about. I do not have the details yet as to timing and the size of the crowd that The President will invite, but we can work that out. You can be sure that Sonny will get a fair share of the credit for this hard-fought legislation.

Thanks for the heads up.

Memo about the signing ceremony.

United States Senate
COMMITTEE ON VETERANS' AFFAIRS
WASHINGTON, DC 20510-6375

July 9, 1987

Ms. Jill Cochran
Professional Staff Member
Committee on Veterans' Affairs
U.S. House of Representatives
Washington, D.C. 20515

Dear Jill,

I wish to express my deep appreciation for your outstanding work on the enactment of "The Montgomery GI Bill" (Public Law 100-48). Committee staff has kept me well informed of the excellent assistance you provided them, beginning last December during our preparations for introducing S. 12, The New GI Bill Continuation Act, right on through the exhilarating 89-to-0 Senate vote in favor of the legislation on May 8 and final passage on May 13.

Your professionalism, good spirit, and sound advice were of great value to me and our Committee. Our relationship with you reminded me of the great esteem I had for your father and how productive and warm our relationship was for so many years.

With warm regards,

Cordially,

Alan Cranston
Chairman

cc: Honorable Sonny Montgomery

Appreciation letter to Ms. Cochran from Senator Cranston.

Mr. Montgomery

In our bicameral legislature, I found it heartening when an elected member of one body took the time to commend a staffer in the other body.

On the previous page is the letter the chairman of the Senate Committee on Veterans' Affairs sent Ms. Cochran of our Veterans' Affairs Committee staff.[26]

I am indebted to Ms. Cochran's considerable skills and good counsel in getting our bill to the White House.

Further, here is the note Vice President George H.W. Bush personally typed to me regarding a Rose Garden signing ceremony… [27]

Vice President Bush

"Dear Gillesp: Keep this to yourself lest it fall through the cracks. I hope they do it when I'm in town. After all my dedicated work at your side on this, I want to be in the front row. Seriously. Well done!"

Bushy

THE VICE PRESIDENT
WASHINGTON

(self-typed)

May 19, 1987

Dear Gillesp:

Keep this to yourself lest it fall through the cracks. i hope they do it when I'm in town. After all my dedicated work at your side on this, I want to be in the front row.

Seriously, Well Done!

Bushy

Mr. Montgomery

Since my first name is Gillespie, the Vice President always called me "Gillesp."

Indeed, Vice President Bush played a valued "behind-the-scenes"-type role within the Administration in getting the legislation passed.[28] And, in the process, I believe he helped give many young Americans a four-year, post-service education opportunity they might not have been able to afford.

ROSE GARDEN

On June 1, 1987, in a Rose Garden ceremony, President Ronald Reagan made what my colleagues and I referred to as a New GI Bill for the All-Volunteer Force the law of the land, as a permanent recruiting and readjustment tool. Said the President:[29]

President Reagan

"Thank you. Welcome to the White House… .In signing this bill, we're providing not only for the future of our service men and women, but for America, too… our military forces are only as

President Ronald Reagan

President Reagan signs the Montgomery GI Bill June 1, 1987.

good as the men and women who man them, and in this high-tech age, we need an increasingly educated and motivated military guarding our country… I've had the privilege these last few years to visit often with our military men and women—from Quantico to the DMZ in Korea—and I can tell you they're among the finest bunch that this country has ever seen… .(applause)"

"I want to pay a special tribute today to Congressman Sonny Montgomery… your great efforts have made this day possible… and now, that's enough out of me. I'll start writing and sign the bill (applause)."

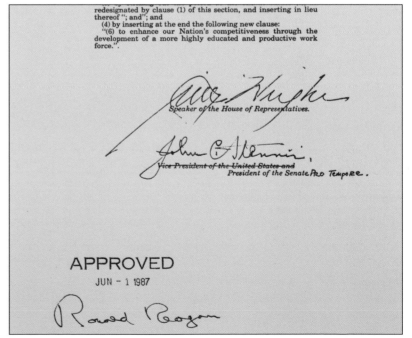

redesignated by clause (1) of this section, and inserting in lieu thereof "; and"; and

(4) by inserting at the end the following new clause:
"(6) to enhance our Nation's competitiveness through the development of a more highly educated and productive work force.".

Speaker of the House of Representatives.

Vice President of the United States and President of the Senate Pro Tempore.

APPROVED

JUN - 1 1987

Ronald Reagan

President Reagan's signature on the Montgomery GI Bill.

ONE OF THE BEST FEDERAL INVESTMENTS SINCE BETSY ROSS BOUGHT NEEDLE AND THREAD

Mr. Montgomery

Was making the GI Bill permanent in 1987 a good public policy?

On June 5, 1990, President George H.W. Bush, flanked by then-Secretary of Defense Dick Cheney, led a ceremony commemorating the one millionth service member to sign up for the Montgomery GI Bill, as of that day. The Montgomery GI Bill is all about the service members. Indeed, they are engaging and resourceful people.[30]

President George H.W. Bush commemorates the one millionth service member to sign up for the Montgomery GI Bill.

Said the President:[31]

"Today, the Montgomery GI Bill ranks among the most practical, cost-efficient programs ever devised and represents one of the best federal investments since Betsy Ross bought thread and needle."

I want to say a few words about Secretary of the Army John Marsh. His quiet leadership was critical to the enactment of the Montgomery GI Bill.

In regard to their leadership style, I think Secretary Marsh and General Max Thurman perhaps, too, were a bit like the "skunk at the picnic" that Secretary Powell referred to earlier.

A former Congressman from Virginia, John Marsh served as Secretary of the Army from January 1981 until August 1989, the longest of any military secretary in U.S. history. Republican President Reagan selected Marsh, a Democrat, for this position.[32]

John and I worked closely together, even though he was part of the Executive Branch and my colleagues and I were in the Legislative Branch. Secretary Weinberger gave Secretary Marsh the support he asked for—and needed—in supporting our legislation.[33]

Mr. Marsh

"Sonny Montgomery knew more members of Congress than anyone else. Sonny had an affable nature. And he liked people. Every time he saw his friend George H.W. Bush he mentioned the need for a New GI Bill. Heck, as a former member, President Bush could have had his own locker in the House gym, but he just shared Sonny's!"[34]

John Marsh

"Sonny was like the 'Fuller Brush salesman' of saving the All-Volunteer Force. If I saw Sonny in the coffee shop or at a Kennedy Center gala, he'd be talking about the same thing—a New GI Bill."[35]

Mr. Montgomery

Colonel Michael Meese, Ph.D., a labor economist and head of the Social Sciences Department at the U.S. Military Academy, sums up:[36]

Col. Meese

"Transitioning to the All-Volunteer Force was the most important change the Army made since World War II; the Montgomery GI Bill was the policy vehicle that allowed this to happen."

Col. Meese and Cadet Shawn Goodin in 2008.

FELLOWSHIP AND CELEBRATION

Writing a law that took seven years called for a celebration and distributing replica versions of the signed law.

Sonny celebrates the signing of the Montgomery GI Bill with Admiral Richard Crowe, chairman of the Joint Chiefs of Staff.

Sonny with Tom Miller, Blinded Veterans Association.

Sonny and HVAC staff Mack Fleming with a replica of the signed Montgomery GI Bill.

From left, Rep. Roy Dyson (D-MD), Sen. Ted Kennedy (D-MA), and Sonny.

Sonny with, from left, Mack Fleming, Rep. Claude Harris, Jr. (D-AL) and HVAC staff member John Brizzi.

Front row, from left, Paralyzed Veterans of America staff Frank DeGeorge, Bob Moran and Gordon Mansfield. In back with Sonny, Doug Vollmer.

Sonny with Mary Stout, Vietnam Veterans of America.

From left, Lt. Col. Al Bemis, Sonny, and Lt. General Bob Elton.

From left, Mylio Kraja, American Legion; Chuck Jackson, NCOA; Cooper Holt, VFW; and Gordon Mansfield, PVA.

Sonny's Lessons Learned

Principle and merit count in a democracy, including when they may hurt the elected official politically.

Even though the military personnel, veterans, and higher education organizations favored our bill, Chairman Glenn still had doubts, as did Sentaors Tower, Nunn and others.

Senator Glenn sponsored the Citizen-Soldier GI Bill amendment as part of the FY 1985 DoD Authorization Act. But Mr. Glenn felt the "economic rent"—that is the annual, recurring cost of an improved post-service education incentive—was too high, relative to the numbers of new enlistees our military would get annually.

In my view, my colleagues and I were right, on principle and merit. And we also had the support of the groups that I mentioned above because they thought we were right on the merits of our proposal as well, especially after we tested the New GI Bill concept for two years.

Nevertheless, I very much appreciate Chairman Glenn's resolve because he continued to carry on the debate with the many groups that opposed his view. He initially could have relented to the pressure they exerted. But he didn't do so. It appears the chairman didn't think the New GI Bill test program was successful enough to make it permanent public policy.

I suspect the chairman would say he put the merits of the issue first. Not everyone would be willing to do so. I admire that.

WHAT'S NEXT

The service branches and the United States Department of Veterans Affairs implement the Montgomery GI Bill. Let's see how well it turns out.

Worth Repeating

"... The often-used Washington saying of 'blood, hair, and eyeballs' all over the floor may very well apply as Senators debated the 'opportunity cost' of the program."

—*Anonymous*

"I'm glad Joe is on your committee... Now, whenever anyone says, 'Who does that darn Kennedy think he is?' —there's a 50-50 chance they don't mean me!"

—*Senator Edward Kennedy*

"I cannot begin to tell the Senate all the machinations, the parliamentary maneuvers, the hearings, the debate, the acrimony involved in getting the GI Bill restored."

—*Senator Bill Armstrong*

"The battle was not an easy one. It came down to the wee hours of the morning on the last day of the conference, and there were those who said they would close down the conference before they would agree to a GI Bill provision. Sonny stood his ground and the test program was accepted."

—*Senator Bill Cohen*

"The Armed Services Committee unanimously approved making the New GI Bill permanent only after a massive lobbying effort by military organizations, lawmakers who supported the bill, and even Pentagon officials who once opposed making the program permanent... ."

—*Rick Maze, Army Times*

"Dear Gillesp... after all my dedicated work at your side on this, I want to be in the front row. Seriously. Well done! Bushy"

—*Vice President George H.W. Bush*

"Thank you. Welcome to the White House... in signing this bill, we're providing not only for the future of our servicemen and women, but for America, too."

—*President Ronald Reagan*

15

SONNY'S
CAST OF
CHARACTERS

*Rick Maze, Congressional
Editor, Navy Times*

*Jim Holley,
Public Affairs Officer,
House Committee
on Veterans' Affairs*

*Honorable George H.W. Bush,
41st President
of the United States*

General Norman Schwarzkopf, U.S. Army

*Honorable Bill Clinton,
42nd President of the United States*

*General John Shalikashvili,
Chairman, Joint Chiefs of Staff*

*Philip Odeen, Chairman,
National Defense Panel*

*Anthony Principi,
Chairman, Congressional Commission
on Service Members and
Veterans Transition Assistance*

*Honorable Gary Hart, Co-Chairman,
U.S. Commission on National Security/
21st Century*

*Vice Admiral Patricia Tracey,
Deputy Assistant Secretary of Defense*

*Representative
Christopher H. Smith
(R-NJ),
Chairman,
Committee on
Veterans' Affairs*

*Representative
Lane Evans (D-IL),
Ranking Democratic
Member, Committee
on Veterans' Affairs*

*Colonel Bob Norton,
U.S. Army (Ret),
Deputy Director of
Government
Relations, Military
Officers Association
of America*

*Nancy Gibbs,
TIME Magazine*

*Ed Elmendorf,
Vice President,
American Assn. of
State Colleges and
Universities*

*Mike McGrevey,
former Vice President,
Mississippi
State University*

1987-Present—
Effect of the Montgomery GI Bill:
Creating a Recruiting and Educational Incentive

SONNY'S SUMMARY

Surveys consistently show the Montgomery GI Bill is the primary incentive to which military enlistees respond and that we continue to recruit youth of uniformly high quality. National study group reports of 1997, 1999, and 2001 all warned of the need for a strong military to protect the United States from attacks by rogue nations and international terrorist groups and the continued need for recruiting high-quality youth into our military.

Through legislation primarily sponsored by Representative Chris Smith (R-NJ) and Senators Arlen Specter (R-PA) and "Jay" Rockefeller (D-WV), President George W. Bush signed H.R. 1291, the Veterans Education and Benefits Expansion Act of 2001, into law, including a record 46-percent increase in the Montgomery GI Bill over three years. House Budget Committee Chairman Jim Nussle (R-IA) and Ranking Member John Spratt (D-SC) authored some $7 billion in direct-spending increases for this bill in the Congressionally approved FY 2002 Budget Resolution.

In addition, from 2002 to 2004 alone, Congress made six major eligibility enhancements to the Montgomery GI Bill.

Lastly, in 2008, Senators Jim Webb (D-VA) and Chuck Hagel (R-NE) primarily authored legislation enacted into law that enhanced the Montgomery GI Bill's purchasing power; and created a more generous "Post 9-11 GI Bill" for enlistees that included two original provisions from H.R. 1400, the proposed Veterans' Educational Assistance Act of 1981.

1987

Mr. Montgomery

Folks, the first three years of Montgomery GI Bill implementation saw continued enthusiasm for it as evidenced by high sign-up rates, including enlistees who scored in the upper quartiles on the Armed Forces Qualification Test.

I was pleased the program was working, as these service members would soon be asked to appear on the world stage, indeed a dangerous place.

NERA ON CAPITOL HILL

by Representative G.V. "Sonny" Montgomery

The new GI Bill becomes permanent

Speaker of the House Jim Wright has stated: "The very best financial investment this country ever made was the GI Bill of Rights at the end of World War II. It sent a whole generation of Americans to college and our country has been reaping the dividends ever since." He is absolutely right, and we want to keep on reaping those dividends.

High technology and sophisticated weaponry in today's Armed Forces demands well-trained, disciplined, and goal-oriented personnel. The primary ingredient for a truly strong military is high quality people. This philosophy was the basis for developing a responsible educational incentive for military recruiting.

For active duty personnel who have joined since June 30, 1985, the latest GI Bill offers $300 a month for up to 36 months--for college, vocational or technical training, or graduate study. In return, individuals must enlist for three years and accept a pay reduction of $100 a month for their first 12 months of service. Thus, an investment of only $1,200 provides a minimum $10,800 return in education. Unless they opt out, all recruits are enrolled automatically, and recruiters explain the program carefully.

Reserve and Guard participants are eligible for $140 a month for up to 36 months in return for a six-year enlistment or re-enlistment. They may use these benefits only at degree-granting institutions of higher learning. There is no pay reduction, however, and benefits can begin after six months service. About 70,000 Guard and Reserve personnel are already going to school under this program. The Veterans Administration funds the basic active duty entitlement, while the Department of Defense funds Guard and Reserve benefits.

Although the current GI Bill was first enacted in 1985, it applied only on a temporary "trial" basis. Made permanent by legislation enacted June 1, 1987, this fourth GI Bill is already credited with a marked increase in high-quality recruits for all service branches.

Representative Montgomery chairs the House Committee on Veterans Affairs and serves on the Armed Services Committee.

Forecasting the Storm

Efforts for a new GI bill began in the late 1970s, when we began to get strong indications on Capitol Hill that available manpower was about to put the All Volunteer Force into big trouble. The plug was about to be pulled from the pool of eligible recruits. According to the Census Bureau, in 1981 there were 8.6 million 18- to 21-year-old men. Today, there are 7.4 million. By 1995, this number will have fallen to only 6.6 million.

Studies were reporting that the Armed Forces would have to recruit as many as *one* of every *two* eligible non-college males just to maintain current strength levels. Meanwhile, an improving employment picture was already beginning to challenge our recruiting capabilities.

Numbers weren't the only problem, either. Quality was already in short supply. Readiness was being eroded by discipline and retention problems resulting from the large number of non-high school graduate and lower mental category recruits coming into military service. This contributed to high attrition rates for mid-level noncommissioned officers. One military official noted: "NCOs look down and see squads moving out from underneath them. They no longer have the same number of soldiers, and they don't see many high school graduates. This has a negative impact on NCO attitude."

In the fall of 1980, we began to respond. Along with staff from the Veterans Affairs Committee, I met with each branch of the Armed Forces to etch a blueprint for a new educational assistance program. I introduced the original bill in 1981 and conducted extensive hearings during which the committee received testimony from nearly 200 witnesses. Three years later, this new GI bill became law. Since its beginning as a test program in July 1985, some 400,000 active duty recruits have signed up, in addition to the 70,000 Guard and Reserve personnel.

Now well into its third year, the Montgomery GI Bill has been termed by one military official "the prime mover in our recruiting and retention efforts." Our "All Volunteer" force is actually an "All Recruited"

force. This new GI Bill has enabled the Armed Forces to open a previously untapped recruiting market—college-oriented young people.

New Alliances

In order to attract quality recruits, the Armed Forces must compete with both an expanding job market and educational institutions. Since implementation of the new GI Bill, however, Congress and the military have forged stronger alliances with community and junior colleges, universities, and other training institutions to ensure individuals who desire to further their education may do so--and do so with the knowledge they earned this opportunity by serving their country.

Article by Sonny in "The Mariner," Jan./Feb. 1998, page 10, a publication of the Naval Enlisted Reserve Association.

1988

The year 1988 was important because it was the first year of implementing the permanent New GI Bill program—now by law called the Montgomery GI Bill.

Here are some excerpts from an article I wrote for the January/February edition of *The Mariner*, the magazine of the Naval Enlisted Reserve Association:[1]

"Since its beginning as a test program in July 1985, some 400,000 active duty recruits have signed up, in addition to 70,000 Guard and Reserve personnel... Our 'All-Volunteer' Force is actually an 'all-recruited' force. This New GI Bill has enabled the Armed Forces to open a previously untapped recruiting market—college-oriented young people...

"... In FY 1980, before implementation of the Montgomery GI Bill, 52 percent of the Army's non-prior service accessions were in the lowest mental category (IV). Contrast this with the **four** percent [emphasis in original] Category IVs being accessed during FY 1986. The number of high school graduate recruits increased from 54 to 91 percent during the same period. In addition, the percentage of higher mental category recruits grew from 26 to 63 percent."

Mr. Rick Maze wrote about the implementation of the Montgomery GI Bill in the March 21, 1988, edition of the *Navy Times:*[2]

Mr. Maze

"The [Montgomery] GI Bill is giving the services people who might not otherwise have enlisted. 'I was going to try to save money for college anyway,' Army recruit Barbara Huntley of Toledo, Ohio, said, 'The GI Bill seemed to be a good way to do it.'"

Rick Maze

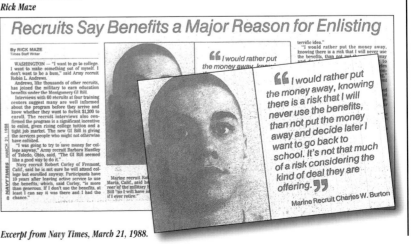

Recruits Say Benefits a Major Reason for Enlisting

By RICK MAZE
Times Staff Writer

WASHINGTON — "I want to go to college. I want to make something out of myself. I don't want to be a bum," said Army recruit Robin L. Andrews.

Andrews, like thousands of other recruits, has joined the military to earn education benefits under the Montgomery GI Bill.

Interviews with 60 recruits at four training centers suggest many are well informed about the program before they arrive and know whether they want to forfeit $1,200 to enroll. The recruit interviews also confirmed the program is a significant incentive to enlist, given rising college tuition and a tight job market. The new GI Bill is giving the services people who might not otherwise have enlisted.

"I was going to try to save money for college anyway," Army recruit Barbara Huntley of Toledo, Ohio, said. "The GI Bill seemed like a good way to do it."

Navy recruit Robert Corley of Fremont, Calif., said he is not sure he will attend college but enrolled anyway. Participants have 10 years after leaving active service to use the benefits, which, said Corley, "is more than generous. If I don't use the benefits, at least I can say it was there and I had the chance."

"I would rather put the money away, knowing there is a risk that I will never use the benefits, than not put the money away and decide later I want to go back to school. It's not that much of a risk considering the kind of deal they are offering."

Marine Recruit Charles W. Burton

Excerpt from Navy Times, March 21, 1988.

Mr. Montgomery

On June 30, 1988, Mr. Jim Holley, Public Affairs Officer for the House Committee on Veterans' Affairs, which I chaired and on which Representative Jerry Solomon (R-NY) served as ranking member, issued a news release. The release commemorated the third anniversary of the New GI Bill, now called the Montgomery GI Bill:[3]

HOUSE VETERANS AFFAIRS COMMITTEE news

335 CANNON H.O.B.
WASHINGTON, D.C. 20515
(202) 225-3527

FOR IMMEDIATE RELEASE   CONTACT: Jim Holley
June 30, 1988

MONTGOMERY GI BILL MARKS THIRD ANNIVERSARY
EDUCATION ASSISTANCE PROGRAM CONTINUES TO ATTRACT BIG NUMBERS AND HIGH QUALITY

WASHINGTON -- Had it not been for its remarkable early success, today might have marked the ending rather than a milestone for the Montgomery GI Bill. The military education assistance program was initially scheduled for a three-year test run when it was implemented on July 1, 1985, but Congress voted last year to make it permanent. President Reagan agreed and enacted it into law in a White House Rose Garden ceremony.

The Montgomery GI Bill has been credited with a marked improvement in the quality of recruits and with giving thousands of young men and women the opportunity to overcome financial barriers to attend college. More than 514 thousand active duty recruits have enrolled in the program and more than 90 thousand reservists have attended school with the benefits.

"We knew it would work, but I don't think we ever dreamed it would work this well," said Rep. G. V. "Sonny" Montgomery (D-MS), the program's author.

The Montgomery GI Bill provides education assistance of $300 a month for up to 36 months in return for a three-year commitment to active-duty service and a $1200 reduction in basic pay over the first 12 months of service; $250 monthly for up to 36 months is provided for a two-year enlistment. Proponents proudly note that the pay reduction for all participants has totaled more than $462 million, which has been returned to the federal treasury and has more than offset the cost of the program thus far. National Guard and Reserve personnel can receive $140 a month for up to 36 months in return for a six-year enlistment or reenlistment, and no pay reduction is required.

Press release issued by House Committee on Veterans' Affairs June 30, 1988.

Mr. Holley

"Had it not been for its remarkable early success, today might have marked the ending rather than a milestone for the Montgomery GI Bill. The military education assistance program was initially scheduled for a three-year test run when it was implemented on July 1, 1985, but Congress voted last

Jim Holley

year to make it permanent.

"The Montgomery GI Bill has been credited with a marked improvement in the quality of recruits and with giving thousands of young men and women the opportunity to overcome financial barriers to attend college. More than 514,000 active

At signing of Montgomery GI Bill in Statuary Hall, Sonny poses with two U.S. Army soldiers.

duty recruits have enrolled in the program and more than 90,000 Reservists have attended school with the benefits…. Proponents proudly note that the pay reduction for all participants has totaled more than $462 million, which has been returned to the federal treasury and has more than offset the cost of the program thus far."

1990

Mr. Montgomery

June 5, 1990, was a wonderful day. President George H.W. Bush held a ceremony honoring the

> *" … TODAY, THE MONTGOMERY GI BILL RANKS AMONG THE MOST PRACTICAL AND COST-EFFICIENT PROGRAMS EVER DEVISED… ."*
> —**President George H.W. Bush**

original GI Bill, as well as the one millionth service member to sign up for the Montgomery GI Bill. Noted the President:[4]

"In October, 1945, Barbara and I joined the ranks of more than 40,000 couples who headed to college that year on the original GI Bill. America's schools were soon swamped with prefab housing and trailers. And by 1946 and 1947, the flood tide had crested, and more than 2.5 million veterans had embarked on getting their education.

"… The GI Bill changed the lives of millions by replacing old roadblocks with paths of opportunity. And in so doing it boosted America's work force, it boosted America's economy, and really, it changed the life of our nation.

"… And I remember some of the tough battles that were fought to get the new bill through Congress. Sonny interrupted one marathon conference session with a rather unique reminder of the needs of the military and of his own commitment to stick it out. He brought in C-rations, and eating them on the Hill is my definition of serious commitment.

"… Today, the Montgomery GI bill ranks among the most practical and cost-efficient programs ever devised… ."

1991

I'd like to share with you three important events that created the New GI Bill, a bill I did not anticipate would include my name in its title.

Sonny visits soldiers during the Persian Gulf War in 1991.

First, during the Persian Gulf War in 1991,[5] I felt honored to go to Kuwait to talk with the many high-quality American soldiers, sailors, airmen, Marines, and Coast Guardsmen of "Operation Desert Storm," who put their lives on the line to liberate that sovereign nation from the occupation by Iraq.

About 95 percent of these soldiers signed up for the Montgomery GI Bill[6] when entering the military; that made my colleagues and me happy!

President George H.W. Bush and troops during Persian Gulf War.

The soldier weeps not for himself.

A daughter reunites with her mother who was captured and taken prisoner by Saddam's Hussein's Iraqi Army.

The Montgomery GI Bill helped bring a new day to the All-Volunteer Force.

First Lady Barbara Bush (center), President Bush, and General Norman Schwarzkopf.

Second, our nation's capital paused to say thanks to the men and women of our country's military, teamed with some 26 coalition countries—including a half-dozen Arab countries—who served during the 1991 Operation Desert Storm to defend Kuwait's sovereignty.[7]

Noted General Norman Schwarzkopf later:

Gen. Schwarzkopf

"It doesn't take a hero to order men into battle. It takes a hero to be one of those men who goes into battle."[8]

"IT DOESN'T TAKE A HERO TO ORDER MEN INTO BATTLE."
—*Gen. Norman Schwarzkopf*

Scenes from the 1991 Desert Storm victory parade in Washington, D.C.

Mr. Montgomery

Richard Darman

And **third**, an interesting experience I had when I left the House floor to take a telephone call from Richard Darman, Director of OMB in the George H.W. Bush White House.

I am pretty sure it was 1992. But I don't think the year is as important as the lesson in communication that Director Darman conveyed.[9]

I was on the House floor with other members who had helped enact the Montgomery GI Bill into law. The House was considering legislation to increase the monthly educational assistance allowance under the Montgomery GI Bill from $350 to $400 per month, as I recall.

I was waiting to ask the House to consider the bill when I was told that OMB Director Darman had telephoned me and was on hold on the phone in the cloak room. So I immediately went to the cloak room and we chatted for five minutes or so.

As I recall, Director Darman said the Administration would support the bill under consideration. But Mr. Darman asked my help in keeping the entitlement cost of the MGIB increase to a figure, I think, of about $200 million.

As I remember it, Director Darman was focusing not so much on the bill we'd pass that day in the House but the cost of the MGIB increase when it came out of conference committee with the Senate.

I believe the Administration wanted to limit the increase to the cost of inflation, as personnel costs, for example, were already more than 50 percent of the DoD budget.[10] I believe I said to Director Darman I especially appreciated his thoughtfulness in personally calling me—and that I'd earnestly consider his request on behalf of the Administration.

I was Democratic Floor Manager for the bill. So, when I got back to my seat in the House chamber, my Committee Chief Counsel Mack Fleming and Deputy Chief Counsel Patrick Ryan asked me the time period over which Director Darman asked Congress to limit the cost.

For example, both the OMB and the Congressional Budget Office project costs of entitlement legislation over one, five and ten years. I said to Mack and Patrick I didn't recall Director Darman specifying a number

Patrick Ryan and Sonny.

of years, although he may have done so. Mack and Patrick immediately assumed it was five years, since that was the usual time frame used for cost estimates.

As I remember it, in the House-Senate conference version of the bill, Congress increased the MGIB by $50 in 1992,[11] so as to spend the $200 million in two years rather than in five or ten years, for example. If we had spread the $200 million in smaller MGIB increases over ten years, it would have had a much more diluted effect, as a financial-aid tool for the veteran student.

I'm not sure our approach was what Director Darman had in mind on a specific cost figure. But I'm not sure either I could have won support from House members by doing it any other way than the way in which the House and Senate ultimately enacted it.

Folks, I share this anecdote with you because it represents some of the reality of lawmaking; the reality of a director, OMB, and a chairman of a committee essentially discussing and negotiating a bill—person to person—while it's under consideration on the House floor.

Direct, informal discussion of this type between the Executive and Legislative Branches represents an effective way to do business, in my view. It cannot happen in every instance; and it may not be something you'll read about in other text books. But it works.

In any case, I appreciated Mr. Darman's forthright and thoughtful communication, as well as his personal involvement. Mr. Darman had a much bigger job than I did. My colleagues and I tried to look after the interests of America's sons and daughters who served in our military in their transition to our civilian economy. Director Darman had to focus on the entire breadth of the United States budget and the nation's vital economic health.

1994

At the celebration, from left, Secretary of Veterans Affairs Jesse Brown, Secret Service agent, President Clinton, Sonny and Garnett Shropshire of the American Legion.

President Clinton and Sec. Brown.

The posting of the colors was a vivid reminder of the men and women who serve.

In June 1994, President Bill Clinton walked from the White House across Lafayette Park to the Department of Veterans Affairs to personally lead a 50th anniversary celebration of the World War II GI Bill.[12]

I'm grateful the President invited me to the occasion.

Army Specialist Mendoza, left, represented Desert Storm veterans.

Secretary of Veterans Affairs Jesse Brown introduced Army Specialist Hugo Mendoza, who represented Desert Storm veterans at the celebration. What an

President Bill Clinton greets VA employees at the 50th anniversary celebration of the WW II GI Bill.

honor to be in Specialist Mendoza's presence.

Secretary Brown was wounded in combat while serving with the U.S. Marine Corps in Vietnam in 1965. He was unable to raise his right arm for the remainder of his life.[13]

Said the President…

President Clinton

"Just as D-Day was the greatest military action in our history, so the GI Bill was arguably the greatest investment in our people in American history.[14]

"The veterans of World War I… got $60 and a train ticket home. The veterans of World War II got a ticket to the American dream."[15]

1995

Mr. Montgomery

Have you heard the term "budget reconciliation?"

In effect, it means that periodically Congress tries to bring federal revenues and spending into line to save money and reduce the federal budget deficit. A more formal definition appears on the U.S. Senate web site:[16]

"[Budget] reconciliation is a process established in the Congressional Budget Act of 1974 by which Congress changes existing laws to

> "JUST AS D-DAY WAS THE GREATEST MILITARY ACTION IN OUR HISTORY, SO THE GI BILL WAS ARGUABLY THE GREATEST INVESTMENT IN OUR PEOPLE IN AMERICAN HISTORY.."
> —*President Bill Clinton*

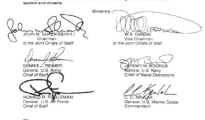

Letter from the Joint Chiefs.

conform tax and spending levels to the levels set in a budget resolution. Changes that are recommended by committees pursuant to a reconciliation instruction are incorporated into a reconciliation measure."

Based on guidance from the Budget Committee, each committee involved has to introduce and mark-up legislation adjusting revenues or spending in their area(s) of jurisdiction.

For example, a proposal under consideration in 1995

Plan to Raise Fee on GI Bill Draws Protest

By Bradley Graham
Washington Post Staff Writer

A Senate move that would require U.S. troops to pay more out of their pockets for GI Bill education benefits has drawn a torrent of protest from Pentagon officials who warn the action would undercut recruiting efforts.

The government's promise to help pay for a college education in return for several years of service ranks as the most popular incentive for joining the military, according to Defense Department surveys. All but about 6 percent of the nation's new privates, seamen and airmen sign up for the program.

But senators have targeted the arrangement as part of an effort to squeeze additional savings from the Veterans Affairs budget, which finances the GI Bill.

Under current law, a servicemember pays $1,200 during his or her first year in the military and, after serving three years, is eligible for nearly $15,000 in education payments. The Senate Veterans' Affairs Committee approved a recommendation last week that would raise from $100 to $133 what new recruits pay monthly into the program, for a total contribution of $1,600. It also would limit the annual rise in the education benefit to half the jump in the cost-of-living index, rather than the full jump added

Proponents of the increase are led by Sen. John D. "Jay" Rockefeller, above. But Gen. John Shalikashvili, chairman of the Joint Chiefs of Staff, below, and other military leaders say recruiting could be affected.

contributions, they say, would constitute a

From the Washington Post, Sept. 29, 1995.

would have increased the $1,200 pay reduction service members pay to be eligible for the Montgomery GI Bill. In this regard, General John Shalikashvili, chairman of the Joint Chiefs of Staff, will speak to his letter of September 28, 1995,[17] to Senator Alan Simpson, chairman, Committee on Veterans' Affairs.

Cosigning the letter were the Vice Chairman of the Joint Chiefs; the Chiefs of Staff of the Army and Air Force; the Chief of Naval Operations; and the Commandant of the Marine Corps.

Although he initially opposed what became known as the Montgomery GI Bill in 1987, Mr. Simpson was one of the first Senators to suggest (some say acknowledge) that the VA—instead of the Department of Defense—would have to fund it. He prevailed! VA funded it because the GI Bill fundamentally is a tool for transitioning from military to civilian life.[18]

As far as I know, Mr. Simpson personally proposed no such cuts in the Montgomery GI Bill under reconciliation.[19] The chiefs wanted to ensure that rank-and-file members of the committee knew their views on possible increases in the $1,200 pay reduction required to be eligible for the Montgomery GI Bill.

Gen. Shalikashvili

"Mr. Chairman, I'll simply highlight a few lines from our 1995 letter to Chairman Simpson:

"As you know, veterans' benefits have provided one of the

Gen. John Shalikashvili

cornerstones of the All-Volunteer Force[20] since its inception and are highly valued by our uniformed personnel.

"In this light, we would like to express our concern for any reduction in the value of the Montgomery GI Bill.

"The significant impact any erosion in benefits will have on our ability to maintain required accession levels and sustain vital force readiness will aggravate an already challenging recruiting environment.

"We strongly urge you to protect benefit levels by maintaining the current individual pay reduction of $1,200 over a 12-month period [and not increasing it under reconciliation].

"In addition to helping us attract the high-quality recruits we need, with your help, the Montgomery GI Bill will continue to enhance our nation's competitiveness through the development of a more highly educated and productive workforce.

"The return to our nation is an investment worth making for national defense, as well as for the training of our nation's future leaders and citizens."

Mr. Montgomery

Ultimately, Congress found **other** reductions in veterans' benefits to meet the reconciliation requirement.[21] Enough said!

AN INCREASINGLY DANGEROUS WORLD...

Fast-forwarding in time shows an increasingly dangerous world, including attacks by terrorist groups over the years on:

- The passenger ship Achille Lauro, 1985;
- Pan Am Flight 193 over Lockerbie, Scotland, 1988;
- The World Trade Center, 1993;
- U.S. embassies in Kenya and Tanzania, Africa, 1993;
- U.S. military personnel at the Khobar Towers housing complex in Saudi Arabia, 1996;
- U.S. Navy ship, USS Cole, 2000; and
- The World Trade Center and the Pentagon, 2001.

Each attack showed how terrorist cells can hurt Americans.

These security vulnerabilities led to compelling reports of expert United States commissions in 1997, 1999, and 2001.

These reports—plus the expert legislative testimony of Vice Admiral Patricia Tracey before the House Veterans' Affairs Committee in 2000—served to shape

significant enhancements to the Montgomery GI Bill from 2000 to 2004.

Each report spoke to the possibility of terrorist attacks within our own borders and the need to recruit quality people to defend us at home.

We, as a nation, would not now only ask civilian police, fire, emergency services, and other first responders to do the job of keeping our cities and communities safe by themselves. We'd ask for our military to play a defined role, as well.

Let's hear from Philip Odeen, chairman of the National Defense Panel. The Panel issued the 1997 report to Secretary of Defense Bill Cohen, *Transforming Defense: National Security in the 21st Century*.[22]

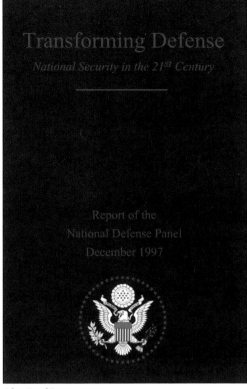

Odeen Panel Report

Mr. Odeen

Philip Odeen

"We must never forget that our people in uniform have been the core of our strength in the past. They, more than any hardware system, form the real defense capability of today and tomorrow.

"Our report also quoted the warnings of Secretary Cohen himself. Here are the Secretary's 1997 words:[23]

"'As the new millennium approaches, we face the very real and increasing prospect that regional aggressors, third-rate armies, terrorist groups, and even religious cults will seek to wield disproportionate power by acquiring and using these weapons that can produce mass casualties. These are neither far-fetched nor far-off threats.'"

[The Transforming Defense report also noted:]

"'We can assume that our enemies and future adversaries have learned from the Gulf War. They are **unlikely** [emphasis added] to confront us conventionally… instead they may find new ways to attack our interests, our forces, and our citizens.'"[24]

1999

Mr. Montgomery

The 1999 report of the bipartisan Congressional Commission on Service Members and Veterans Transition Assistance examined the federal benefits our military earns for its service.[25]

Here's Commission Chairman Anthony Principi. Mr. Principi went on to serve with distinction for four years as President George W. Bush's Secretary of Veterans Affairs and later headed the 2005 [Department of Defense] Base Closure and Realignment Commission:[26]

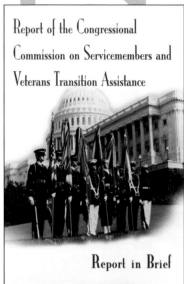

Report of the Congressional Commission on Servicemembers and Veterans Transition Assistance

Report in Brief

Mr. Principi

Anthony Principi

"To defend the country in the 21st century, the Armed Forces must recruit high-quality high school graduates of college caliber. The chief vehicle for accomplishing these goals is the Montgomery GI Bill, a direct descendent of the great World War II GI Bill that helped transform the nation… .

"In enacting the Montgomery GI Bill, a farsighted Congress under the inspired leadership of veterans' champions like Congressman G.V. 'Sonny' Montgomery, severed the link between [strictly] wartime service and education benefits… .

"However, most college-bound youth and their families see a tour of military service as a detour from their college plans, not as a way to achieve that goal… .

"The commission believes the Montgomery GI Bill represents an untapped opportunity for the nation. An enhanced Montgomery GI Bill that would pay for tuition, books, fees, and a monthly subsistence allowance would differentiate, on the basis of quality of education, the educational assistance benefits earned through military service from benefits available to the general public."

Mr. Montgomery

Ladies and gentleman, what the commission recommended was a return to a World War II-type GI Bill. A GI Bill in which—as Chairman Principi said—"veterans of our military could attend any school in America, limited only by their own aspirations, ability and initiative."[27]

NEW WORLD COMING: AMERICAN SECURITY IN THE 21ST CENTURY

The U.S. Commission on National Security/21st Century was initiated over two years ago out of a conviction that the entire range of U.S. national security policies and processes required examination in light of new circumstances that lie ahead.

Phase 1 (July 1998 - August 1999)
The Phase I Report is dedicated to understanding how the world will likely evolve over the next 25 years. It describes global trends in scientific, technological, economic, socio-political and military security domains and the interplay of these developments on U.S. national security.

- MAJOR THEMES AND IMPLICATIONS
- SUPPORTING RESEARCH & ANALYSIS (Adobe Acrobat file)
- STUDY ADDENDUM (Adobe Acrobat file)

Phase 2 (August 1999 - April 2000)
The Phase II Report devised a U.S. national security strategy to deal with the world in 2025. The purpose of the Phase II Report is to define an American strategy based on U.S. interests and key objectives. It develops a strategy for America to reap the benefits of a more integrated world to expand freedom, security, and prosperity and to dampen the forces of instability.

- SEEKING A NATIONAL STRATEGY: A CONCERT FOR PRESERVING SECURITY AND PROMOTING FREEDOM, Phase II Report

Also in 1999, another expert group called the United States Commission on National Security/21st Century and headed by former Senators Gary Hart and Warren Rudman, issued its report titled *New World Coming: American Security in the 21st Century*.[28]

The report also raised concerns about military recruiting by observing:[29]

Mr. Hart

Gary Hart

"Today, the military is having even greater difficulty recruiting quality people than the civilian sector of the government. Despite significant post-Cold War force reductions in recruiting goals, the services have missed their quotas in some recent years. Moreover, recruiting costs have risen by nearly one-third over the last four years… ."

2000

Mr. Montgomery

Here is the testimony of Admiral Tracey in 2000 before the Subcommittee on Benefits, House Committee on Veterans' Affairs, then-chaired by Representative J.D. Hayworth of Arizona:[30]

Vice Admiral Tracey

Vice Admiral Patricia Tracey

"Money for college consistently ranks as the major reason young men and women give for enlisting... ."[31] There is little doubt that the Montgomery GI Bill has met or even exceeded the expectations of its sponsors and has been a major contributor to the success of the All-Volunteer Force.

"The remarkably low unemployment rate, the booming economy, and the increasing propensity for high school seniors to enroll in college immediately upon graduation are such that we now face difficult challenges."

Mr. Montgomery

Students, I would just note for you that "unemployment declined from 7.3 percent in 1992 to 4.7 percent in 1998; about 65 percent of high school graduates ages 18-19 now enroll in higher education."[32]

Out of a universe of say, 100 17- to 21-year-old males, how many do you think the service branches get to recruit from? About 14, as of 2001.

The testimony of Lt. General Timothy Maude,[33] U.S. Army, on May 24, 2001, is instructive:[34]

"... We believe that probably only 14 percent, or about 14 out of every 100, is our target audience when we go about our recruiting... after you eliminate those that are below the aptitude, the mental and moral disqualifications, those in jail, those already in the military, those in college, that leaves about 14 percent of the population, who meet those qualifications."

2001

Lastly, let's cite the 2001 findings and recommendations of the U.S. Commission on National Security/21st Century[35] in its report titled *Road Map for National Security: Imperative for Change.*

Co-chairman Hart, would you please share with our students the commission's findings and recommendations regarding recruiting and an educational incentive?

ROAD MAP FOR NATIONAL SECURITY: IMPERATIVE FOR CHANGE

THE UNITED STATES COMMISSION ON NATIONAL SECURITY/21ST CENTURY

Mr. Hart

"Thank you, Mr. Chairman.

"We must change the ways we recruit military personnel. This means putting greater effort into seeking out youth on college campuses and providing grants and scholarships for promising candidates.[36]

"Congress should significantly enhance the Montgomery GI Bill... .

"The [Montgomery] GI Bill is both a strong recruitment tool and, more importantly, a valuable institutional reward for service to the nation... .

"GI Bill entitlements should equal, at the very least, the median education costs of four year U.S. colleges, and should be indexed to keep pace with increases in those costs. Such a step would have the additional social utility of seeding veterans among the youth at elite colleges... ."[37]

Montgomery GI Bill
The Legacy of Service: The Future of Freedom

Mr. Montgomery

Students, I wanted you to know about the 1997-2001 findings and recommendations of each of these commissions. Their recommendations inspired enhancements to the Montgomery GI Bill, especially in light of the tragic events of September 11, 2001.

By 2003, the United States and its partner nations had liberated Iraq from its brutal dictator, Saddam Hussein.

I was so proud of our soldiers, sailors, airmen, Marines, and Coast Guardsmen who liberated Iraq. I think Nancy Gibbs of *TIME* Magazine said it best in her 2003 "Person of the Year" article:

Ms. Gibbs

"For uncommon skills and service, for the choices each one of them has made and the ones still ahead, for the challenge of defending not only our freedoms but those barely

Nancy Gibbs

stirring half a world away, the American soldier is *TIME's* 'Person of the Year.'[38]

"They swept across Iraq and conquered it in 21 days. They stand on streets potholed with skepticism and rancor. They caught Saddam Hussein. They are the face of America, its might and good will, in a region unused to democracy.[39]

"To have pulled Saddam Hussein from his hole in the ground brings the possibility of pulling an entire country out of the dark.[40]

"… Our pilots and soldiers and sailors are, for starters, all volunteers, in contrast to most nations, which in 2003 conscript those who serve in their armed forces.[41]

"Liberty can't be fired like a bullet into the hard ground. It requires, among other things, time and trust and a nation scarred by tyranny and divided by tribe and faith is not going to turn into Athens overnight.[42]

"It now falls to the Iraqis themselves to decide what they are willing and able to do with the chance they have been given, and the rest of the world to decide how to help."[43]

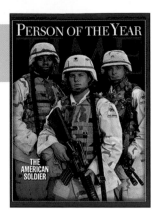

Mr. Montgomery

Representatives Christopher Smith and Lane Evans will speak to enhancements they've championed to the Montgomery GI Bill from 2000 to 2005. The high-energy leadership of these two legislators on behalf of our fellow Americans who have worn the military uniform has been exceptional.

2004

Mr. Smith

Christopher Smith

"We've each served in Congress for about 22 years. Lane offered the amendment at committee mark-up in 1987 to name the New GI Bill the 'Montgomery GI Bill' and I was a cosponsor with the chairman in 1981 when he introduced the New GI Bill legislation.

"We also had the good fortune to follow in Mr. Montgomery's footsteps by serving as chairman and ranking Democratic member, respectively, of the House Veterans' Affairs Committee from 2001-2004."

A C-17 transport plane named the "Spirit of Sonny Montgomery."

Mr. Evans

Lane Evans

"As Chris and I see it, the Montgomery GI Bill and the spirit and vision of Sonny Montgomery indeed represent part of the continuing legacy of the World War II GI Bill—the law that works!

"We worked with Senate Veterans' Affairs Committee Chairman Arlen Specter (R-PA) and Ranking Minority Members Jay Rockefeller (D-WV) (through 2002) and then Senator Bob Graham (D-FL) (through 2004), in making the Montgomery GI Bill even more comprehensive.

"On December 27, 2001, President George W. Bush signed into law H.R. 1291, the Veterans Education and Benefits Expansion Act of 2001. Public Law 107-103 boosted Montgomery GI Bill education benefits from $24,192 in December 2001 to $35,460 in October 2003, an increase of $11,268. This was the largest increase in the Montgomery GI Bill's history. The Congressional Budget Office estimated the cost of these increases over 10 years at $6.8 billion."[44]

Mr. Smith

"I was very grateful for President Bush's support in signing H.R. 1291—and to Jim Nussle (R-IA) and John Spratt (D-SC), chairman and ranking member of the House Budget Committee.

"I met with Chairman Nussle at every opportunity; in his office, on the House floor, and seemingly each time I saw the chairman I made the empirical case for the 46-percent Montgomery GI Bill increase over three years embodied in H.R. 1291, which I introduced as a bipartisan measure.

"Chairman Nussle and Ranking Member Spratt included the bill's ultimate $6.8 billion 'direct spending' increase in the House- and Senate-passed budget blueprint for FY 2002. Jim and I also discussed the inclusion of the Montgomery GI Bill increase in the budget blueprint in the colloquy on the House floor, as documented in the *Congressional Record*.

Rep. Chris Smith and Sonny in 1987.

"It would have been impossible for Lane, me and HVAC Subcommittee on Economic Opportunity Chairman Mike Simpson to have identified some $6.8 billion in offsets over 10 years to pay the bill.

"Nevertheless, From 2000-2004 alone, Congress enhanced the Montgomery GI Bill in six major areas, each time meeting pay-as-you-go requirements. Congress, for example:

- Accelerated Montgomery GI Bill benefits payments for high-cost, high-technology courses;[45]

- Protected against loss of Montgomery GI Bill benefits resulting from military mobilization or deployment;[46]

- Enabled use of the Montgomery GI Bill for entrepreneurship courses offered by U.S. Small Business Development Centers;[47]

- Enabled use of these benefits for occupational licensing and credentialing testing[48]; and

- Updated significantly the Montgomery GI Bill on-job training and apprenticeship benefits to reflect business and industry today, including competency standards."[49]

Mr. Montgomery

Representative Smith has been a New GI Bill leader from the beginning. And I know of no member of Congress who has authored more improvements to the Montgomery GI Bill than former Marine, Representative Lane Evans.

Sonny and Lane Evans in 2004.

Michael Michaud   *Henry Brown*

Representatives Jack Quinn (R-NY), J.D. Hayworth (R-AZ), Mike Simpson (R-ID), Bob Filner (D-CA), Silvestre Reyes (D-TX), Henry Brown, Jr. (R-SC), and Michael Michaud (D-ME) all played leadership roles in improving selected aspects of the Montgomery GI Bill.[50]

As we continue to rely more and more on the Guard and Reserve, I think we need to make their education benefits more equal to our regular, active-duty military.

2006

Let's hear from Bob Norton, deputy director of government relations for the Military Officers Association of America and a principal in the Partnership for Veterans' Education, a Washington-based organization made up of military personnel associations, veterans' organizations, and higher education associations.

I'd note, too, that Mr. Larry Rhea, legislative director of the Non Commissioned Officers Association of the U.S.; Mr. Sid Daniels, legislative director of the Veterans of Foreign Wars of the U.S.; Mr. Don Sweeney, legislative director of the National Association of State Approving Agencies; and Dr. Steve Kime, president of the Servicemembers Opportunity Colleges, were among the principals in forming the Partnership for Veterans' Education in 2000.

Mr. Norton

Bob Norton

"The father of the modern GI Bill named for him, Representative G.V. 'Sonny' Montgomery, long-time chairman of the House Veterans' Affairs Committee, envisioned that Guard and Reserve men and women deserved to participate in the GI Bill program in exchange for their voluntary service. But at the time, there was 'pushback' on the issue of 'veteran status' for Reservists. Moreover, leaders then did not anticipate today's routine usage of Guard and Reserve forces for active duty missions. Some groups felt that Reservists who had not served on active duty had not earned veterans (readjustment) benefits. Chairman Montgomery forged a compromise that resulted in placing the new Reserve GI Bill programs into the Armed Forces Code, Title 10... .

"A new architecture is needed to align the Montgomery GI Bill with the realities of the Total Force policy in the 21st century."[51]

Mr. Montgomery

2008

A Partnership for Veterans' Education member, the American Association of State Colleges and Universities, has assisted the partnership in its recommendations regarding a "Total Force" Montgomery GI Bill. Vice President for Governmental Relations Ed Elmendorf will give us some insight, then Mike McGrevey, former vice president of Mississippi State University.

2008 Public Policy **Agenda**

Mr. Elmendorf

Ed Elmendorf

"The AASCU supports amendments to the Montgomery GI Bill that would equalize the benefits for active and Reserve components, including to:[52]

• "Benchmark Montgomery GI Bill benefits to the cost of attendance at public four-year institutions;

• "Consolidate active duty and Reserve Montgomery GI Bill programs in Title 38, U.S. Code for Veterans Benefits, and align benefit rates with type and length of service (A "Total Force GI Bill");

• "Close the growing benefit gap between Chapter 1606, Educational Assistance for Members of the Selected Reserve, in Title 10 and Chapter 30, Montgomery GI Bill-Active Duty, in Title 38;

• "Transfer Chapter 1607, the Reserve Educational Assistance Program (REAP), to Title 38, U.S. Code for Veterans Benefits, from Title 10 U.S. Code for [the] Armed Services, and adjust the rate formula to provide one month of active duty benefits under Chapter 30 for every month mobilized; and

• "Authorize the use of Reserve Montgomery GI Bill benefits earned during mobilization for a period of ten years after leaving the service—equal to current portability for active duty members."

Mr. McGrevey

Mike McGrevey

"Mississippi State University student and Reservist Staff Sergeant Kimberly Island is an example of the Guard and Reserve members nationwide who would benefit from a "Total Force" Montgomery GI Bill. As Colonel Norton and Mr. Elmendorf have said, we need a new architecture to close the benefit gap between regular, active-duty service and Reserve service.

Kimberly Island

"There are rarely easy issues in the art of legislating during a 2008 Presidential election year when creating or adding to new entitlement benefits is involved.

An education for veterans

President Bush and the Democrat-controlled Congress can each be faulted for turning the debate over a Montgomery G.I. Bill update into an election-year political football. At this time of war and with the costs of tuition increasing, expanded educational opportunities for veterans are in order. And yet, Mr. Bush busily issues veto threats against a viable bipartisan Senate proposal, ostensibly on grounds of fiscal prudence, while, to their equal discredit, Democrats make deceptive charges about an alternative proposal from the Republican minority which also has merits. Rather than admit honest differences and examine them, the partisans instead use the occasion to suggest, wrongly, that Sen. John McCain seeks to short-change American veterans. Nice going, Washington.

The proposal in the Senate is bipartisan, championed by the Democratic leadership and sponsored by Sen. James Webb of Virginia. It would measurably improve veterans' educational opportunities. At a cost of $2.5 million to $4 billion, S. 22, the "Post 9/11 Veterans Educational Assistance Act," matches the highest in-state tuition rates for beneficiaries, waives a $1,200 enrollment fee, pays for books and fees, and furnishes a modest living stipend. S. 22 echoes the post-World War II educational benefits that today are rightly credited on both sides of the aisle with helping make postwar middle-class prosperity attainable for a very wide swath of American veterans. After six and more years of repeated deployments and interrupted lives — to say nothing of stagnant middle-class incomes — redressing the G.I. bill is most welcome. The Veterans of Foreign Wars calls the Senate proposal "the right bill at the right time."

The Republican bill, the "Enhancement of Recruitment, Retention and Readjustment Through Education Act," is sponsored by Sens. Lindsay Graham and Richard Burr and endorsed by Mr. McCain. Two key differences are a national payment formula, as opposed to S. 22's state-specific one, and a provision to make benefits transferrable to the spouses and dependents of service members. We don't support the legacy entitlement.

But we instead hear the same partisans grinding familiar axes. Last week, the Senate's supremely partisan Majority Leader Harry Reid was heard caterwauling that "Senators McCain, Graham and Burr have finally been dragged into the debate over providing proper support for our troops." This follows former Gen. Wesley Clark's co-authored Los Angeles Times Op-Ed three weeks ago suggesting that Mr. McCain's failure to sign on to S. 22 is "casting doubt on his own commitment to the newest generation of American heroes." The powers in the Senate are now threatening to attach the bill to the war supplemental, though there's widespread agreement in Washington that the benefits should be improved, opinions differ over the form of the improvements.

The most popular approach, championed by Sen. James Webb, D-Va., and leading veterans' groups, would give vets about $2,000 every month spent in college, or enough cover the most expensive four-year public university. Veterans would also receive ,000 yearly stipends for books and a ,000 monthly housing allowance.

This is an appealing package, particularly an election year and at a time when servicemembers have borne the brunt of the rden in Iraq and Afghanistan. There are

If the White House and Congress can set aside partisanship on just one issue, this should be the one.

Veterans' benefits are too important an issue to be torn asunder. Our fighting men and women deserve passage of a clean war supplemental bill that tells them "America has your back." Likewise, they deserve a benefits bill that delivers on the original intent of the Montgomery G.I. Bill — and that is to offset some higher education costs.

USA TODAY

Today's debate: College for servicemembers

Vets deserve better benefits, but don't drain the military

Our view:
Costly education aid plan would bust the budget, hurt retention.

To put himself through Virginia's Radford University, Chris House works 35 hours a week at a local Pizza Hut. During summers, e takes a second job as a farm hand.

Despite those jobs, House will owe about 15,000 in college debt when he graduates next year. His would be part of a struggling student, except for one thing: House, 25, is an raq war veteran who erved with the 82nd Airborne.

Aren't vets like House opposed to get college aid for when they leave e military?

That's how it worked under the fabled G.I. Bill of 1944. Eight million World War II veterans got an education under a generous program that covered tuition, fees, books and some living expenses.

Today's education benefits receive about $1,100 a month when they are in school, enough to cover about 60% of the costs of the average four-year public college.

GI Bill benefits

Current education aid for servicemembers:
► Active-duty members who have continuously served for at least two years, and who forfeit $1,200 of their pay in one year, are entitled to receive $1,101 a month as a full-time student for up to 36 months, which is equivalent to four academic years.
► In general, the benefit must be used within 10 years of leaving the service.
► Part-time students receive less, but can stretch the benefit over a longer amount of time.

Source: The Associated Press

only two problems with it: It's not affordable, and it would worsen the volunteer military's already serious problem with retention.

The non-partisan Congressional Budget Office estimates the plan would cost $51.8 billion in the next 10 years, piling a costlier entitlement program onto the nation's already unsustainable mountain of debt.

Moreover, the generous benefits in the Webb approach would lure 8,000 soldiers a year out of the Army, a top Pentagon manpower official says. Although those same benefits might attract 2,000 more soldiers, that still leaves a 6,000-soldier gap that could cost $100 million a year in new retention bonuses to fill.

An alternative approach, backed by Sen. John McCain, R-Ariz., and the Bush administration, is more closely tailored to the needs of today's volunteer military. Veterans leaving active service would see their monthly education benefits rise to $1,500, enough to cover the average public university. To boost retention, this plan would allow members who served six years or more to transfer part or all their post-service education benefits to a spouse or child. There's no official cost estimate for this alternative, but government analysts had calculated that such a program would run $1 billion to $2 billion a year.

That's a more reasonable price tag, but given the nation's $400 billion annual deficit, it, too, needs to be paid for. In this case, the first place to look is the Pentagon's own bloated weapons procurement programs, such as the Navy's new coastal combat ship, which are riddled with cost overruns.

War veterans such as Chris House have made great sacrifices to serve their country, and they deserve more help to further their education and get on with their lives. Now it's time to ask taxpayers or defense contractors to sacrifice a little so that can happen.

"Legislating also is not easy when there are multiple 'dimensions' to a public policy issue. *The Washington Times* and *USA Today* 2008 editorials (previous page) raise dimensions of educational opportunity, politics, partisanship/bipartisanship, stagnant middle-class incomes, student debt, military recruitment and retention, national debt, dependent spouse and child transferability of benefits, and workforce development. Below, an editorial by George Lisicki, VFW National Commander, speaks to the issues.

"Do you see other 'dimensions' to this debate as well?

"When Congress passes legislation to change the Montgomery GI Bill, veterans can go to *www.gibill.va.gov* to get information or refer to booklets produced by the VA as well.

"For all veterans' benefits, publications like *For Service to Your Country* are helpful.

POST 9-11 GI BILL

Mr. McGrevey

"H.R. 2642, the *Iraq Supplemental Appropriations Act*, that President George Bush signed into law June 30, 2008, (Public Law 110-252) both increased the Montgomery GI Bill to $1,321 per month, and established a generous, new 'Post-9-11 GI Bill' for persons who enlist after August 1, 2009.

"Senators Jim Webb (D-VA) and Chuck Hagel (R-NE) furnished the bipartisan leadership for the improvements, which were derived from an amended version of S. 22, the proposed Post-9-11 Veterans Education Assistance Act, that they—and 37 other Senators—initially introduced January 4, 2007.

"Happily, Senators Webb and Hagel included two provisions in the Post 9-11 GI Bill that Chairman Montgomery and his colleagues originally introduced in H.R. 1400, the proposed Veterans' Educational Assistance Act of 1981 we have discussed in earlier chapters. One of these provision no longer requires new enlistees to pay in $1,200 to be eligible for the Post 9-11 GI Bill. The other provision allows the service member to transfer GI Bill benefits to a spouse or a child.

"Indeed, President Bush called for the 'transferability' provision in his January 28, 2008, State of the Union Address. I'd note, too, that former Senator Max Cleland (D-GA) had been a longstanding advocate for the provision.

"Even though Congress created a new Post 9-11 GI Bill, Congress did not repeal the Montgomery GI Bill for new enlistees or those service members and veterans already eligible."

Reduce financial burdens

Opposing view:
Webb's more generous proposal would reward troops for service.

By George Lisicki

There is no argument in Washington that the Montgomery GI Bill has not kept pace with rising college costs — it provides for less than 70% of public tuitions and 30% of private — but there is debate on how to improve the benefit. That is where two Senate colleagues and fellow Vietnam War veterans — James Webb, D-Va., and John McCain, R-Ariz. — are at odds.

Webb's plan would pay the highest in-state tuition; provide for fees, books and a living stipend; boost Guard and Reserve benefits; and match private institution rates dollar-for-dollar. McCain's proposal would also increase education benefits, especially for those who stay in uniform longer, and would allow the benefit to transfer to spouses or children.

Fearing a mass exodus of first-term enlistees, the Defense Department is against Webb's bill, to the point that the department is reticent to even acknowledge that a better benefit might attract more qualified applicants, which could boost both recruiting and retention goals.

A compromise might be on the horizon, but until then, my organization remains solidly behind Webb's bill because it meets a top legislative goal for a new GI Bill for the 21st century. We appreciate the efforts of Sen. McCain and others who are trying to update this benefit, but the Pentagon needs to focus on reality — one being that young people enlisting today will go to war, come home, then reintegrate into society. Another is that not everyone will make the military a career, nor would everyone be allowed.

In his University of Texas campus newspaper this month, LBJ School of Public Affairs professor Edwin Dorn said, "The GI Bill is an incentive … (that) becomes less of an incentive if you talk to an 18-year-old about what's going to happen 12 years from now."

Webb's bill is the right legislation at the right time. It would ease transition, reduce financial burdens, and introduce educated and highly motivated employees into the American workplace. It has strong bipartisan support in Congress and the endorsement of every major veterans' organization. It is something the troops expect from their nation, and it is something all Americans should demand that their Congress deliver.

George Lisicki, a Vietnam War veteran from Carteret, N.J., is the national commander of the 2.3 million-member Veterans of Foreign Wars.

George Lisicki, VFW National Commander

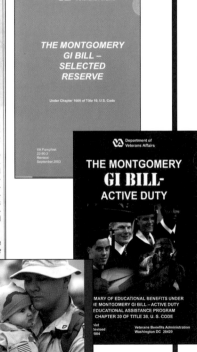

FOR SERVICE TO YOUR COUNTRY
The Insider's Guide to Veterans' Benefits
★ ★ ★ ★
PETER S. GAYTAN & MARIAN EDELMAN BORDEN
Foreword by Senator Bob Dole

THE MONTGOMERY GI BILL – SELECTED RESERVE

Department of Veterans Affairs

Under Chapter 1606 of Title 10, U.S. Code

VA Pamphlet 22-90-2 Revised September 2003

THE MONTGOMERY GI BILL- ACTIVE DUTY

Department of Veterans Affairs

SUMMARY OF EDUCATIONAL BENEFITS UNDER THE MONTGOMERY GI BILL – ACTIVE DUTY EDUCATIONAL ASSISTANCE PROGRAM CHAPTER 30 OF TITLE 38, U.S. CODE

Veterans Benefits Administration Washington DC 20420

Marine recruits training at Parris Island, SC, in 2009.

WE MAKE MARINES

Sonny's Lessons Learned

A law that works can always work better.

Coupled with other factors, since 1987 the youth of America has responded to an improved Montgomery GI Bill educational incentive, as we thought they would.

And the Montgomery GI Bill served as the economic investment that we thought would help service members transition to civilian life. Indeed, it has accomplished what its statutory purpose clauses said it should do.[53]

More pointedly, who would have thought that in 2008—27 years after we introduced our original New GI Bill legislation (H.R. 1400 in 1981)—that the new, 2008 Post 9-11 GI Bill enacted into law would contain two provisions from H.R. 1400 that the Senate continuously opposed? These two provisions were (1) no $1,200 pay reduction to gain eligibility, and (2) "transferability" of the benefit to the service member's spouse or child.[54]

Worth Repeating

"It doesn't take a hero to order men into battle. It takes a hero to be one of those men who goes into battle."
—*General Norman Schwarzkopf*

"Just as D-Day was the greatest military action in our history, so the GI Bill was arguably the greatest investment in our people in American history."
—*President Bill Clinton*

"We must never forget that our people in uniform have been the core of our strength in the past. They, more than any hardware system, form the real defense capability of today and tomorrow."
—*Chairman Philip Odeen*

"We can assume that our enemies have learned from the Gulf War. They are <u>unlikely</u> [emphasis added] to confront us conventionally. … instead they may find new ways to attack our interests, our forces, and our citizens."
—*Chairman Philip Odeen*

WHAT'S NEXT

In Chapter 16 we look at the role of the Montgomery GI Bill in developing America's workforce to help the United States compete in a world economy.

"So veterans of our military could attend any school in America, limited only by their own aspirations, ability, and initiative."

—*Anthony Principi*

"There is little doubt that the Montgomery GI Bill has met or even exceeded the expectations of its sponsors and has been a major contributor to the success of the All-Volunteer Force."

—*Vice Admiral Patricia Tracey*

"From 2000-2004 alone, Congress enhanced the Montgomery GI Bill in six major areas..."

—*Chairman Christopher Smith*

16

SONNY'S CAST OF CHARACTERS

Faith DesLauriers, Past President, National Association of Veterans' Program Administrators

James Bombard, Past President, National Association of State Approving Agencies

Jerome Sullivan, Executive Director, American Association of Collegiate Registrars and Admissions Officers

Kathy Snead, President, Service Members Opportunity Colleges

Major General (Ret) Robert F. Cocklin, U.S. Army, Legislative Director, Association of the U.S. Army

Master Sergeant (Ret) Michael Cline, Executive Director, Enlisted Association of the National Guard of the U.S.

Dennis Douglass, Deputy Director (Ret), Education Service, U.S. Department of Veterans Affairs

Bill Stephens, Chief, Veterans' Education, Pennsylvania Department of Education

Chad Schatz, Director, Veterans' Education, Missouri Department of Elementary and Secondary Education

Anthony Principi, Secretary of Veterans Affairs, 2001-2005

Don Wilson, President and CEO, Association of Small Business Development Centers

Walt Blackwell, CEO, National Veterans Business Development Corporation

1987-Present— Effect of the Montgomery GI Bill: Affording Postsecondary Education

SONNY'S SUMMARY

Initiative breeds opportunity, Alan Cranston said. Surveys show that military service gives young Americans a four-year, post-service education and training benefits some could not have afforded otherwise. More than 2.3 million veterans have used the Montgomery GI Bill since 1985. At the collegiate level, about 45 percent of those are enrolled in programs for two-year degrees, typically in specialized technologies.

But that's not all. Many soldiers do not wait until they leave the military to enroll in college or technical training. For example, 798,971 active-duty service members were pursuing associate's, bachelor's, or master's degrees during off-duty hours in fiscal year 2005. Further, the Montgomery GI Bill helps veterans "earn and learn" with employers through structured, on-job learning of up to two years, and competency based apprenticeships of up to about five years.

Mr. Montgomery

Folks, our previous chapter talked mostly about how the Montgomery GI Bill has worked effectively as an educational incentive for joining our military.

In this chapter, we'll talk about the extent to which the Montgomery GI Bill has fulfilled one of three new statutory requirements known as "purpose clauses." The House and Senate approved these purpose clauses in H.R. 1085 when sending it to President Reagan's desk in 1987.

---

§ 3001. Purposes

The purposes of this chapter [38 USCS §§ 3001 et seq.] are--

(1) to provide a new educational assistance program to assist in the readjustment of members of the Armed Forces to civilian life after their separation from military service;

(2) to extend the benefits of a higher education to qualifying men and women who might not otherwise be able to afford such an education;

(3) to provide for vocational readjustment and to restore lost educational opportunities to those service men and women who served on active duty after June 30, 1985;

(4) to promote and assist the All-Volunteer Force program and the Total Force Concept of the Armed Forces by establishing a new program of educational assistance based upon service on active duty or a combination of service on active duty and in the Selected Reserve (including the National Guard) to aid in the recruitment and retention of highly qualified personnel for both the active and reserve components of the Armed Forces;

(5) to give special emphasis to providing educational assistance benefits to aid in the retention of personnel in the Armed Forces; and

(6) to enhance our Nation's competitiveness through the development of a more highly educated and productive work force.

Excerpt from Title 38, USC.

Our visual highlights the three new "purpose clauses"[1] Congress added for the Montgomery GI Bill, as it appears in Title 38, United States Code, Veterans Benefits.[2]

Title 38 governs the provision of veterans' benefits and services, primarily by the Departments of Veterans Affairs and Labor.

Our focus will be the purpose clause on affording postsecondary education. We'll discuss the new Montgomery GI Bill purpose clause regarding workforce development and global competitiveness in Chapter 17.[3]

I've had many veterans tell me how the Montgomery GI Bill helped them pursue college or technical training, including through an apprenticeship or on-job training.

Some say they may not have pursued additional training but for the Montgomery GI Bill. Others tell me they planned to pursue postsecondary training, in any case, and the Montgomery GI Bill made it financially more feasible to do so.[4]

Let's hear from the leaders of six professional organizations that have staff located on college campuses or otherwise interact everyday with service members or veteran students.

First, we'll hear Ms. Faith DesLauriers, past president, National Association of Veterans Program Administrators (NAVPA), founded in 1975.[5]

The NAVPA is a nationally recognized professional organization for administrators working at both campus and community based settings that assists veterans, dependent widows, and children of deceased service members, and active-duty military personnel.

Ms. DesLauriers is university director of veterans' affairs at Embry-Riddle Aeronautical University in Daytona Beach, FL. Embry-Riddle is perennially ranked the top aeronautical engineering university in America.[6]

Ms. DesLauriers

"My experience is that veteran students enter college not necessarily counting on the Montgomery GI Bill to pay tuition and fees, but to pay living expenses. The Montgomery GI Bill is a big help in that way.

"I think many veteran students come from families who would struggle to send their children to college. Plus, many of these veteran students come from smaller towns. They see the military and the Montgomery GI Bill as an opportunity to have a world experience, as well as an education experience."[7]

Faith DesLauriers

Mr. Montgomery

Second, we'll hear Dr. Jim Bombard, a disabled combat infantry officer and past president, National Association of State Approving Agencies, founded in 1948.[8]

Under federal law, State Approving Agencies (SAAs) approve educational institutions for veterans' training under the Montgomery GI Bill and other VA educational assistance programs. SAAs exist in each state and also approve on-job training (OJT) and apprenticeships for veterans through private/public-sector employers, conduct outreach to veterans, and assist occupational licensing and credentialing entities in their states.

Mr. Bombard

Jim Bombard

"Yes, I suspect there are lots of veterans who—except for their military service—may not have had the opportunity to pursue postsecondary education and training as paid by their parents, for example. That said, America's sons and daughters who choose to wear the military uniform are highly motivated individuals. When they leave the military after four years they are eager to catch up with their non-veteran peers who chose not to serve. That's in part why so many veterans go to school year around."[9]

Mr. Montgomery

Third, Mr. Jerome Sullivan, longstanding executive director, American Association of Collegiate Registrars and Admissions Officers (AACRAO), founded in 1910, speaks.

"The AACRAO is a non-profit, voluntary professional association of more than 10,000 admissions and registration professionals who represent approximately 2,500 institutions."[10]

A professional usually assigned to the campus Office of the Registrar often serves as the Department of Veterans Affairs "certifying official." This person helps veterans, as well as service members serving on active-duty or Reserve-duty, to electronically complete VA Montgomery GI Bill application forms. After VA determines the applicant eligible, the on-campus official certifies to VA that the veteran is enrolled, is pursuing an educational program at the institution, and is maintaining academic progress. In effect, the certifying official is the person veteran students seem to seek out first for help, no matter what the issue.

Mr. Sullivan

Jerome Sullivan

"I don't think there's any question that the Montgomery GI Bill helps young people access higher education who otherwise might not have done so. Veterans also can qualify for grants and loans like other students. The Montgomery GI Bill, coupled with other federal or state grants and loans, is a powerful package. Since World War II, our on-campus certifying officials have taken pride in their partnership with veteran students. Working with them is special because of the commitment and maturity they bring to campus."[11]

Mr. Montgomery

Fourth, we'll hear from Dr. Kathy Snead, president, Servicemembers Opportunity Colleges (SOC), founded in 1972.

SOC is a consortium of more than 1,800 colleges and universities that provide educational opportunities to service members who may have unique challenges meeting academic residency requirements for a college degree due to periodic change of duty station or deployments. Through SOC, military students enroll in courses in their off-duty hours at or near military installations in the United States, overseas, and on Navy ships.[12]

LEARNING: ON BASE, ON SHIP, ON LINE[13]

Dr. Snead

Dr. Kathy Snead

"A service member who perhaps was not financially positioned to pursue postsecondary education or training after high school is positioned to do so while in the military due to the Department of Defense Tuition Assistance program, administered under Title 10, USC.

"Each service branch administers this program through a civilian education services officer stationed at U.S. military installations here and throughout the world. Under federal law, while on active duty, service members may use tuition assistance paid for by their service branch to pursue off-duty education.

"Service members may also use their Montgomery GI Bill while on active duty. But many service members like to save their Montgomery GI Bill eligibility for when they leave the military.

"In fiscal year 2006, 798,971 service members used the tuition assistance program while serving on active duty.[14] And during the year, 26,633 earned associate degrees, 7,958 earned bachelor's degrees, and 8,822 earned master's degrees.[15]

"Noted Anthony Principi, former chairman of the Congressional Commission on Service Members and Veterans Transition Assistance and also former Secretary of Veterans Affairs, 'Our highly engaging and resourceful military represents America's largest university. Larger than all the Ivy League schools combined... .'"[16]

Mr. Montgomery

Fifth, Major General (Ret) Robert Cocklin, legislative director, The Association of the U.S. Army, speaks.

Established in 1950,[17] The Association has a long-standing record of advocacy for educating soldiers, both during and after military service.

Maj. Gen. Cocklin

Major General (Ret) Robert Cocklin

"A college education is the dream of a large segment of our youth… and their parents… . For many the cost is prohibitive, and for some they have not yet discovered a field of endeavor in which to focus their time, talents, and efforts. It seems to us there is not a more economical and socially constructive way for the government to apportion precious resources than to reward military service to the nation by providing the financial means for higher education of America's top-quality young men and women. It is not a grant; it is not a giveaway program; it is smart business and a prudent investment in human resources."[18]

Mr. Montgomery

Sixth, National Guard Master Sergeant (Ret) Michael Cline, executive director, Enlisted Association of the National Guard of the United States:[19]

Master Sgt. Cline

Master Sergeant (Ret) Michael Cline

"The National Guard, established on the village green in Salem, MA, in 1636, is an enduring part of America's heritage. The Guard represents a valued contingency force whether it's for a natural disaster, war-time service, or peace-time emergencies.

"The Selected Reserve aspect of the Montgomery GI Bill[20] gives Guard and Reserve members the opportunity to pursue postsecondary education and training for up to a 14-year eligibility period while an active member of a Guard or Reserve unit.

"The Montgomery GI Bill gives Guard and Reserve members the opportunity to use education benefits as they are serving—rather than having to wait until after they complete their service obligation.

"In this sense it: first, provides the Guard or Reserve member access to postsecondary education, and, second, serves as a retention tool because once the Guard or Reserve member leaves the Selected Reserve, Montgomery GI Bill benefits discontinue.

"Congress specifically designed the Montgomery GI Bill program with these two purposes in mind."[21]

Mr. Montgomery

Folks, I'll conclude this section by agreeing with Ms. DesLauriers, Dr. Bombard, Mr. Sullivan, Dr. Snead, Major General Cocklin, and Master Sergeant Cline.

Initiative breeds opportunity.[22] Many service members and veterans who did not have the financial access to postsecondary education and training simply have gone out and created that opportunity for themselves.[23] It's an earned opportunity valued in 2008 at about $39,636[24] through the Montgomery GI Bill.

I'm going to ask Mr. Dennis Douglass, deputy director (Ret) of the Department of Veterans Affairs program that administers the Montgomery GI Bill, to give us a breakdown of the types of training the 2.3 million veteran students have pursued under the Montgomery GI Bill since 1985.[25] In essence, they've gained skills that help build both their post-military careers and our national workforce.

Mr. Douglass

Dennis Douglass

"Mr. Chairman, I am honored to do so.[26]

"Of the 2,332,577 veterans who have used the Montgomery GI Bill since 1985, 1,991,653 have trained at the college level. This is broken down by 894,120 who have enrolled at two-year colleges, 959,381 at four-year institutions, and 147,612 at graduate institutions.

"As the numbers indicate, at the college level about 45 percent (894,120 of 1,991,653) choose education and job training that often gives them marketable skills in two years. Classroom training, especially in two-year specialized technology degrees, can go a long way toward meeting the workforce needs of private-sector employers.

"At institutions other than two- or four-year colleges, another 153,014 veterans have used the Montgomery GI Bill for vocational-technical training, on-job training, apprenticeship, correspondence, or flight training."

> "… 2.3 MILLION VETERANS HAVE USED THE MONTGOMERY GI BILL SINCE 1985."
> —*Dennis Douglass, Deputy Director (Ret), Dept. of Veterans' Affairs*

THREE WAYS TO USE THE MONTGOMERY GI BILL THAT ARE NOT WELL-KNOWN

Mr. Montgomery

I'd like to focus now on three ways to use the Montgomery GI Bill that, in my opinion, are not that well-known: occupational licensing and certification; apprenticeship; and on-job learning. Then I'd like to talk about entrepreneurship.

First, let's discuss the occupational licensing and certification aspect of the Montgomery GI Bill that helps veterans obtain the professional credentialing they need to perform their skills in our civilian economy.

The Department of Veterans Affairs reimburses a veteran up to $2,000 for the cost of an occupational licensing and certification test.

In today's business and governmental climate, a license is required for most professions and for jobs that are subject to state or other government regulations.

Whether you are a heavy equipment operator, medical technician, computer network engineer, public accountant, teacher, plumber, or surgeon, you'll need to successfully pass a "competency" test to be certified to practice your profession.

Led by Representatives Jack Quinn (R-NY) and Bob Filner (D-CA), Congress enacted the licensing and credentialing program aspect of the Montgomery GI Bill in 2001.[27] In 2005, VA reimbursed 4,706 veterans for the cost of their tests.[28]

Here are two final questions to close this section on licensing and credentialing.

Does a service member's military occupational specialty help in civilian life? May a service member "transfer" that skill to a civilian career for which he or she might need to pursue a civilian occupational license?

Yes and yes!

As of January 2005, 92 percent of Army military occupational specialties have civilian job equivalents that are subject to licensure or certification; and 95 percent of the Army's more than 400,000 enlisted soldiers serve in these specialties.[29]

A second—and often overlooked—way for using the Montgomery GI Bill is through an apprenticeship program[30] in which veterans "earn and learn" simultaneously.[31]

The U.S. Department of Labor reports that today 858 professions[32] can be mastered through apprenticeships. Apprenticeships and the Montgomery GI Bill represent an opportunity to build a career.

Under the Montgomery GI Bill, VA pays the veteran a monthly amount that, by design, attempts to close the gap between the training wage paid at the entry level and the wage of the journey worker who has completed his/her apprenticeship.

For the first six months of the apprenticeship, VA augments the apprentice's training wage by $825 per month, for the second six months by $605, and for the third and any successive six months by $385.[33]

Notes Bill Stephens of the Pennsylvania Department of Education:[34]

Mr. Stephens

Bill Stephens

"As Mr. Montgomery said, under the law, VA provides monthly assistance to supplement the training wage until the journey worker wage is reached and the training program is finished. For most apprenticeships you have to demonstrate competencies for each training module before you can go on to the next one. Some apprenticeships, such as those in the electrical and avionics fields, for example, are very rigorous and about five years in length. VA pays the veteran monthly until he or she completes his training objective, qualifying as a journey worker. It's a fantastic way to learn not just a job—but to build a career."

Mr. Montgomery

A third way to use the Montgomery GI Bill is through the on-job training (or on-job learning) program. Veterans may participate in this structured training for up to two years. The Montgomery GI Bill pays the veteran the difference between the trainee wage and the journey worker wage.

Notes Chad Schatz of the Missouri Department of Education:[35]

Mr. Schatz

Chad Schatz

"Employers like the employees they get under VA's apprenticeship and OJT program. The National Association of State Approving Agencies received survey responses from 496 employers in 14 states.

"One question we asked was whether employment and training of VA/OJT benefits recipient(s) was beneficial to their company. On a five-point scale with one meaning strongly disagree and five meaning strongly agree, 235 employers marked a five and 172 employers marked a four.

"Another question we asked was whether the skills and knowledge attained from this OJT or apprenticeship training have enhanced the employee's earned income and potential. Two hundred forty-two gave a five score, and 165 gave a four.

"Learning is earning under the Montgomery GI Bill, Mr. Chairman!"

Mr. Montgomery

Lastly, the Montgomery GI Bill empowers veterans by helping them start and grow small businesses. As Anthony Principi noted in his aforementioned Commission's 1999 report to Congress:

Mr. Principi

President George W. Bush and Anthony Principi.

"Small businesses are the bedrock of our economy.[36]

"We as a nation want to ensure that veterans have a full opportunity to participate in our free-enterprise system their military service has sustained."[37]

Mr. Montgomery

Small Business Development Centers and The National Veterans Business Development Corporation help in this way.

Notes Don Wilson, longstanding president and CEO of the Association of Small Business Development Centers:[38]

Mr. Wilson

Don Wilson

"Mr. Chairman, small business **success** is **our** success at our nation's Small Business Development Centers (SBDCs).[39]

"Congress created the Small Business Development Program in 1980 under Public Law 96-302. Located in every state, the Small Business Development Center network provides management and technical assistance to more than 1.3 million small business owners and aspiring entrepreneurs each year.[40] In Fiscal Year 2006, our SBDCs furnished face-to-face business consulting of an hour or more to more than 201,823 clients, including 18,367 veterans; and training sessions for 465,837 attendees, including 23,224 veterans.[41]

"For those who have fought to protect our personal, political and economic freedoms… it is extremely important they be afforded every opportunity to prosper economically in this free society with its free market economy that they have invested so much to protect.[42]

"The veterans who we assist each year are well positioned to add value to our economy because of the challenges they have met in the military.

"Indeed, the small business sector of our economy currently accounts for 52 percent of the nation's gross national product.[43] Fifty-one percent of non-farm, private-sector workers are employed by small businesses.[44] Small businesses in the last decade accounted for roughly 70 percent of the new jobs created in our economy.[45]

"And the best part is that veterans can use their Montgomery GI Bill to enroll in the many courses our centers offer in starting and growing small businesses.

"… It's very easy to start a business in the United States. A recent study by the World Bank shows that the United States, at five days, ranks behind only Canada and Australia in terms of the number of days required to start a business, and has the fourth lowest administrative costs to start a new business."[46]

Mr. Montgomery

Congress established The National Veterans Business Development Corporation in 2000 under Public Law 106-50.[47] Notes Walt Blackwell, CEO of the Corporation:[48]

Mr. Blackwell

Walt Blackwell

"Mr. Chairman, when veterans succeed America succeeds.[49]

"Mr. Chairman, Congress created The Veterans Business Development Corporation—known as The Veterans Corporation[50]—to give veterans and disabled veterans the tools they need to start and grow small businesses, including:

- Access to capital;
- Access to business services; and
- Access to entrepreneurial education.

"The success rate of veterans' business start-ups is high compared to other business startups, partially due to the experience veterans have gained in our military.

"Data from various national surveys, including the November 2004 SBA-sponsored Waldman Associates Survey, indicated approximately 5.5 million veterans, including 759,000 service-disabled veterans, currently own small businesses.

"Veterans and service-disabled, veteran-owned small businesses contribute more than $202 billion to the U.S. economy per year. You can see state-by-state figures at *www.veteranscorp.org*.[51]

"Mr. Chairman, through our very small headquarters staff and partners,[52] TVC furnished face-to-face services to 14,206 veterans in 2006.[53]

"With the advent of Internet-based, on-line services, the publicly funded service delivery model changed dramatically, allowing TVC to reach service members anywhere in the world, at any time. In FY 2006, through *www.veteranscorp.org*, 119,431 current and former service members received value-added information on starting and growing small businesses.[54]

"Add in TVC's Virtual Business Incubator, Virtual Business Center (in cooperation with SBA's SCORE program), and Virtual Veteran Resource Center, and we furnished information and assistance to another 325,982 veterans.[55]

"Thank you, Mr. Chairman."

Sonny's Lessons Learned

The stated purposes or objectives of a law—as expressed in the law itself—can be many and varied. Multiple purposes, as was the case in the Montgomery GI Bill, can strengthen—not dilute—what Congress wants laws to accomplish.

Worth Repeating

"I don't think there's any question that the Montgomery GI Bill helps young people access higher education who otherwise might not have done so."
—*Jerome Sullivan, Executive Director, American Association of Collegiate Registrars and Admissions Officers*

"The National Guard, established on the village green in Salem, MA, in 1636, is an enduring part of America's heritage. The Guard is a valued contingency force whether it's for a natural disaster, war-time service, or peace-time emergencies."
—*Michael Cline, Executive Director, Enlisted Association of the National Guard of the U.S.*

"Small businesses in the last decade accounted for roughly 70 percent of the new jobs created in our economy."
—*Don Wilson, President, Association of Small Business Development Centers*

"Approximately 5.5 million veterans, including 759,000 service-disabled veterans, currently own small businesses."
—*Walt Blackwell, CEO, The Veterans Corporation*

WHAT'S NEXT

In Chapter 17, we look at the effect of the Montgomery GI Bill as a tool in developing the U.S. workforce.

17

Senator Bill Cohen (R-ME)

*Charles Ciccolella,
Former Assistant
Secretary of Labor for
Veterans' Employment
and Training*

Senator John Kerry (D-MA)

*Charles Murray,
Scholar,
American Enterprise
Institute*

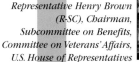
*Representative Henry Brown
(R-SC), Chairman,
Subcommittee on Benefits,
Committee on Veterans' Affairs,
U.S. House of Representatives*

*George W. Bush,
43rd President of
the United States*

*Beth Buehlmann, former Vice
President and Executive
Director, Center for Workforce
Preparation, U.S. Chamber of
Commerce*

*Representative Steve
Gunderson (R-WI)*

*Bob Lutz, Vice Chairman,
Product Development,
General Motors*

*Tom Speicher, Writer,
One College Avenue,
Pennsylvania College
of Technology*

*Steve Wohlwend,
Senior Division Manager,
Industrial Relations,
John Deere & Company*

*Anne Campbell,
Lt. Col. (Ret), USAF*

*Wesley Poriotis, Chief
Executive Officer, Wesley,
Brown & Bartle Global
Executive Recruiting*

*Representative John
Paul Hammerschmidt
(R-AR)*

Also featured in this chapter:
Kevin Horigan
Robert C. Crawford

*Harold Scott, Vice President,
Human Resources, Harley-
Davidson Motor Company*

*Evan Gaddis, President,
National Electrical
Manufacturers Association*

*Patricia Klemm, President,
Klemm Analysis Group*

1987-Winter 2008—
Effect of the Montgomery GI Bill:
Developing the U.S. Workforce

SONNY'S SUMMARY

While the mortgage crisis with U.S. banks has adversely affected the world economy and us at home, America's economy has historically shown remarkable resilience, flexibility, and the ability to rebound even stronger. The challenge to America's world economic leadership has never been greater. If we are going to grow and compete in a world economy in which other countries produce goods and services more cheaply and about 95 percent of the world's customers live outside our borders,[1] we have to open more international markets for the goods and services we produce and eliminate trade barriers. As baby boomers reach retirement, our competitive edge depends upon developing a skilled workforce, especially in sophisticated new-growth industries.

To this end, veterans personify economic strength. Just as ten WW II veterans won a Nobel Prize in science,[2] so current and future veterans, trained under the Montgomery GI Bill, represent part of our ongoing potential for achieving world leadership in current and emerging fields such as nanotechnology, robotics, biotechnology, communications, engineering, health care, logistics, transportation, and manufacturing. The 200,000[3] or so service members who leave the military each year (about 72 percent[4] of whom will use the Montgomery GI Bill) represent a unique national resource and competitive business asset. Fundamentally, hiring former service members represents a good business decision.[5] Hiring them for patriotic reasons expresses appreciation and respect. Hiring them for business reasons gets results.[6]

Mr. Cohen

Bill Cohen

"We should remember that when GI Bill benefits were established in 1944, they were the initial step in the federal provision of educational assistance. Until 1965, the GI Bill stood virtually alone as a source of aid to postsecondary education students. And as late as 1975, the Vietnam-era GI Bill provided over 50 percent of all student aid to those in postsecondary education."[9]

> **"UNTIL 1965, THE GI BILL STOOD VIRTUALLY ALONE AS A SOURCE OF AID TO POSTSECONDARY EDUCATION STUDENTS."**
> —*Senator Bill Cohen, Maine*

Sonny's Scene Setter
Former members of our military serve as a competitive business asset in a global economy.

DEVELOPING A HIGHLY EDUCATED AND PRODUCTIVE WORKFORCE

Mr. Montgomery

Here's the second, new "purpose clause" we'll focus on that Congress created for the Montgomery GI Bill, as it appears in Title 38, United States Code:

> "To enhance our nation's competitiveness through the development of a more highly educated and productive workforce."[7]

In this chapter, first, we'll learn that veterans represent a valued business asset and personify economic strength.

Second, we'll learn what the future may hold (including for veterans) as we compete with other nations on the world economic stage.

And third, we'll learn what we need to do to compete successfully and the role veterans/the Montgomery GI Bill can play.

Are you surprised that enhancing our nation's competitiveness through the development of a more highly educated and developed workforce is a statutory purpose of the Montgomery GI Bill? I was a bit surprised when I first learned of the idea of using a GI Bill program in this way. But then, as I thought about it, I agreed with it.

Chairman Cranston and Ranking Member Murkowski proposed the competitiveness purpose clause as an amendment to the New GI Bill Continuation Act (S. 12)[8] during Senate Committee on Veterans' Affairs mark-up on February 26, 1987. As we learned in Chapter 13, the committee approved the bill, as amended, by a vote of 12-0.

I appreciated the committee's vision and foresight in recognizing the economic significance of the program. America's need to compete in a global economy that was emerging in 1987 is now economic reality.

As Senators Bill Cohen and John Kerry observed on the Senate floor in May 1987 during the Senate vote on S. 12, (as amended when the Senate passed it 89-0) the role of the modern GI Bill in financially supporting national workforce development was not new. Noted the Senators:

Mr. Kerry

John Kerry

"The GI Bill has made an enormous contribution to our nation in the past through the education and training of our citizenry, and through increased productivity, gross national product, and tax revenues. Almost 20 million veterans have trained under GI Bill programs since World War II. Passage of the New GI Bill Continuation Act will extend these benefits into the future, and will enhance America's economic competitiveness."[10]

COMPETING IN THE GLOBAL MARKET PLACE

> **"THE GI BILL HAS MADE AN ENORMOUS CONTRIBUTION... THROUGH INCREASED PRODUCTIVITY, GROSS NATIONAL PRODUCT, AND TAX REVENUES."**
> —*Senator John Kerry, Massachusetts*

Mr. Montgomery

The Committee Report on S. 12—the proposed New GI Bill Continuation Act—filed by Chairman Cranston and Ranking Member Murkowski on March 17, 1987, explains why the committee added the global competitiveness purpose clause to what would become the Montgomery GI Bill on June 1, 1987:[11]

"The challenge to American economic world leadership has never been greater. Our competitive edge depends upon a skilled labor force.[12] Critical, sophisticated, new-growth industries[13]—computers, robotics, and biotechnology to name a few—demand workers skilled in technology and a populace conversant with the rudiments of science.

"The speed and complexity of trade in the information age also requires worker —and management—versatility and a higher level of reasoning and analytical skills than that demanded by any other age in our history. Our nearest competitor, Japan, recognized the importance of education for its own future 25 years ago, when its Economic Council declared, 'Economic competition among nations is a technical competition that has become an **educational competition** [emphasis added].'"

The report filed by Chairman Cranston and Ranking Member Murkowski continues:

"Global leadership today demands managerial excellence, expert management of information and resources, foreign language skills, and a mastering of emerging technologies at every level. The challenge must be met through education and training, particularly—in view of level of competency required—at the college and university level. The more Americans who desire the opportunity for a higher education and are given encouragement and access to pursue it, the more effective will be America's response to the global challenge."

The Committee Report on S. 12 concludes with:

"The members and veterans of, and Reservists in, the All-Volunteer Force who could be trained through the resources of the New GI Bill can make or break our competitive effort. They represent an enormous potential for

> "... THE ALL-VOLUNTEER FORCE... REPRESENTS AN ENORMOUS POTENTIAL FOR CONSOLIDATING OR ACHIEVING WORLD LEADERSHIP IN SCIENCE, ENGINEERING, MATHEMATICS..."
> —*Senator Alan Cranston & Senator Frank Murkowski*

consolidating or achieving world leadership[14] in science, engineering, mathematics, business management, and the full range of arts and humanities. We cannot afford to have them undereducated, underskilled, and underemployed."

VETERANS AS VALUED BUSINESS ASSETS

When we consider the 2.3 million veterans who have used the Montgomery GI Bill for many different types of training, along with an infusion of about 200,000 service members discharged into our domestic economy annually,[15] what do we get?

Let's hear from six of America's leaders in business and industry, starting with Congressman Henry Brown of South Carolina:[16]

Mr. Brown

Henry Brown

"Thank you, Mr. Chairman.

"You know, I speak **slowly**. It's a **Southern** thing!

"What we ultimately get from veterans in our domestic economy is leadership and dependability. In what other segment of our society do 20-year-olds maintain billion-dollar military aircraft; operate and troubleshoot billion-dollar nuclear ships; and operate and maintain space-based technologies to keep us safe in an increasingly unsafe world?

"To me, that says a lot."

Ms. Buehlmann

Beth Buehlmann

"I'm Beth B. Buehlmann, former vice president and executive director, Center for Workforce Preparation, (now Institute for a Competitive Workforce) U.S. Chamber of Commerce.

"Over 200,000 military personnel transition into the civilian workforce annually... .[17]

"Veterans bring added value to the American workforce because veterans have; training that meets industry standards... knowledge of cutting-edge technologies that are of concern to employers as they evaluate the abilities of their current workforce in meeting the skill needs of the future marketplace... education and certification credentials necessary in a global economy... and demonstrated leadership skills and managerial experience.[18]

"[And] hiring veterans is simply good business sense... [19]

"Veterans are attractive because of the skills acquired through their highly effective military training. In addition, these men and women offer the vital, intangible attributes of strong work ethics, resourcefulness, ability to follow orders, flexibility, and accountability and dedication to mission.[20]

"I use the word resourcefulness because veterans do quite well with respect to earning power, as compared to their non-veteran peers.

"For example, Department of Veterans Affairs researcher Robert E. Klein, Ph.D., has published often on this topic. In his 1989 analysis that I believe is still relevant today, Dr. Klein found:[21]

- 'Veterans in general fare better than non-veterans with respect to both personal and family income, and have done so consistently for many years;

• 'Veterans' median personal income during the [earlier Klein] analysis in 1987 was 27 percent higher than non-veterans' median personal income; and

• 'Except for the youngest [recently-separated from military service] men in 1988, veterans have higher median income than non-veterans at each age and in each year [between 1978 and 1988].'

"In my opinion, Dr. Klein's data is instructive as to why employers strive to hire veterans."

VETERANS PERSONIFY ECONOMIC STRENGTH...

Mr. Lutz

Bob Lutz

"I'm Bob Lutz, vice chairman of General Motors.

"Veterans personify economic strength... veterans represent the ready work force for the 21st century... veterans, regardless of their generation, have the soft skills that every employer seeks: team players with a strong work ethic, loyalty, the ability to start a job and get it done all the way through."[22]

Mr. Wohlwend

Steve Wohlwend

"I'm Steve Wohlwend, senior division manager of Industrial Relations for John Deere & Company, a 167-year-old global enterprise.

"When citizen/soldiers return home and bring their added skills, training, and work ethic, they assist our company in meeting the competitive challenges of the global marketplace."[23]

Mr. Poriotis

Wes Poriotis

"I'm Wes Poriotis, CEO of Wesley, Brown & Bartle Global Executive Recruiting.

"... over 4 million veterans have transitioned [through March 2004] from the armed services since the end of the first Gulf War. This is a great deal of talent being infused into the workforce at a rate of 1,000 continuing every work day."[24]

Mr. Scott

Harold Scott

"I'm Harold Scott, vice president of human resources for Harley-Davidson Motor Company, a company with a century old tradition of making great motorcycles.

"At Harley-Davidson, we experience the positive contributions of military veterans every day. From leadership positions throughout every level of the company, military veterans have brought in a work ethic reflective of the training and experiences that they have acquired... ."[25]

Mr. Horigan

"I'm Kevin Horigan, group vice president, Public Services, PeopleSoft, Inc.

"Our veterans have critical skills not easily accessible to the private sector, skills including communications, encryption, security, and other computer technology skills, health care logistics and manufacturing... . But there are other characteristics as well that make veterans an attractive group for recruitment and employment—loyalty, stress management, discipline, and leadership."[26]

Mr. Crawford

"I'm Robert C. Crawford, vice president for staffing, Prudential Financial Services—an industry leader for 126 years.

"America's veterans have been, and continue to be, an extraordinary source of the diverse qualities and skills that Prudential knows it needs to compete and prosper... .We recognize the emphasis in today's military on leadership at all levels, decision-making, problem-solving, team work, resourcefulness, dependability, and loyalty."[27]

> "AMERICA'S VETERANS HAVE...
> SKILLS THAT PRUDENTIAL
> KNOWS IT NEEDS TO
> COMPETE AND PROSPER..."
> —*Robert C. Crawford,*
> *vice president for staffing,*
> *Prudential Financial Services*

Mr. Montgomery

Veterans also help meet America's workforce and economic competitiveness needs—including competing in the world economy—through 420[28] military occupational skills that are directly transferable to our civilian economy.

Electronics technician, jet engine mechanic, avionics specialist, nuclear propulsion specialist, hospital corpsman, procurement specialist, human resources specialist, logistician, finance specialist,

> "... 420 MILITARY OCCUPATIONAL SKILLS... ARE DIRECTLY TRANSFERABLE TO OUR CIVILIAN ECONOMY."
> —*House Committee on Veterans' Affairs*

and military police officer are just a few examples.

Notes Major General (Ret) Evan Gaddis, president, National Electrical Manufacturers Association:[29]

Maj. Gen. Gaddis

Evan Gaddis

"Part of my earlier responsibility as head of Army Recruiting Command—and that of my top-notch team—was to tie military training to the civilian world for soldiers and employers.

"We learned the importance of doing so from focus groups that we held with enlistees who had been in the Army for about one year. We simply asked our soldiers what was important to them. They told us they wanted the Army to develop a link between their military jobs and civilian employers **before** they enlisted so opportunities would be there **after** they left the military.

"So we contacted companies like Pepsi Cola, Frito-Lay, and John Deere & Company—among many others—who made commitments to hire soldiers in many different technical specialties **before** they enlisted because the companies needed those same technical skills when the soldiers left the military.

"We also established linkages with civilian, competency based apprenticeship programs so that a soldier's military time in those specialties would count toward fulfilling apprenticeship requirements. Private-sector firms were very happy to establish the link because they ultimately wanted former service members in their ranks as established performers."

The New York Times

Execs With Military Background Do Best

New Haven, Conn. — On November 13, a panel of distinguished journalists and military officials will meet in an open forum at Yale's Luce Hall Auditorium, 34 Hillhouse Avenue, to discuss ethical issues surrounding media coverage of events in a time of war.

Beginning at 7:45 p.m., the forum is a continuation of a symposium on the media and the war on terrorism held on the Yale campus last year.

"How do you maintain truth-telling in th[e]... fundamental question to be debated, sa[id]... political science department who has or[ganized]...

"Finding the balance between satisfying the public's r[ight]... respecting the responsibility of intelligence agencies a[nd]... sensitive information, is an ongoing concern for journ[alists]... more critical in a war against terrorism," says Flink.

Participants in the forum are former Under Secretary [of State] Townsend Hoopes; James F. Hoge, Jr., editor of Fore[ign Affairs]... Bernard E. Trainor, Lt. Gen. USMC(Ret); and vetera[n]... Wilson.

Brief biographical sketches of the participants follow[:]

Senior Fellow of Washington College, Hoopes is a re[cognized expert on] international security. He has had a long career in gov[ernment]... international consulting firm Cresap, McCormick and [Paget]... Deputy for International Security Affairs at the Penta[gon]... Subsequently, he served as president of the Associati[on of]... Americans for SALT and director of the American C[ommittee]... numerous works on international affairs and contem[porary issues]... Intervention" (on the Vietnam War), "The Devil and J[ohn Foster Dulles]... and Times of James Forrestal" (co-authored with Dou[glas Brinkley]... won the 1992 Theodore and Franklin D. Roosevelt N[aval History Prize]... collection of his essays and speeches was published i[n "Adventures in] the Creation of the UN" (co-authored with Brinkley)[...]

Hoge spent three decades in newspaper journalism, se[rving as a]... correspondent, editor-in-chief and publisher of the Ch[icago Sun-Times]... then publisher and president of the New York Daily N[ews]... the editor of Foreign Affairs in 1992. He was a Fello[w at the]... Kennedy School of Government in 1991, a Senior Fe[llow]...

LOS ANGELES BUSINESS JOURNAL

Ex-Soldiers Are Recruited Again (and Eagerly) for Civilian Jobs

By EILENE ZIMMERMAN
Published: June 19, 2006

A confluence of events — media coverage of the Iraq war, a patriotic desire to support the troops and corporate America's struggle to fill jobs and groom leaders — has hiring managers tapping one of the nation's most diverse and well-trained talent pools: the 220,000 men and women who leave military service each year.

Job boards for former military personnel are expanding rapidly — Military.com is growing about 50 percent a year and RecruitMilitary about 35 percent a year. Sales at VetJobs, which charges employers to post jobs on its Web site, are up 200 percent over last year. The Destiny Group, which operates more than 100 veteran-specific career sites, reports a 250 percent increase in its business over the last year.

Extensive coverage of the war, recruiters say, has created a largely positive perception of the military. "They aren't a bunch of grunts sitting in the woods smoking, with all kinds of things on their helmets," said Bill Gaul, Destiny's

Mr. Montgomery

The headlines of two 2006 articles in the *Los Angeles Business Journal* and *New York Times* tell it all: "Execs With Military Background Do Best" and "Ex-Soldiers Are Recruited Again (and Eagerly) for Civilian Jobs."[30]

With about 200,000 talented and resourceful service members leaving our active-duty military each year—many of whom have high-tech skills—the hiring of veterans fundamentally represents a good business decision for our economy.[31]

Folks, I'll close this part of our chapter by noting again that about 2.3 million service members have used the Montgomery GI Bill while also transferring their hard and soft skills to our civilian economy.

With respect to economic investment, the Klemm Analysis Group, Inc., released its year-long evaluation of the Montgomery GI Bill in April 2000. Klemm conducted the analysis under a contract from the Department of Veterans Affairs.

The Legislative and Executive Branches use program evaluations to assess how well public programs are working.

Noted project director Rebecca Klemm:[32]

Ms. Klemm

"The federal government realizes a sizable financial gain on its investment for benefits users [veterans and service members] who complete a traditional academic program [two- or four-year degree]. The ratio of government benefits to cost is more than $2 received for every $1 spent. Private [economy] returns are even higher (more than $7 to $1)."

Rebecca Klemm

Mr. Montgomery

Elected officials function as stewards of the public trust with regard to taxpayer-financed programs, such as

"THE RATIO OF GOVERNMENT BENEFITS TO COST IS MORE THAN $2 RECEIVED FOR EVERY $1 SPENT."
—*Rebecca Klemm, Ph.D.*

the Montgomery GI Bill. The Klemm finding said to us that we successfully used public dollars to generate an investment in both public and private dollars.

OUR WORKFORCE AND DOMESTIC ECONOMY TODAY

Let's hear now from former Assistant Secretary of Labor for Veterans' Employment and Training Charles "Chic" Ciccolella. Mr. Ciccolella has an excellent vantage point on our domestic economy because his agency is "responsible for helping veterans make the transition from the military to good civilian jobs."[33]

Mr. Ciccolella

"Mr. Chairman, before we talk about what the future holds, I'd like to talk about where we are at with respect to our workforce and domestic economy.

"To help us, here are seven factual nuggets I have gleaned from the economic reports of the President submitted to Congress in 2008, 2007, and 2006. You may view the reports on-line.[34] The 2008 report focuses on our 2007 economy, the 2007 report on the 2006 economy, and the 2006 report on the 2005 economy.

Charles Ciccolella

2008 REPORT

"The 2008 report is the most recent—and probably the most visible one—as it serves as background to the H.R. 5140, the Economic Stimulus Act of 2008, a short-term economic stimulus package. President George W. Bush signed H.R. 5140 into law on February 13, 2008.[35] Now the nuggets.

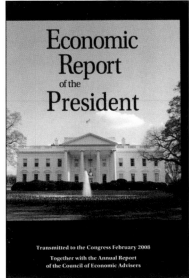

2008 Report

"First, the 2008 report notes 'economic expansion continued for the sixth consecutive year in 2007. The economic growth came despite a weak housing sector [widespread mortgage foreclosures due to subprime loans], credit tightening, and high energy prices.... Projections of weaker growth in the first half of 2008 and near-term risks of a broader economic slowdown, however, led the President to call on the Congress to enact a short-term economic growth package.'[36]

"However, the 2007 and 2006 reports provide greater information on the workforce development issues; issues in which we are interested. So, we'll focus on those issues, including the U.S. economy proper, unemployment, information technology, productivity, workforce capability, and workforce availability.

2007 REPORT

"Second, 'The **United States economy** continues to demonstrate remarkable resilience, flexibility, and growth. Having previously endured a stock market collapse, recession, terrorist attacks, and corporate scandals, this year [2005] the economy showed strong growth and robust job creation in the face of higher energy prices and devastating natural disasters. This is the hard work of America's workers, supported by pro-growth tax policies.... .

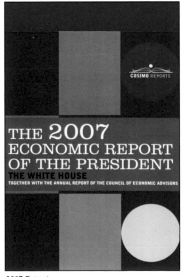

2007 Report

"'Further, the economic expansion continued for the fifth consecutive year in 2006. This economic growth comes despite numerous headwinds, and results from inherent U.S. economic strengths and pro-growth policies.'[37]

"Third, regarding **unemployment**, 'The average unemployment rate in 2006 (4.6 percent) was below the averages of the 1970s, the 1980s, and the 1990s.... . The number of long-term unemployed fell by 263,000 during the year.'[38]

"Fourth, regarding **information technology**, 'The United States has gained more from rapid advances in information technology than the other major industrialized countries because its culture of entrepreneurship and its flexible markets for products, capital, and labor have allowed American businesses to make the most of these changes.'[39]

2006 REPORT

"Fifth, '**Productivity**—how much workers produce per hour—has accelerated since 2000. In the past five years, productivity has grown faster than in any other major industrialized country[40] since 2001... .[41]

"'Productivity growth will be even more important as new technologies accelerate global economic integration and **as the population ages** [emphasis added].'[42]

"Sixth, regarding **workforce capability**, 'A recent study of U.S. economic growth between 1950 and 1993 found that one-third of productivity growth over this period was due to increased levels of education.[43]

"'Both economic research and common sense suggest that workers' skills play a critical role in economic growth and individual well-being. In the

2006 Report

past, rapid increases in schooling levels helped to raise the U.S. standards of living, but in recent years improvements in educational attainment have slowed. Unless the United States can improve the educational achievement of its residents, it may be difficult to sustain rapid economic growth in the future.[44]

"'Workers often obtain training at community colleges, generally two-year post-secondary institutions that offer certificates and associate's degrees. Community colleges play an important role in providing training to workers both directly and through employers. Of individuals age 30 and older attending college, about half go to a community college, compared with one-third of traditional college age.'[45]

"Mr. Chairman, seventh and last, is **availability of workforce**. 'Participation in the labor force—by working or looking for a job—declines as workers age through their 50s and 60s.[46]

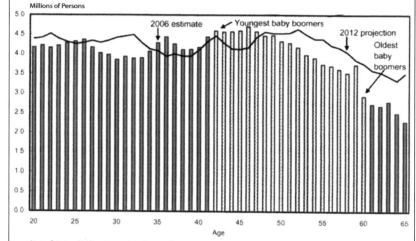

U.S. Population By Age
Because of the aging of the baby-boom generation, the U.S. population in 2012 will have many more people of ages 55-65, and fewer of ages 35-45.

Note: October 2006 estimates from Census Bureau. The 2012 population is projected using growth factors from Census Bureau's 2004 Interim Projections applied to 2006 population estimates.
Sources: Department of Commerce (Census Bureau) and Council of Economic Advisers.

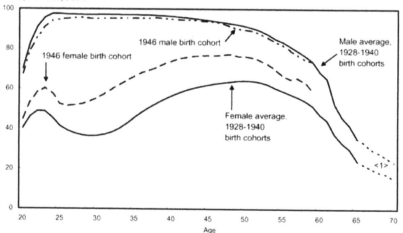

Labor Force Participation Rates By Age
This age-participation profile follows the same birth cohorts as they get older. Participation rates for men and women edge down during their 50's and fall sharply during their 60's.

<1> Not all 13 cohorts are included in participation estimates for age 65 and older because some cohorts are still too young. These participation rates have been adjusted to account for the reduced number of cohorts.
Source: Department of Labor (Bureau of Labor Statistics) with interpolations by Council of Economic Advisers.

"'As baby boomers (those born between 1946 and 1964) reach retirement, growth in total hours of work across the U.S. economy will slow, and the United States will have to depend increasingly on productivity growth to drive increases in gross domestic product. While labor force growth will slow, the elderly population will expand relatively quickly. Strong GDP growth must continue in order to maintain the standards of living for both the working age and dependent populations.[47]

"'Because of the aging of the baby-boom generation, the U.S. population in 2012 will have many more people of ages 55-65, and fewer of ages 35-45.[48]

"'The large baby-boom cohorts are now 42 to 60 years old, and their aging will shift a sizeable fraction of the population into age brackets with lower [workforce] participation rates, thus decreasing the share of the population in the high [workforce]-participation ages.'"[49]

Mr. Montgomery

WORKFORCE CHALLENGES AHEAD

We heard above that while our U.S. economy is resilient, it is not operating at full throttle. The U.S. workforce development landscape has to change **now** if we are going to be able to compete in a world economy in which other countries produce goods and services more cheaply; especially "since 95 percent of the world's customers live outside of our borders, opening international markets to our goods and services is critical for our economy."[50]

Tony Zeiss, president of Piedmont Community College (PCC) in Charlotte, NC, observed in 2005 that "America is about to experience the greatest labor shortage in history. At the same time, today's skilled workers—already too few in number—are more independent and mobile than ever."[51]

Beth Buehlmann, who spoke earlier, notes: "There will be a shortage of 10 million workers to meet projected job growth by 2010. The Bureau of Labor Statistics predicts there will be only 157 million people… to fill 167 million jobs."[52]

Here's more. The consequences of a tight labor market have already emerged.

Notes President Zeiss: "A serious lack of workers will begin in 2005 and grow to 5.3 million by 2010 and to 14 million by 2015. If the need for unskilled workers is included, the shortage will be 7 million in 2010 and 21 million by 2020. Shortages will be most acute among managers, who are approaching retirement, and skilled workers in high-tech jobs.[53]

"The pressure to find and keep skilled workers is already becoming serious and will get progressively worse. Baby boomers are retiring in record numbers, and there are not enough people in succeeding generations to fill the need. In fact, by 2010 some 30 million workers will be older than 55, and organizations both public and private are facing a dual challenge of decreasing workers and declining worker skills.[54]

"In addition, only 20 percent of American jobs require a bachelor's degree or higher, yet 75 percent require technical skills training beyond high school."[55]

Scholar Charles Murray of the American Enterprise Institute observes:[56]

Mr. Murray

Charles Murray

"Our culture puts a false premium on the [four-year] college degree; for a few occupations, a college degree still certifies a qualification. For example, employers appropriately treat a bachelor's degree in engineering as a requirement for hiring engineers. But a bachelor's degree in a field such as sociology, psychology, economics, history or literature certifies nothing.

"One glimpse of the future is offered by the nation's two-year colleges. They… provide courses that meet [student] needs more explicitly. Their time frame gives them a big advantage—two years is about right for learning many technical specialties, while four years is unnecessarily long.

"The spread of wealth at the top of American society has created an explosive increase in the demand for craftsmen… . Finding a good carpenter, painter, electrician, plumber, glazier, mason—the list goes on and on—is difficult, and it is a seller's market.

"Journeymen craftsmen routinely make incomes in the top half of the income distribution while master craftsmen can make six figures. They work even in a soft economy. Their jobs cannot be outsourced to India."

Mr. Ciccolella

"Noted President George W. Bush speaking in Charlotte, NC, in 2004:"

President Bush

"We're not training enough people to fill the jobs of the 21st century. There is a skills gap. And if we don't adjust quickly and if we don't do smart things with the taxpayers' money, if we don't properly use our community colleges, we're going to have a shortage of skilled workers in the decades to come."[57]

President George W. Bush

Mr. Ciccolella

"Lastly, let me share with you the (still instructive) February 2004 remarks of former Representative Steve Gunderson (R-WI):"

Mr. Gunderson

"We're in a silent crisis regarding labor shortages and skills gaps. By 2006 the business community will be shouting to Congress for greater job training.[58] We're in a workforce revolution."[59]

Steve Gunderson

Mr. Ciccolella

"Here's more from the Economic Report of the President transmitted to Congress in February 2008:"[60]

President Bush

"In 2005, the federal government spent nearly $15 billion (excluding Pell grants) on job training and employment programs. These programs assist many workers in getting the training and other services they need to advance their careers.

"However, these programs can be strengthened. The $15 billion in job training money is spread among nine different government agencies and more than 40 different programs, most with their own rules, eligibility requirements, administrative staff, and overhead costs. **Much of this money is not used to support job training programs** [emphasis added] but instead funds job-referral services or job-search assistance.

"To get more job training dollars into the hands of workers, eliminate unnecessary duplication of services, and improve accountability, [I have] proposed consolidating several large job training and employment programs into a single grant that would be used to provide job training vouchers.

"These vouchers, known as Career Advancement Accounts, would be administered by each state but controlled largely **by the worker** [emphasis added], who could use the account to pay for education and training. The education and training could take place either at postsecondary institutions or through apprenticeships or other work-based training… ."

Mr. Ciccolella

"Representative Gunderson also revealed some disturbing trends:"[61]

Mr. Gunderson

"… While the United States will graduate 2.3 million students from college in 2005, China will graduate 2.7 million, and India will graduate 2.1 million.

"As former second- and third-world countries increase the knowledge levels of their populations, they will not only be positioned to take jobs from the United States, but they will also become more creative about producing their **own new** technologies [emphasis added]."

Mr. Ciccolella

"Policies that welcome the world's 'best and brightest' can contribute to future U.S. competitiveness. More than one-fifth of America's scientists and engineers come from abroad.[62] But that number is declining.

"In 2003, almost 150,000 students from abroad were enrolled in science and engineering graduate programs at U.S. universities. Nonetheless, in a post-911 world, new enrollment of such students has been falling. Between 2001 and 2003 (the latest year available), first-time international graduate student enrollment in U.S. science and engineering programs declined by 13 percent."[63]

NANOTECHNOLOGY

Mr. Montgomery

As Chairman Brown and our business leaders said earlier, many in our military have jobs or responsibilities that use high technology, especially information technology. And veterans are poised to help fill the void in science and engineering.

I look to veterans to take their information technology skills to the next level by acquiring additional skills and training in nanotechnology, for example. It would be a logical progression. Mr. Tom Speicher of Pennsylvania College of Technology—an affiliate of Pennsylvania State University— helps us with this:

Mr. Speicher

"Broadly defined as the manipulation of individual atoms and molecules to form or enhance functional technology,

Tom Speicher

nanotechnology focuses on a world about 80,000 times smaller than a strand of hair but large enough to potentially dwarf the advancements of the 20th century.[64]

"… the National Science Foundation estimates that 2 million workers will be needed to support nanotechnology industries worldwide within the next 15 years.[65]

"According to Lux Research, which brands itself as the world's leading technology research and advisory firm, by 2014, products incorporating nanotechnology will account for $2.6 trillion, or 15 percent, of the world's manufacturing output.[66]

"Today, examples of nanotechnology's influence are evident in fields ranging from agriculture to automotive. As the Web site *www.nanotechwire.com* points out, super small materials and devices facilitated by nanotechnology can result in ultra-compact data storage and faster computing, more effective drug delivery, more efficient solar energy conversion, and stronger and tougher manufacturing materials."[67]

Mr. Ciccolella

"Lastly, let's read what *U.S. News and World Report* had to say in May 2006:[68]

U.S.News & WORLD REPORT

"'Last fall, The National Academies, experts on science, engineering, and medicine, issued a report aptly titled, *Rising Above the Gathering Storm.*

"'It warned that unless the United States moves fast, China, India, and others rapidly will catch up with us competitively. America maintains commanding leads in high technology; but we've gone from a $54 billion **surplus** [emphasis added] in 1990 to a $50 billion **deficit** [emphasis added] today. Last year, American investors put more money in foreign stock funds than in domestic.

"'Part of the reason our rivals are catching up with us is their lower costs.

"'A high-tech company in the United States, says the national commission, can now find and employ eight young engineers in India for the cost of just one in America. But another reason is that China and India are aggressively preparing for the future through education. Within five years, observers believe, 90 percent of all of the world's scientists and engineers will live in Asia.'"

Mr. Montgomery

So in a nut shell, here is what I think we've heard in this chapter from our many experts:

• First, the 180,000 or so veterans of our military who join our domestic economy each year add value to it through the hard and soft skills they possess, and also from the skills they bring to our economy gained through the Montgomery GI Bill;

• Second, employers look to veterans to play leadership roles in the composition of our domestic economy/workforce, as baby boomers retire in record numbers creating a labor shortage; and

• Third, to compete on the world economic stage in continuously emerging technologies—and especially nanotechnology— veterans of our high-tech All-Volunteer Force are poised to play a value-added, leadership role.

THANK YOU, STUDENTS!

Folks, I'll close this section of our final chapter by thanking you for having me in your classroom. Thanks for the opportunity to talk with you directly about the challenges of writing laws. I've greatly enjoyed the journey with you. I earnestly hope you've learned some things along the way about working across the aisle and the art of legislative leadership.

Lt. Col. Campbell

"Ladies and gentlemen, my name is Anne Campbell.[69]

"The Montgomery Institute and Mississippi State University have provided the needed financial support for Mr. Montgomery's case study.

"They have asked me if I would speak on behalf of the 2.3 million

Sonny and Lt. Col. Anne Campbell.

former service members who have used the Montgomery GI Bill so far. I'm honored to do so.

"After graduating from the Air Force Academy, I served for 20 years as an Air Force officer and have used the Montgomery GI Bill.

"What is so helpful about the Montgomery GI Bill is one can use it for either full- or part-time study, for either undergraduate or graduate work, for technical school, for on-job learning and apprenticeship, or for starting and growing a small business. The Montgomery GI Bill enables former service members to pursue their education and new careers without being saddled with huge student loan debts.

"I am honored to say on behalf of both service members and veterans across America who have used the Montgomery GI Bill that Mr. Montgomery and his colleagues and supporters have our deepest thanks and respect."

Mr. Hammerschmidt

John Paul Hammerschmidt

"Folks, I'm John Paul Hammerschmidt.

"On November 9, 2005, George W. Bush presented Mr. Montgomery with the Presidential Medal of Freedom, the highest award America gives to civilians. Noted the President:"[70]

President Bush

"During his three decades as a member of the House of Representatives from Mississippi, Sonny Montgomery was a tireless champion for America's veterans.

"A decorated veteran of World War II and the Korean War, Sonny Montgomery brought his personal experience and expertise to his service on the Veterans' Affairs Committee and the Armed Services Committee. He sponsored the landmark Montgomery GI Bill, which has helped make higher education and professional and vocational training accessible to millions of America's veterans.

"The United States honors Sonny Montgomery for his service to his country and for his dedicated work to honor and improve the lives of the men and women who we owe our liberty."

President Bush presents Sonny with the Presidential Medal of Freedom during a White House ceremony, November, 2005.

Sonny's Lessons Learned

Write laws for tomorrow—not just today. Frank Murkowski and Alan Cranston figured this out with respect to the workforce development purpose clause they added to the Montgomery GI Bill. Now you have, as well!

Worth Repeating

"Our nearest competitor, Japan, recognized the importance of education for its future 25 years ago, when its Economic Council declared, 'Economic competition among nations is a technical competition that has become an educational competition.'"

—Alan Cranston, chairman,
and Frank Murkowski, ranking member
Report of the Senate Committee on Veterans' Affairs
on the New GI Bill Continuation Act, March 1987

"Veterans personify economic strength... veterans represent the ready workforce for the 21st century... veterans, regardless of their generation, have the soft skills that every employer seeks: team players with a strong work ethic, loyalty, the ability to start a job, and get it done all the way through."

—Bob Lutz, vice chairman General Motors

"... Over four million veterans have transitioned from the armed forces since the end of the first Gulf War... this is a great deal of talent being infused into the workforce at a rate of 1,000 continuing every work day."

—Wes Poriotis, CEO,
Wesley, Brown & Bartle Global Executive Recruiting

"The rate of government benefits to [the Montgomery GI Bill's] cost is more than $2 received for every $1 spent. Private [economy] returns are even higher (more than $7 to $1)."

—Dr. Rebecca Klemm

AFTERWORD

FROM MACK FLEMING

Chairman Montgomery created educational opportunity for millions of young men and women of our military who otherwise may not have had that opportunity. Indeed I think the Chairman would have described the Montgomery GI Bill's Oct. 19, 2009, 25th anniversary, fundamentally as a testament to them and their initiative.

Mack Fleming

Chairman Montgomery ensured that America's veterans were represented at the highest councils of government by championing legislation, with Rep. Gerald B.H. Solomon, that made the Veterans Administration a cabinet department.

Working with fellow Chairman Alan Cranston, Mr. Montgomery played a valued role in enacting The Veterans Judicial Review Act of 1988, which created the U.S. Court of Appeals for Veterans Claims.

A citizen-soldier his entire adult life, Mr. Montgomery worked tirelessly for the National Guard and Reserves and their valued role in responding to natural disasters at home and military threats abroad.

But I think Chairman Montgomery's enduring legislative achievements represented just one part of this unique man. He made many trips to South Vietnam to be with our soldiers. After the war ended, Mr. Montgomery led a delegation to North Vietnam on four occasions in search of American soldiers and airmen who were missing in action.

Lastly, the Chairman's quiet bearing, polite manner, and down-home friendliness made people feel comfortable. House colleagues described Mr. Montgomery as "an island of calm in a sea of contentiousness" when debate boiled over. He was the person political allies and adversaries alike turned to. And he never got wrapped up in what we might call his own importance. The legions of Americans that Mr. Montgomery befriended indeed knew they had a friend for life.

Mack G. Fleming
Staff Director and Chief Counsel
Committee on Veterans' Affairs
U.S. House of Representatives—1981-1994
Sewanee, South Carolina
October 2010

FROM ROBERT (BOB) BAILEY

I worked with Representative Montgomery in community, educational, military, and business settings for some 40 years. Sonny was more than a treasured friend. Like so many Mississippians, I considered Sonny a valued teacher and mentor.

Bob Bailey

Four irreplaceable values shaped Sonny's life: faith, patriotism, relationships, and perseverance. These values and his gentle demeanor served him well in 41 years of public service.

Sonny never forgot where he came from or the opportunities afforded him as a young man. Sonny's legacy of leadership and service lives on through the G.V. "Sonny" Montgomery Foundation, which furnishes scholarships and provides leadership recognition at Sonny's alma mater, Mississippi State University. The enduring qualities of this unique man continue to empower our citizens, even in his passing.

Robert (Bob) Bailey
President, The G.V. "Sonny" Montgomery Foundation
Yazoo City, Mississippi
October 2010

What's the True Secret of Good Leadership? There Is None.

Bookstores are filled with hundreds of volumes on leadership and management, many promising the "secret" to being an effective leader. But there are no secrets to good leadership, other than common sense and hard work. Do you remember that first Town Hall meeting when I arrived at State over a year ago? We talked about the qualities and demands of leadership. I laid out some of the principles that are important to any organization if it is to succeed in its mission and maintain the highest morale among its ranks. Let me recap and add a little more.

Dare to be the skunk at the picnic. Every organization should tolerate rebels who tell the emperor he has no clothes. This is not a license to be mean or rude. But make the tough decisions, confront people who need it, reward those who perform best. Speak your mind. Work toward consensus building and don't hide from reality.

The day people stop bringing you their problems is the day you have stopped leading them. Open your door and encourage folks to come in with their ideas and opinions. Let them argue with you. The people in the field, in the trenches, are closest to the problem and that is where the real wisdom lies.

It is people who get things done. Plans don't accomplish work. Organizational charts don't either. People do. That's why every individual is important. Set yourself the goal of creating an environment where the best, the brightest, the most creative are attracted, retained and unleashed.

Challenge people to reinvent their jobs. Even large organizations can wither when leaders won't challenge the old, comfortable ways of doing things. Effective leaders create a climate where people's worth is measured by their willingness to learn new skills and see new responsibilities, thus constantly reinventing their jobs.

Perpetual optimism is a multiplier. Do not pollute the atmosphere with pessimism. The ripple effect of a leader's enthusiasm and optimism is incredible. The Marines call this a gung ho attitude: we can change things, we can achieve the impossible, we are the best. The Marines are right. Avoid whining and blaming. Embrace optimism.

In any crisis, occasionally stop and step away from the confusion and shouting. Ask yourself two simple questions: What am I doing that I shouldn't be doing? and, What am I not doing that I ought to be doing to influence the situation in our favor? Work actively to shape the crisis and create success.

Come up for air. Demand excellence from people but also insist that they have lives outside the office. You don't have to prove to anybody that you can work 16 hours a day if you can get it done in eight. Surround yourself with people who take their work seriously, but not themselves.

Of all the little lessons above, the one about people as the ingredient that makes the recipe work stands out. People are the most important part of any organization. That is why leadership is an art; management a science. At the end of the day, leadership is getting people to use their full talents to support your shared objective. That requires all that we've said above, to be sure; but above all it requires caring deeply about the people you are leading—about their training, quality of life, their todays, and their tomorrows. Without that caring, it's all dull science—and doomed to fail sooner or later.

During the past year, we've explored ways to bring this philosophy of leadership to the State Department in a more structured way. Part of that effort is what we're doing at the Foreign Service Institute. FSI's revised Leadership and Management Training Continuum, its Training Continuum for Foreign Service Generalists (see *State Magazine* for December 2001, page 34) and the recently released (online) Training Continuum for Civil Service Employees provide guidance on the training and education in leadership that is essential throughout an individual's career.

A key element of this approach is the integration of leadership training at all stages of an employee's professional life, rather than waiting until the employee assumes a senior position. Much of this training and education will be mandatory. Moreover, an employee's leadership skills will be weighed when he or she is being considered for an assignment or promotion. Merely attending a leadership course or class will be insufficient.

The tenets of good leadership must be made part of our daily routine, integrated into everything we do. It is essential that superb leadership become a hallmark of the Department of State. Our shared challenge is to make it so.

—State Magazine, February 2002

Colin L. Powell served as Chairman of the Joint Chiefs of Staff under President George H.W. Bush and Secretary of State under President George W. Bush.

ENDNOTES

CHAPTER 1

This is "Sonny:" Honorable Bill Cohen

1

Senator Cohen acknowledged Montgomery's vision and leadership in a letter to G.V. Montgomery on May 6, 1987, saying, "You can take great pride in what you have done to make what many considered the impossible a reality." Further, in a May 15, 1987, letter Senator Cohen said, "This legislation is a lasting monument to you, your persistence, and your commitment to the young men and women serving in our armed forces." Letters accessed from House Committee on Veterans' Affairs (HCVA) Internal Historical File on the Montgomery GI Bill. As an internal, working file and not one intended to be archived, the files/folders are not uniformly numbered or titled, nor are the contents of the files itemized by subject. However, the contents of the files generally are aggregated by year. The authors do not repeat this caveat in further notes.

2

Mr. Montgomery used the words *politics* and *possibilities* in referring to the longstanding chief counsel and staff director of the House Committee on Veterans' Affairs, Mack G. Fleming, as well: "His [Mr. Fleming's] was the deep commitment of the true believer tempered by a unique practical sense of political possibilities and opportunities." See *Congressional Record*, April 16, 1985, E823. "Politics is the art of the possible" is attributed to Otto Von Bismarck (1815-1898), first chancellor of Germany. See The Quotations Page, "Quotations by Author Otto Von Bismarck" at http://www.quotationspage.com/quotes/Otto_von_Bismarck; (accessed May 11, 2007).

3

For additional information on the lifetime public service of Sonny Montgomery, see Mississippi State University, "Salute to a Patriot: G.V. Sonny Montgomery," http://msuinfo.ur.msstate.edu/alumni/sonny/salutetoapatriot; (accessed March 22, 2006).

4

Military.com, "Advocate for America's Vets Dies," May 15, 2009, www.military.com/NewsContent/0, 13319,97216.00.html; (accessed October 6, 2009).

5

Michael B. Ballard and Craig S. Piper, *Sonny Montgomery: The Veteran's Champion* (Mississippi State University Libraries: University Press of Mississippi, 2003), 62.

6

Light-hearted humor often characterized the friendship of George H.W. Bush and G.V. Montgomery. For example, at a September 18, 1996, farewell salute in honor of Montgomery's 30 years in Congress, both former President Bush and First Lady Barbara Bush told stories: "George Bush delighted the audience with tales of Montgomery's visits to Bush family Thanksgiving dinners at Camp David—especially when he noted that Sonny's blessings before the meals were lengthy in the extreme. Commenting on Montgomery's attire for the [farewell salute] evening, which included his extensive military decorations on the pocket of his tuxedo and the Medal of Freedom he recently won around his neck, Bush quipped: 'I almost didn't recognize Sonny tonight, I thought he was one of those Latin American dictators.' Barbara Bush stole the hearts of East Central Mississippians who have passed the gargantuan sign designating Meridian's G.V. Montgomery National Guard Complex on Interstate 20 for [many] years when she recounted the story of accompanying her husband to the facility's dedication: 'When we arrived, George leaned over to me and whispered, 'We really didn't have to come to this, we could have seen the sign from the White House lawn,' Mrs. Bush said to gales of laughter from Montgomery's Meridian area friends." See "Sharing a Laugh with Sonny," *Starkville Daily News*, September 18, 1996, page number not evident on photocopy. President Bush reportedly has also needled his friend Montgomery by saying, "There are only two things on earth visible from outer space: The Great Wall of China and the sign that says 'G.V. Montgomery National Guard Complex.'"

7

Mississippi State University, "Salute to a Patriot: G.V. 'Sonny' Montgomery," http://msuinfo.ur.msstate.edu/alumni/sonny/salute9.htm. Also, "When Sonny was elected to Congress in 1966, American soldiers were fighting in the war in Vietnam. He demonstrated his concern for those who were involved in that dangerous and deadly region by spending Christmas in Vietnam each year with the soldiers. On these trips, Sonny would carry blank cards with him, and when he ran into young soldiers from Mississippi, he would ask them to write the names and addresses of their families on these cards. When Sonny returned home he would take the time to call each soldier's family to let them know he had seen their son or daughter and relay any stories or news that might interest them. Today, people still thank Sonny for those calls." Ballard and Piper, *Sonny Montgomery: The Veteran's Champion*, 197.

8

Congressional Record, May 8, 1987, S6209. See also *Congressional Record*, November 16, 1979, S16896-S16898 for Mr. Cohen's introductory statement on S. 2020 that would create a non-contributory New GI Bill. Senator Cohen testified on S. 2020 and Senator Armstrong on S. 2596 in the Senate Committee on Veterans' Affairs, June 19, 1980, chaired by Senator Cranston. The hearing's topic was *Educational Incentives and the All-Volunteer Force.*

9

Ibid.

10

For additional information about William S. Cohen, see The Cohen Group, http://www.cohengroup.net.

11

Ibid., 9.

12

Mr. Cohen's Congressional papers and his papers as Secretary of Defense are housed at the University of Maine's Fogler Library. The University also houses the William S. Cohen Center for International Policy and Commerce. See http://www.umaine.edu/cohen/default.html.

13

Congressional Record, May 8, 1987, S6209. Presidents George H.W. Bush and Bill Clinton also used the broad concept of "journey" in referring to the outcome of The *Servicemen's Readjustment Act of 1944.* At a June 5, 1990, ceremony honoring the GI Bill, President Bush said, "The [World War II] GI Bill changed the lives of millions by replacing old road blocks with paths of opportunity. And, in so doing, it boosted America's work force, it boosted America's economy, and really, it changed the life of our nation." *Public Papers of the Presidents of the United States, Administration of George Bush, 1990* (Washington, DC: Government Printing Office, 1991, 777 of Book I.) In a June 22, 1994, ceremony commemorating the 50th anniversary of the GI Bill of Rights, President Clinton said, "The veterans of World War I got… $60 and a train ticket home. The veterans of World War II got a ticket to the American dream." See *Public Papers of Presidents of the United States, Administration of William J. Clinton, 1994* (Washington, DC: Government Printing Office, 1994, 1103 of Book I). Also, in a February 4, 1997, address before a joint session of the Congress on the State of the Union, President Clinton again referenced the GI Bill and the journey metaphor: "We must expand the frontiers of learning across a lifetime; all our people, of whatever age, must have the chance to learn new skills. Most Americans live near a community college. The roads that take them there can be paths to a better future. My GI Bill for America's workers will transform the confusing tangle of federal training programs into a simple skill grant to go directly into eligible worker's hands." *Public Papers of Presidents, William J. Clinton*, 1997, 112.

14

Andrew Carnegie, "[Teamwork] is the fuel that allows common people to attain uncommon results."

15

Congressional Record, March 17, 1987, H1302. Noted Mr. Montgomery, "Mr. Speaker, let me first thank the many people in this chamber for making this day possible. This was a **team** effort and so many deserve credit for this historic bill." [emphasis added]. Additionally, at H1313, Mr. Montgomery said, "I do appreciate the wonderful, kind things that have been said here today. It is really not me, it has been a **team** effort totally." [emphasis added]. Lastly, at H1318, Montgomery said, "There are many, many members of the House of Representatives and other laymen who have participated and made the bill possible. It is not one individual's efforts. As I keep repeating, it has been a **team** effort all the way."

16

"Military personnel groups" are civilian organizations that represent active duty, Reserve, or retired military persons. Some examples include the Association of the U.S. Army, Navy League, Fleet Reserve Association, Air Force Association, the Marine Corps League, the Non Commissioned Officers Association of the United

States, the Military Officers Association of America, National Guard Association, Enlisted Association of the National Guard of the United States, and Reserve Officers Association.

17

Nineteen was the uniform age at which young men were drafted at the time through the United States Selective Service System. From August 1964 until February 1973, the United States drafted 1,857,304 young men into military service. Selective Service System, "History & Records," http://www.sss.gov/induct.html; (accessed May 7, 2007).

18

The authors document this statement in Chapters 15, 16, and 17.

19

VEAP took effect on January 1, 1977, enacted as Public Law 94-502. VEAP was a five-year pilot program. The Montgomery GI Bill (MGIB) took effect as a permanent program on June 1, 1987, enacted as Public Law 100-48. Neither VEAP nor MGIB were enacted as "war-time" legislation that would inactivate at a war's conclusion. The MGIB was the single, ongoing permanent program from 1987 until 2008 when Congress also created the Post-9/11 GI Bill in Public Law 100-252, which took effect August 1, 2009.

20

Memorandum from Ted Van Hintum, assistant director for program management, Education Service, Department of Veterans Affairs, April 17, 2007, 1. Memorandum in possession of Mississippi State University.

CHAPTER 2

The World War II GI Bill: The Legacy Begins

1

The characters listed at the beginning of each chapter primarily are those who played a role at the time the events portrayed in the chapter took place. However, the authors include more modern-day figures here, too, when such persons can offer insight. For example, among others in this chapter, the authors include the Honorable Anthony Principi, Secretary of Veterans Affairs, 2001-2005.

2

"New GI Bill Would Repay Nation's 'Freedom Debt,'" *Stamford (CT) Advocate*, July 8, 2003. Similar articles appeared in the *Fredericksburg (VA) Free Lance Star* on July 5 and the *Victorville (CA) Press Dispatch* on July 6. Articles are (1) provided by Burrelles Information Service; (2) furnished to the authors by the late Michael G. Bennett; and (3) in possession of Mississippi State University.

3

Dwight Young, ed., *Dear Mr. President: Letters to the Oval Office from the Files of the National Archives* (Washington, DC: *National Geographic*, 2006), 75. Many of the American men who were called to arms were drafted. "America's first national military conscription law was enacted in 1862, but it wasn't until World War I that the U.S. relied primarily on the draft to build and maintain its armed forces. The fall of France in 1940 spurred Congress to adopt the first peacetime draft, calling up men aged 21 to 35 for a one-year hitch. Just a year later, with the threat of war looming bigger every day, Congress voted—by a one-vote margin in the House of Representatives—to keep draftees in uniform beyond the end of their one-year term. After the Japanese attack on Pearl Harbor, all able-bodied men aged 18 to 38 were subject to conscription for the duration of the war… .The peak year for conscription, [was 1943] when more than 3.3 million men were drafted… .Almost 10 million men were drafted from 1940 through 1945."

4

In a broad sense, Paul Dickson and Thomas B. Allen suggest the 45,000 World War I veterans who descended on Washington, D.C. during the summer of 1932 planted the seeds that created the 1944 World War II GI Bill of Rights. Dickson and Allen note the "Bonus Army" soldiers "demanded immediate payment of a cash bonus promised them eight years earlier for their wartime service." The ex-soldiers lived in shanty towns and rallied nearly for two months: "On July 28, 1932, going beyond presidential orders, Army Chief of Staff Douglas MacArthur drove the veterans out of the city with tanks, tear gas, and soldiers wielding bayonet-tipped rifles." Dickson and Allen further note "the bonus was finally paid in 1936 when Congress overruled [Franklin Roosevelt's] fourth veto. But the Bonus Army legacy came in 1944 when Congress passed the GI Bill of Rights…" Paul Dickson and Thomas B. Allen, *The Bonus Army: An American Epic* (New York: Walker and Company, 2004), 266-277 and the book's inside cover. For an additional description of these Depression-era veterans who in 1932 formed the Bonus Expeditionary Force ["Bonus Army"] to lobby Congress, see U.S.

Department of Veterans Affairs, *The Veterans Benefits Administration: An Organizational History: 1776-1994,* November 1995, 21-22. Lastly, Janet Maslin observes "for all the defeats that the Bonus Army endured, its struggle paved the way for the GI Bill of Rights." See "Home from the War, Yet the Battle is Just Beginning," *New York Times*, February 21, 2005.

5

Milton Greenberg, *The GI Bill: The Law That Changed America* (New York: Lickle Publishing, 1997), 12. In Chapter 11 of this Montgomery text, Professor Charles Moskos similarly refers to the GI Bill as "valuable in terms of name recognition and positive symbolism… ." "The words GI Bill signify commitment to enhancement of the citizen soldier even in an all-volunteer format." We note Milton Greenberg, is professor emeritus of government at The American University, Washington, D.C., where he served as provost and interim president. We cite below other instructive publications Dr. Greenberg has authored on the GI Bill. First, he served as guest editor of a special fall, 1994 issue of the American Council on Education Magazine, *Educational Record*, titled "The GI Bill's Lasting Legacy," on the bill's 50th anniversary. We cite the Educational Record herein at chapter 2 notes 19 and 55, note 6 of chapter 3, and note 15 of chapter 5. Second, Dr. Greenberg authored an article "How the GI Bill Changed Higher Education," published in *The Chronicle of Higher Education*, June 18, 2004, which commemorates the 60th anniversary of the GI Bill. Third, his article "The New GI Bill Is No Match for the Original," published in *The Chronicle of Higher Education*, July 25, 2008, compares the new and older versions of the historic legislation. And fourth, his chapter titled "The GI Bill of Rights: Changing the Social, Economic Landscape of the United States" is part of the U.S. Department of State book, *Historians on America*, April 3, 2008. The book discusses 11 "tipping points" in American history.

6

The Bill of Rights is the first 10 amendments to the U.S. Constitution containing guarantees of essential rights and liberties. Library of Congress, "Primary Documents in American History," http://www.loc.gov/rr/program/bib/ourdocs/billofrights.html; (accessed May 9, 2007).

7

The authors use the words Army and soldiers frequently throughout the text of this book. Instructive is the manner by which Army leaders refer to the everyday soldiers who represent the heart of the Army. Four examples are as follows. *First*, noted Chief of Staff of the Army General Creighton Abrams, Jr., "People are not in the Army, they **are** the Army." [emphasis added]. Creighton Abrams, "From Agawam to Chief of Staff," *Washington Post*, September 5, 1974. *Second*, observed Abrams, "We are, at root, an Army of people, not of machines nor policies, nor structures." Abrams, "Emphasis Is on Readiness," *Army*, October 1974, 9. *Third*, noted Abrams, "By people I do not mean personnel… . I mean living, breathing, serving, human beings." See Lieutenant General Harris Hollis, U.S. (Ret), "The Heart and Mind of Creighton Abrams," *Military Review* LXV, no. 4 (April 1985): 63. *Fourth*, observed recent Chief of Staff of the Army (2003-2007) General Peter Shoomaker, "Humans are more important than hardware. We must always remember that soldiers **are** the Army." [emphasis addcd]. Shoomakcr in the Wcst Point Society of the District of Columbia, "CSA Remarks of October 7, 2003, to Association of U.S. Army at Eisenhower Luncheon," furnished to co-author, Darryl Kehrer, by Keith Fulk, USMA 1976, October 11, 2003.

8

Information about American veterans of both World War I and II and subsequent military conflicts is available through the Veterans History Project (VHP) at the Library of Congress. The VHP mission is to collect and archive the personal recollections of U.S. wartime veterans to honor their service and share their stories with current and future generations. The VHP also collects stories from home front civilians who worked in support of our armed forces. Donated collections take the form of war veterans' firsthand oral histories, memoirs, photographs, letters, diaries, official separation documents, and other historical documents from World War I through current conflicts. Next-of-kin may furnish information on deceased veterans, as well.

9

Greenberg, *The GI Bill*, 12: "In a legendary effort, he drafted the essence of the law on the back of hotel stationary in room 507 of the Mayflower Hotel." Also, see Michael J. Bennett, *When Dreams Came True—The GI Bill and the Making of Modern America* (Washington, London: Brassey's, 1996.) Notes Bennett at 135: "Writing the bill—as Colmery did in Suite 570 of the Mayflower Hotel—was the first essential step toward passage, 'No one alive knows how long it took him to write—in longhand and on hotel stationary—the first draft of what would become introduced as the Servicemen's Readjustment Act of 1944,' *The American Legion Magazine* of June 1984 reported." Greenberg cites room 507, and Bennett cites 570. The engraved plaque commemorating the bill's historic drafting resides in room 570.

10

Greenberg, *The GI Bill*, 11. In July 1943, President Roosevelt spoke to the nation: "Veterans must not be mobilized into an environment of inflation and unemployment, to a place on a bread line or on a corner selling apples. We must this time have plans ready."

11

Testifying before the House Committee on World War Veterans Legislation on March 29, 1944, Mr. Colmery observed in three statements: in the *first* at 396 of the 1944 hearing record on H. R. 3917 and S. 1767, "Bridging of the gap between actual separation and the getting of them back into gainful employment or education, the idea is to see that the veteran is not penalized by reason of his service, and that he is given a fair break toward getting to the position where otherwise he would have been, through, first, education; and second, in the field of employment—job counseling and an opportunity to get back into gainful employment; third, through the various provisions in Title IV; and then lastly, through a readjustment allowance section, as we call it;" in the *second* statement at 399 of the same hearing record, Mr. Colmery says, "In the matter of employment—economic freedom, the opportunity to earn a competent livelihood for one's self and those dependent upon him, is the very cornerstone of all freedoms. Without them [our] civil, political, and religious liberties are just mere sales talk;" in the *third* statement at 400 of the same hearing record, Mr. Colmery says, "For the period of reconversion of industry back to peace-time operation, the absorption of ten or more million [former service members] into pursuit of commerce and industry, the reshifting of many more, both geographically and occupation-wise, the personal dislocation which will create individual problems of adaptability, mental and physical readjustment, and recharting of courses in life—all will create uncertainties and a great potential of anxiety, despair, [and] suffering want, which may be devastating to individual and community life and stability." House Committee on World War Veterans Legislation, *Hearings on H.R. 3917 and S. 1767 to Provide Federal Government Aid For the Readjustment in Civilian Life of Returning World War II Veterans*, January 11, 12, 13, 17, 18; February 24; March 9, 10, 27, 28, 29, 30, 31, 1944. Specifically, hearing of March 29, Testimony of Harry W. Colmery, past commander, The American Legion, 397-400. Documents are contained in the published "History of Veterans Laws; Public Laws 346, 78C, 483, 78C; Veterans Administration, Vol IX; "Tab PL 346, 78C; Department of Veterans Affairs, Office of General Counsel, Legislative Services Division, Washington, D.C.

12

Ibid., 397, 400. House Committee on Veterans' Affairs, *Committee Spotlight: GI Bill 60th Anniversary*, "Statement of the Honorable Henry E. Brown, Jr. of South Carolina on Posthumously Awarding the Medal of Freedom to Harry W. Colmery." July 6, 2004, as excerpted from the *Congressional Record*, http://veterans.house.gov/benefits/gi60th/hbrown.html; (accessed July 18, 2006). Sponsored primarily by Representative Jim Ryun of Kansas, the Colmery-Medal-of-Freedom legislation passed the House in 2004 but did not pass the Senate.

13

For information on House Committee on Veterans' Affairs chairmen and chairwomen since World War II, see http://veterans.house.gov/about/history/pastchairmen.html. Also see endnote 21 in this chapter.

14

After World War II, through the Legislative Reorganization Act of 1946, Congress changed the name of the House Committee on World War Veterans' Legislation to the Committee on Veterans' Affairs. National Archives and Records Administration, *Guide to the Records of the United States House of Representatives at the National Archives—1789-1989 Bicentennial Edition*, Document No. 100-245, 100th Cong., 2nd sess.,1989, 269-271. For a discussion of the creation of the Senate Committee on Veterans' Affairs, see notes for Chapter 12.

15

Michael J. Bennett, *When Dreams Came True: The GI Bill and the Making of Modern America* (Washington, London: Brasseys, 1996), 113. Also, observed Representative Thomas G. Abernethy of Mississippi regarding Rankin: "No member of this or any preceding Congress has been more intently interested in the welfare of the veteran than the gentleman from Mississippi [Mr. Rankin]. For more than 20 years he has fought the battle of veterans on Capitol Hill. He still fights their battles. For his many achievements in their behalf I congratulate him… . In an effort to write the best possible bill, our committee has had this measure under consideration for several months. We have worked hard, unceasingly, and untiringly. For almost three weeks, immediately prior to its being reported out, we went over the bill, in executive session, line by line and paragraph by paragraph." Abernethy statement excerpted from May 18, 1944, *Congressional Record*-Appendix at A2637.

Further, observed Representative Walter Granger of Utah, "I want to join my colleagues in expressing my sincere appreciation to the chairman of the committee, the gentleman from Mississippi [Mr. Rankin], not only for his painstaking effort in the preparation of this bill, but for his long years of unselfish and devoted service given in the interest of veterans of other wars, especially the disabled and their dependents." *Congressional Record*, May 12, 1944, 4531.

16

Ibid. Russell Whelan, "Rankin of Mississippi," *The Nation*, July, 1944, quoted in Bennett, *When Dreams Came True*, 113.

17

Bennett, *When Dreams Came True*, 154.

18

Ibid.

19

The American Council on Education (ACE) and the 55 educational organizations it represented opposed what it perceived would be federal control of institutionally based education and training of veterans on numerous occasions during their public testimony. For example, see 121-123 of the published hearing transcript of the Committee on Education and Labor, United States Senate, December 13, 14, and 15, 1943, on S.1295 and S.1509 regarding The Servicemen's Education and Training Act of 1944. The ACE also expressed such opposition at 308-310 and 313-317 of the published transcript of hearings held by the Committee on World War Veterans Legislation, House of Representatives, March 29, 1944; and at 130-131 of testimony before the Senate Finance Committee on February 11, 1944. The ACE wanted each state—not the federal Veterans Administration—to administer through federal funds what would become known as the GI Bill. Noted ACE President George F. Zook at the aforementioned 313, "In the allocation of powers to the federal government, education was not included, and the founders, therefore, of our republic had very seriously in mind that education was one of those powers which should be reserved to the states and to the people." The ACE also wanted the U.S. Office of Education—rather than the Veterans Administration— to be the federal entity that coordinated the program with the states. Some of Dr. Zook's explicit testimony took on a parochial—if not problematical—tone not evident in the testimony of other council member organizations. For example, at 122 of the published hearing transcript of hearings on the Veterans' Omnibus Bill (S. 1617) before the Subcommittee of the U.S. Senate Committee on Finance, January 14, 15, 21, 24; February 11, 14, 23; March 8 and 10, 1944, Dr. Zook testified on January 14 that "The council has attempted to be familiar with this **problem** of the education of returning veterans… ." [emphasis added]. Further, at the aforementioned 312, Dr. Zook observed that "we suggested that this group of 21 [education] organizations which were specifically interested in this **problem** [of education of returning veterans] might be brought together." [emphasis added]. As early as 1942, Dr. Zook wrote "The executive committee… has authorized the appointment of two temporary committees—one to explore what possible action might be taken for education reconstruction in the United States, including the **problem** of the education of servicemembers after their period of service…" [emphasis added]. See [ACE] *President's Annual Report* 1941-1942, p. 21, as cited in *Educational Record, The Magazine of Higher Education*, Fall 1994, "The GI Bill's Lasting Legacy," 19. In addition, Representative Walter H. Judd of Minnesota defended the view of the ACE: "The set-up for providing education and training for veterans as proposed in Title II of the GI Bill of Rights makes it possible for the Veterans Administration to exercise a control over the education of the veterans which certainly is not necessary to the success of the program and which cannot give the veteran any better service, and might give him a lot worse service than if the actual conduct of the program is through the state and local agencies of education already established, experienced, and operating efficiently." *Congressional Record*-Appendix, May 10, 1944, A2463. Lastly, at the aforementioned 131, Senate Finance Committee Subcommittee on Veterans' Legislation Chairman Bennett Champ Clark observed that "fundamentally, we are concerned about the interest of the veterans… and not the interests of your educational system. In other words, I am perfectly willing to utilize and expand the educational system and supply the money, but I say the administration ought to be in the hands of some federal agency who is interested primarily in the interests of the veteran rather than expanding the universities and colleges."

20

Ibid., 160. Observed Chairman Rankin, "If the bill [S. 1767] passes in its present form [as approved by the Senate] agricultural high schools in the district which I represent will not be included. I would rather have a graduate of one of those high schools in my community than to have some of these sociology professors that I see come in here from what they call the higher educational institutions of the nation; because they [those who attend agricultural high schools] are the ones on whose shoulders rests the responsibility of sustaining the nation in time of peace and fighting its battles in time of war. I am afraid you are getting ready to make this thing top-heavy. I am tired of a few crack-brained professors of the country looking down the noses at the masses of the people who are furnishing the sweat and toil to support the nation in times of peace and whose sons fight for us in time of war, and I want to be particularly careful that we do not aid or abet that philosophy in writing this bill. If the boy from the Long View High School or from the Carolina rural school district wants to go back to that school, he has just as much right to do so as one would to go to Yale or Harvard. That is one thing I want to be particularly careful about." U.S. House of Representatives, Committee on World War Veterans Legislation, *Hearings on H.R. 3917 and S. 1767 to Provide Federal Government Aid for the Readjustment in Civilian Life of Returning World War II Veterans*, January 11, 12, 13, 17, 18; February 24; March 9, 10, 27, 28, 29, 30, 31, 1944. More specifically, note the published Record of Hearing on March 31, at 432 and 433, as contained in published "History of Veterans Laws; Public Laws 346, 78C, 483, 78C; Veterans Administration, Vol IX;" Tab PL 346, 78C; Department of Veterans Affairs, Office of General Counsel, Legislative Services Division, Washington, D.C.

21

Office of the Historian, U.S. House of Representatives, *Women in Congress, 1977-1990* (Washington, DC: Government Printing Office, 1991), 219-220.

22

Mrs. Rogers went on to chair the Committee on Veterans' Affairs during 1947-1948 and 1953-1954.

23

We quote Representative Rogers from the *Congressional Record*, as contained in The House Committee on World War Veterans Legislation published legislative history document on The Servicemen's Readjustment Act of 1944, located in room 340, Cannon House Office Building, Washington, D.C. At the time of the (Montgomery) book's publication, the document is not shelved in room 340, and the authors have been unable to obtain the page number of the Rogers quote. The authors also note James B. Conant, president, Harvard University, asserted the GI Bill "could flood the college campuses with the least capable of the war generation." Bennett, *When Dreams Came True*, 133 and 240. Robert M. Hutchins, President of the University of Chicago, saw the GI Bill as a "threat to American Education." Dickson and Allen, *The Bonus Army-An American Epic*, 272. Hutchins speculated that "colleges and universities will find themselves converted into educational hobo jungles. And veterans, unable to get work and equally unable to resist putting pressure on the colleges and universities, will find themselves educational hobos.... Education is not a device for coping with mass unemployment." Keith W. Olson, *The GI Bill: The Veterans and The Colleges* (University of Kentucky Press, 1974), 25. Lastly, the higher education establishment, headed by Conant and Hutchins, wanted to have direct control of GI Bill money. Noted Representative John Rankin of Mississippi, chairman of the Committee on World War Veterans' Legislation: "This is a bill for veterans, not educators." Bennett, *When Dreams Came True*, 155. Bennett also notes that "as a bill for veterans, not educators, the GI Bill would become a permanent force in American society, as Clark Kerr, former president of the University of California, observed 50 years after the bill's passage. It did so by financing higher education **through students** rather than **through institutions** [emphasis is Kerr's]. Bennett, *When Dreams Came True,* 156. Per Bennett, also at 156, Kerr favored "financing higher education by giving money directly to individuals and, therefore, markets rather than institutions." In addition, Bennett observes at 157 that "the basic pattern of personal rather than institutional financing, first adopted in the GI Bill, has been reaffirmed in subsequent federal programs, such as Pell grants. 'As a result, the intent of the GI Bill lives on,' as Kerr observed." Lastly, Bennett notes at 134 that [the GI Bill was] "so extensive and sweeping that it can be compared only to Lyndon Johnson's Great Society and Civil Rights Legislation. Of course, the great difference was the GI Bill vested control directly in the hands of individuals rather than new federally sponsored community action programs."

24

Interestingly, *sentimental* and *awakening* appear elsewhere in the debate. Noted Representative Emanuel Celler of New York commenting on May 3, 1944, on S. 1767 that had passed the Senate and was under consideration by the House: "No man has yet bought groceries, paid his rent, gone to school or married on a 'thank you.' We are faced with the solemn obligation to assure them those very things they are fighting for, among them, freedom from want, [and] freedom from fear. It is not a question of **sentimental** slobbering over their sacrifices, too many pompous phrases have already covered that. [emphasis added]. It is a question of facing realistically, honestly, without compromise and without flinching, what every fighting man and woman in our armed forces is asking now: 'Where do we go from here, boys?'" Statement excerpted from May 3, 1944,

Congressional Record, A2284, "Servicemen's Readjustment Act," General, Part III, Pub. 346, 78th C., Department of Veterans Affairs, Office of General Counsel, Legislative Services Division. Also, notes Bennett in *When Dreams Came True* at 123: "That was the atmosphere [in February of 1944 of contentiousness between President Roosevelt and a coalition of conservative Democrats and Republicans] in which the GI Bill was wending its way through committee, having been introduced the month before. The New Deal and all of its works had become anathema to the vast majority of members. Even FDR's few stalwart defenders, such as Senator Claude Pepper, had shown some suspicion about the administration's education plans for GIs. The overall feeling was perhaps best expressed by Senator Kenneth Wherry (R-NE): 'The New Deal and this Administration is having its wings clipped and from now on you can expect Congress to continue to do the clipping. I do think we have had quite an **awakening** and I think that the Senate realizes that we must cause a halt to government by executive order.'" Bennett attributes the Wherry quote to David Camelon in "The Fight for Mustering Out Pay" and "A Surprise Attack" that appeared in *American Legion Magazine* (September, October, November 1949).

25

Bennett, *When Dreams Came True*, 120-121.

26

House Committee on Veterans' Affairs, "Excerpts from *When Dreams Came True* and other writings by Michael J. Bennett," http://veterans.House.gov/benefits/gi60th/wdct.html; (accessed March 16, 2005).

27

Greenberg, *The GI Bill*, 12. Further, the view of the Disabled American Veterans (DAV) is found throughout the legislative history of the Servicemen's Readjustment Act. *First*, at 71, of his January 24, 1944, testimony before the Subcommittee on Veterans' Legislation of the Senate Committee on Finance, Millard W. Rice, DAV national service director, said, "The bill now before the committee, S. 1617, the so-called Legion omnibus bill, is just such a bill, the enactment of which we fear very much might have a detrimental effect upon the administration of legislation for disabled men. We are particularly fearful that it might prove prejudicial to the interests of the service-connected and service-connectible veterans because of the numerous other problems that will be imposed upon the Veterans' Administration if the provisions of this bill will be enacted into law." *Second*, at 264 of the House Committee on World War Veterans Legislation published hearing document on H.R. 3917 and S. 1767, the committee (at the request of Millard W. Rice, national service director, Disabled American Veterans) inserts into the record an editorial that appeared on the front page of the *Disabled American Veterans Semimonthly*, issued on February 26, 1944, titled "Keep the Veterans' Administration for the Disabled." *Third*, at 265, the committee quotes numerous Detroit disabled veterans from information furnished by Mr. Rice: "It is not fair to the service-connected disabled to load up the Veterans Administration budget with benefits for the able-bodied discharged veteran, as set forth in the GI Bill.... Many of us are Legionnaires as well as members of the Disabled American Veterans and, when we speak, it is not against the Legion and their program for aid to the able-bodied discharged veteran in the shape of the greater education program or in unemployment insurance benefits. We do feel, however, that the cost of this program for the able-bodied veteran should not be included in the Veterans Administration budget. Also, that the administration of same be handled by other departments of the government." *Lastly*, Representative Joseph P. O'Hara of Minnesota placed into the April 25, 1944, *Congressional Record* at A2121-22, "What is Wrong with the So-Called GI Bill of Rights?" The entry cites the views of aforementioned Millard W. Rice as delivered over radio station WINX, Washington, D.C., April 5, 1944: "First things should be done first. I submit to you that America's disabled veterans have not yet been adequately provided for, nor have their dependents.... The Veterans Administration has heretofore been the one federal agency delegated primarily to deal with the problems of service-disabled veterans including vocational rehabilitation where needed, and, if it is also given the same responsibility as to millions of able-bodied veterans, it will naturally be apt to give less attention to the more complicated problems of disabled veterans. Post-war education for the able-bodied veterans should more appropriately be assumed by the various states, or, if federal assistance is needed, by the Office of Education."

28

Congressional Record, House, June 13, 1944, 5933-5935. Title I: Hospitalizations, Claims, and Procedures; Title II: Education; Title III: Loans for the Purchase or Construction of Homes, Farms, and Business Property; Title IV: Employment; Title V: Readjustment Allowances for Former Members of the Armed Forces Who Are Unemployed; and Title VI: General Administrative and Penal Provisions.

29

Olson, *The GI Bill, The Veterans, and The Colleges*, 25. Fifty-six national education institutions under the

American Council on Education initially also opposed the GI Bill legislation due to perceived, excessive federal control. Notes Bennett at 160: "If the professional educators' language in calling the provision 'the most serious threat to the existing state and local control of education that has yet appeared in this country' was extreme, so was Rankin's reaction. It transfigured him into a champion of unrestricted access to education—even for blacks." Further, the current-day Center on Education Policy also cites the Servicemen's Readjustment Act of 1944 at 8 in "A Brief History of the Federal Role in Education: Why it Began and Why It's Still Needed." Notes the center, "The federal government has entered the field of education when a vital national interest was not being met by states or localities, or when national leadership was required to address a national problem."

30

Ms. Borchardt served as a vice president, American Federation of Teachers, from 1924 through 1962. Ms. Borchardt's papers are housed at the Walter P. Reuther Library, Wayne State University, Detroit, MI. http://www.reuther.wayne.edu/ward/aft/people.html.

31

President Dr. Marvin was also chairman, Commission of National Education Associations on Post-War Education that was looking at educational opportunities for former GIs. Following World War I, Marvin served as a dean at the University of California. One of his duties was to administer the vocational rehabilitation training program for disabled, World War I veterans. Marvin, too, was concerned about potential, excessive federal control of education after World War II, as evidenced by his March 29, 1944, testimony at 308 of the published hearing record of the House Committee on World War Veterans Legislation. Noted Marvin: "[We] recommend that this bill have powers defined so that the administrator, the Veterans Administration, cannot reach down into the several states and dominate the state educational system." But, unlike Zook and others, as a college president, Marvin especially seemed to appreciate that education under the GI Bill should not be limited only to colleges. At 307, he testifies that "there will be demand in the vocational schools and in the technical training schools and in apprenticeship training." At 317, Marvin testifies that "have in mind that today I am not speaking of colleges and universities. I am speaking of education. If that boy needs a six-month course on how to plant something in a technical school in Texas, or how to plant alfalfa in Wisconsin, let us make sure he gets it." Marvin's focusing on the veteran—rather than institutions—seemed to gain him credibility with the House Committee on World War Veterans Legislation. Testifying in the Senate Finance Subcommittee before Chairman Bennett Champ Clark, Vice President Borchardt also seemed focused on the veterans rather than institutions: "When the first draft of the training bill came before us we were simply shocked at many of the unfortunate provisions in it, and many of the vitally essential principles that were omitted from it. We are very happy to see that most of those unfortunate provisions have been deleted. For example, the original bill would have denied 93 percent of the men in the service the benefit of training by a stilted process of selection. That bill provided that those servicemen who were 'selected' should have training." (Ms. Borchardt was testifying on a Veterans' Omnibus bill, S. 1617, "a bill to provide federal government aid for the readjustment in civilian life of returning World War II veterans" on which the subcommittee held nine hearings during January-March, 1944.)

32

Congressional Record - March 28, 1944, A1680.

33

Hearings before Senate Subcommittee of Committee on Finance on S. 1617, 78th Cong., January 14, 15, 21, 24; February 11, 14, 23; March 8 and 10, 1944. Hearings before the [House] Committee on World War Veterans Legislation on H.R. 3917 and S. 1767, 78th Cong., January 11, 12, 13, 17, 18; February 24; March 9, 10, 27, 28, 29, 30, 31, 1944. Compilation of dates cited from Memorandum for File, 7-11-47, L.R. & R. "Servicemen's Readjustment Act," History of Veterans/Laws Public Laws, 346, 78th C, 483, 78th C, Tab PL 346 78C, Roosevelt Transmittal, HDCO 344 78th C., Department of Veterans Affairs, Office of General Counsel, Legislative Services Division.

34

U.S. Department of Veterans Affairs, "GI Bill 50th Anniversary 1944-1994" (History subsection), June 1994, 2.

35

Ballard and Piper, *Sonny Montgomery: The Veteran's Champion*, 71.

36

John Vogel, undersecretary for benefits, U.S. Department of Veterans Affairs, noted still another visionary law in his 1994 Veterans' Day remarks at California University of Pennsylvania: "Presidents Lincoln and Roosevelt were instrumental in shaping the role of government in veterans' affairs, particularly in higher education. In 1862, President Lincoln signed the Land Grant College Act, which has been described as prying 'higher education from the ivied realm of the privileged' and creating 'peoples colleges' where millions of Americans had the opportunity for the first time to go to college… with [Roosevelt] signing the GI Bill in 1944, higher education would again change dramatically." Mr. Vogel's remarks are in possession of Mississippi State University.

37

Administrator of Veterans Affairs Frank T. Hines sent a letter on June 19, 1944, to the Honorable Samuel Rosemann, special counsel to the President, "with an enclosure in draft form, which furnishes data for a statement that the President may desire to issue in connection with the signing of the GI Bill… there are two statements enclosed: one in considerable detail, and the other more consolidated. Servicemen's Readjustment Act," General, Part IIIa, Pub 346, 78th C., Department of Veterans Affairs, Office of General Counsel, Legislative Services Division.

38

House Committee on Veterans' Affairs, *Montgomery GI Bill: Report to Accompany H.R. 1085*, 100th Cong., 1st sess., 1987, 9. Current-day presidential historian Michael Beschloss commented on Roosevelt's role: "The amazing thing is that Roosevelt really didn't spend much time on this. He signed this bill two weeks after D-Day. He had spent much less thought on this than he did on most of the New Deal, but if you look at the effect of this, this had much greater impact on bringing Americans into the middle class than everything Roosevelt had tried to do over eight years in the 1930s." PBS online *News Hour*, "The GI Bill's Legacy July 4, 2000," http://web-cro5.pbs.org/newshour-//bb/military/july-dec00/gibill-7-4.html. It appears Roosevelt had an experience based reference point for his "avoid veterans selling apples on street corners" statement. Note Dickson and Allen on the front dust cover of *The Bonus Army—An American Epic* (Walker & Company, 2004), "During the summer of 1932, in the depths of the Depression, some 45,000 World War I veterans descended on Washington, D.C. to demand immediate payment of a cash bonus promised them eight years earlier for their war-time service… . Roosevelt proved even more determined than President Hoover not to pay the bonus, and bonus armies returned in the first three years of his administration. Seeking a solution, Roosevelt sent many to work camps in Florida, where, on Labor Day 1935, the worst hurricane ever to strike the United States [until that time] killed some 250 unprotected vets, prompting a New Deal whitewash and cover-up of the facts." Also instructive are observations by Janet Maslin: "And although Presidents Herbert Hoover and Calvin Coolidge ('Patriotism which is bought and paid for is not patriotism') had been loftily opposed to the high price of veterans' bonuses, Franklin Delano Roosevelt was no more helpful. 'The veteran who is disabled owes his condition to the war,' Roosevelt said, as he vetoed a bonus bill. 'The healthy veteran who is unemployed owes his troubles to the Depression.'" "Home from the War, Yet the Battle Is Just Beginning," *New York Times*, February 21, 2005.

39

Service members learned about this GI Bill idea in various ways during the war. Making sure service members knew about it during the height of the war seemed secondary to the political urgency at hand for both the Congress and the President, at least in the eye of one individual who wrote what is regarded as the seminal document on the World War II GI Bill: "With respect to timing and the character of its actions, Congress supported a GI Bill only when there were sustained casualty lists." Olson, *The GI Bill, The Veterans, and The Colleges*, 108.

40

Vogel, "1994 Veterans' Day Remarks," 10, 11.

41

One of the effects was hope. Notes Stephen Ambrose in *Band of Brothers* at 113 and 114: "For the first time in the Army [during the July 13-September 16, 1944, period after D-Day], and to his delight, [Pvt. David Kenyon Webster] found men who talked about going to college after the war, including Corporal Dukeman and Sergeants Muck, Carson, and Malarkey… and Lieutenant Compton had convinced the college-bound group that UCLA was the only place to go for an education."

42

Olson, *The GI Bill, The Veterans, and The Colleges*, 38. President Roosevelt understandably was preoccupied with matters associated with the war itself: "The White House quietly approved the bill but offered no leadership." Michael Bennett notes that, fortunately, Congress created the GI Bill before millions of our troops came home rather than waiting until after they came home: "Veterans 'will be a potent force for good or evil in the years to come,' [American Legion] National Commander Atherton said during a radio address on May 2. 'They can make our country or break it. They can restore our democracy or scrap it.'" Mr. Bennett notes that "Eleanor Roosevelt had also foreseen the potential threat. As early as April 1942, she warned that veterans could 'create a dangerous pressure group in our midst.'" Bennett, *When Dreams Came True*, 129.

43

American women at home played a vital role in our winning the war. Mary Blauser Meilwes of Boynton Beach, FL, describes her war-time life: "In 1942, I worked for Curtiss-Wright in Columbus, OH, where the firm designed and built the SB2C Helldriver carrier-borne attack plane for the Navy. As a clerk in the engineering/planning department, I earned 40 cents an hour for 40 hours. We worked nine hours for five days and eight hours on Saturdays… Gasoline was rationed, so it was necessary to carpool to obtain gas coupons… Shoes also were rationed… The plant cafeteria served good food. For breakfast, it offered the best fried mush for 5 cents… lunch cost about a quarter… liquor also was rationed." *Reminisce Magazine*, "The Magazine That Brings Back More Good Times," (January 2007), 63.

44

Air & Space Smithsonian, February/March, 2007, p. 68. The 3,812 figure includes "a scattering of U.S. War Department employees, Red Cross workers, Merchant Marine sailors, and one war correspondent whose bodies were recovered in the United Kingdom during World War II. Another 5,126 are listed on the Wall of the Missing. The authors also note "roughly 70 percent of the burials drew from the U.S. Army Air Forces, and most of these came from the 8th Air Force. It was the nature of the 8th's long-distance bombing campaign, says [cemetery associate Arthur] Brookes, that many fell unseen into remote country, coastal waters, or their burning targets below. By war's end, more than 10,000 Americans had been buried here. In 1945, the U.S. government offered the next of kin of deceased overseas personnel the option of repatriation; about 60 percent accepted. Yet the buried and the missing at Cambridge represent only a fraction of the 8th's 26,000 dead."

45

Such cemeteries are maintained by the American Battle Monuments Commission, which Congress established in 1923 to "commemorate the service achievements and sacrifice of U.S. armed forces where they served overseas since 1917, and within the U.S. when directed by public law." The Commission maintains "24 overseas military cemeteries that serve as resting places for almost 125,000 American war dead; on Tablets of the Missing that memorialize more than 94,000 U.S. servicemen and women; and through memorials, monuments, and markers." American Battle Monuments Commission, "Time Will Not Dim the Glory of Their Deeds," http://www.abmc.gov/home.php; (accessed January 18, 2007).

46

Olson, *The GI Bill, The Veterans, and The Colleges*, 99. Seymour E. Harris, Harvard professor, was one of many who wanted to limit the scope of the GI Bill: "In education, however, the GI Bill carried the principle of democratization too far." Olson disagreed, as he notes: The GI Bill paid "rich dividends to society and the concept of democracy." Olson, 110. Some 35 years later, the president of the American Association of Community and Junior Colleges (AACJC) offered a general observation about the role of postsecondary education: "Contrary to the elitist form of education, lifelong education is **universal** in character. It represents **democratization of education** [emphasis added]." Edmund G. Gleazer, Jr., *The Community College: Values, Vision & Vitality* (1980), 182.

47

Michael J. Bennett, "An International GI Bill Could Turn Third World's Emerging Military into Middle-Class Citizens," Paper in possession of Mississippi State University, page 3.

48

The 7.8 million veterans who used the GI Bill exceeded all expectations with respect to numbers of participants. However, the follow-up analysis of the GI Bill's effectiveness years later was cast in much broader terms: "A Congressional study under Congressman Olin E. Teague concluded that the original GI Bill had achieved the specific purposes for which it was written: prevention of any serious problems of unemployment, unrest, and dissatisfaction among veterans, and restoration of human resources lost or retarded by war." U.S. Department of Veterans Affairs, "History of the GI Bill," http://www.75anniversary.va.gov/history/gi_bill.html; (accessed July 7, 2007).

49

Veterans Administration, Information Service, "GI Bill of Rights 25th Anniversary 1944-1969" (Fact Sheet for Editors, Broadcasters, Writers), (Washington, D.C., 1969), 9.

50

Ibid., 8.

51

Greenberg, *The GI Bill*, 47.

52

Ibid. The following observations all comport with Greenberg: "Veterans demanded more practical college course work, and this need led to a changed concept of higher education, with more emphasis on degree programs like business and engineering." *West's Encyclopedia of Law*, 2nd ed., "GI Bill." Suzanne Mettler's research in *Soldiers to Citizens: The GI Bill and the Making of the Greatest Generation* on page 71 also reinforces the Greenberg statement: "Veterans pursued more practical fields than students of the past, gravitating especially towards business administration, followed by professional fields such as law, medicine, dentistry, and teaching, and then in almost equal numbers, engineering, architecture, the physical sciences, the humanities, and the social sciences." At 213, Note 60, Mettler cites three sources for the aforementioned statement. *First*, President's Commission on Veterans' Pensions, *Readjustment Benefits: Education and Training and Employment and Unemployment*, 84th Cong., 2nd sess., 1956, 27-29. *Second*, "The GI Bill: In 10 Years, 8 Million," *Newsweek*, October 1954, 90." *Third*, Lloyd C. Emmons, "College Curricula of World War II Veterans," *School and Society*, August 1946, 152-53.

53

Olson, *The GI Bill, The Veterans, and The Colleges*, 102. Many veterans were the first in their families to pursue postsecondary education, and in so doing, they changed the definition of what constituted a college student: "Veterans embedded in higher education the concept of the married student."

54

Bennett, "An International GI Bill Could Turn Third-World's Emerging Military into Middle-Class Citizens," 6.

55

Anthony Principi, keynote address, National Association of Veterans' Program Administrators 25th Annual Conference, San Diego, CA, October 20, 2000. The following reinforce the Principi observation: *First*, "Non-veterans at Stanford called veterans 'DARs' for Damn Average Raisers." Keith W. Olson, "The Astonishing Story: Veterans Make Good on the Nation's Promise," *Educational Record* (Fall 1994, p. 24). *Second*, "Here is the most astonishing fact in the history of American higher education… .The GIs are hogging the honor rolls and the Dean's lists; they are walking away with the top marks in all of their courses… far from being an educational problem, the veteran has become an asset to higher education." Benjamin Fine, *New York Times*, November 1947, quoted in Olson, *The GI Bill, The Veterans, and The Colleges*, 41; and Bennett, *When Dreams Came True*, Chapter 8. *Third*, "Similar traditions [such as at Columbia University of climbing a greased pole to fetch an object that Mettler cites at 71] disappeared on other campuses such as the freshman dink (skullcap or beanie) at UCLA… ." The G.I. Bill: In 10 Years, 8 million," 88, quoted in Suzanne Mettler, *Soldiers to Citizens*, 213. Mettler also notes at 67 that "many universities and colleges began offering courses throughout the entire year rather than only during the traditional nine-month schedule, thus permitting veterans to complete their degree in less than the typical four years." At page 212, note 37, Mettler cites "Readjustment Benefits: Education and Training," 24-25, as the source of this statement.

56

Here are two examples. *First*, Rob Norton speaks to consequences of many different types of public policies ranging from quotas on imported steel to limitations on roadside billboards. The Library of Economics and Liberty, "*Unintended Consequences: The Concise Encyclopedia of Economics*," http://www.econlib.org/library/Enc/UnintendedConsequences.html; (accessed September 18, 2008). *Second*, the novel *Unintended Consequences*, written by John Ross and first published in 1996 by Accurate Press, is a novel about gun control legislation and unintended consequences of same.

CHAPTER 3

The World War II GI Bill and Beyond: The Legacy Continues

1

We do not discuss in the text how educators, government officials, and others dramatically underestimated the extent to which World War II veterans would use the GI Bill after the war. Six examples follow: *First*, "so little investigation of this situation has been made, and the best guess that we can find, at the present time is that at least 1 out of every 10 of these veterans who return will want some kind of educational and training opportunities, so that you can easily see that if that estimate is anywhere near correct that more than a million men will be involved in this educational program." House Committee on World War Veterans Legislation, *Hearings on H.R. 3917 and S. 1767 to Provide Federal Government Aid for the Readjustment in Civilian Life of Returning World War II Veterans*, January 11, 12, 13, 17, 18; February 24; March 9, 10, 27, 28, 29, 30, 31, 1944, hearing of March 29, testimony of Dr. George F. Zook, president, American Council on Education, 311. *Second*, "[Donald] Eberly pointed out 'Earl McGrath, a future commissioner of education, predicted that 640,000 of the 15 million veterans would pursue further education under the GI Bill. The number who actually did so was 7.8 million. Mr. McGrath… did not account for the fact that the educational appetites of millions of veterans had been whetted by their service experience." *Building a Consensus on National Service*, 1993, 18. *Third*, Mettler notes the following in *Soldiers to Citizens*, 204-205, note 2: "Veterans Administration Chief Frank T. Hines predicted that 700,000 students—less than 5 percent of all service members—would attend college on the GI Bill." *Fourth*, an internal March 21, 1944, memorandum regarding S. 1767 from the Executive Assistant to the Administrator of Veterans Affairs to Solicitor Odom states, "If the assumption of the solicitor is correct in regard to the total strength of the armed forces (including Army, Navy, Marine Corps, Coast Guard and the components thereof) and that approximately 10 percent of the veterans would be granted the educational benefits… ." "Servicemen's Readjustment Act," General, Part III, Pub. 346, 78th C., Department of Veterans Affairs, Office of General Counsel, Legislative Services Division. *Fifth*, U.S. Commissioner of Education Earl McGrath voiced an even more conservative figure of 640,000. Earl J. McGrath, "The Education of the Veteran," *Annals of the American Academy of Political and Social Science*, March 1945, 84. (It appears Mr. McGrath quotes himself). *Sixth*, Representative Emanuel Celler offered an observation like no other. He referred to Title II, the education aspect of the Servicemen's Readjustment Act of 1944, as "no empty provision. A survey conducted by Research Branch of the Moral Service Division indicates that 7 percent of the men think they will actually go back to full-time school or college after the war. It is conceded, however, that married men and those over 25 are least likely to do so." *Congressional Record*, May 3, 1944, A2284.

2

As discussed in the text, more veterans enrolled in and graduated from trade, business, and high schools than colleges and universities. But the popular media of the 1940s and 1950s understandably were more intrigued with veterans home from war who enrolled in college and university programs. So that's what media tended to write about. In this chapter, we focus more on collegiate veterans, as well as what media referred to as "elites" of the higher education community who were vocally skeptical about enrolling veterans.

3

Several speakers in this chapter furnish information to reinforce this statement, including Conant, Pusey, Ellis, and Drucker. Also instructive are statements made by legislators at the time: "I regard the GI Bill of Rights, passed by the Senate in March and now in conference between the Houses, as one of the most important measures that has ever come before Congress." Honorable Harry S Truman quoted in the statement by Senator Bennett C. Clark of Missouri, *Congressional Record*, June 12, 1944, A3196. In addition, "we are now in executive session on that [GI] bill, which is probably the most explosive and most far-reaching measure of its kind ever produced in Congress. We are going over it line-by-line and paragraph-by-paragraph." Honorable John Rankin, *Congressional Record*, April 20, 1944, 3654.

4

House Committee on World War Veterans Legislation, *Hearings on H.R. 3917 and S. 1767*, March 29, 1944, 317.

5

Senate Subcommittee of the Committee on Finance, *Hearings on S. 1617, Veterans' Omnibus Bill*, January 14, 15, 21, 24; February 11, 14, 23; March 8 and 10, 1944, 221-222. The Thomas bill appeared to be a bill based on the recommendations of a committee of educators working under the auspices of the Navy and War departments, that President Roosevelt convened on November 13, 1942, regarding postwar education opportunities of service personnel. *The Preliminary Report to the President of the United States from the Armed Forces Committee on Post-War Educational Opportunities for Service Personnel*, June 30, 1943. The report recommended at 2: "The federal government should make it financially feasible for every man and woman who has served honorably for a minimum period in the armed forces since September 16, 1940, to spend a period of up to **one calendar year** [emphasis added] in a school, a college, a technical institution, or in actual training in industry, so that he can further his education, learn a trade, or acquire the necessary knowledge and skill for farming, commerce, manufacturing, or other pursuits. In addition, the federal government should make it financially possible for a **limited number** [emphasis added] of ex-servicemen and women selected for their special aptitudes to carry on their general, technical or professional education for a

further period of one, two or three years." Representing the American Federation of Teachers, Ms. Borchardt objected to the recommendation that only a small percentage of veterans would be selected for education and training beyond one year. Her testimony in regard to 93 percent of veterans not being allowed to enroll in training beyond a **single year** [emphasis added] appears to be in response to the following statement in the *Report of the President's Committee*, at 10: "It seems a reasonable assumption that if the nation mobilizes an Army and Navy of about 12,000,000, a minimum of 1,000,000 may be expected to be interested in resuming interrupted courses of education or in applying to new educational courses abilities uncovered and developed by their experience in the armed forces. Should demobilization begin in 1945, it seems likely that the Army's and Navy's share of the educational deficit will be relatively overcome if 200,000 ex-service personnel are enabled to carry on their education for a second year after discharge, approximately 165,000 for a third year, and about 150,000 for a fourth year." Further, Ms. Borchardt appears to object to the report's recommendation at 14: "Establish quotas for training after the first year and apportion the subquotas to the several states." House Committee on Education, *Post-War Educational Opportunities for Service Personnel*, 78th Cong. 2, 10.

6

Bennett, *When Dreams Came True*, 161; Dickson and Allen, *The Bonus Army*, 272; Olson, *Educational Record*, 22.

7

Dickson and Allen, *The Bonus Army*, 275.

8

Ibid., 276.

9

Veterans Administration, "GI Bill of Rights 25th Anniversary 1944-1969," 11.

10

Bennett, *When Dreams Came True*, 239, quoted in Karen Thomas', *The GI Bill of Rights: The Law That Changed America* (Washington, D.C.), unpublished manuscript for a television documentary.

11

Sergeant Messiah studied architecture most likely as part of a baccalaureate degree program. However, the World War II GI Bill furnished education and training assistance in many areas, including for a high school diploma, on-the-job training, trade and business school, and graduate study. The Veterans Administration promulgated and then published numerous definitions associated with the explicit language expressed in the law and the administration of the GI Bill program. Defining the terms used in the law fulfilled an important function in administering such a large and complex program. *Veterans Administration Index, Digest of Decisions of the Administrator of Veterans Affairs* (Omar N. Bradley), March 1, 1931, to June 30, 1946, 96-101. The period between 1931 and 1944 furnished definitions for the vocational rehabilitation of disabled veterans that predated enactment of the Servicemen's Readjustment Act of 1944, as well.

12

Greenberg, *The GI Bill*, 71.

13

Veterans Administration, "*GI Bill of Rights, 1944-1969*," 12.

14

House Committee on Veterans' Affairs, "Some Notable Beneficiaries of the GI Bill," http://veterans.house.gov/benefits/gi60th/notbenef.html; (accessed March 16, 2005).

15

House Committee on Veterans' Affairs, http://veterans.house.gov/benefits/gi60th.wdet.html; (accessed March 16, 2005).

16

Ibid. Also, the authors note that Dwight Young at 91 in *Dear Mr. President, Letters to the Oval Office from the Files of the National Archives* expands on the Bennett statement: "Almost as soon as the fighting ended in 1945, the United States started working to help war-shattered Germany restart its economy and help the German people rebuild their lives. Today, discussion of America's contribution to postwar European recovery usually focuses on the amazing accomplishments of the Marshall Plan, which funneled an estimated $13 billion into various programs to help Europe get back on its feet. Less well known is the fact that the U.S. spent nearly an equal amount—almost $11 billion—on European recovery during the years between 1945 and 1948, before the Marshall Plan was launched. Among those early and largely unheralded efforts was a program that got under way in the spring of 1947 to provide food to German school children. To mark the first anniversary of the program, more than a million Bavarian children took part in a drawing competition to show their gratitude for America's generosity. The 50 best drawings were sent to [President Harry S Truman] at the White House."

17

Edited by Philip Scranton and published by University of Georgia Press, Athens, GA, 2001.

18

Department of Veterans Affairs, 60th anniversary [news release], June 18, 2004.

19

Ben Callison with Jaunita Winkler, Sandy Kelly, Dena Balsama, Erin Rulli, and Esther Walenta, *Ben: The Life and Times of Benjamin Callison*, 33. Mr. Callison attended Michigan Tech in the early 1940s as part of the Army Air Corps commissioning program. Decorated in 1945 by the 8th Army Air Corps for "courage, coolness, and skill in combat," Mr. Callison went on to serve from 1947 to 1974 as a firefighter and officer in the Los Angeles Police Department. Thereafter, he served with the Office of California Fire Marshal from 1974 to 1979. In 1999, while visiting his granddaughter, Tara, and her family in South Carolina, Mr. Callison visited the Mighty 8th Air Force Museum in Savannah, GA. Dedicated in 1996, the museum honors the 350,000 members of the 8th Air Force, including 26,000 who were killed in action and 28,000 who became prisoners of war.

20

Bennett, *When Dreams Came True*, 7.

21

Greenberg, *The GI Bill*, 51.

22

Suzanne Mettler, *Soldiers to Citizens: The GI Bill and the Making of the Greatest Generation*, (New York: Oxford University Press, 2005), 7. Dr. Mettler cites Putnam in *Bowling Alone*, at 268 as the source for the 80 percent figure.

23

Suzanne Mettler, interview by Kehrer (co-author), July 14, 2004.

24

Public Law 550, the "Veterans Readjustment Assistance Act of 1952," signed by President Harry S Truman, July 16, 1952.

25

Public Law 358, the "Veterans Readjustment Benefits Act of 1966," signed by President Lyndon B. Johnson, March 3, 1966. Mettler suggests at 195, note 30 of *Soldiers to Citizens*, that for an assessment of the effects of the Vietnam-era GI Bill program, see Sar A. Levitan and Joyce K. Zickler, *Swords to Plowshares: Our GI Bill*, (Salt Lake City: Olympus, 1973).

26

Olin "Tiger" Teague represented Texas's 6th Congressional district from 1946 to 1978. He served as chairman, Committee on Veterans' Affairs, and also as chairman, Committee on Science and Technology. Noted Secretary of Veterans Affairs James Nicholson in remarks regarding the 25th Annual Olin E. Teague Award on October 12, 2005, "By the time he left the chairmanship of the Committee on Veterans' Affairs, Congressman Teague had authored more veterans' legislation than any member preceding him." The Olin E. Teague Veterans' Center in Temple, TX, is a full-service teaching hospital and the headquarters of the Central Texas Veterans Health Care System. Olin Teague's Congressional papers are preserved at the Texas A&M University Archives, and the Olin E. Teague Building houses the offices of the Associate Provost for Information Technology, among others. To learn more about the extraordinary public service of Olin Teague, see the *Biographical Directory of the United States Congress, 1774-present*.

27

The authors note that Guy H. McMichael III served as chief counsel to the Senate Committee on Veterans' Affairs, 1971 to 1977. Van Hartke (D-IN) served as chairman and Strom Thurmond (R-SC) as ranking member at that time. Among other duties, Mr. McMichael advised the committee with respect to numerous improvements to the Vietnam-era GI Bill enacted into law. He then served as Veterans Administration general counsel during the tenure of Max Cleland, Administrator of Veterans Affairs in the Carter presidency. Among later assignments, Mr. McMichael also would serve as chairman, Board of Contract Appeals, and acting under secretary for Benefits (Veterans Benefits Administration) at the United States Department of Veterans Affairs.

28

Department of Veterans Affairs, FY 2008 *Congressional Budget Submission*, Volume 11, 2B-13.

CHAPTER 4

Producing Legislative "Widgets:" Committees, Bills, and Bipartisanship

1

A statement in a January 3, 2007, article titled "What the Congress Can Do for America" by President George W. Bush published in *The Wall Street Journal* may be instructive for students: "The majority party gets to pass the bill it wants. The minority party, especially where the margins are close, has a strong say in the form bills take."

2

This is a phrase heard in the nation's Capitol from time to time and isn't exclusive to G.V. Montgomery.

3

Rules Committee of the House of Representatives, "Glossary of Terms in the Federal Budget Process," http://www.rules.house.gov/archives/glossary_fbp.html; (accessed June 12, 2007).

4

Ibid.

5

Ibid., 6.

6

Ibid., 14.

7

Ibid., 10.

8

Ibid., 17.

9

The visual basically is replicated from *Our American Government*, Foreword by Robert W. Ney and Saxby Chambliss, Chairman and Vice Chairman, respectively, Committee on House Administration, (U.S. House of Representatives, Doc. 108-94, Washington, D.C.: U.S. Government Printing Office, 2003), 30. The House Rules Committee generally is not directly involved in veteran's legislation and is not depicted here.

10

The use of the term *legislative widgets* is not exclusive to the authors.

11

During the 1987 Senate consideration of Montgomery GI Bill legislation (S. 12 and H.R. 1085), Alan Cranston was the Democratic (majority) Whip, and Alan Simpson was Republican (minority) Whip. Mr. Cranston and Mr. Simpson served as the chairman and ranking member of the Senate Committee on Veterans' Affairs. "Dual-hatted" members such as Mr. Cranston and Mr. Simpson helped move the legislation along.

12

For an example of a "whip notice," see http://republicanwhip.house.gov. The House Majority Whip for the 110th Congress was Representative James Clyburn of South Carolina. The House Minority Whip was Representative Roy Blunt of Missouri. The Senate Majority Whip for the 110th Congress was Senator Richard Durbin of Illinois. The Senate Minority Whip was Senator Trent Lott of Mississippi (who later resigned from Congress).

13

Per the official rules of the House of Representatives, suspension of the rules is a procedure used on the House floor to pass relatively noncontroversial bills: "This procedure is governed primarily by Clause 1 of House Rule XV. When a bill or some other matter is considered under suspension, floor debate is limited, all floor amendments are prohibited, and a two-thirds vote is required for final passage." Congressional Research Service, *Suspension of the Rules in the House: Principal Features*, 2006, 1. Further, for a listing of Congressional Research Service reports on the legislative process in the House, see http://www.rules.house.gov/archives/crs_reports.html. Topics include: Congress: The House; Introduction and Origin of Legislative Measures; House Floor Proceedings; House Committees; Special Rules and the Rules Committee; Budget Process; Congress: The Senate; Relations with the Senate; and Presidential Relations. For additional information on the legislative process, see http://www.crs.gov/products/guides/guidehome.html.

14

Charles W. Johnson, *How Our Laws Are Made*, (U.S. House of Representatives, Doc. 108-93, Washington, D.C.: U.S. Government Printing Office, 2003), 34, 35. The authors note that Mr. Johnson served with distinction in the House for 40 years under seven successive speakers, including 10 years as Parliamentarian.

15

United States Senate, "Reference Home/Glossary," http://www.senate.gov/reference/glossary/_term/conference_committee.html; (accessed June 13, 2007).

16

Michael J. Malbin, *Unelected Representatives: Congressional Staff and the Future of Representative Government*, (Basic Books, 1980), Chap. 5, "Detailed Negotiations: The Phantom Conference on the GI Bill."

17

Ibid.

18

Ibid., 79.

19

Ibid., 80. However, Malbin notes the original source of the Teague statement as quoted in Colman McCarthy, "'Tiger' Teague and the Veterans Compromise," *Washington Post*, November 19, 1977. Also William H. Harader, in his 1968 Johns Hopkins University doctoral dissertation, found that Representative Olin Teague was respected by Senators and Senate staff, as far back as the 1960s and perhaps earlier. At 180, Harader quotes one Senator assigned to one of the several committees having jurisdiction over veterans' issues prior to when the Senate formed the Committee on Veterans' Affairs in 1973: "The House committee is a real buffer, protecting both bodies. Many of us see Teague as a real God-send." At 184, Harader quotes one member of the House Committee: "[Senator Russell] Long comes to a conference with his hand full of proxies, all set to hold his ground. Then, we start discussing the bill, [and] Teague has to spend hours explaining the thing and what it will do to him [Long]. Then, we have to explain what his changes will do to the [veterans' benefits] program. Only after we educate him, can we talk about the substance of the conference. He usually comes around after a respectable length of time." Harader then concludes that "the influence of the House is based on the expertise of its committee. The Senate has no comparable experts." William H. Harader, "The Committee on Veterans' Affairs: A Study of the Legislative Process and Mileau as They Pertain to Veterans Legislation" (Ph.D. diss., Johns Hopkins University, 1968), 180, 184. For further information on the House Committee on Veterans' Affairs, see Wallis, Anthony A. and Beuttler, Fred. W., *A History of the House Commitee on Veterans' Affairs: 1794-2009*. Washington, D.C.: Government Printing Office, 2010.

20

When the House and Senate Veterans' Affairs Committees would consider the bills passed by their respective chambers, the two bodies often merged all the separate bills into one large bill, sometimes called an omnibus bill. The Joint Explanatory Statement (JES) would explain how the House and Senate combined the bills and the results of their negotiations on each provision in each bill; the two bodies could adopt the provisions by not changing them, amending them, or dropping them.

21

The bill's legislative language itself would be an important part of the compromise-agreement package, as expressed through the JES. But the JES often took on the role of explanatory vehicle because it would be written in everyday, pedestrian language rather than bill language. Congress issues the JES jointly as a single House-Senate published document.

22

U.S. Government Info/Resources, "Census 2000 Apportionment Data Released," http://usgovinfo.about.com.library/weekly/aa122800a.html; (accessed January 19, 2007).

23

Otto Von Bismarck (1815-1898), Chancellor of Germany, 1871-1890, is credited with saying "Laws are like sausages. It's better not to see them being made." The Quotations Page, "Quotations by Author Otto Von Bismarck," http:www.quotationspage.com/quotes/Otto_von_Bismarck, (accessed May 11, 2007).

24

Edgar Potter, *Cowboy Slang*, (Phoenix, Golden West History), 1986, 63.

25

Colin L. Powell, "What's the Secret to Good Leadership," *State Magazine*, February 2002, 2.

26

Senators John Tower of Texas and Sam Nunn of Georgia—among many others—did not share this view.

CHAPTER 5

1980-1983—Road to Enactment: How to Fix a "Hollow" Army

1

House Committee on Veterans' Affairs, 97th Cong., 1st sess., 1981, 14, 15, *Report to Accompany H.R. 1400 Veterans' Educational Assistance Act of 1981*. The Vietnam Conflict ended in 1973, but the Vietnam-era period continued for GI Bill education benefits until 1975. Plus, the draft ended in 1973. The balance of the cited footnote furnished some historical background; "In February 1970, the Gates Commission recommended that the country complete the transition to an All-Volunteer Force by July 1, 1971. Though President Nixon accepted the goal of an All-Volunteer Force in principle, the pressures of the Vietnam War and the need for a more orderly transition to an All-Volunteer Force necessitated deferral of the target date from July 1, 1971, to July 1, 1973. Actual inductions of men into the Armed Forces ended on December 31, 1972; and on June 30, 1973, with certain minor exceptions, the authority of the President to induct men into the Armed Forces expired. Standby [military] draft registration continued until April, 1975, when it was terminated by executive order of President Gerald R. Ford. Although the draft ended in 1973, entitlement to the Vietnam Era GI Bill continued to be extended to those joining the All-Volunteer Force. On May 7, 1975, President Ford issued a proclamation terminating the Vietnam wartime period… ." "The Veterans Administration in its report on H.R. 6806… to terminate accrual of [Vietnam era] educational benefits stated… with the signing of the cease-fire agreement and implementing protocols of January 27, 1973, which ended our involvement in hostilities in Vietnam… it is appropriate to terminate the current [Vietnam era] readjustment program."

2

United States Department of Defense, *Report of Secretary Elliot L. Richardson on the FY 1974 Defense Budget and FY 1974-1978 Defense Program*, Senate Committee on Appropriations—Department of Defense Subcommittee, unnumbered table titled "Draft Calls," March 26, 1973, 120.

3

Beginning in 1970, a lottery drawing determined the order in which males born from 1944 to 1950 would be drafted. Selective Service System, "History and Records—Induction Statistics," http://www.sss.gov/induct.html; (accessed May 8, 2007).

4

House Committee on Veterans' Affairs, *Veterans' Educational Assistance Act of 1981*, 97th Cong., 1st sess., 1981, 15.

5

Ibid., 22.

6

Senate Committee on Veterans' Affairs, *Educational Incentives and the All-Volunteer Force*, 96th Cong., 2nd sess., 1980.

7

Ibid., 47. Testimony by Honorable William S. Cohen, a U.S. Senator from the state of Maine (prepared statement for the record).

8

General Meyer was a highly accomplished and professional military leader and he believed strongly in the Army and its soldiers. He took no joy in using the word "hollow" to describe the Army. He felt he had no choice. General "Shy" Meyer, interview by Kehrer (co-author), Arlington, VA, 2006.

9

Darryl W. Kehrer, "Symposium on The GI Bill and the Revolution in American Higher Education," presentation, the Harry S Truman Library Institute, St. Louis, MO, January 19, 1996.

10

Veterans' Educational Assistance Act of 1981, Committee on Veterans' Affairs to Accompany H.R. 1400, 97th Cong., 1st sess., 14.

11

Department of the Army, Continental Army Command (CONARC), "Reports on Modern Volunteer Army (MVA)—Concept, Experiments, Quality Army," undated, 1. Boxed information on Volunteer Army (VOLAR) Evaluation Project, Fort Ord, archived at the U.S. Army Military History Institute, Carlisle Barracks, Carlisle, PA. For information on contents of the project, see United States Army, Army Heritage Collection Online Research Catalog at http://ahecwebopac.carlisle.army.mil.

12

General William C. Westmoreland knew combat soldiers and the Army well: "In 1964, General Westmoreland was appointed Deputy Commander, Military Assistance Command, Republic of Vietnam. Six months later, he was promoted to General and designated as Commander, U.S. Military Assistance Command, Vietnam and Commanding General, United States Army, Vietnam, where he served for four years." The authors note "in 1968, General Westmoreland returned to the United States to assume the Army's highest post—Chief of Staff. Charged by President Nixon to convert the Army to an all volunteer force, he successfully guided the Army as it transitioned from a Vietnam-oriented, conscripted force to an Army of volunteer professionals, trained, equipped, and focused on protecting the vital interests of the nation." Further, during his 36 years of military service, he served as First Captain at West Point from which he graduated in 1936; saw extensive combat in the North African and European Theater of Operations throughout World War II, including at the Kasserine Pass; commanded the 101st Airborne Division; was appointed by President Dwight D. Eisenhower as 45th Superintendent of the United States Military Academy; and commanded the Army's 18th Airborne Corps, the Army's strategic rapid reaction force. In 1965, *Time* magazine named him Man of the Year. Among other books, he is author of *A Soldier Reports*, a memoir of 40 years in uniform. General Westmoreland died on July 18, 2005, at age 91. He is buried at West Point. The quotations above are cited from Association of Graduates, U.S. Military Academy, Citation: William Childs Westmoreland, http://www.aog.usma.edu/AOG/AWARDS/DGA/96-Westmorl.html; (accessed January 20, 2007). "Gen William Childs Westmoreland USA (Ret.), March 26, 1914-July 18, 2005," http://west-point.org/users/usma1936/10571/.

13

Ibid., 1, 2.

14

"On June 30, 1973, the Armed Forces would be comprised of 2,252,846 men and women: approximately 801,000 in the Army, 564,000 in the Navy, 196,000 in the Marines, and 691,000 in the Air Force… . Of the men who signed on with all services in June 1973, 18.3 percent were black, compared with 13.5 percent among all males of military age. Blacks favored the Army most and Navy least in June recruitments: 24.1 percent of Army recruits were black; 17.2 percent in the Marines; 15.4 percent in the Air Force, and 11.2 percent in the Navy." "Volunteer Army—Is It Working," General Creighton W. Abrams, Chief of Staff, U.S. Army, *U.S. News and World Report*, August 6, 1973, 41. With respect to women, "we are also making strides in upgrading and enlarging the contribution of women in the Army. More occupational specialties have been opened to them. Of the 482 occupational specialties in the Army, 434, or approximately 90 percent, are now open to women." Statement of General Creighton W. Abrams, Chief of Staff, U.S. Army, before the Subcommittee on Defense, Senate Committee on Appropriations, March 29, 1973, 22.

15

G.V. Montgomery, "The Montgomery GI Bill: Development, Implementation, and Impact," *Educational Record*, 1994: 49.

16

Ibid., 60.

17

The bill number was H.R. 7726, introduced in the 94th Congress.

18

U.S. House of Representatives, *Report of the Committee on Veterans' Affairs to Accompany H.R. 1400*, 15.

19

Ibid., 15-17.

20

In this parenthetical, the House Committee on Veterans' Affairs Report to accompany H.R. 1400 at page 17 used the words "about 1 out of every 4 eligible enlistees;" 23.3 is the actual percentage.

21

Ibid., 17.

22

Ibid.

23

Ibid., 19.

24

G.V. Montgomery cites the seven years in a June 1, 1987, letter to Honorable Alan Simpson saying, "The development and enactment of this legislation has taken a little more than seven years." Montgomery also thanks Senator Simpson "for the major role you played in helping get the bill enacted into law." Mr. Montgomery and Mr. Simpson had attended the Montgomery GI Bill signing ceremony at the White House earlier that day. House Committee on Veterans' Affairs, Internal Historical File on the Montgomery GI Bill.

25

Every two years as a new Congress convenes, bill numbers begin with one. Subsequent bills are assigned a number in sequence as they are introduced. In the House, a staffer hand carries the bill with the member's signature on it to a small area on the House floor where a clerk hand writes the bill number at the top of the bill and deposits it in a box. The bill and number are officially printed a few days later.

26

Congressional Record, February 11, 1987, H676. "On January 28, 1981, I first introduced the new GI Bill, H.R. 1400. Prior to that date, the staff had worked for approximately eight months with the military service departments to lay the groundwork for this legislative proposal. It has proven to be time well spent." Mr. Montgomery made this observation as part of his introductory statement on H.R. 1085 on this date on behalf of himself and 174 original cosponsors.

27

"Alan was very helpful in establishing educational benefits for veterans who completed their military obligation, and he saw to it that the educational benefits go to the actives as well as National Guard and Reserve." Excerpt from statement of G.V. Montgomery at Memorial Tribute to Alan Cranston, U.S. Senator, 1969-1993, February 6, 2001, Hart Senate Office Building, Washington, D.C. Joint Committee on Printing, *Memorial Tributes and Addresses in Eulogy of Alan Cranston, Late a Senator from California* (Washington, D.C.: U.S. Government Printing Office, 2001), 96. The Senate document number is 107-2.

28

Mack G. Fleming, interview by Kehrer (co-author), February 2, 2006, and letter of January 15, 1981, from E.C. Meyer, General and Chief of Staff, United States Army, to Honorable Alan Cranston.

29

Mr. Fleming interview by Kehrer (co-author) and letter of February 21, 1981, from T.B. Hayward, Admiral, U.S. Navy, Chief of Naval Operations, to Honorable Alan Cranston.

30

Mr. Fleming interview by Kehrer (co-author) and letter of January 19, 1981, from Lew Allen, Jr., General and Chief of Staff, U.S. Air Force, to Honorable Alan Cranston.

31

Mr. Fleming interview by Kehrer (co-author) and letter of January 13, 1981, from R.T. Barrow, General, U.S. Marine Corps, Commandant of the Marine Corps, to Honorable Alan Cranston.

32

Mr. Fleming interview by Kehrer (co-author) and letter of January 10, 1981, from David C. Jones, General, U.S. Air Force and Chairman of the Joint Chiefs of Staff, to Honorable Alan Cranston.

33

Letter of January 15, 1981, from Robert B. Pirie, Jr., Assistant Secretary of Defense (MRA and L), to Honorable Alan Cranston.

34

Letters of December 31, 1980, from David Harlow of Air Force Sergeants Association and January 9, 1981, from Richard Johnson of Non Commissioned Officers Association, to Honorable Alan Cranston.

35

Letters of January 14, 1981, from Donald Schwab of the Veterans of Foreign Wars of the United States, and Mylio Kraja of The American Legion, to Honorable Alan Cranston.

36

These stated functions most likely were a reference to furnishing health care to veterans and disabled veterans.

37

Letter of January 8, 1981, from John Mallan of the American Association of Colleges and Universities, to Babette Polzer, professional staff member, Senate Committee on Veterans' Affairs Committee, Alan Cranston, Chairman.

38

When introduced in 1981, H.R. 1400 proposed a monthly educational assistance allowance of $300. VEAP's allowance was $225.

39

Garrison Nelson and Clark H. Benson. As stated, this was Representative Simpson's 2002 observation rather than the timeframe that this chapter in the text discusses. The reference document used throughout the text on Committee assignments is "Committees in the U.S. Congress 1947-1992," Vol. 1: Committee Jurisdictions and Member Rosters, *Congressional Quarterly* (1993).

40

Convening the Mayflower Hotel commemoration were Representatives Christopher Smith, Chairman, and Lane Evans, ranking member, Committee on Veterans' Affairs. Among the persons participating were former Senator Bob Dole, G.V. Montgomery, Secretary of Veterans Affairs Anthony Principi, Representative Mike Simpson, and American Legion National Adjutant Bob Sponogle.

41

Representative Simpson also was the prime author of the *Jobs for Veterans Act* enacted on November 7, 2002, Public Law 107-288. The act redesigned the delivery of veterans' employment and training services by the states around themes of increased accountability, flexibility, incentives, and results. Lastly, Mr. Simpson authored the legislation that created in law Department of Labor Transition Assistance Program services to our service members serving at U.S. bases overseas, enacted as Public Law 108-183.

42

The authors do not support the notion that the peers of veterans are those of the same age who enter the workforce and do not pursue postsecondary education. For example, VA data shows that almost 7 of 10 of the 9.3 million Vietnam-era veterans used the GI Bill to pursue various forms of postsecondary education after separation from the military. The peers of veterans are those who pursued postsecondary education.

43

Mr. Matsunaga was a member of the U.S. House of Representatives before becoming a U.S. Senator.

44

The persons cited do not constitute a comprehensive listing.

45

Colonel Michael Meese, Ph.D. and head, Social Sciences Department, U.S. Military Academy, interview by Kehrer (co-author), West Point, NY, October 19, 2005. The legislative history of the Montgomery GI Bill offers numerous insights from General Thurmond on the importance of an educational incentive. Elected officials quoted him often. Observed Professor Philip B. Carter, chair of the faculty, North Carolina State University, "the late General Max Thurman who coined the greatest recruiting slogan of our time 'Be All You Can Be,' had the vision of nanotechnology for the soldier 25 years ago." Statement cited at North Carolina State University, "General Faculty Meeting February 5, 2002, http://www.fis.ncsu.edu/facultysenate/05febgf.html; (accessed August 1, 2006). For an overview of General Thurman's 37-year Army career, see http://www.arlingtoncemetery.net/mthurman.html.

46

House Committee on Veterans' Affairs, *Veterans' Educational Assistance Act of 1981,* 97th Cong., 1st sess., 1981, 22. General Meyer's name virtually is synonymous with value-added educational incentives cited in the legislative history. Elected officials often cited his views in public debate. General Meyer served one combat tour in Korea and two in Vietnam. His military career is summarized at The Association of Graduates, U.S. Military Academy: http://www.westpointaog.org.

47

General (Ret.) John Wickham, interview by Kehrer (co-author), January 10, 2006. The information cited in the text paragraph is secondary to General Wickham's overall advocacy, as selected Senators quoted General Wickham frequently on the Senate floor, in legislative reports, and in other ways. Students may learn more about General John A. Wickham, Jr. at The Association of Graduates, U.S. Military Academy: http://www.aog.usma.edu/aog/awards/dga/05cit/wickham.html.

48

Ibid.

49

Cosponsoring were Senators Henry Bellmon, Rudy Boschwitz, David Durenberger, Barry Goldwater, Sam Hayakawa, Roger Jepsen, Paul Laxalt, Pat Leahy, George McGovern, and Patrick Moynihan. Senate Committee on Veterans' Affairs, *Educational Incentives and the All-Volunteer Force,* 96th Cong., 2nd sess., S. 2020 and S. 2596, 1980, 26, 44.

50

Ibid., 27. Noted Senator Cohen in this same published hearing document at 50: "The old [Vietnam-era] GI Bill helped recruit 25 to 30 percent of the volunteers entering the Armed Forces. In December 1976, the last month for the old GI Bill, a record 27,585 youths enlisted in the Army. The year before, only about half that many—14,173—enlisted."

51

Congressional Record, March 7, 1983, 4075. During his introductory statement on S. 691, the proposed Veterans Education Assistance Act of 1983, Senator Cohen said, "It has been estimated that the old GI Bill helped recruit between 25 to 36 percent of the volunteers entering the Armed Forces. In December 1976, the last month the GI Bill was in effect, a record 27,585 individuals enlisted in the Army alone. The approximately 100,000 youths who joined the uniformed services were about twice the normal first time enlistment." Also, see *Congressional Record*, July 13, 1983, on an unsuccessful effort by Senators Armstrong and Cohen to create a new GI Bill through a Senate floor amendment (as part of the FY 1984 DoD Authorization Act) when Senator Matsunaga stated, "Second, I do not know how it can be argued that the GI Bill might have a detrimental effect on military recruiting. It has been estimated that the Vietnam-era GI Bill during the initial years of the volunteer system helped to recruit between 25 and 36 percent of the volunteers entering the Armed Forces. In December 1976, the last month the old [Vietnam-era] GI Bill was in effect, approximately 100,000 recruits joined the military services, with the Army receiving more than 27,000 enlistees. I think this more than demonstrates the great attractiveness of the GI Bill educational benefits to the recruit and the return on investment to the military."

52

House Committee on Veterans' Affairs, *Veterans' Educational Assistance Act of 1981,* 93-96.

53

Public Law 95-566 "brought college loans to the middle class by removing the income limit for participation in federal aid programs." The Brookings Institution, "Research Topics: Education/Increase Access to Post-Secondary Education," http://brook.edu/gs/cps/research/projects/50ge/endeavors/postsecondary.html, (accessed November 28, 2006).

54

Ibid., 48, 51. *Congressional Record*, May 8, 1987, S. 6210. Senator Cohen further gave credit to the National Association of State Approving Agencies: "A number of individuals and organizations have also been essential to this effort. I cannot name them all, but there are two I would like to pay special tribute to… the Non-Commissioned Officers Association… . The other organization is the National Association of State Approving Agencies, whose president, Don Sweeney, is a constituent, serving as coordinator of veterans' education programs for the state of Maine. Don has spent many, many hours working with me and my staff, and with the staffs of other Senate and House leaders, in this effort." Senator Cohen also stated that "Representative Bob Wilson (R-CA) has introduced a similar measure [to mine], H.R. 4676, in the House."

55

Senate Committee on Veterans' Affairs, *Educational Incentives and the All-Volunteer Force,* 96th Cong., 2nd sess., S .2020 and S. 2596, 1980, 11-14 and 23-26.

56

Congressional Record, June 11, 1984, S15639.

57

Congressional Record, December 12, 1980, S33826.

58

Congressional Record, June 13, 1984, 16068. "Senator Armstrong entered President Reagan's statement into the Record: 'I will ask Congress to reinstate the GI Bill, a program which was directly responsible for the most rapid advance ever in the educational level of our population.' Ronald Reagan, televised address to the nation, October 19, 1980." Senator Kennedy at 16094 also quotes President Reagan: "During his address before the 1980 annual American Legion convention in my home state of Massachusetts, then-candidate [for President] Ronald Reagan stated: 'We must provide the resources to attract and retain superior people in each of the services. We should take steps immediately to restore the GI Bill, one of the most effective, equitable, and socially important programs ever devised.'"

59

Office of Management and Budget, "The Mission and Structure of the Office of Management and Budget," http://www.whitehouse.gov/omb/organization/mission.html; (accessed October 21, 2006).

60

Office of Management and Budget, "Jobs at OMB," http://www.whitehouse.gov/omb/recruitment/index.html; (accessed October 21, 2006). "The [OMB] contains significant numbers of both career and politically appointed staff; OMB staff provide important continuity within the EOP [Executive Office of the President] since several hundred career professionals remain in their positions regardless of which party occupies the White House. Six positions within OMB—the Director, the Deputy Director, the Deputy Director for Management, and the Administrators of the Office of Information and Regulatory Affairs, the Office of Federal Procurement Policy, and the Office of Federal Financial Management—are Presidentially appointed and Senate-confirmed (PAS) positions."

61

Congressional Record, June 11, 1984, S15639.

62

March 17, 19, 24 and 25, and April 6 and 23, 1981. See Congressional Information Service (CIS)/Annual 1984, *Legislative Histories of U.S. Public Laws*, CIS/Index Legislative Histories, January-December 1984, Public Law 98-525, Department of Defense Authorization Act-1985, 98th Cong., 2nd sess., P.L. 98-525 Debate, 504.

63

Congressional Record, July 8, 1981, 15027. Mr. Montgomery noted the following regarding Mr. Edgar: "Mr. Speaker, Bob Edgar has worked diligently in bringing his bill through the committee. He and his subcommittee listened to well over 100 witnesses in Washington and in the field. Although H.R. 1400 was initially introduced by me, the bill as amended in committee has Bob Edgar's stamp on and many features of the bill as amended are those recommended by him following extensive hearings."

64

These were field hearings. Both Republicans, the two members most likely testified as individual members of the Armed Services Committee and encouraged the Armed Services Subcommittee to hold a hearing in their respective Congressional districts.

65

Congressional Record, July 8, 1981, 15027, 15028.

66

Ibid.

67

Under the Vietnam-era educational assistance program, veterans received 45 months (five academic years) of entitlement and additional subsistence allowance for each dependent. There was no service member financial contribution or buy-in to establish eligibility.

68

Ibid.

69

Ibid.

70

U.S. Army Chief of Staff General "Shy" Meyer notes earlier in this chapter that such attrition is high for non-high school graduates. But the 1979 GAO figure of $5.2 billion is not limited to non-high school graduates.

71

CIS/INDEX Legislative Histories, Department of Defense Authorization Act of 1985, January-December 1984, 504.

72

Beyond the beltway is a colloquial phrase used in Washington, D.C., for communities in America that are not dominated by politics and federal funding.

73

House Committee on Armed Services, *Veterans' Educational Assistance Act of 1982*, 97th Cong., 2nd sess., 1982, 39. Page 39 notes such minor amendments (generalized here with Senate provision stated first) as the following: (1) *basic benefit*: education benefits paid for by VA of $200 per month versus $300 per month in the House Committee on Veterans' Affairs (HCVA)-reported version of H.R. 1400; (2) *kickers*: up to $400 paid for by DoD for difficult-to-recruit-for-skills with certain limitations versus no such limitations in the HCVA-reported H.R. 1400; (3) *supplemental benefit*: $100 per month for certain additional years of service versus $300 of such benefit in the HCVA-reported bill; (4) *transferability*: paid for by DoD on a discretionary and targeted basis versus entitlement for all servicemembers who complete 10 or more years of service in the HCVA-reported bill; (5) *cash out* paid for by DoD under various circumstances versus no similar HCVA-reported provision; (6) *in-service tuition reimbursement*: paid for by both DoD and VA—reduces benefit for which otherwise would be eligible with same provision in HCVA-reported bill; (7) *Guard and reserves*: $140 per month paid for by DoD versus no similar HCVA-reported provision; and (8) *accrual funding*: requires service branches to set aside funds in budget as obligation is incurred versus no similar HCVA-reported provision.

74

Ibid., 178, for the 40-1 full committee vote and p. 100 for the 12-1 subcommittee vote. Report number is 97-46, May 17, 1982.

75

Ibid., 99

76

Ibid., 154

77

House of Representatives, Mr. Nichols from the Committee on Armed Services, Report 97-80 to Accompany H.R. 1400, Part 2, May 11, 1982, *Veterans' Educational Assistance Act of 1982*, 54.

78

Report No. 97-46, 159-160.

79

Died in committee is a phrase that both the proponents and opponents of a bill would be prone to use.

80

In introducing a bill, a member or his or her staff takes a copy of the bill to the House floor and drops it in the bill box to the right of the Speaker's chair on the rostrum (to the left as one observes from the House floor). A bill cannot be dropped off in advance and held until the desired bill number becomes available. The bill must be introduced only on the day the desired bill number emerges. The bill clerk keeps a list of bill numbers that have been reserved. When a reserved number gets close to becoming available, the bill clerk's office contacts the member's office. Robert Cover, Office of the Parliamentarian, House of Representatives, interview by Kehrer (co-author), Washington, D.C., June 5, 2007.

81

Congressional Record, June 11, 1984, S15639.

82

Congressional Record, July 13, 1983, S18991.

83

Ibid., S19018.

84

Senator Armstrong and his fellow cosponsors of both S. 691 and the July 13 proposed amendment viewed themselves as being part of an informal team with their House counterparts. We note Senator Armstrong's introductory statement on S. 691: "As before, the Armstrong-Cohen-Matsunaga bill is a carefully thought out compromise which blends the best features of GI bill proposals introduced by Senators Cohen, Hollings, and myself in the 97th Congress, and which is compatible with the provisions of H.R. 1400, the leading GI Bill proposal in the House of Representatives." *Congressional Record*, March 7, 1983, 4074.

85

Congressional Record, March 7, 1983, S4073-6.

86

The five issues are based on readings of the debate in the July 13, 1983, *Congressional Record*, S18991 to

S19018. Examples of the issues are furnished in the next five notes. The debate was not without interesting personal observations by Senators. With respect to the political issues that emerged in the debate, Senator Simpson humored his colleagues, as recorded at S19003: "I would only share with you that I have the flickering of something like: Woe is me, the emaciated form of the chairman of the Veterans' Affairs Committee, speaking against the peacetime GI bill; the hint of, again, muffled drums on the parade ground. The decommissioning ceremonies will be cranking up again. I can hear them now." And with respect to the cost of the amendment, Senator Domenici shared with fellow Senators, as recorded at S19011… . "Many members in this Senate who are prone to vote for this are constantly, persistently, consistently saying the problem with the U.S. budget is the entitlement programs, which are out of control. Once you create them, you cannot do anything about them. They are automatic. Presidents cannot veto them. Appropriators cannot do anything with them. If you are entitled to a benefit, you get it. If you have the right color eyes, the right stature, the right age, they will write you a check. That is what an entitlement is." Lastly, with respect to the need for the amendment, Senator Cohen shared with Senators, as recorded at S4074 on March 7, 1983, when he joined with Senator Armstrong in introducing S. 691: "In the mid-1970s, Congress and the administration looked at the All-Volunteer Force (AVF), saw how well it was doing, and, with a feeling of confidence, dealt a series of body blows to it which almost put it in its grave. The AVF is doing so well, the reasoning went, that we can cap pay, end the GI bill, and reduce recruiting and advertising money. Those actions, coupled with the Pentagon's implementation of a new recruit qualification test which was incorrectly calibrated, proved disastrous. By the late 1970s, the number of high school graduates entering the Army had plummeted and the percentage of Category IV recruits, the lowest accepted into the service, had sky rocketed."

87

As noted in the debate at S19008 and S19015, July 13, 1983, *Congressional Record*, Chairman Tower and Senator Denton, respectively, thought it inappropriate for Senator Armstrong, et. al. to bring the bill to the floor in the form of an amendment without having had hearings on the measure in the Armed Services Committee. Conversely, also at S19008, Senator Cohen and others thought it appropriate that Chairman Tower scheduled no hearings on the Armstrong amendment, as Cohen and Armstrong introduced such legislation in 1979 and in subsequent years.

88

As noted in the debate at S19007 and S19011, Senators Exon and Domenici, respectively, argued that Congress fixed past military pay issues that had hurt recruitment and that 1983 military recruitment and retention issues were not problematical. Conversely, at S18998 and S19009, Senators Armstrong and Matsunaga, respectively, argued that due to demographics and economic issues, by 1987 military recruiting and the All-Volunteer Force would be in jeopardy, absent a quality educational incentive.

89

As noted in the debate at S19005, Senator Simpson observed that the United States had never enacted a GI Bill educational assistance program for the purpose of military recruitment and retention; past GI Bill programs helped veterans readjust to civilian life after service in a war period. Conversely, Senator Matsunaga at S19010 argued that a GI Bill for recruiting purposes was needed to avoid a peacetime draft.

90

As noted in the debate at S19011, Senator Domenici argued that that the federal deficit and entitlement programs (such as a permanent GI Bill Senator Armstrong proposed) were out of control. Conversely, at S19010, Senator Matsunaga argued that Congress was considering too many costly weapons systems that may not be essential to our national security.

91

As noted in the debate at S19008, Senator Tower observed that he wouldn't vote for the Armstrong amendment simply because doing so would be politically popular in Texas with its many military bases and veterans. Conversely, also at S19008, Senator Cohen observed that the Armstrong amendment he (Senator Cohen) cosponsored was not politically motivated and that he introduced similar legislation in 1979 when he was not running for re-election, the first year of his service in the Senate.

CHAPTER 6

Late Spring 1984—Road to Enactment: House Passes a New GI Bill Unopposed

1

Congressional Information Service (CIS)/Annual 1984, *Legislative Histories of U.S. Public Laws*, CIS/Index

Legislative Histories, January–December 1984, Public Law 98-525, Department of Defense Authorization Act, 1985, 98th Cong., 2nd sess., P.L. 98-525 Hearings, 504.

2

See Mr. Edgar's statement at 12295, May 15, 1984, *Congressional Record*: "During the 97th Congress [1981-1982]… my subcommittee conducted a minimum of eight hearings on the bill [H.R. 1400, The Veterans' Educational Assistance Act of 1982]." The April 12, 1983, hearing actually was part of the 98th Congress. It was titled "Proposals to Establish a New Educational Assistance Program for Veterans and Members of the Armed Forces, and Review of the Veterans' Educational Assistance Program (VEAP)." CIS/Index Legislative Histories, January-December 1984, 505.

3

House Committee on Armed Services, *Department of Defense Authorization Act, 1985,* 1984, H.R. 5167, 262-265.

4

Ibid.

5

Ibid.

6

Cong. Inf. Serv., 98th Cong., 2nd sess., 1984, P.L. 98-525 Debate, 504.

7

Congressional Record, Index Volume 130, part 24, January 23, 1984, L-2 and History of Bills, 2425.

8

The authors reviewed the content of 81 documented instances in the *Congressional Record* in which H.R. 5167 was discussed, debated, or amended in the House and found no opposition to a New GI Bill. The pages in which such instances appear begin on H5691 and end on H14680 of the 1984 *Congressional Record*. *Congressional Record*, Index Volume 130, part 124, January 23, 1984, to October 12, L-Z and History of Bills, 2425. At 11463 and 11464 of the May 30 *Record*, Representative Barney Frank engages Mr. Montgomery in a discussion regarding extending, under certain circumstances, the 10-year eligibility period under the Vietnam-era GI Bill. Mr. Montgomery pledges public hearings on the matter, but this was not a New GI Bill issue.

9

Congressional Record, May 15, 1984, 12296.

10

Ibid., 12286.

11

Congressional Record, May 15, 1984, 12266-12267.

12

The Senate had not adopted the first concurrent budget resolution on the fiscal year 1985 budget, either. See Senate debate in this regard in Chapter 9.

13

Congressional Record, May 15, 1984, H12267.

14

Students will note that when the House Veterans' Affairs Committee had its committee-passed bills on the House floor for a vote that the regular rules were suspended by agreement of both the House majority and minority parties. Under suspension of the rules, no amendments were permitted. For House consideration of the FY 1985 DoD Authorization Act, the opposite was true. Under the open rule, amendments were permitted and, in fact, dozens were offered during debate on the bill from April 19 to May 31, 1984.

CHAPTER 7

Summer 1984—Road to Enactment: Senate Passes Glenn Test Citizen-Soldier Education Program 96 to 1—First Vote

1

John Glenn became a member of the Senate Armed Services Committee in the 99th Congress, at which time he had served in the U.S. Senate for 11 years. The 99th Congress commenced in January 1985. Garrison Nelson and Clark H. Benson, "Committees in the U.S. Congress 1947-1992," Vol. 1: *Committee Jurisdictions and Member Rosters, Congressional Quarterly,* (1993): 52.

2

THOMAS (Library of Congress), "S. 2723," http://thomas.loc.gov/cgi-bin/bdquery/z?d098:SN02723:@@@Z, (accessed January 16, 2006). "S. 2723. Title: An original bill to authorize appropriations for the military functions of the Department of Defense and to prescribe personnel levels for the Department of Defense for fiscal year 1985. Sponsor: Tower, John [TX] (introduced 5/31/1984) Cosponsors (None), Latest Major Action, 6/21/1984 Senate floor actions. Status: Indefinitely postponed by Unanimous Consent. Floor Action 5/31/84 Reported to Senate from the Committee on Armed Services, S. Rept. 98-500, 5/31/1984 Placed on Calendar in Senate… 6/11/1984 Measure considered in Senate… 6/13/84 Measure considered in Senate. Thomas also notes the following: "The Senate considered the Glenn and Armstrong amendments on 6/11/84 and 6/13/84. However, on another THOMAS Internet site with the same identifier as above except for the last four digits (@@@S) appears the following wording: 'ALL ACTIONS: 5/24/1984: Committee on Armed Services ordered to be reported an original measure in lieu of S. 2414, S.2364, and S. 2459.'"

3

The act carries the same name each year while substituting the appropriate fiscal year.

4

Congressional Record, June 13, 1984, S16085. "Federal Legislative History: A Quick Guide to Reference Sources."

5

Congressional Record, June 11, 1984, S15628-15642 and *Congressional Record* June 13, 1984, S16060. Since these pages are the only source of Senatorial debate in this chapter, the authors have not provided endnotes for each Senator's statement each time he or she speaks. However, the authors do endnote the page of the *Congressional Record* that records a vote when a vote occurs.

6

United States Senate, "Reference Home/Glossary," http://www.senate.gov/pagelayout/reference/b_three_sections_with_teasers/glossary.html; (accessed September 11, 2008). "The *Daily Digest* is the key to finding information in the *Congressional Record.* It is much like a table of contents in a book, but is found in the back of each daily edition of the *Record.* The permanent edition of the *Record* includes a *Daily Digest* volume which cumulates each issue for the year. Chamber and committee activities are summarized separately for the Senate and House. Measures introduced and passed, amendment activity, appointments, nominations, and roll call votes from the previous meetings are listed with page numbers to those actions within the *Record's* full text."

7

Not taking a vote was a professional courtesy that Senators Glenn, Tower, and Nunn extended to Senator Armstrong, given Mr. Armstrong's absence.

8

Language such as *Conclusion of Morning Business* in this and the next two chapters is verbatim from the *Congressional Record* of June 11 and June 13, 1984.

9

John Tower represented Texas in the United States Senate from 1961 to 1985. His career in public service included appointments as chairman of the Senate Armed Services Committee, chair of the President's Foreign Intelligence Advisory Board, and strategic nuclear arms negotiator with the Soviet Union. The John G. Tower Congressional papers are housed at the A. Frank Smith, Jr. Library Center, Southwestern University, Georgetown, TX. Southern Methodist University sponsors the *John Goodin Tower Center for Political Studies* and the *Tower Center Teaching Fellows Program.*

10

Amendment No. language of this type in this and the next two chapters is also verbatim from the *Congressional Record.*

11

The Senator Glenn amendment language consumes pages 15630-15632 of the June 11, 1984, *Congressional Record.* Senator Tower's perfecting amendment to the Glenn amendment made the Glenn-proposed Citizen-Soldier Educational Assistance Program, a pilot (test) program limited to 12,500 enlistees.

12

Assuming the Chair means that the Senator was now presiding over the debate from the chair and is

addressed as "Mr. President" or "Madam President." In the House, the presiding officer is addressed as "Mr. Speaker" or "Madam Speaker." Only members of the majority party preside over debate in both the House and Senate.

13

As a general matter, in this debate, the Senate referred to *bill* in lower case. Conversely, the House generally would capitalize the first letter.

14

The *Congressional Record* for Senate debate generally spells a Senator's name in uppercase letters when making reference to the senator. The authors do not do so here.

15

Senate Committee on Armed Services, *Omnibus Defense Authorization Act of 1985*—Report to Accompany S.2723, 98th Cong., 2nd sess., 1985, 516.

16

As a general matter, again in this debate the Senate referred to "new" GI Bill in lowercase. The House generally would capitalize the first letter, as in "New" GI Bill.

17

The authors make reference to this vote at the end of Chapter 5. The Armstrong amendment failed 52 to 46 in some part because the Senate Armed Services Committee had not taken testimony on his bill, S. 691.

18

The Senator Alan Simpson alternative proposal essentially was one to establish a high-level study. The alternative "would have required the President to report to Congress at such time as he determines that there are recruitment and retention problems in the Armed Forces that are contrary to the national interest, but in no event later than July 1, 1987, as to the nature and extent of those problems and the usefulness of the new educational assistance program in addressing them." *Congressional Record,* June 11, 1984, S15637.

19

This bill is referenced at the "Legislative Journey guide" on pages 10-11.

20

Congressional Record, June 11, 1984, S15639.

21

Senate Committee on Veterans' Affairs, *Hearing on Educational Incentives and the All-Volunteer Force* (S.2020 and S.2596 and all related bills), 96th Cong., 2nd sess., 1980, 11-14 and 23-26.

22

Sam Nunn went on to serve as co-chairman and chief executive officer of the Nuclear Threat Initiative (NTI), a charitable organization working to reduce the global threats from nuclear, biological, and chemical weapons. Mr. Nunn served as an United States Senator for 24 years (1972-1996). In addition to his work with NTI, Senator Nunn has continued his service in the public policy arena as a distinguished professor at the Sam Nunn School of International Affairs at Georgia Institute of Technology and as chairman of the board of the Center for Strategic and International Studies in Washington, D.C.

23

Congress terminated the Vietnam-era GI Bill on December 31, 1976, as the Vietnam Conflict had concluded and the United States no longer drafted young men into its military. Initially, Congress did not appear to believe it owed a GI Bill-type educational assistance program to volunteers in the all-volunteer force that took effect on January 1, 1973. However, Congress would create the Post-Vietnam-era Educational Assistance Program in this regard.

24

Students may observe an actual roll call vote on C-SPAN.

25

Congressional Record, June 13, 1984, S16060.

26

Students may also wish to note the exceptionally formal and courteous language used by Senators during floor debate. Decorum, professionalism, and civility are important.

CHAPTER 8

Summer 1984—Road to Enactment:

Senate Fails to Table Armstrong Peacetime Veterans' Educational Assistance Act 51 to 46—Second Vote

1

This chapter of the text is drawn verbatim from various statements of U.S. Senators during the debate, as expressed at pages S16060 to S16095. Because the debate as expressed in the June 13, 1984, *Congressional Record* is the only source of each statement, each individual statement does not have an endnote. However, we do endnote the recorded votes.

2

As a general matter, we do not include in the text instances of the presiding officer recognizing a Senator to speak except at the beginning of a chapter of text or when a Senator asks the Chair for a vote on a measure.

3

The Chair and the Presiding Officer are the same person.

4

The *Congressional Record* does not document or state the name of the Senator who seconds a motion.

5

This appears to be a reference to the senior Senator from Massachusetts, Mr. Kennedy.

6

The Army furnished the additional $8,000-$12,000 in each instance. In 1984, the Army was the only service branch to develop a special educational fund of this type to augment VEAP.

7

Ballard and Piper, *Sonny Montgomery: The Veteran's Champion,* 206. Mr. Weinberger consented to an interview for this book but passed away in 2006 prior to the interview. In 2003, Ballard and Piper quoted Mr. Weinberger with respect to Mr. Montgomery retiring from Congress after 30 years: "I was sorry indeed to learn of your decision to leave the Congress next year, but of course can completely understand it. However, I could not let the event pass without writing to tell you how deeply I have appreciated not only your many personal kindnesses and friendship to me, but the really great service you have performed for the country.... You were always a strong, clear voice for the kind of legislation and kind of moral support that our troops need. I was deeply grateful to you then and am still."

8

Mr. Montgomery and colleagues agreed with Senator Simpson on this statement of fact but for a different reason. Both felt a paradigm shift was in order. Senator Simpson and colleagues believed that since the United States never had a so-called permanent, peacetime GI bill that we should not have one now. Montgomery and colleagues used essentially the same argument as the reason the United States should have one now. Nonetheless, Simpson and Montgomery had a good relationship. Alan Simpson attended the White House signing ceremony when President Reagan signed H.R. 1085, as amended, creating the Montgomery GI Bill in 1987. Like George H.W. Bush, Alan Simpson liked to joust with Montgomery: "With Sonny here, another dear friend on the other side of the aisle.... Sonny used to sit next to me [at public events with veterans' organizations, for example] and say: 'Don't do it, pal. I know what you're going to do. Just shut up, won't you?' I know we're not going to let that get away now, Sonny." Excerpt from statement of Alan Simpson at Memorial Tribute to Alan Cranston, U.S. Senator, 1969-1993, February 6, 2002, Hart Senate Office Building, Washington, DC. Joint Committee on Printing, *Memorial Tributes and Addresses in Eulogy of Alan Cranston, Late a Senator from California* (Washington, D.C.: Government Printing Office, 2001), 84.

9

Senator Nunn seemed to be referring to the Army College Fund.

10

Air-Launched Anti-Satellite Missile, a unique U.S. Air Force space vehicle. This weapon was designed to destroy orbiting satellites that threaten the U.S.

11

Senator Armstrong is referring to the peacetime period from the conclusion of the Vietnam Conflict in 1973 until December 31, 1976. Persons entering our military during this period were eligible for the Vietnam-era GI Bill, even though the conflict was over. Their eligibility occurred largely in the absence of an intervening GI Bill policy decision by Congress.

12

Alan Cranston, *Congressional Record,* June 11, 1984, S15640. S. 1747 to which Senator Pressler refers "was introduced on August 3, 1983, by Senators Armstrong, Cohen, Hollings, Matsunaga, and Cranston and which is [was] cosponsored by Senators Bradley, D'Amato, DeConcini, Dole, Hart, Hawkins, Kasten, Kennedy, Mitchell, Boschwitz, and Pressler. The amendment would amend Title 38, United States Code, to establish two new programs of educational assistance designed to assist the Armed Forces in recruiting and retaining highly qualified men and women."

13

Congressional Record, June 13, 1984, S16095.

CHAPTER 9

Summer 1984—

Road to Enactment: Senate Passes Amended Glenn Citizen-Solider Test Education Program 72 to 20—After Third, Fourth, Fifth and Sixth Votes

1

The *Congressional Budget and Impoundment Control Act of 1974* (Public Law 93-344).

2

The selected floor debate as contained in this chapter may be found at pages S16095 to S16107 of the June 13, 1984, *Congressional Record.* As stated earlier, the authors have noted the pages in which a vote occurred.

3

Federal budget function 050 is national defense.

4

A major part of the Annual Budget Resolution is to identify new areas of direct spending based on new legislation, especially entitlements. As the majority leader noted, the Senate had not yet adopted a budget resolution for fiscal year 1985 so there was no spending blueprint for the Senate Appropriations Committee to follow. In the annual Congressional budget resolution process, the various authorizing committees (including Armed Services) mark up a proposed new fiscal year budget first, then the Budget Committee and the full Senate do so. Finally, the Appropriations Committee does so. The House follows the same process.

5

This appears to be a reference to the *Congressional Budget and Impoundment Control Act of 1974,* which Senator Domenici will discuss specifically later in this chapter.

6

The authors regret we have been unable to determine the name of the $21 billion and $23 billion entitlement programs to which Mr. Domenici refers.

7

Six and one-half hours into the debate, the Senate had taken two of the five votes.

8

Senator Goldwater admirably tried to take a middle-of-the-road position here between the Armstrong advocates and the Tower advocates. He attempted to mediate. One of the more popular sayings regarding a middle-of-the-road position is attributed to Representative Jim Hightower, a populist Democrat from Texas: "The only things in the middle of the road are yellow stripes and dead armadillos!" "Fate of Two Joes Reflects Drive for Partisan Purity," *USA Today,* August 10, 2006.

9

Congressional Record, June 13, 1984, S16104.

10

Ibid., S16105.

11

James Dykstra, interview by Kehrer (co-author), Washington, D.C., January 23, 2007. Students will note that Vice President George H.W. Bush had assumed the chair as presiding officer of the Senate. It would appear the Vice President was presiding in anticipation of close votes in the next section of the debate on President Reagan's Strategic Defense Initiative, the MX missile, and the like.

12

Ibid., S16106.

13

Of the 46 Senators who voted **to table** the Armstrong amendment the first time (*Congressional Record*, June 13, 1984, S16095), all voted to table it the second time (*Congressional Record*, June 13, 1984, S16106); but with the addition of Senators Gorton, Kassebaum, and Johnston (who initially voted not to table it) and Senators Stafford and Bumpers (who didn't vote the second time but voted to table it the first time). So the second vote netted 47 votes to table. Of the 51 Senators who voted **not to table** the Armstrong amendment the first time, Senators Gorton, Kassebaum, and Johnston switched their votes (as stated above). Plus, Senators Tsongas, Kennedy and Weicker (who initially voted not to table it) didn't vote the second time. So the second vote netted 45 votes to table. At S16106, Senator Stevens announced that "if present and voting, the Senator from Wisconsin (Mr. Kasten) would have voted 'nay'; thus yielding 46 votes not to table, but still one vote short of the 47 votes to table."

14

Ibid., S16108. Illustrative of the stark contrast between consideration of a New GI Bill—as part of the FY 1985 DoD Authorization Act—and other necessary provisions of the act was the next item for Senate consideration: "Cost-effective funding of nuclear weapons."

15

The authors discussed in Chapter 3 of our text that the House and Senate Committees on Veterans' Affairs often used a staff negotiation process rather than a formal House-Senate Conference Committee to negotiate House-Senate-passed bills. The New GI Bill aspect of the FY 1985 Omnibus DoD Authorization Act was under the jurisdiction of the House and Senate Armed Services Committees, which hold formal conferences.

CHAPTER 10

Fall 1984—Road to Enactment: House-Senate Conference on the FY 1985 DoD Authorization Act

1

Kim Wincup, interview by Kehrer (co-author), McLean, VA, June 1, 2006.

2

The G.V. Montgomery tribute to Mack Gerald Fleming, longstanding confidant, appears in the April 6, 1995, *Congressional Record* at E823. In addition to Montgomery acknowledging Mr. Fleming for "his intuitive sense of timing and ability to reach an effective compromise" is the credit Montgomery gives to his chief counsel for the legislation enacted into law that elevated the Veterans' Administration to cabinet status and legislation creating a New GI Bill. (Montgomery did not use the word "Montgomery" regarding the GI Bill, even though Congress named it in his honor.) Most instructive about Mr. Fleming and his "extraordinary career in public service" is what Montgomery said about the man himself: "We all know Mack thrived in and was energized by the rough and tumble of politics, and he loved nothing better than a good fight on behalf of a cause he championed. He nevertheless was not swallowed up or overwhelmed by the sometimes heady Capitol Hill existence. There was something in his background or the way he was raised that kept him solidly grounded, and that made the difference: the difference between a boastful person and one whom people boast of knowing; the difference between a cynical man and one who only sees the good he can do for other people; and the difference between a man who looks for credit for his accomplishment and a man who accomplishes much." Lastly, persons who have worked with Mr. Fleming likely would appreciate the following Montgomery statement: "Serene is not a word I associate with Mack, but he never retreated from the consequences of his conviction."

3

"Joint Explanatory Statement (JES) of the Committee of Conference on H.R. 5167, the FY 1985 DoD Authorization Act," September 26, 1984, 179. The JES is part of Conference Rep. No. 98-1080.

4

House Committee on Armed Services, *Department of Defense Authorization Act of 1985*, 1984, H.R. 5167, 262-265. *Report Together with Additional and Dissenting Views to Accompany H.R. 5167*.

5

Senate Committee on Armed Services, *Omnibus Defense Authorization Act, 1985-Report to Accompany S. 2723*, 98th Cong., 2nd sess., 1985, S. Rep. 98-500.

6

Cong. Inf. Serv., *Department of Defense Authorization Act of 1985*, 98th Cong., 2nd sess., P.L. 98-525 Debate, 504.

7

For example, Congressman Dellums led an effort "to strike all procurement funding ($7.1 billion) for the B-1B Bomber and to delay any further development of ground-launched cruise missiles or Pershing II missiles in Western Europe… the Bennett-Mavroules amendment to delete all production funds for the MX missiles… . The Weiss amendment to delete research and development for the Trident II/D5 missile… . The Brown amendment to halt anti-satellite weapon flight test in space… and the Bethune-Porter-Fascell amendment to delete all production money for chemical weapons." Walter Fauntroy, *Congressional Record*, May 16, 1984, 12503. Also at 12503, Delegate Fauntroy notes that "in 1953, Dwight David Eisenhower warned: 'Every gun that is made, every warship that is launched, every rocket fired, signifies a theft for those who hunger and are not fed, those who are cold and are not clothed. This world in arms is not spending money alone. It is spending the sweat of its laborers, the genius of its scientists, the hopes of its children.'"

8

For example, "Speaker Jim Wright (D-TX) on 8 February 1988… announced that the first person to say the Pledge of Allegiance on the House Floor would be Representative Sonny Montgomery (D-MS) and that it would rotate Democrat then Republican each day to recite the Pledge. The first Pledge done by Mr. Montgomery was recited the next legislative day, which was on 13 September 1988." Baptist minister Francis Bellamy wrote the Pledge of Allegiance on September 7, 1892. President Benjamin Franklin Harrison recognized the pledge with a proclamation on October 12, 1892, stating that the pledge was to be first used in public schools. *The History of the Pledge of Allegiance*, Office of the Historian, U.S. House of Representatives, September 7, 2006.

9

Charles W. Johnson, interview by Kehrer (co-author), Washington, D.C., March 20, 2008. Mr. Wincup observed that many held this view about Mr. Montgomery's leadership, including Charles W. Johnson, Parliamentarian of the House. Mr. Johnson served with distinction in the Office of the Parliamentarian for 40 years beginning in May 1964, including 10 years as Parliamentarian under the appointments of three successive Speakers. The House of Representatives resolution honoring Mr. Johnson, as well as Speaker Hastert's personal tribute, may be viewed in the May 20, 1994, *Congressional Record* at H3394 and successive pages.

10

CIS Index of Legislative Histories, January-December 1984, 504.

11

House Committee on Armed Services, Conference Report to Accompany H.R. 5167, *Department of Defense Authorization Act of 1985*, 1984, H.R. 5167, 352-354. Pages 352 and 353 lists 13 members from the House Armed Services Committee. Page 354 lists 18 members from the Senate Armed Services Committee. Page 354 also lists nine additional House members, appointed as part of the conference for discussion of the New GI Bill provision and two additional Senators for same. The "Calendars of the United States House of Representatives and History of Legislation, Final Edition, 98th Congress" confirms on pages 2-14 "Bills Through Conference" that Simpson and Cranston served as conferees "soley for consideration of any benefits to be paid by VA." On pages 2-15, the Calendars publication notes the following House conferees "soley for consideration of Title VII of the House bill and Sec. 1606 of the Senate amendment: Edwards of California, Edgar, Sam B. Hall, Jr. of Texas, Leath of Texas, Shelby, Applegate, Hammerschmidt, Wylie, and Solomon. The nine House conferees and the two Senate conferees listed in 'Calendars' are the same individuals who signed the 'Conference Report.'"

12

Ibid. Most of these weapons systems are part of Title I-Procurement or Title II-Research, Development, Test, and Evaluation.

13

Conference Report No. 98-1080.

14

Ballad and Piper, *Sonny Montgomery: The Veteran's Champion*, 74. Mr. David Lyles, then a principal staff member on the Senate Armed Services Committee, expressed a different view regarding Chairperson Tower scheduling the GI Bill issue as the last item. David Lyles, interview by Kehrer (co-author), Washington, D.C., July 11, 2006. Observed Mr. Lyles: "The GI Bill matter would have been discussed before the final negotiating session of the conference. The GI Bill was part of the final session because conferees could not come to agreement during earlier discussions of it."

15

Congressional Record, June 11, 1984, S15638. Observed Senator Tower regarding the June 11, 1984 "debate" before the formal debate on the proposed amendment itself: "We have looked into the matter of the GI Bill quite a bit. It is our view that it is not cost-effective at this time. But I also have the very pragmatic view that something is likely to pass and I want to minimize the budget impact."

16

The 31 members from the House and Senate Armed Services Committees were appointed for the full bill plus 11 more from the House and Senate Veterans' Affairs Committees for the New GI Bill provisions. See note 11 above.

17

Congressional Record, June 13, 1984, S16089-90. The authors repeat for the reader one of the Alan Simpson quotes here as well: "It cannot be emphasized strongly enough that this is not a GI Bill like any previous GI Bills. The goal in the past has always been to assist veterans to readjust to civilian life after service in a period of war. No GI Bill has ever been enacted solely in order to assist the Armed Forces in recruitment and retention."

18

Mack Fleming, interview by Kehrer (co-author), February 2, 2006, and October 28, 2010.

19

Congressional Record, June 21, 1984, 17708-17709. Speaker of the House Thomas "Tip" O'Neill appointed House conferees on H.R. 5167, *Department of Defense Authorization Act of 1985* on June 21, 1984.

20

Pages 352 and 353 of the Conference Report on H.R. 5167. House Report No. 98-1080.

21

Ballard and Piper, *Sonny Montgomery: The Veteran's Champion,* 73-74. Mr. Fleming's observation is also confirmed by the following: "I [Montgomery] immediately asked the Speaker of the House to name additional conferees from the Veterans' Affairs Committee so that each Committee would have the same number.… .The Speaker permitted me to do this."

22

See previous note 11 and *Congressional Record,* June 25, 1984, 18536.

23

See previous note 11: Representatives Don Edwards, Bob Edgar, Sam B. Hall, Jr., Marvin Leath, Richard Shelby, Douglas Applegate, John Paul Hammerschmidt, Chalmers P. Wylie, and Gerald B.H. Solomon.

24

The Parliamentarian organizationally is part of the Speaker's office. For information on Parliamentarians of the House 1857 to present, see U.S. House of Representatives, Office of the Clerk, "House History— Parliamentarians of the House," http://clerk.house.gov/art_history/house_history/parliamentarians.html; (accessed September 25, 2008).

25

The proxie shown in the visual is for illustrative purposes. It is a proxie Representative John Paul Hammerschmidt furnished Chairman Montgomery for a July 15, 1985, House-Senate Armed Services Committee Conference on S. 1160, the proposed National Defense Authorization Act for Fiscal Year 1986, which the authors discuss at the end of this chapter. The proxies applied only to discussion of section 522 on New GI Bill program matters.

26

Congressional Record, May 15, 1984, 12285. Mr. Montgomery expressed his thanks to Chairman Price and ranking member Dickinson for this opportunity in part through Mr. Montgomery's support for H.R. 5167, the Fiscal Year 1985 DoD Authorization Act.

27

Edgar Potter, *Cowboy Slang*, (Phoenix: Golden West History, 1986), 46.

28

Honorable John Marsh, interview by Kehrer (co-author), Culpeper, VA, August 26, 2005. Then-Secretary of the

Army John Marsh said he "may" have furnished the MREs in the interest of helping conferees come to closure on a meaningful educational incentive.

29

Ballard and Piper, *Sonny Montgomery: The Veteran's Champion,* 74. Staff were intrigued at conferees eating MREs. Karen Heath, interview by Kehrer (co-author), Arlington, VA, January 2, 2006. Observed Ms. Heath of the House Armed Services Committee majority staff: "I must say, I was surprised to see the venerable Senator Warner, for example, squeezing peanut butter onto a cracker from a metal tin!" Ms. Heath would serve as assistant secretary of the Navy after her service on the House Armed Services Committee.

30

Interview by Kehrer (co-author) with person present at the House-Senate Conference, June 20, 2006; name withheld by mutual agreement.

31

Anthony Principi, interview by Kehrer (co-author), June 27, 2006. John Sullivan, interview by Kehrer (co-author), Washington, D.C., December 27, 2007.

32

Mack Fleming, interview by Kehrer (co-author), February 2, 2006.

33

Ron Dellums represented California's 9th District in Congress from 1971 to 1998. He served in a number of leadership positions in Congress, including chairman, House Services Committee, 1995-1996. Mr. Dellums is an U.S. Marine Corps veteran and administers the Ronald V. Dellums Chair in Peace and Conflict Studies at University of California at Berkeley.

34

Mack Fleming, interview by Kehrer (co-author), October 28, 2010.

35

See Chapters 7-9.

36

Mack Fleming, interview, by Kehrer (co-author), February 2, 2006, and October 28, 2010.

37

Ballard and Piper, *Sonny Montgomery: The Veteran's Champion*, 75.

38

James Dykstra, interview by Kehrer (co-author), Washington, D.C., June 7, 2006.

39

Anthony Principi, interview by Kehrer (co-author), June 27, 2006. G.V. Montgomery, interview, by Kehrer (co-author), Meridian, MS, December 15, 2004.

40

Ballard and Piper, *Sonny Montgomery: The Veteran's Champion*, 75.

41

Ibid.

42

Ibid.

43

G.V. Montgomery, interview by Kehrer (co-author), Meridian, MS, December 15, 2004.

44

Ballard and Piper, *Sonny Montgomery: The Veteran's Champion*, 76.

45

HCVA Internal Historical File on the Montgomery GI Bill. Senator William S. Cohen corroborates the 2 a.m. timeframe in a March 14, 1986, letter to G.V. Montgomery: "I'm hopeful that we'll be as successful as we were at the 2 a.m. session a couple years ago."

46

We believe the date was September 25 because Mr. Montgomery points out in Ballard and Piper at 77 that "at that hour, with the conference agreement going to the floor for a vote the next day [September 26]… the *1984 CIS/INDEX of Legislative Histories*, Public Law 98-525, at 504 shows the House agreeing to the conference report on the FY 1985 DoD Authorization Act (P.L. 98-525) on September 26. The conference report to accompany H.R. 5167 on this act was ordered to be printed September 26, 1984, Rep. No. 98-1080.

47

Ibid., 77.

48

Congressional Record, March 19, 1987, H1498. For example, noted Mr. Montgomery on the House floor, March 19, 1987: "Mr. Bob Cover of the Legislative Counsel's office did all the drafting of the first bill I introduced in January 1981, H.R. 1400. Mr. Joe Womack of the Legislative Counsel's office did all of the drafting of H.R. 1085 and legislation enacted last year to improve the program. If the New GI Bill is made permanent, Bob Cover and Joe Womack will have played a major role in helping to bring about this new education program for our armed services. It is fitting that Bob and Joe are members of the team since they are responsible for a lot of legislation that comes out of the House Armed Services Committee, as well as the Committee on Veterans' Affairs… . I'm also grateful to Mr. Hugh Evans, Senate legislative counsel, who worked with Bob in putting together the conference agreement as part of the DoD Authorization Act of 1984."

49

Karen Heath, interview by Kehrer (co-author), Arlington, VA, January 2, 2006. Mr. Montgomery is speaking to the mechanics of the legislative drafting process, as it very much involved professional staff of the Armed Services and Veterans' Affairs Committees and the House and Senate Offices of Legislative Counsel.

50

Ibid. Mr. Montgomery again is speaking to the mechanics of the drafting process.

51

Congressional Record, September 27, 1984, 27437. As is discussed later in this chapter, Mr. Cranston observed the following: "I very much regret the way that this matter was handled [in conference] and the outcome that Mr. Montgomery had to accept at the 11th hour in order to salvage the entire conference report… . I still believe he was not treated properly on this issue."

52

Ballard and Piper, *Sonny Montgomery: The Veteran's Champion*, 77. Mr. Wincup, Ms. Heath, and Mr. Fleming had the same recollection as Mr. Montgomery. Kim Wincup, interview by Kehrer (co-author), June 1, 2006. Karen Heath, interview by Kehrer (co-author), January 2, 2006. Mack Fleming, interview by Kehrer (co-author), February 2, 2006.

53

Ballard and Piper, *Sonny Montgomery: The Veteran's Champion*, 77.

54

Senator Alan Cranston addresses this matter from the Senate floor at S27427 of the September 27, 1984, *Congressional Record*.

55

Ballard and Piper, *Sonny Montgomery: The Veteran's Champion*, 77.

56

See page 27241 of the *Congressional Record*, September 26, 1984, for the record of conferees presenting the conference report to House members and subsequent discussion and agreement.

57

See page 27304 of the *Congressional Record*, September 27, 1984, for the record of conferees presenting the conference report to the Senate and discussion/agreement. Also, see *Congressional Record*, Index, Volume 130 – Part 24, January 23, 1984, to October 12, 1984, L-Z and History of Bills (Washington, DC: U.S. Government Printing Office, 1984) at 2425 for an extensive listing of dates associated with H.R. 5167, a bill to authorize appropriations for Fiscal Year 1985 for the armed forces.

58

Congressional Record, September 26, 1984, 27304.

59

Ballard and Piper, *Sonny Montgomery: The Veteran's Champion*, 74. Observed Mr. Montgomery: "The House and Senate conferees met to work out differences between the two bodies on the Authorization bill. What a conference it was—unlike any I had ever attended during my tenure in the House."

60

Congressional Record, September 27, 1984, 27428.

61

Ibid., 27428 and 27429. Senator Nunn thanked staff of the Armed Services Committee: majority staff members Jim McGovern and Arnold Punaro and minority staff members Bill Hoehn, Jeff Smith, David Lyles, John Hamre, Russell Miller, Patty Watson, Pam Powell, Cathy Bognovitz, Shelley Turner, and Debbie Paige-Dubose.

62

Ibid., 27428.

63

Ibid., 27427. Senator Cranston acknowledged majority staff members of the Veterans' Affairs Committee: Jon Steinberg, Ed Scott, and Babette Polzer; minority staff member Tony Principi; and majority staff of the House Veterans' Affairs Committee Mack Fleming, Frank Stover, Richard Schultz, and Jill Cochran.

64

Ballard and Piper, *Sonny Montgomery: The Veteran's Champion*, 77.

65

The description of the compromise agreement between the conferees appears at pages 306-307 of the Conference Report on H.R. 5167, as cited earlier. This description became the basis for the new educational assistance provision in the conference version of the legislation signed by the President after the House and Senate concurred in the conference report. *Public Papers of The Presidents of the United States, Ronald Reagan, 1984* (Washington, D.C.: Government Printing Office, 1984), 1582 of Book II. In signing H.R. 5167 into law, President Reagan made no reference to the New GI Bill program. President Reagan offered the following tribute to Chairman Tower: "There is one Senator whose contributions to our nation's defense over the years has been unique and enduring—that Senator is John Tower. The final passage of this Defense Authorization Act marks one of the last milestones in a legislative career spanning nearly 24 years in the Senate. His lasting contributions, and especially those during his outstanding service as chairman of the Committee on Armed Services, bear the mark of a true statesman and an extraordinary American. We can only hope that he will not consider his retirement from the Senate to be a retirement from public life. Thank you, John."

66

A copy of this letter appears in the HCVA Internal Historical File on the Montgomery GI Bill.

67

"The New GI Bill and the New Army College Fund," Brochure, U.S. Army, 1985; "New GI Bill Plus Army College Fund," News Release, Office of the Assistant Secretary of Defense (Public Affairs), No. 112-85, March 1, 1985; "New GI Bill to Begin July 1, 1985," News release, Veterans Administration, Office of Public and Consumer Affairs, Washington, DC, June 17, 1985. However, the New GI Bill plus the Army College Fund would produce benefits of $25,200. The Army College Fund was available to enlistees who were "a high school graduate, score 50 or more on the Armed Forces Qualification Test, and enlist for… training in one of 80 selected Army specialties."

68

National Center for Education Statistics, *Digest of Education Statistics 2002* (Washington, D.C.: U.S. Government Printing Office, June 2003), 354.

69

Fiscal Year 1986 would begin on October 1, 1985.

70

Senate Committee on Veterans' Affairs, *Report to Accompany H.R. 752, New GI Bill Amendments of 1985*, 99th Cong., 1st sess., 1985, 6. This committee made some amendments to the House-passed bill but still embraced the House's major provisions. The Senate Committee on Veteran's Affairs legislative activity occurred after the House action. The report of the House Committee on Veterans' Affairs to accompany H.R. 752 is No. 99-1, March 7, 1985. The report of the House Armed Services Committee (HASC) to accompany H.R. 752 is No. 99-17, part 2, March 20, 1985. The HASC referred to the amendments made by H.R. 752 as "New GI Bill Amendments of 1985."

71

1985 CIS Annual Abstracts of Congressional Publications, CIS/Index, January-December 1985, 552.

72

Frank Murkowski chaired the committee, and Alan Cranston was ranking member.

73

Barry Goldwater chaired the committee, and Sam Nunn was ranking member.

74

HCVA Internal Historical File on the Montgomery GI Bill. File includes 1985 letters of April 12 from Sam Nunn to G.V. Montgomery, April 12 from Barry Goldwater and Sam Nunn to Majority Leader Bob Dole, April 23 from Barry Goldwater to G.V. Montgomery, and June 26 from Frank Murkowski and Alan Cranston to Majority Leader Bob Dole. There is also a May 21, 1985, letter from Mr. Murkowski and Mr. Cranston of the Committee on Veterans' Affairs to Barry Goldwater, Chairman of the Armed Services Committee regarding "outside conferees" to the House-Senate conference committee for consideration of the National Defense Authorization Act for Fiscal Year 1986 regarding section 522.

75

Mack Fleming to G.V. Montgomery, memorandum, August 12, 1985, HCVA Internal Historical File on the Montgomery GI Bill.

76

Alan Cranston, *Congressional Record*, June 5, 1985, S7517-S7518.

77

In his June 5, 1995, statement cited above, Senator Cranston explains the lack of support for the amendments approved by the Senate Armed Services Committee. For example, the test program automatically enrolled the service member in the New GI Bill unless the service member specifically disenrolled, as many service members later would regret not being eligible for $10,800 in education benefits. In addition, the New GI Bill was established as an educational assistance program and not as a savings plan from which to withdraw funds for impulse purchases that are not uncommon to youth. Senator Cranston also expressed regret—on behalf of himself and Senator Murkowski—that the Parliamentarian didn't accord the Veterans' Affairs Committee sequential referral on section 522 of S. 1160, as the Parliamentarian accorded the Armed Services Committee sequential referral of H.R. 752. Noted Mr. Cranston at 7517: "I am advised by the Parliamentarian that the fact that this provision is included in a measure that has been reported from the [Armed Services] Committee as an original bill, rather than as a bill previously introduced and reported, precludes us from doing so successfully. I believe that there is no doubt that section 522 invades the jurisdiction of the Veterans' Affairs Committee and that a point of order to that effect would have been sustained by the chair were this not an original bill." Mr. Cranston further observed that "our committee has agreed to honor the request of that [Armed Services] Committee and agree to a limited sequential referral of H.R. 752.... That same spirit of accommodation is not being exercised regarding the pending [S. 1160] measure, however."

78

Alan Cranston to G.V. Montgomery, July 18, 1985. HCVA Internal Historical File on the Montgomery GI Bill. Senate Committee on Veterans' Affairs support for Montgomery's efforts in opposition to the Senate-passed section 522 is evidenced. Cranston also notes his frustration in not being named an outside conferee on the FY 1988 DoD Authorizations Act with respect to section 522—proposed New GI Bill changes under the jurisdiction of the Veterans' Affairs Committee: "Frank's [Murkowski] and my efforts to be named conferees on the Senate side regarding these matters, as Al Simpson and I were last year, have been unsuccessful thus far."

79

Such persons/organizations include but are not limited to military personnel associations, veterans' service organizations, higher education associations, and the service branches. "Four years" is a reference to Mr. Montgomery/cosponsors commencing the bill's initial development through informal 1980 meetings with the service branches and higher education/veterans'/military personnel associations through the January 28, 1981, introduction of H. R. 1400, the proposed Veterans' Educational Assistance Act of 1981; and finally to the October 17, 1984, enactment of the three-year New GI Bill program in Title VII of the Fiscal Year 2005 National Defense Authorization Act (Public Law 98-525).

80

To view all of the visuals from this event, see University Libraries, Mississippi State University at http://library.msstate.edu. Select the Congressional and Political Research Center tab; digital collections; Stennis-Montgomery collection; and GI Bill photos.

81

The Coast Guard then was organizationally part of the U.S. Department of Transportation. The Coast Guard is now part of the U.S. Department of Homeland Security.

CHAPTER 11

1985-1986—Road to Enactment:
Implementing the Three-Year New GI Bill Program

1

"Format letters 170AA," June 25, 1985, HCVA Internal Historical File on the Montgomery GI Bill. The second paragraph of this letter notes the New GI Bill's comprehensive nature: "The new GI Bill is an important program that will help keep our military strong and stable, will enrich the lives of our service members, will meet the challenges to recruiting presented by an improved economy and demographic factors, and will benefit taxpayers. I think it is a program that you may want to publicize in your Congressional district."

2

Office of Assistant Secretary of Defense (Public Affairs), "New GI Bill Plus New Army College Fund" [News Release], March 1, 1985. HCVA Internal Historical File on the Montgomery GI Bill. We emphasize that the Department of Defense and/or service branches using the words "veterans' education benefits" instead of "New GI Bill" was not applicable in every instance. This particularly seemed the case when the information addressed both the New Army College Fund and the New GI Bill as a package.

3

Charles Moskos to Honorable G.V. Montgomery, January 13, 1985, HCVA Internal Historical File on the Montgomery GI Bill. Mr. Moskos, Professor of Military Sociology at Northwestern University, saw a difference in the language, too: "Calling the new legislation a GI Bill makes sense from every standpoint. First, the terminology is consistent with that of previous veterans' educational packages for those who served during the Korean and Vietnam era (none of which had the exact words "GI Bill" in the formal legislation yet still used such wording). Second, the new legislation is a qualitative, not incremental, improvement over the status quo, and should be recognized as such. Third, the term 'GI Bill' itself is valuable in terms of name recognition and positive symbolism.... What is at stake is more than a terminological quibble. The words 'GI Bill' signify commitment to enhancement of the citizen-solider concept even in an all-volunteer format."

4

Carl T. Rowan, "The Investment in Education," *Washington Post*, February 13, 1985. "I went to Oberlin College and got a degree in mathematics and to the University of Minnesota and earned a master's in journalism, thanks to the life-changing existence of a federal education program for former sailors and soldiers... given the fact that until war dragged me out of McMinnville, TN, I had never been able to get a job that paid more than 25 cents an hour. This is a great, rich, awesome nation, in part because 7.8 million veterans of World War II got higher education through the GI Bill. So did 2.4 million who fought in the Korean War and 8 million veterans of the Vietnam War. If we have learned anything about the educational benefits made available because of those wars, it is that America never made any better investments."

5

G.V. Montgomery to Secretary of Defense Caspar Weinberger, January 22, 1985, and G.V. Montgomery to the Secretaries of the Army (Mr. Marsh), Navy (Mr. Lehman), and Air Force (Mr. Orr), January 23, 1985, each found in HCVA Internal Historical File on the Montgomery GI Bill. In letters to Weinberger, Marsh, Lehman, and Orr., G.V. Montgomery asked for help in resolving this issue. The text of the first paragraph of each letter says the following: "I am very concerned about reports I have received that DoD is considering using a name other than GI Bill for the new educational program. As you know, this legislation had strong support in Congress. The term GI Bill was used repeatedly, if not exclusively, throughout the debates and consideration of this legislation. In my opinion, that is the reference most appropriate." Each letter also notes the following: "I have had an opportunity to mention my concern to Vice President Bush."

6

As a general matter, it is not unusual for legislative branch committee staff to consider such report language as akin to the force of law.

7

"Military College Remedy," the photocopied version of this two-column article in the HCVA Montgomery GI Bill Internal Historical File obscures the newspaper name and page number. It appears to be the *Washington Times.*

8

Michael B. Tanner, "Army College Fund Meeting Its Objectives?" *JSTOR Industrial and Labor Relations Review 41, No.1*, 50-62: "The Army College Fund is a program started in 1981 that offers post-service educational benefits to eligible recruits. It was hoped the program would increase the quality of Army recruits by attracting more of the college-oriented. Using data from three Army sources, Tanner examines enrollment and financial participation in the program from 1981 to 1985. He finds that "enrollment grew rapidly during that time and that the quality of Army recruits, as measured by Armed Forces Qualification test scores, also drastically increases." Tanner found the "program may turn out to be more expensive than anticipated, however, because the number of participating soldiers—those making the co-payments necessary to receive benefits later—has exceeded expectations."

9

"New GI Bill Succeeds in Attracting Recruits," *USA Today*, November 25, 1985.

10

The $1,200 pay reduction did not apply to Reservists.

11

Department of Defense, "New GI Bill (NGIB) Participation (first 15 months) versus VEAP Participation (first nine months)," [White paper], October 16, 1986, HCVA Internal Montgomery GI Bill Historical File. The measurement period for VEAP participation was 1977 and for NGIB was July 1985 to September 1986.

12

Honorable John Marsh, interview by Kehrer, (co-author), Culpeper, VA, September 26, 2005.

13

"Implementation of the New GI Bill," undated, HCVA Montgomery GI Bill Internal Historical File.

14

"GI Bill, Once a Reward, is Now a Lure to Sign Up," *New York Times*, December 5, 1986.

15

House Committee on Veterans' Affairs, *Report to Accompany H.R. 1400, Veterans' Educational Assistance Act of 1981*, 99th Cong., 1st sess., 1981, 18.

16

Representative G.V. Montgomery to Honorable Barry Goldwater, May 5, 1986, HCVA Internal Historical File on the Montgomery GI Bill.

17

"Some Democrats Weigh Reviving Draft to Bolster Armed Services and Make Mark on Defense," *Wall Street Journal*, November 17, 1986.

18

H. Lawrence Garrett, III, general counsel, U.S. Department of Defense, to Honorable Thomas P. O'Neill, Speaker, U.S. House of Representatives, March 28, 1986. Seven pages of proposed legislation accompany the letter.

19

U.S. General Accounting Office (National Security and International Affairs Division), "The New GI Bill: Potential Impact of Ending It Early" (Washington, D.C.: U.S. Government Printing Office, March 25, 1986), 2. The report also noted with respect to recruiting and retention impacts of the New GI Bill: The comparison of Navy Selected Reserve accessions shows a "5.4 percent increase in the percentage of accessions from the highest two mental categories and a 10.8 percent decrease in the percentage from the lowest mental category," 8; "Air Force Reserve non-prior service [NPS] enlistments, which are for a period of 6 years, increased by 17.2 percent," 10; "Army Reserve enlistees who were high school graduates increased by 11.2 percent," 10; and "Army National Guard shows the number of NPS accessions who were high school graduates increased by 15 percent." GAO report number is B-222339.

20

"Lawmaker Goes to War to Preserve GI Benefits," *Washington Post*, March 21, 1986.

21

Ibid.

22

The words "serious impact" and "send a clear signal" were also quoted in a March 24, 1986, *Army Times* article written by Rick Maze. But the article, titled "Services' Opinions Differ on Value of New GI Bill," takes a different approach than the *Washington Post* article cited in the text. Mr. Maze writes in the first paragraph of the March 24 article that "Army and Navy Manpower officials told a House [Armed Services military personnel and compensation] subcommittee [on March 12] that they want the New GI Bill continued because the program has aided recruiting, but Air Force and Marine Corps officials said they don't need it." Maze writes further, though, that "Congressional sources said all of the services, including the Air Force and Marine Corps, have privately appealed to lawmakers to continue the New GI Bill. 'What they are saying here is not what they have said privately,' one congressional staffer said." The Maze article then cites the internal Air Force memo. A *New York Times*, April 16, 1986, article, titled "Conflict Over Aid to Veterans Seen—Army and Navy Push College Funds as Administration Seeks Cut in Program," also seems to mirror the March 24 *Army Times* article. Notes *The Times*: "The Army and Navy have begun advertising special college tuition benefits that are tied to a veterans' assistance law that President Reagan is seeking to eliminate." The special college tuition benefits are a reference to the Army College Fund and the Navy Sea College program, which are designed to raise from $10,800 to "$17,000 the total amount that soldiers and sailors could get for college." The article notes that beyond the $10,800, "the Air Force and Marine Corps offer no special benefits."

23

"OMB to Review Plan to Kill New GI Bill," *Army Times*, April 21, 1986.

24

"OMB Defers Effort to Kill GI Bill," *Army Times*, June 9, 1986, 2.

25

However, *Army Times* continued writing about this topic throughout 1986. "Pressure to Minimize Spending Clouds Future of New GI Bill," October 27, 1986, 16; "Recruiters Exceed Quality, Quantity Goals in Fiscal '86," October 27, 1986, 3; and "Montgomery Links Fate of GI Bill to Its Effectiveness," December 1, 1986, 8.

26

Representative G.V. Montgomery to Honorable Barry Goldwater, May 5, 1986, HCVA Internal File on the Montgomery GI Bill.

27

"Military Draft is Not Unmentionable Anymore: Democrats in Congress Weigh Alternatives," *New York City Tribune*, December 17, 1986.

28

Congressional Record, February 7, 1985, S1266. The bill number was S. 424.

29

Ibid., S1269. General Rogers made the statement in the October 1, 1984, edition of *U.S. News and World Report*.

30

"Military Draft Is Not Unmentionable Anymore: Democrats in Congress Weigh Alternatives," *New York City Tribune*, December 17, 1986.

31

"Some Democrats Weigh Reviving Draft to Bolster Armed Services and Make Their Mark on Defense," *Wall Street Journal*, November 17, 1986.

32

"Goodbye, All-Vol," *Air Force Times*, December 1, 1986, editorial page. The *Air Force Times*—an independent newspaper serving Air Force persons—most likely viewed the number of military leaders who supported a return to the draft as a limited number, as well: "The All-Volunteer Force has operated successfully for 13 years, and the Republican administration is satisfied with it. So are most military leaders."

33

Ibid.

34

Colonel Robert Gordon, Director, Political Science, U.S. Military Academy, interview by Kehrer (co-author), West Point, NY, October 20, 2005. AmeriCorps and our AVF both placed a priority on recruiting 18- to 22-year-olds. Nevertheless, the military helped AmeriCorps with initial "training of trainers." Chairman of the Joint Chiefs of Staff Colin Powell convened the Chiefs on March 2, 1993, at the Pentagon for a meeting with Eli Segal, head of the White House Office of National Service. Major Robert Gordon, U.S. Army, a White House Fellow assigned to the White House Office of National Service, arranged the meeting. Dr. Segal sought staff help and Chairman Powell committed to providing it. Over the long term, Chairman Powell cited Junior ROTC programs across

America as a conceptual training model for local AmeriCorps initiatives. In the short term, the service branches furnished planning and logistical help for the Summer of Service training that AmeriCorps provided in 1993 at Treasure Island, CA. Joint Chiefs liaison officer Lt. Colonel Randy Larson, USAF, served as project officer. Then-Major Gordon observed that "the ethic of service is important to society" [in whatever form it takes]. For example, "AmeriCorps provides Americans who cannot meet the physical requirements of military service an opportunity to serve the nation."

35

Steven Waldman, *The Bill: How the Adventures of Clinton's National Service Bill Reveal What Is Corrupt, Comic, Cynical—and Noble—about Washington* (New York: Viking, 1995). See 198, 226, and 227 for Mr. Stump's legislative actions in this regard and 101, 227 for Mr. Montgomery's active support of such actions.

36

"We know with some certainty how much the federal government will hand out in Pell Grants ($13.4 billion next year)." See "Uncle Sam's Students Loans," *Wall Street Journal*, August 1, 2005. For a viewpoint on a better GI Bill for both our military and national service opportunities such as AmeriCorps, see "Uncle Sam Wants You," *The Boston Globe*, December 7, 2005. For a viewpoint on a better GI Bill for military service, see "Why Skimp on the GI Bill," *Los Angeles Times*, November 11, 2005. For a viewpoint on national service, see "Require All Young People to Serve the Nation," *The Baltimore Sun*, May 14, 2006. The aforementioned articles are noted courtesy of City Year (Michael Brown, president and cofounder): Investing in Civic Leadership, National Service Policy Forum, sponsored by McCormick Tribune Foundation, June 15, 2006 and Professor Suzanne Mettler.

37

The authors furnish three examples of such service and attendant veterans' benefits. *First*, "since the earliest days of our Republic, veterans' benefits have served as incentives for military recruiting. During the American Revolution, George Washington offered pensions and grants of land—benefits of great value in an agricultural age." See Oral Statement of Anthony J. Principi, chairperson, Congressional Commission on Servicemembers and Veterans Transition Assistance, House Committee on Veterans' Affairs, February 23, 1998, 4. The four-page oral statement from which Mr. Principi testified is in possession of Mississippi State University. *Second*, "veterans' benefits, in fact, date back to the earliest days of our history. In 1636, the Pilgrims declared: 'If any person shall return maimed he shall be maintained competently by the Colony during his life.' Early in the Revolutionary War, the Continental Congress created the first veterans' benefits package which included life-long pensions for both disabled veterans and dependents of soldiers killed in battle. Education benefits for veterans date back to cover the beginning of the 20th Century. Congress recognized that military service prevented young people from receiving training for employment or a vocation and passed the Rehabilitation Act of 1919. This act gave veterans disabled in World War I a monthly education assistance allowance." See Department of Veterans Affairs, "The GI Bill: From Roosevelt to Montgomery," Historical Perspective, http://www.gibill.va.gov/education/gibill.html, (accessed March 15, 2005). *Third*, "during the American Colonial Period, legislatures had found it prudent to induce volunteers into military service by promising pensions and other benefits, a practice that was continued by the Continental Congress. This practice was based on traditions dating back as early as 9th-Century England and a body of statutes relating to the benefits of military service that had evolved throughout English history. The English practices themselves found precedent in still earlier traditions of compensation to veterans in Greece and Rome. With the start of the War for Independence, the first national pension law was enacted to ensure the survival and effectiveness of the Continental Army at a critical time. In order to encourage enlistment and to keep morale up and the numbers of deserters down, the Continental Congress, by means of a resolution passed on August 26, 1776, promised pensions to soldiers and officers who were disabled during the course of service." Department of Veterans' Affairs, *The Veterans Benefits Administration: An Organizational History: 1776-1994*, 6. The text of this latter publication endnoted the reference to veterans in Greece and Rome. The endnote states, "See U.S. Library of Congress, Federal Research Division, *Veterans Benefits and Judicial Review: Historical Antecedents and the Development of the American System* (Holly Snyder, Walter R. Iwaskiw, Ihor Y. Gawdiak, and Robert L. Worden, authors.) (Washington: March 1992), 2, 13-14."

38

The National Guard, "About the National Guard—1636 The First Muster," http://www.ngb.army.mil.About/default.aspx; (accessed May 13, 2006).

39

"Battle for Iwo Jima," http://www.geocities.com/Pentagon/7338usmc.html; (accessed May 16, 2007). Of the 20,000 Japanese defenders, only 1,083 survived.

40

Paige McManus, subcommittee staff director, Committee on Veterans' Affairs, U.S. House of Representatives, interview by Kehrer (co-author), Washington, D.C., September 17, 2005.

41

To learn more about the late-Representative Bob Stump, a former chairman of both the Veterans' Affairs and Armed Services committees, see The White House, "(Presidential) Statement on Congressman Bob Stump," http://www.whitehouse.gov/news/releases/2002/06/20030624.html; (accessed September 9, 2006). In addition, Arizona State University (West) is establishing the Bob Stump Chair in Southeastern Cultural History. See Arizona State University, "ASU West Bob Stump Endowed Chair Fund Commemorates Congressman, Arizona History," http://westcgi.west.asu.edu/publicaffairs/publicrelations/news/prstump0603.html; (accessed May 11, 2006).

42

Per Title 38, United States Code, among other duties, "state approving agencies" approve educational institutions and employers for on-the-job training and apprenticeship under the Montgomery GI Bill and other VA educational assistance programs. The authorizing legislation for adding on-the-job training and apprenticeship to the New GI Bill was S. 962, introduced on April 22, 1985, and H.R. 3747 in the House. See *Congressional Record*, Senate, October 8, 1986, for information on the incorporation of the on-the-job training and apprenticeship provision from S. 962 into S. 1887. Among others, George McMullen, David Hulteen, and Donald Sweeney furnished technical assistance in writing the legislation to the House and Senate Committees on Veterans' Affairs on behalf of the National Association of State Approving Agencies.

CHAPTER 12

Fall 1986-Winter 1987—
Road to Enactment: Gaining House and
Senate Veterans' Affairs Committees' Approval

1

Public Law 100-48, enacted on June 1, 1987, made the New GI Bill permanent and named it the Montgomery GI Bill.

2

Deputy Chief of Staff of the Army to the Assistant Secretary of Defense (Force Management and Personnel), memorandum, November 12, 1986, HCVA Internal Historical File on the Montgomery GI Bill.

3

Dr. Charles Moskos is the originator of this phrase.

4

Beth J. Asch, M. Rebecca Kilburn, Jacob A. Klerman, *Attracting College-Bound Youth Into the Military—Toward the Development of New Recruiting Policy Options*, (Santa Monica: RAND, 1999), 23.

5

The Mensel letter applauded the aggressive efforts of the National Guard, as Guard and Reserve members were eligible for a GI Bill for the first time, per the statutory three-year "test" program. Guard recruiters wanted it and needed it to sustain quality recruiting. Mr. Mensel would also author an article in the February/March *AACJC Journal* titled "New GI Bill Inspires U.S. Army's New Educational Philosophy."

6

University Libraries of Mississippi State University, *United States Research Guide*. The Guide cites "U.S. Government Manual" as the source of the information.

7

William H. Harader, "The Committee on Veterans' Affairs: A Study of the Legislative Process and Mileau as They Pertain to Veterans Legislation" (Ph.D. diss., Johns Hopkins University, 1968). Although Congress created the House Committee on Veterans' Affairs through the Reorganization Act of 1946, Congress did not create the Senate Committee on Veterans' Affairs until 1973. The 1968 research of William H. Harader is instructive. *First*, at 147, Harader observes that "Veterans' legislation in the Senate is usually handled by one of three committees: Finance, Labor and Public Welfare, and Banking and Currency. In no instance is it a primary concern for any of these committees. In fact, only the Committee on Labor and Public Welfare bothers to maintain a subcommittee on veterans' affairs." *Second*, at 163, Harader notes that "as early as 1933,

Congressional leaders were suggesting that the veterans' program could best be handled by a single committee in each house of Congress [Dr. Harader endnotes 1933 hearings in this regard]. This suggestion has been a long time gaining acceptance. Only after World War II did it receive serious consideration, being included in a reorganization bill in 1946. The bill, as submitted by the Joint Committee on Legislative Reorganization, would have created complimentary committees on veterans' affairs. This proposal passed the House intact but ran into obstacles in the Senate. Senators George and Johnson of the Finance Committee blocked the consolidation in the Senate. Each claimed an interest in veterans' programs and regretted that the new rules would limit them to two committees, preventing their membership on the new group." *Third*, Harader notes at 165, "in 1963, one member…. Senator Vance Hartke (D-IN) urged that the Senate create a single committee to oversee the problems of some 20 million veterans." (Harader cites the *New York Times*, October 2, 1963, at 48 in this regard.)

8

As noted in Chapter 5, Senator Cranston introduced S. 3263, the proposed All-Volunteer Force Educational Assistance Act of 1980 on December 12, 1980, after extensive consultation with interested parties.

9

Kehrer (co-author) served as a professional staff member with the Senate Committee on Veterans' Affairs at the time and is the source of this information. Working through the Office of Legislative Liaison at the Department of Defense and at the direction of Committee Chief Counsel Jonathan Steinberg on behalf of Chairman Cranston, committee staff invited representatives from each service branch to visit the committee. The purpose was to discuss informally the draft bill and to ask the service branches to furnish information/data that Chairman Cranston potentially could cite in support of what would become S. 12. The service branches did so. Staff from the minority side of the committee participated in this meeting, as well.

10

There was a printer's error on some of the copies of S. 12 that cited the date of introduction as January 6, 1985, instead of 1987. Mr. Charles Glasgow of the General Counsel's office, Department of Veterans Affairs, furnished the legislative file that contained the bill with the error. File title is PL 100-48, 101 Stat, Leg History, New GI Bill Continuation Act, 17-1 Peacetime-General.

11

Congressional Record, January 6, 1987, S230-S232. Alan Cranston assumed the chairmanship from Al Simpson when the Democratic Party won a majority in the November 1986 Senate elections.

12

Mettler, *Soldiers to Citizens*, 166. The Mettler analysis makes a similar observation: "The fundamental idea behind the GI Bill, and the key to the program's stunning success, was that in a democracy, reciprocal obligations bind citizens and government. Beneficiaries' deservingness was premised on their willingness to fulfill their civic duty, their commitment toward the polity; it bestowed on them for giving of themselves for the common good…. The GI Bill… treated recipients with dignity and respect, as rights-bearing beneficiaries."

13

Congressional Record, January 6, 1987, S232, S233. Mr. Murkowski became the ranking Republican at the same time Alan Cranston became chairman.

14

Darryl Kehrer, eyewitness account. The wit and insights of Senator Simpson also may be observed in his book titled, *Right in the Old Gazoo: A Lifetime of Scrapping with the Press* (New York: William Morrow, 1997). Two fairly common examples of such insights are as follows: "If you have integrity, nothing else matters. If you don't have integrity, nothing else matters." Further, "I graduated not cum laude, but thank laude!" Source of examples is M.A. Settlemire, American Association of Community Colleges, transmittal to Darryl Kehrer, May 11, 2006. For more information on Mr. Simpson, see The Alan K. Simpson Institute for Western Politics and Leadership, University of Wyoming at http://ahc.uwyo.edu/about/departments/simpson.html.

15

University of Hawaii at Manoa, "Senator Spark M. Matsunaga Papers—Finding Aid," http://libweb.hawaii.edu/libdept/archives; (accessed September 4, 2006). Readers may learn more about Senator Spark Matsunaga at Hawaii Congressional Paper Collection, Archives and Manuscripts Department, University of Hawaii at Manoa Library, dated January 2005. Page 1 of the archived papers offers the following introductory information: "Spark Matsunaga (1916-1990) was a member of Congress from Hawaii, serving in the U.S. House of Representatives (1963-1976) and the U.S. Senate (1977-1990). He started his political career as an assistant public prosecutor in Honolulu (1952-1954), was a Representative in the Territory of Hawaii

Legislature (1954-1959), worked tirelessly for Hawaii statehood, and was also a lawyer in private practice. He served in the U.S. Army, in the famed 100th Infantry Battalion during WWII, receiving the Bronze Star and two Purple Hearts. He married Helene Hatsumi Tokunaga in 1948 and had five children." Further, at 3, the Hawaii Congressional Paper Collection notes that "after the war, he [Mr. Matsunaga] legally changed his [first] name [from Masayuki] to Spark, taken from his childhood nickname based on a cartoon character…. He was a powerful member of the influential [House] Rules Committee; House Majority Leader Hale Boggs quipped, 'It's getting to the point where you have to see Sparky Matsunaga to get a bill passed around here.' Mr. Matsunaga died in 1990 at the age of 73. Shortly thereafter, the Institute for Peace at the University of Hawaii at Manoa was renamed the Spark Matsunaga Institute for Peace."

16

Darryl Kehrer (co-author), eyewitness account. The Senate Veterans' Affairs committee had no subcommittees. Senator Matsunaga chaired the hearing at Chairman Cranston's request. Mr. Matsunaga's impromptu observation spoke to the long distance Bertie Rowland and Lynn Denzen traveled to testify at the hearing on behalf of the National Association of Veterans' Program Administrators. Ms. Rowland was veterans' affairs officer at Chico State University, Chico, CA, and Ms. Denzen at the University of Denver.

17

The Library of Congress has an excellent database for legislation/sponsors: http://thomas.loc.gov.

18

Ibid.

19

Edgar Potter, *Cowboy Slang*, (Phoenix: Golden West History, 1986), 40. The quoted language in the text may be original to Edgar Potter as well but is derived from "purrin' like a blind cat in a creamery," 40.

20

Senate Committee on Veterans' Affairs, *Hearing on New GI Bill Continuation Act* (S. 12), 100th Cong., 1st sess., 1987, iii-iv.

21

Ibid., 68. Chief Benefits Director R.J. Vogel testified to the administration's view. The administration proposed in the president's FY 1988 Budget Submission to Congress that DoD—not VA—should assume responsibility for funding the basic New GI Bill benefit. The committee disagreed. On March 3, 1987, Mr. Vogel also testified before the Subcommittee on Military Personnel and Compensation of the House Armed Services Committee recommending the administration's position that DoD pay for the Montgomery GI Bill benefit rather than VA. The subcommittee disagreed.

22

The draft statement that the Defense Department submitted to OMB for Assistant Secretary of Defense for Force Management and Personnel Chapman Cox's testimony contained a paragraph to which VA objected: "Placing both management and fiscal responsibility for the New GI Bill within the Department of Defense will permit a concentrated approach to using educational benefits which emphasizes their effectiveness as a recruiting incentive." The notes and annotations of VA Assistant General Counsel James P. Kane show that Mr. Kane obtained internal VA comments on DoD's draft testimony from each of VA's Education Service—the organization with hundreds of staff across the country which administered the Montgomery GI Bill three-year "test" program, the Chief Benefits Director, and the Office of General Counsel unit with responsibility for handling policy/legislative matters associated with VA educational assistance programs. All objected to placing "management" of the Montgomery GI Bill in the Defense Department, as DoD proposed. (DoD had never administered a GI Bill program previously.) Mr. Kane asked OMB legislative analyst Bob Pellici to remove the entire objectionable paragraph cited above, which Mr. Pellici did. See James P. Kane, Memorandum for File on Proposed DoD Testimony, February 2, 1987. Information accessed through Department of Veterans Affairs, Office of General Counsel, File on PL 100-48, 101 Stat 331, Leg History, New GI Bill Continuation Act, 17-1 Peacetime-General.

23

Senate Committee on Veterans' Affairs, *Hearing on New GI Bill Continuation Act (S. 12)*, 100th Cong., 1st sess., 1987, 22-23.

24

Senate Committee on Veterans' Affairs, *Report to Accompany S. 12, New GI Bill Continuation Act*, 100th Cong., 1st sess., 1987, 7.

25

Ibid.

26

Ibid.

27

Senate Committee on Veterans' Affairs, *Hearing on New GI Bill Continuation Act (S. 12)*, 100th Cong., 1st sess., 1987, 76. See 18 for Mr. Shaw's oral testimony.

28

Ibid., 68, 72.

29

Ibid.

30

The focus of the Department of Defense legitimately is on the needs of current service members and their military mission—not veterans who are no longer part of the military. Administering a veterans' benefits program arguably did not comport with DoD's mission.

31

Allan Ostar, interview, by Kehrer (co-author), August 28, 2006. As a young man, Mr. Ostar's unit, the 42nd Infantry Regiment, was thrown into the line in November 1944 with the 7th Army during Operation Nordwind—Hitler's last offensive in Alsace, France. Due to the dire need for infantrymen, Mr. Ostar's regiment received little training after arriving in the European Theater of Operations and went directly into combat in brutal winter weather. Nordwind saw 40,000 German and American casualties. After the war, Mr. Ostar earned a master's degree using the GI Bill.

32

Senate Committee on Veterans' Affairs, *Hearing on New GI Bill Continuation Act (S. 12)*, 100th Cong., 1st sess., 1987, 48, 138.

33

Darryl Kehrer, eyewitness to the committee developing the invitation letter requesting the service branch representatives to testify before the committee.

34

Darryl Kehrer, eyewitness account. The policy position of each service branch did not necessarily comport with the DoD or OMB-directed policy position.

35

There is no OMB clearance process for executive branch witnesses in this instance because witnesses submit no prepared, written testimony. Witnesses respond orally to questions at the hearing based on the position of the witness's service branch, thus having greater latitude in what witnesses say.

36

U.S. Army Armor Center, Fort Knox, KY; Navy Recruit Training Center, Orlando, FL; Marine Corps Recruit Depot, Parris Island, SC; and Military Training Center Lackland Air Force Base, San Antonio, TX.

37

House Committee on Veterans' Affairs, *The New GI Bill; Its Implementation and Effectiveness, Trip Report to the Committee on Veterans' Affairs*, 100th Cong., 1st sess., 1987, 3.

38

Ibid., 9.

39

G.V. Montgomery, interview with Kehrer (co-author), Meridian, MS, December 15, 2004. Mr. Montgomery did not prefer to use the phrase "inextricably linked," as it sounded artificial.

40

Senator Armstrong also used the word "peacetime" in the title of S. 1747, the proposed Peacetime Veterans' Educational Assistance Act. Senator Armstrong would unsuccessfully offer this proposed new Peacetime Veterans' Educational Assistance Act amendment on the Senate floor on June 13, 1983, (See *Congressional Record*, June 13, 1983, 18991). As the authors discuss in this text's Chapter 8, Senator Armstrong again offered as an unsuccessful floor amendment on June 13, 1984 (See *Congressional Record*, June 13, 1984, 16060). Both amendments used the word "peacetime."

41

Drew Douglas, "Congress Moving to Retain Highly Successful New GI Bill," *Congressional Quarterly*, February 28, 1987, 364. "On February 26, both the Senate Veterans' Affairs Committee and a subcommittee of the House Veterans' Affairs Committee approved a bill (S. 12 as amended, and H.R. 1085 as amended, respectively) to continue the program indefinitely. The full House is expected to follow suit March 4."

42

Senate Committee on Veterans' Affairs, *Report to Accompany S. 12, New GI Bill Continuation Act*, 100th Cong., 1st sess., 1987, 80. See Page 2 for the legislative language of the purpose clauses the committee added.

43

Mr. Yoder subsequently served as deputy director, Republican staff, Senate Committee on Veterans' Affairs; as a panel staff director of the Commission on Servicemembers and Veterans Transition Assistance; and as counsellor to the Secretary of Veterans Affairs.

44

This phrase is attributable to Anthony Principi who chaired the Congressional Commission on Servicemembers and Veterans Transition Assistance established pursuant to Public Law 104-275.

45

Senate Committee on Veterans' Affairs, *Report to Accompany S. 12, The New G.I. Bill Continuation Act*, 100th Cong., 1st sess., 1987, 8. See 9 for the following: "The first two of these purposes are derived from sections 1651(2) and (3) of Title 38, declaring the purposes of Chapter 34 of title 38, the so-called 'Vietnam-era GI Bill.'" See 8-10 for an explanation of why the committee added these two purpose clauses.

46

Ibid., 9.

47

For example, see Robert M. Cyert and David C. Mowery, Eds., *Technology and Employment—Innovation and Growth in the U.S. Economy* (Washington, DC: National Academy Press, 1987). See also Senate Committee Meetings by Date Compiled from the *Congressional Record* Daily Digests, "100th Congress (1987-1988), January 6-December 22, 1987," http://www.lib.ncsu.edu/congbibs/senate/100dgst11.html; (accessed October 13, 2007). See, for example, January 13, 1987, entry for "[Senate] Committee on Finance: Committee began hearings on the world economy and trade issues… ;" January 16, 1987, entry for "[Senate] Committee on Finance: Committee resumed hearings on the world economy…receiving testimony from… John Young… on behalf of the President's Commission on Industrial Competitiveness;" and February 10 entry for "[House] Committee on Education & Labor; Committee began hearings on 'Education and Training for American Competitiveness Act of 1987… .'"

48

See Public Law 100-48, June 1, 1987.

49

CIS/INDEX Legislative Histories, Public Law 100-48, January-December 1987, 86.

50

Ballard and Piper, *Sonny Montgomery: The Veteran's Champion*, 79.

51

Abstracts of Congressional Publications, 1987, Congressional Information Service, Armed Services, Vol. 18, No. 1-12. Rep. H203-1, *New GI Bill*, March 11, 1987.

52

Photocopy of testimony of R.J. Vogel, chief benefits director, to the Subcommittee on Military, Personnel, and Compensation, House Armed Services Committee, May 3, 1987, 5. Photocopy in possession of Mississippi State University.

53

House Committee on Armed Services, Report to Accompany H.R. 1085, (Part 2), New GI Bill, 100th Cong., 1st sess., 1987, 3.

CHAPTER 13

Spring 1987—
Road to Enactment:
House Passage and Senate Armed Services Committee Approval

1

HCVA Internal Historical File on the Montgomery GI Bill, Listing of Persons Attending May 4, 1987, Meeting. As S. 12, as amended, and H.R. 1085, as amended, worked their way along the legislative road toward permanent enactment, House Veterans' Affairs Committee staff worked with VA and DoD program administrators regarding how VA and the service branches were administering the existing $1,200 service member pay reduction to gain program eligibility under the ongoing New GI Bill three-year test program that began July 1, 1985. Marianne Deignan of the Congressionl Budget Office also attended the meeting. The outcome of the meeting is unknown. The House Veterans' Affairs Committee professional staff appeared to want an update regarding the pay reduction process.

2

Senators Alan Cranston and Frank Murkowski to Senator John Glenn, March 12, 1987, HCVA Internal Historical File on the Montgomery GI Bill. There was an exchange of letters between Senate Armed Services Subcommittee Chairman John Glenn and Senate Veterans' Affairs Committee Chairman Alan Cranston and Ranking Member Frank Murkowski on February 18 and March 12, 1987, respectively. Chairman Glenn expressed his subcommittee's interest in the military recruitment and retention aspects of S. 12 and his interest in holding a subcommittee hearing on those topics. Doing so would require a sequential referral of S. 12 to the Armed Services Committee by the Parliamentarian. Senators Cranston and Murkowski agreed that the Parliamentarian should accord the Glenn subcommittee sequential referral of the bill, as the Glenn subcommittee had primary jurisdiction over military manpower and force management/structure matters such as recruiting and retention. Further, Cranston and Murkowski desired favorable consideration on S. 12 so the two committees jointly could take S. 12 to the full Senate for a vote. Cranston and Murkowski sent an identical letter to Senator Pete Wilson, Senator Glenn's ranking member. Senators Cranston and Murkowski furnished a courtesy copy of both letters to House Veterans' Affairs Committee Chairman G.V. Montgomery.

3

Jill Cochran, memorandum to Chief Counsel Mack G. Fleming, March 24, 1987. The Senate Armed Services Committee did not publish a committee document recording verbatim testimony at this hearing, nor is the hearing recorded in the *CIS Index to Unpublished US Senate Committee Hearings 1977-1980.* The index does not extend that far.

4

The one exception on a sequential referral is if one of the committees waives its jurisdiction on the matter.

5

Representative Bob Edgar ran unsuccessfully for U.S. Senate in Pennsylvania against Arlen Specter and later served as general secretary of the National Council of Churches of Christ in New York City. The Council represents more than 100,000 local congregations and 45 million persons in the United States. Mr. Edgar currently heads *Common Cause* based in Washington, D.C. Mr. Edgar's role in developing the Montgomery GI Bill proved significant. Richard Fuller subsequently served with distinction as legislative director, Paralyzed Veterans of America (PVA). Mr. Fuller's vision and recommendations for veterans' health care over some 25 years are well documented in public hearing and legislative documents of the House and Senate Committees on Veterans' Affairs. Mr. Fuller furnished the leadership for the *Independent Budget* developed annually by national veterans' service organizations, a comprehensive budget and policy document created by veterans for veterans. First published in 1986, the *Independent Budget* is produced by PVA, the Veterans of Foreign Wars of the United States, Disabled American Veterans, and AMVETS. In 2008, 54 organizations publicly supported the *Independent Budget.* Mr. Fuller passed away in 2008.

6

Chairman Cranston's tribute to Ms. Cochran appears in Chapter 14.

7

Jill T. Cochran, memorandum to Mack G. Fleming, March 24, 1987, HCVA Internal Historical File on the Montgomery GI Bill.

8

Ibid. Notwithstanding Ranking Member Wilson's concerns, Senator Wilson voted in favor of S. 12 at the subcommittee and full committee level of Armed Services and on the Senate floor.

9

Ibid., 2.

10

Ibid.

11

Ibid.

12

There is one other issue regarding the Senate Armed Services Committee not publishing the proceedings of the hearing. The authors found no public record of (1) the testimony of witnesses submitted for the record, (2) a transcript of witness's oral testimony, or (3) subcommittee members' questions and witnesses answers. The HCVA Internal Historical File on the Montgomery GI Bill contained a photocopy of the Statement for the Record of Dr. Singer. The authors' 2006 review of the listing of John Glenn public papers housed at Ohio State University shows no entry for this hearing in the summary of archived material.

13

The language Mr. Montgomery uses regarding "data cannot be sorted so specifically as to attribute behaviors with regard to joining the military to one factor alone" and "the New GI Bill was the centerpiece of a recruiting package that needed to be held together" is attributed to subcommittee staff director Jill Cochran in a spring 1987 internal briefing paper produced for Mr. Montgomery.

14

For example, see published Congressional delegation trip summary referenced in Chapter 12.

15

Congressional Record, March 17, 1987, H1326.

16

Darryl Kehrer (co-author), eyewitness. Indeed during Senate consideration of S. 12, as amended on May 8, Senator Chafee of Rhode Island and Senator Glenn asked (both via unanimous consent) to be cosponsors during the process of the floor debate.

17

Two days later after the March 17 400-to-2 vote, on March 19, 1987, the *MacNeill-Lehrer News Hour* included a segment called "I Want You." With a permanent New GI Bill having passed the House two days earlier after the military services had been testing it for about two years, one of the points made in the segment was the unwillingness of the military simply to concede college-bound students to the colleges. Observed MacNeill: "One major recruiting inducement is money for college, now available under the new GI bill." And noted Spencer Michaels of public station KQED in San Francisco: "Navy recruiters like Harry Garvin can offer more than seeing the world. They now can dangle a premium: money for a school—a strategy to attract college-bound youngsters." Further, the announcer from an Army ad said, "Now there's a new route to college; the GI Bill plus the new Army College Fund. If you qualify, you can earn over $25,000 for college while you learn things no one can put a price on. The New GI Bill plus the new Army College Fund." Quotes accessed from facsimile text of *MacNeill-Lehrer News Hour,* March 19, 1987, 10. The authors note that 25 years later in 2002, Representative Mike Simpson of Idaho, chairman of the Subcommittee on Benefits, Committee on Veterans' Affairs, offered a tribute to the late Lt. General Timothy Maude, who had enunciated the same college-but-serve-first theme: "The last time this subcommittee had the good fortune to receive testimony from the service branches was on May 24 of last year [2001]. The issue was H.R. 1291, the proposed 21st Century Montgomery GI Bill Enhancement Act. Representative J.D. Hayworth of Arizona was chairman of the subcommittee at that time. The first witness that day was the late Lieutenant General Timothy J. Maude, U.S. Army. He was a forceful advocate for an improved Montgomery GI Bill. At the subcommittee's request, General Maude shared with Chairman Hayworth, Ranking Member Reyes, Mr. Smith, Mr. Evans, Mrs. Brown, and the late Floyd Spence, the data on how few 17- to 21-year-old males the service branches actually get to recruit. This is because so many go to college right out of high school. What struck me in reading the transcript of that hearing was that General Maude was unwillingly simply to give up—to give, if you will, college-bound students to the colleges. That was very clear. He just wanted them in the Army first. And if a person went to college right out of high school and decided to stop out, he wanted them back in college while in the Army. Why? I suspect because of what the Army had to offer them, real life experiences perhaps more noble than an 18-year-old might be able to imagine. As you know, General Maude died at the Pentagon on the morning of September 11, at the age of 53, while doing what he liked best, looking after the interests of soldiers; not surprising for an individual who rose from the rank of private to general officer; not surprising for a man who was a Vietnam veteran and a Bronze Star winner. I attended the memorial service for General Maude and other selfless Americans who died at the Pentagon on September 11. I respectfully pay tribute to this man by noting that H.R. 1291, the bill on which he personally testified, is now the law of the land, and contains the largest increase ever in the Montgomery GI Bill. And in General Maude, I would say the youth of America had a wonderful friend. I thank everyone for indulging me." House Committee on Veterans' Affairs, *Hearing on Transition Assistance Program and the Disabled Transition Assistance Program*, 107th Cong., 2nd sess., 2002, 10, 11.

18

Ibid., H1304, H1305. Representative Dowdy served as chairman, Subcommittee on Education, Training, and Employment, 1987 and 1988. His role in developing the Montgomery GI Bill proved significant.

19

Ibid., H1306. Representative Penny served as chairman, Subcommittee on Education, Training, and Employment beginning in the 101st Congress in 1989. Mr. Penny co-authored with Major Garrett *Common Cents: A Retiring Six Term Congressman Reveals How Congress Really Works and What We Must Do to Fix It* (Little J. Brown and Company, 1995). A Senior Fellow at the Hubert H. Humphrey Institute of Public Affairs, University of Minnesota, Mr. Penny teaches courses in Public Budgeting and Being Effective in the Legislative Process, and the Politics of Social Security. Mr. Penny also serves as president of the Southern Minnesota Initiative Foundation, which fosters economic growth and community development.

20

Ibid., H.5755. Representative Hammerschmidt served in Congress from 1967 to 1993. North Arkansas College hosts the John Paul Hammerschmidt Lecture Series and houses the John Paul Hammerschmidt Business and Conference Center. For additional information, see http://www.northark.net/lecture_series/default.html.

21

Ibid., H 5764. An analysis of enhancements to the MGIB from 1985 to 2006 likely would show that Representative Evans sponsored and cosponsored more enhancements than any member of Congress.

22

Ibid., H5759. Mr. Smith was ranking member on the Dowdy subcommittee. In Public Law 107-103, the Veterans Education and Benefits Expansion Act of 2001, Chairman Christopher Smith and Ranking Member Lane Evans were original authors (joined by Representative Mike Simpson (R-ID), Representative Bob Filner (D-CA) and others) of the largest (46 percent) increase in the MGIB monthly benefit in the program's history. See http://chrissmith.house.gov/lawsandresolutions/vetsedandbenefitsexpansion.html.

23

Ibid., H5754. Representative Byron also served as a conferee on the FY 1985 DoD Authorization Act.

24

Ibid., H5760. Representative Gray served also as chairman of the Budget Committee.

25

Ibid., H5753. Representative Panetta went on to serve as chief of staff to President Clinton and also as director, Office of Management and Budget.

26

Ibid., H5765.

27

Ibid., 5766. Mr. Montgomery offered similar remarks in reference to the team effort at 5760 and 5762. Mr. Montgomery didn't limit his thanks to elected officials. He thanked House and Senate staff members at 5751; a representative of a national higher education association at 5752, and military GI Bill program managers, also at 5752. The co-authors repeat Mr. Montgomery's words regarding the program's managers here: "Mr. Speaker, if I may, I would like to pay special tribute to some of the people who devoted an enormous amount of time and energy behind the scenes to ensure the success of the New GI Bill. Without their support, and without the information and statistics they have supplied, the New GI Bill would not be the effective program it is today. ACTIVE FORCES: LTC Al Bemis - Army; LTC Joe Selman - Army; LTC Ron Johnston - Army; Mr. George Karasik - Air Force; Ms. Jude Korol - Navy; Major Al Pingree - Marine Corps; Ms. Gail Christiansen - Coast Guard. RESERVE COMPONENTS: SFC Mike Graves - Army National Guard; Major E.L. Robertson - U.S. Army Reserve; CDR Jin Spanogle - U.S. Navy Reserve; MSG Fred Richardson - Air National Guard; Major Fred Reinero - U.S. Air Force Reserve; Major Dan Franklin - U.S. Marine Corps Reserve; CDR Isele

- Coast Guard Reserve; DEPARTMENT OF DEFENSE: COL William A. Scott - Director of Education Policy; Dr. Lenore Saltman - Coordinator, Voluntary Education." Lastly, with respect to Mr. Karasik, on December 14, 1987, the *Air Force Times* at 14 contains an article titled "Air Force's 'Mr. GI Bill' Leaves Pentagon for Kirtland." The article chronicles Mr. Karasick's longstanding leadership at the Pentagon in Air Force education programs. Article secured from HCVA Internal Montgomery GI Bill Historical File.

28

The subcommittee to which Mrs. Byron refers actually is part of the Committee on Veterans' Affairs.

29

Ibid., H5767.

30

The Woodrow Wilson National Fellowship Program, Princeton, NJ, administers the Woodrow Wilson Public Service Program: http://www.woodrow.org/.

31

Darryl Kehrer (co-author), "The Enactment of the Montgomery GI Bill: A Senate Staffer's Perspective," presentation at the Conference on the GI Bill and the Revolution in American Higher Education, St. Louis, MO, January 19-20, 1996.

32

"Lobby" is in quotation marks because its usage here is not the traditional usage of organizations outside of government that lobby the Legislative Branch.

33

Congressional Record, May 8, 1987, S6206.

34

Learn about John Glenn's extraordinary career in public service through the John Glenn School of Public Affairs, The Ohio State University: http://glenninstitute.osu.edu/washington/Index.html. John Glenn's U.S. Senate papers are housed at The Ohio State University Libraries/University Archives: http://library.osu.edu/sites/archives/glenn/collection/senate/glennsenate.php.

35

John O. Marsh Jr., to the Deputy Secretary of Defense, memorandum, October 22, 1986, HCVA Montgomery GI Bill Internal Historical File. This correspondence also appears at 82 of the published hearing record on S. 12, February 4, 1987, S. Hrg. 100-87.

36

"Senate Votes to Make GI Bill Permanent," *Army Times*, May 18, 1987, 1, 4.

37

Edgar Potter, *Cowboy Slang*, (Phoenix: Golden West History), 52.

38

Recollection of Darryl Kehrer (co-author), then-professional staff member, Senate Committee on Veterans' Affairs. Kent Talbert served as Senator Thurmond's legislative assistant on veterans' matters at the time. On September 27, 2005, President Bush George W. Bush nominated Mr. Talbert to be general counsel, U.S. Department of Education, and he was confirmed by the U.S. Senate on May 19, 2006. In Kehrer's March 9, 2007, Washington, D.C., telephone interview with Mr. Talbert, Mr. Talbert said he "didn't remember" if Representative Montgomery called or visited Senator Thurmond roughly in March 1987 regarding support for H.R. 1085 and S. 12. However, Mr. Talbert said it was "very possible" that Representative Montgomery contacted Senator Thurmond, as Senator Thurmond "highly respected Mr. Montgomery" and they shared many common interests regarding America's military and veterans.

39

Congressional Record, May 8, 1987, S6208. A member of the Veterans' Affairs and Armed Services Committee, Senator Thurmond was an early cosponsor of S. 12. Senator Thurmond eventually offered the motion in the full Armed Services Committee markup session to approve S. 12, as amended.

40

Our Campaigns, "Candidate - J. Strom Thurmond," http://www.fec.gov/pres96/pres1b.jpg; (accessed July 22, 2007).

41

G.V. Montgomery to John McCain, April 6, 1987, HCVA Internal Historical File on the Montgomery GI Bill. Noted Mr. Montgomery: "I enjoyed very much our telephone call and am very pleased that you will take the lead in the subcommittee to oppose any amendment that may be offered to test the New GI Bill for another three years. It has been tested long enough. It is working and we should proceed to make it permanent."

42

Representative Marcy Kaptur (D-OH) to Senator John Glenn (D-OH), May 7, 2007, HCVA Internal Historical File on the Montgomery GI Bill. Representative Kaptur wrote to the Senator in his capacity of representing Ohio, rather than in his capacity as chairman, Subcommittee on Manpower and Personnel, Senate Committee on Armed Services.

43

On March 30, 1987, Chairman Montgomery's staff met in the committee hearing room with representatives of 13 military personnel associations, six veterans' service organizations, one higher education association, Lt. General Robert M. Elton, Deputy Chief of Staff, U.S. Army, and Lt. Colonel Al Bemis, program manager for the New GI Bill, Department of the Army. The purpose of the meeting was to encourage the parties present to contact members of the Senate Armed Services Committee regarding their support for S. 12. Of the 20 members of the committee, the various organizations identified 11 that an organization present agreed to contact. See HCVA Internal Historical File on Montgomery GI Bill, three-page list of attendees and membership list of Senate Armed Services Committee/staff annotations as to senators to contact/organizations volunteering to do so.

44

Darryl Kehrer (co-author), eyewitness account while serving as professional staff member, Committee on Veterans' Affairs, U.S. Senate.

45

Ibid. It was not unusual for the Pentagon to furnish information to committee staff when requested in the chairman's name.

46

"Unholy troika" is a part-serious, part-fun phrase heard on Capitol Hill from time to time. Generally, the phrase humorously refers to three legislators who band together on a public policy issue but whose political views generally differ.

47

Congressional Record, May 8, 1987, S6206. Senator Glenn says the following at S6206: "We approved it [S. 12] out of subcommittee with my vote in favor of it." Mr. Glenn's statement furnishes no date for the Force Management and Personnel Subcommittee's markup, nor does Thomas.loc.gov under "S. 12" or the Legislative Histories of U.S. Public Laws for 1987, CIS/INDEX Legislative Histories, January/December 1987, under "New GI Bill Continuation Act." However, the HCVA Montgomery GI Bill Internal Historical File contains an April 22, 1987, letter from G.V. Montgomery to Representative Kaptur. "The Senate Armed Services Subcommittee on Manpower and Personnel voted five to two to make the New GI Bill a permanent program. We understand Senator Glenn voted in support of the measure, and I know that your conversations with him helped him reach this decision."

48

Ibid. However, initially there was one member who objected, and his objection garnered the support of others. Senator Glenn speaks to this matter in greater detail in Chapter 14.

49

HCVA Internal Montgomery GI Bill Historical File. On May 1, 1987, Mr. Montgomery sent a letter to Dr. Dale Parnell, president, American Association of Community and Junior Colleges informing him of the 12-0 Senate Armed Services Committee vote on S. 12. "I want to again thank you and your organization for your help and support. Without it, we certainly would not have gotten the overwhelming vote we got today."

50

U.S. Senate, [News release], *GI Bill* (Washington, DC, May 4, 1987). Mr. Flander served on Senator Cranston's staff in the Senator's capacity representing California. However, in this instance he issued the news release on behalf of Senator Cranston as Veterans' Affairs Committee Chairman.

51

This statement is based in part from the observations of Darryl Kehrer, eyewitness account to the views of the legislative assistants handling S. 12/H.R. 1085 for the three Senators. It is also based on Mr. Kehrer's recollection of spring 1987 discussions with Mr. Chris Yoder of Ranking Member Murkowski's committee staff.

52

Congressman Kennedy accompanied Chairman Montgomery on a Congressional delegation visit to four

recruit training bases on February 12-13, 1987, to speak with enlistees about the New GI Bill program. Congressman Kennedy's letter to Chairman Montgomery of February 19, 1987, furnishes Mr. Kennedy's observations from the delegation's visit regarding the structure of New GI Bill legislation. The letter appears at page 35 of the House Veterans' Affairs Committee's published trip report of March 25.

53

"Biographical Directory of the United States Congress, 1774-Present," Biography, Kennedy, Robert Francis, (1925-1968); http://bioguide.congress.gov/scripts/biodisplay.pl?index=k000114; (accessed October 14, 2009).

CHAPTER 14

Summer 1987—

Road to Enactment: Senate Passage, Conference, and Rose Garden

1

The quote here is illustrative of a difficult debate on an issue. Senator Alan Simpson was known to use this humorous phrase, although the authors do not attribute it to him in this instance. The Senate Armed Services Committee delayed its vote on S. 12 due to an interest in continuing to test the New GI Bill. Noted Senator Glenn, "There was a considerable debate. We put off a final vote until another day. The objection that was raised in the first meeting was removed at the second meeting, and we voted out unanimously to approve this bill." *Congressional Record*, May 8, 1987, S6206.

2

Copies of these letters are contained in the committee's Montgomery GI Bill Internal Historic File.

3

Congressional Record, May 8, 1987, S6216. This vote was on a Friday with only 89 senators present.

4

Ibid., S6202. In Chapter 3, Professor Suzanne Mettler notes that World War II veterans who used the GI Bill were active as civic leaders 50 percent more frequently than those who did not use the GI Bill. Oxford University Press published Mettler's seven years of research in 2005; Mettler's insights represented data that was not available to Chairman Cranston in 1987. Observes Mettler at 174 of *Soldiers to Citizens*: "For the sake of democracy itself, we need to consider how public programs could foster social inclusion, increase opportunity, and stimulate civic engagement. Policies are often subjected to economic cost-benefit analyses, but their political implications are typically ignored. Henceforth, the civic effects of programs should be probed as well by assessing what kinds of resource and civic effects they are likely to generate and how those might affect civic engagement. The policy alternatives to be pursued today are not obvious, but it is imperative that we begin to deliberate about what they might be." Nevertheless, in one sense, Cranston in 1987 and Mettler in 2005 broadly seem to make the same point. At S6202 after noting the return of $3 to $6 for every dollar invested in the WWII GI Bill, Cranston says, "A permanent GI Bill [will] produce a richer social fabric for our nation." Further, Mettler at 128-131 furnishes examples of how the WWII GI Bill had the unanticipated effect of joining citizens together creating a form of social capital. Lastly, at 128, Mettler also notes that such capital "fosters connections between people… and fosters social trust" that otherwise may not have existed. Mettler furnishes several examples, as well.

5

Ibid., S6204. Frank Murkowski represented Alaska in the U.S. Senate from 1980 to 2002. He also served as Governor of Alaska from 2002 to 2006.

6

Ibid., S6205-6. Also at S6206, Chairman Glenn acknowledges Armed Services Committee staff members on both sides of the aisle who worked on this legislation for many years: Fred Pang, David Lyles, and Pat Tucker.

7

It appears Senator Armstrong is referring to when he first offered an amendment (in 1983) to the FY 1984 DoD Authorization Act rather than when he first introduced S. 2596, the proposed Veterans' Educational Assistance Act of 1980.

8

In a May 29, 1987, letter to G.V. Montgomery, Senator Armstrong noted, "There are very few issues about which I feel as keenly or as well satisfied as the GI Bill. I want to compliment you for your tremendous sustained leadership… ." HCVA Montgomery GI Bill Internal Historical File.

9

Ibid., S6206-7. Senator Armstrong assumed the presidency of Colorado Christian University on August 15, 2006.

10

Ibid., S6207.

11

Ibid., S6208. Strom Thurmond served in the U.S. Senate for 48 years. See the Strom Thurmond Institute of Government & Public Affairs, Clemson University. http://www.strom.clemson.edu.

12

At S6210, Senator Cohen acknowledges that "The Non Commissioned Officers Association has been perhaps the leading organization in this important effort. Through its Washington staff, Mack McKinney and Dick Johnson, in particular, it has done much of the behind-the-scenes work in bringing us to where we are today." Senator Cohen further noted: "The other organization [essential to this effort] is the National Association of State Approving Agencies, whose president, Don Sweeney, is a constituent, serving as coordinator of veterans' education programs for the State of Maine. Don has spent many, many hours working with me and my staff, and with the staffs of other Senate and House leaders, in this effort."

13

Ibid., S6211.

14

Ibid., S6214.

15

Ibid., S6215.

16

Ibid., S6213.

17

This was a vote on S. 12 as amended since the Senate voted on H.R. 1085, as amended had struck out all of the H.R. 1085 language after the enacting clause. The progression of the S. 12/H.R. 1085 vote in the May 8, 1987, *Congressional Record* is as follows: At S6200, Mr. Byrd said, "Mr. President, Mr. Cranston and Mr. Murkowski are on their way to the floor to proceed with debate and action on S. 12." Further at S6216: "The committee amendment [to S. 12] in the nature of a substitute was agreed to." Also at S6216, this statement was followed by: "The text of S. 12, as amended, is inserted in lieu of the text of H.R. 1085." Lastly at S6216, after the 89 yeas and 0 nays were announced, the Presiding Officer (Mr. Breaux) said, "So the Bill (H.R. 1085), as amended, was passed."

18

"Senate Votes to Make GI Bill Permanent," *Army Times*, May 18, 1987, 1, 4.

19

1987, Legislative Histories of U.S. Public Laws, Congressional Information Service, CIS/INDEX Legislative Histories, January-December 1987, *New GI Bill Continuation Act*, 87.

20

Ibid., 86.

21

House Committee on Veterans' Affairs, one-page typed list of Members Attending Statuary Hall Signing Ceremony as of May 15. HCVA Internal Historical File on Montgomery GI Bill.

22

Ibid., two-page typed List of All Other Parties.

23

Memorandum from James M. Frey, OMB Assistant Director for Legislative Reference to Legislative Liaison Officers at Defense and VA, May 20, 1987, Department of Veterans Affairs, Office of General Counsel, legislative file titled PL 100-48, 101 Stat 331, Leg History: *New GI Bill Continuation Act*, 17-1 Peacetime General.

24

Letter from Thomas Turnage to James Miller III, May 20, 1987, Department of Veterans Affairs, Office of General Counsel, Legislative file.

25

HCVA Internal Historical File on the Montgomery GI Bill contained a photocopy of this memorandum.

26

Ibid.

27

HCVA Internal Historical File on the Montgomery GI Bill, photocopy.

28

HCVA Internal Historical file on the Montgomery GI Bill contains a photocopy of an unsigned October 26, 1987, five-paragraph letter from Chairman Montgomery to Vice President Bush. The first paragraph reads: "As you requested, enclosed is a brief summary of the historical development of the New GI Bill." The second paragraph reads: "All of us who worked so hard for this educational assistance program are grateful to you for the help you gave us overcoming the opposition of the Office of Management and Budget to the New GI Bill. I recall very well your personal conversations with Dave Stockman urging him not to oppose the legislation establishing this program. On more than one occasion you encouraged the President to sign the DoD Authorization bill which included the original three-year test program for the New GI Bill. Your conversations with [OMB Director] Jim Miller helped convince him to back off from his recommendation that the test program be repealed. Finally, you urged the President to sign H.R. 1085, amended, a bill making the New GI Bill permanent, and to hold a bill signing ceremony because of the importance of the legislation." It would appear that Mr. Montgomery signed and dispatched this letter to the Vice President, but we are unable to discern so from the historical file. In any case, the letter appears to represent Mr. Montgomery's views on Vice President Bush's role in the New GI Bill legislation.

29

U.S. Office of Press Secretary, The White House, Remarks by The President in Signing Ceremony for H.R. 1085 *New GI Bill Continuation Act.* (Washington DC, June 1, 1987).

30

See Chapters 16 and 17 for testaments to the engaging and resourceful nature of service members and veterans as a class of individuals.

31

Public Papers of the Presidents of the United States, Administration of George Bush, 1990 (Washington, D.C.: Government Printing Office, 1991), 777 of Book I.

32

John Marsh was commissioned a lieutenant in the United States Army at age 19 and served 1944-1947 with occupation forces in Germany. Biographical Directory of the United States Congress, http://bioguide.congress.gov. The source of information on Mr. Marsh's tenure as Secretary of the Army is http://techcenter.gmu.edu/about/contacts/marsh.john.html. Shenandoah University maintains the Marsh Institute for Government & Public Policy. See http://www.su.edu/marsh/.

33

At the Senate Veterans' Affairs Committee hearing on S. 12 on February 4, 1987, Senator Murkowski presented to the committee a letter from Secretary Marsh stating the Army would pay for a new, improved GI Bill from its own funds (rather than VA funds). Darryl Kehrer (co-author), eyewitness account. This letter does not appear in the published hearing record.

34

Honorable John Marsh, interview by Kehrer (co-author), Culpeper, VA, August 26, 2005.

35

Ibid.

36

Colonel Michael Meese, Ph.D., Head of Social Sciences, U.S. Military Academy, interview by Kehrer (co-author), West Point, NY, October 19, 2005.

CHAPTER 15:

1987-Present—

Effect of the Montgomery GI Bill:
Creating a Recruiting and Educational Incentive

1

The Mariner, January/February, 1998, 10.

2

Navy Times, "Recruits Say Benefits a Major Reason for Enlisting," March 21, 1988. 90000

3

House of Representatives, Committee on Veterans' Affairs, *Montgomery GI Bill Marks Third Anniversary-Education Assistance Program Continues to Attract Big Numbers and High Quality*, June 30, 1988. Note: Technically, it was not until June 1, 1987, (Public Law 100-48) that Congress named the New GI Bill the Montgomery GI Bill by designating its official name as "The Montgomery GI Bill Act of 1984."

4

Public Papers of the Presidents of the United States, Administration of George Bush, 1990 (Washington, D.C.: Government Printing Office, 1990), 777 of Book I.

5

"On August 2, 1990, Iraqi troops invaded Kuwait. Fearing that Saddam Hussein's militancy posed a threat to America's Middle Eastern allies and the region's oil supplies, George H.W. Bush organized a multinational coalition and began a massive buildup of troops and equipment in Saudi Arabia. After weeks of devastating air attacks on targets in Kuwait and Iraq, the ground offensive—Operation Desert Storm—was launched on February 24, 1991. Three days of fierce combat drove the invaders out of Kuwait, and fighting ended with Iraq's acceptance of cease-fire terms on March 3." Dwight Young, *Dear Mr. President-Letters to the Oval Office from the Files of the National Archives*, 169. At 168 and 171, Young publishes letters to President George H.W. Bush of November 27, 1990, from Patricia J. Elvin of Tampa, FL, and February 12, 1991, from Lance Corporal Eric Colton, USMC, serving in Operation Desert Storm in Saudi Arabia. Notes Young at 169, 170: "Patricia Elvin's letter to President Bush expresses neither the gung-ho enthusiasm of a hawk nor the pained disapproval of a dove… . In the second letter, the uncertainties of a civilian on the home front are replaced by the calm self-assurance of a U.S. Marine on the battlefront." Lastly, Young notes at 170, "Eric Colton came home safe and sound. Almost 300 other Americans died in the Gulf War."

6

House Committee on Veterans' Affairs, *21st Century Montgomery GI Bill Enhancement Act*, 107th Cong., 1st sess., 2001, 92. Annually, the percentage can fluctuate roughly between 93 percent and 97 percent. For example, in her 2001 testimony, Deputy Assistant Secretary of Defense (Military Personnel Policy) Vice Admiral P.A. Tracey cited a 2001 sign-up rate of 97 percent.

7

United States military units marched in the parade in the order in which they had deployed to the Persian Gulf.

8

Norman Schwarzkopf written with Peter Petre: *It Doesn't Take A Hero: The Autobiography of General H. Norman Schwarzkopf* (New York: Bantam Books, 1993 paperback), xiii as excerpted from a television interview with Barbara Walters, March 15, 1991.

9

Patrick Ryan, Deputy Chief Counsel, Deputy Staff Director, Committee on Veterans' Affairs, U.S. House of Representatives, interview by Kehrer (co-author), Washington, D.C., July 25, 2007. Mr. Ryan was present with Mr. Montgomery on the House floor for the debate on the bill.

10

By way of comparison, "In 2006 direct and indirect military manpower costs are about $.70 on the dollar. There is continued cost growth in benefits for retirees, for example. That leaves only about $.30 on the dollar for technology, research and development, procurement, and other essential functions." Honorable Frederic Pang, interview by Kehrer (co-author), Arlington, VA, January 2, 2006.

11

Section III of the Veterans Benefits Act of 1992, enacted as Public Law 102-568. Section 301 increased the monthly educational assistance for full-time training under the Montgomery GI Bill from $350 to $400 per month. The original bill number was H.R. 5008. House report (Veterans' Affairs Committee) No. 102-753(I), July 29, 1992. For a more comprehensive legislative history, see *United States Code and Administrative News*; 102nd Cong., 2nd sess., 1992, Vol. 6, and *Legislative History: Public Laws 102-551 to 102-590*, West Publishing Co., St. Paul, MN. Consult 3646 of *Public Laws* for legislative history, 3656-7, 3661, and 3666-3667 for Montgomery GI Bill increases furnished in Public Law 102-568.

12

The Department of Veterans Affairs closed the street in the front of its headquarters at 810 Vermont Avenue adjacent to Lafayette Park. VA erected a large tent for the celebration. Mr. James Jensen of VA's Veterans Benefits Administration was a principal planner of this historic event.

13

The late Jesse Brown served as President Clinton's Secretary of Veterans' Affairs, January 1993 to July 1997. Prior to directing the second largest agency (VA) in the federal government, Mr. Brown served for 25 years with the Disabled American Veterans, including as executive director from 1989 to 1993. The Arlington National Cemetery web site notes: "His tenacity made him a driving force in improving the circumstances for generations of veterans and caused the *Wall Street Journal* to feature him on its front page under the banner 'You Don't Mess With Jess.' The web site further notes: "His managerial talent instilled a new pride among VA employees as well, and his promotion of 'Putting Veterans First' still resonates within the agency." Lastly, "An honors graduate of Chicago City College, he also attended Roosevelt University in Chicago and Catholic University in Washington, D.C." Mr. Brown died at age 58 on August 15, 2002. To learn more about Mr. Brown's exceptional life of service, see http://www.arlingtoncemetery.net/jesse-brown.html.

14

Public Papers of the Presidents of the United States, Administration of William J. Clinton, 1994 (Washington, D.C.: Government Printing Office, 1994), 1103, of Book I. President Clinton made these remarks to the U.S. Business Roundtable.

15

Ibid., June 22, 1994, 1115. President Clinton made these remarks commemorating the 50th anniversary of the GI Bill of Rights.

16

United States Senate, "Reference Home and Glossary," http://www.senate.gov/reference/glossary_term/reconciliation_process.html.

17

Photocopy of letter in possession of Darryl Kehrer (co-author).

18

See Senator Simpson's statement at *Congressional Record*, S16084, June 13, 1984. Noted the Senator: "And then, as I mentioned the other day, if anybody really believes that the Department of Defense is going to keep this in their budget, they are really wrong because this is going to end up in the Veterans' Administration budget and it is going to come out of some existing veterans' benefit." Noted Mr. Montgomery during the House vote on H.R. 1085 on March 17, 1987: "Had Senator Simpson not agreed that the Veterans' Administration should pay for the basic benefit, we probably would not have the program today." *Congressional Record*, H5751.

19

Notes the September 29, 1995, *Washington Post* article: "A Senate move that would require U.S. troops to pay more out of their pockets for GI Bill education benefits has drawn a torrent of protest from Pentagon officials who warn the action would undercut recruiting efforts." Senator John D. "Jay" Rockefeller IV, ranking Democrat on the committee, proposed raising from $100 to $133 per month what new recruits pay monthly into the program, for a total contribution of $1,600. The changes were projected to save "$80 million in 1996 and $933 million over seven years," per the article. The article further notes: "Led by Rockefeller, ranking Democrat on the veterans' committee, proponents say the hike in monthly contributions is not too much to ask, given that the out-of-pocket sum has remained frozen for a decade while military pay has climbed 48 percent and the education benefit has risen 33 percent. Charging more for the GI Bill, Rockefeller contends, is the fairest of the hard choices committee members are facing to meet a veterans affairs budget ceiling imposed by Senate and House conferees… . Leading the opposition on Capitol Hill to raising GI Bill fees is Rep. G.V. 'Sonny' Montgomery, who sponsored the bill in 1985. The House Veterans' Affairs Committee, on which Montgomery serves, yesterday approved an alternate package of adjustments in veterans' benefits that members said would achieve the same savings as the proposed GI Bill changes." "Plan to Raise Fee on GI Bill Draws Protest," *Washington Post*, September 29, 1995. The authors note that although Senator Rockefeller desired to increase the 12-month pay reduction, he went on to author or coauthor many Montgomery GI Bill enhancements, especially in the 1999-2005 period. Mr. Rockefeller also was an original cosponsor of S. 12 in 1987.

20

For a review of the all-volunteer force over its first 20 years, see Roger Little, J. Eric Fredland, Curtis Gilroy, and W.S. Sellman, *Professionals on the Front Lines: Two Decades of the All-Volunteer Force*, (Washington, D.C.: Brassey's, 1996).

21

A September 29, 1995, news release by the House Committee on Veterans' Affairs did not specify the nature of the savings in veterans' programs generated through reconciliation, but no savings were generated through revisions to the Montgomery GI Bill: "The House Committee on Veterans' Affairs has acted on its recommendations to the Budget Committee… by a vote of 21 to 8." The release noted: "The VA Committee has always met its budget mandate in a responsible and bipartisan manner," said Rep. Bob Stump (R-AZ), chairman of the Committee…. The savings made by the budget resolution could have been much worse,' Stump said. 'The budget conferees could have gone with the House passed budget target of $6.4 billion [for veterans' programs] over seven years, or the Senate target of $9.4 billion over seven years. We asked the House conferees to fight for the lower number, and they won.' Rep. G.V. "Sonny" Montgomery (D-MS), ranking member of the committee stated that 'the package which Mr. Stump and I are proposing is as good as veterans could ask for under the circumstances. This package should reassure veterans and their dependents that Congress has not forgotten their sacrifices or the results from their service to the country.'" See House Committee on Veterans' Affairs, "VA Committee Sends Reconciliation Recommendations to Budget Committee," http://veterans.house.gov/news/104/relrec.html; (accessed June 14, 2007).

22

National Defense Panel, *Transforming Defense: National Security in the 21st Century* (Arlington, Virginia, 1979), iii.

23

Ibid., 42.

24

Ibid., 11.

25

Public Law 104-275 established the Commission on Servicemembers and Veterans Transition Assistance. Per the statute, the chairman and ranking members of the House and Senate Veterans' Affairs and Armed Services Committees individually named members to the commission rather than the Secretaries of Veterans' Affairs and Defense doing so, for example. The House Committee on Veterans' Affairs held a public hearing to receive the Commission's report on February 23, 1999. http://commdoes.house.gov/committees/vets/hvr022399.000/hvr022399_0.html.

26

Congressional Commission on Servicemembers and Veterans Transition Assistance, "Report to Congress," http://www.va.gov/vetbiz/library/Transition%20Commission%20Report.pdf. The "To Defend the Country" paragraph appears at 24; the "In enacting the Montgomery GI Bill" paragraph also appears at 24; the "However, most college-bound youth" paragraph appears at 27; and the "The commission believes" paragraph appears at 31.

27

Keynote Address, National Association of Veterans' Program Administrators 25th Annual Conference, October 20, 2000, 13.

28

The commission issued its reports in three phases: Phase I described "the world emerging in the first quarter of the 21st century;" Phase II designed "a national security strategy appropriate to that world;" and Phase III proposed "necessary changes to the national security structure in order to implement that strategy effectively." *New World Coming: National Security in the 21st Century,* http://www.fas.org/man/does/nwe/nwc.html; (accessed August 17, 2006).

29

The U.S. Commission on National Security/21st Century (The Hart-Rudman Commission), Phase III Report, *Road Map for National Security: Imperative for Change,* February 15, 2001, Washington, D.C., 102, 103, http://www.fas.org/man/docs/hwc; (accessed October 2, 2008).

30

House Committee on Veterans' Affairs, Hearing on H.R.1291—*The 21st Century Montgomery GI Bill Enhancement Act,* 108th Cong., 1st sess., 90, 92.

31

The single analysis the authors identified that said education was not a primary incentive for joining the all-volunteer military was a survey of two infantry battalions that were stationed at Fort Lewis, WA, during the summer of 2002. Survey responses from 257 enlisted soldiers revealed that 73.9 percent of respondents listed "adventure/challenge" as the main motivation to serve; 65.8 percent listed "serve country;" and 61.1 percent listed "money for college." Nine other motivations scored lower than money for college. Woodruff, et. al., "Propensity to Serve and Motivation to Enlist Among American Combat Soldiers," *Armed Forces & Society* 32, No. 3, (April 2006): 359.

32

U.S. House of Representatives, House Republican Conference, "Fixing the Military Recruiting Problem and Harnessing the Unique Abilities of Veterans Through an Enhanced GI Bill," National Security—Member's Message of the Month for January 2000, Representative Bob Stump, http://hillsource.house.gov/NationalSecurity/MemberMessage; (accessed January 10, 2006). The RAND Corporation uses a figure of 67 percent: "High school graduates are enrolling in college at record rates. In 1975, only 51 percent of recent high school graduates entered college within a year of graduation; by 1997, that figure had grown to 67 percent." RAND Research Brief, *The Montgomery G.I. Bill–Assessing Proposed Changes,* RB 7538 (2000).

33

Lt. General Timothy Maude died while serving America headquartered at the Pentagon on September 11, 2001. The 2nd Infantry Division, Camp Casey, Korea, dedicated the Lt. Gen. Timothy J. Maude Soldier Support Center on March 11, 2002. The U.S. Army Europe, Heidelberg, Germany, dedicated the Lt. Gen. Timothy J. Maude Center for Human Resources at Campbell Barracks on April 30, 2003. News release, Department of Defense, U.S. Army Europe Public Affairs, "Sept 11 Fallen Warrior Memorialized in Building Dedication," April 30, 2002.

34

Committee on Veterans' Affairs, Hearing on H.R. 1291, 17.

35

The document cited is the Phase III report issued on March 15, 2001. The commission issued its Phase II report on April 15, 2000, titled "*Seeking a National Security and Providing Freedom.*" The commission issued its Phase I report "*New World Coming: American Security in the 21st Century,*" September 15, 1999.

36

The Phase III Report of the U.S. Commission on National Security/21st Century, "*Road Map for National Security: Imperative for Change,*" March 15, 2001, 105.

37

Ibid., 107.

38

Nancy Gibbs, "[2003] Person of the Year: The American Soldier," *Time* magazine, December 29, 2003, http://aolsvc.news.aol.com/news/article.adp?id=20031210134909990001; (accessed April 7, 2004), p. 2.

39

Ibid., p. 1.

40

Ibid.

41

Ibid., 2.

42

Ibid., 3.

43

Ibid.

44

Congressional Budget Office—Pay-As-You-Go Estimate, H.R. 1291 *Veterans Education and Benefits Expansion Act of 2001* (as cleared by the Congress on December 12, 2001), December 28, 2001, 1.

45

Section 104 of the *Veterans Education and Benefits Expansion Act of 2001,* enacted on December 27, 2001; Public Law 107-103.

46

Ibid., Section 103.

47

Section 305 of the *Veterans Benefits Act of 2003*, enacted on December 16, 2003; Public Law 108-183.

48

Section 122 of the *Veterans Benefits and Healthcare Improvement Act of 2000*, enacted on November 1, 2000; Public Law 106-419.

49

Title I of the *Veterans Benefits Improvement Act of 2004*, enacted on December 10, 2004; Public Law 108-454.

50

Representatives Quinn, Hayworth, and Filner in *Sonny Montgomery: The Veteran's Champion* at 86. The documented leadership of Representatives Simpson and Brown and Reyes and Michaud, Subcommittee on Benefits Chairmen and Ranking Members, respectively, emerged after the Mississippi State University Libraries published/University Press of Mississippi distributed Mr. Montgomery's book in 2003.

51

Written testimony of Vice Admiral Norbert Ryan, Jr., national president, Military Officers Association of America, on behalf of the Partnership for Veterans' Education, before the joint hearing of the Military Personnel Subcommittee of the House Armed Services Committee/Economic Opportunity Subcommittee of the House Veterans' Affairs Subcommittee, September 27, 2006, 4.

52

2008 Public Policy Agenda, American Association of State Colleges and Universities, pp. 24-26.

53

US News & World Report and John F. Kennedy School of Government, *National Leadership Index 2005: A National Study of Confidence in Leadership*, October 18, 2005. This national public opinion poll conducted by TSC, a division of Yankelovich, Inc., asked American adults about the state of leadership in the country today, their views on what is important in good leadership, and their confidence in various leaders. In response to the question "How much confidence do you have in the following leaders?," the military placed first, followed by medical, executive branch, educational, religious, nonprofit and charity, Congressional, local government, state government, business, and the press. Point of contact is Hal Quinley, PhD, Yankelovich, Inc., telephone 909-624-0912. http://www.usnews.com/usnews/news/features/051022/22leaders.pdf.

54

U.S. Department of Veterans Affairs, *Program Evaluation of the Montgomery G.I. Bill*, 38 U.S.C., Chapter 30, April 17, 2000.

CHAPTER 16:

1987–Present—

Effect of the Montgomery GI Bill: Affording Postsecondary Education

1

U.S. Senate, Committee on Veterans' Affairs, Report on S. 12, *New GI Bill Continuation Act*, 100th Cong., 1st sess., 1987, 8. "Section 4 of the committee bill would add three new purpose clauses to the current declared purposes of the New GI Bill chapter 30 program, as set forth in section 1401 of Title 38, United States Code. These new clauses are: (1) to extend the benefits of a higher education to qualifying men and women who might not otherwise be able to afford such an education; (2) to provide for vocational readjustment and to restore lost educational opportunities to those service men and women who served on active duty after June 30, 1985; and (3) to enhance our Nation's competitiveness through the development of a more highly educated and productive workforce." The legislative language itself of the three new purpose clauses appears at 1, 2.

2

Section 3001 (2). The full citation is Title 38 – Veterans' Benefits; Part III – Readjustment and Related Benefits; Chapter 30 – All-Volunteer Force Educational Assistance Program; Subchapter I – Purposes; Definitions.

3

The authors do not discuss in the text the new purpose clause "to provide for vocational readjustment and restore lost educational opportunities to those service men and women who served on active duty after June 30, 1985."

4

For examples of feedback that veterans personally shared with Mr. Montgomery, see Ballard and Piper, 82, 83, 84.

5

http://www.navpa.org. 2006 president was Mr. Jack Mordente, Southern Connecticut State College; 2008/2009 president is Mr. R.K. Williams, Boise State University.

6

U.S. News and World Report ranks Embry-Riddle's aerospace engineering program "No. 1 among the nation's aerospace engineering programs without doctoral degrees." "Six Embry-Riddle alumni are current or former astronauts." Embry-Riddle Aeronautical University, "Points of Pride," http://www.erau.edu/er/abouterau/pointsofpride.html.

7

Ms. Faith DeLauriers, interview by Kehrer (co-author), February 6, 2006, Daytona Beach, FL.

8

http://www.saavetrain.org/index.html. 2007 president was Ms. Joan Ryan, Illinois; and 2008/2009 president was Mr. Charles Rowe, New Jersey.

9

Dr. James Bombard, interview by Kehrer (co-author), Arlington, VA, February 26, 2006.

10

http://www.aacrao.org.

11

Dr. Jerome Sullivan, interview by Kehrer (co-author), Washington, D.C., November 8, 2006.

12

http://www.soc.aascu.org. Institutional participation in SOC is not limited to schools located near military bases.

13

U.S. Department of Defense, "DoD Voluntary Education: A Broad Overview," Carolyn L. Baker, Chief of Continuing Education, March 2005, 4, http://www.voled.doded.mil/voled_web/voledhome.asp; (accessed November 9, 2006).

14

Dr. Kathy Snead, interview by Kehrer (co-author), Washington, D.C., August 23, 2006. The source of this data is the FY 06 Department of Defense Voluntary Education Fact Sheet. http://voled.doded.mil/voled_web/voledhome.asp; (accessed August 23, 2006).

15

We have not cited in the text 39 service members who received GEDs and 15 who received doctoral degrees.

16

Testimony of Anthony J. Principi, Subcommittee on Economic Opportunity, House Committee on Veterans' Affairs, December 7, 2006, 9. Mr. Principi also noted at page 9, "36,415 service members received college degrees in fiscal year 2005 while carrying out their military duties on a full-time basis." And in addition to the 819,256 service members pursuing degrees during off-duty hours under the DoD Tuition Assistance Program, "during fiscal year 2005 another 20,607 active-duty service members were pursuing college degrees during off-duty hours using their Montgomery GI Bill… ."

17

http://ausa.org. 2007 president is Gordon R. Sullivan.

18

Senate Committee on Veterans' Affairs, *Report on S. 12*, 9.

19

MSG (Ret.) Michael Cline, interview by Kehrer (co-author), Washington, D.C., February 13, 2008.

20

Chapters 1606 and 1607, Title 38, United States Code.

21

Major General Ronald Young, director, Manpower and Personnel, Joint Staff, National Guard Bureau, elaborates on this access to postsecondary education/Guard and Reserve retention concept in July 31, 2007, testimony before the Senate Committee on Veterans' Affairs, at page 2 of his statement for the record. http://www.veterans.senate.gov/public/, "hearings," "July, 2007," "Hearing: VA and DoD Education Issues;" (accessed January 7, 2008).

22

Senate Veterans' Affairs Committee Chairman Alan Cranston used this phrase, as well, during the 1987 Senate floor debate on S.12. See *Congressional Record*, May 8, 1987, S6202.

23

Also instructive is what employers expect from veterans and nonveterans alike who pursue postsecondary education. See Bill Coplin, *10 Things Employers Want You to Learn in College* (Berkeley/Toronto: Ten Speed Press, 2003).

24

U.S. Department of Veterans Affairs, "Chapter 30 Rates–January 1, 2008." http://www.gibill.va.gov; (accessed February 13, 2008). The monthly rate for full-time institutional training is $1,101 times 36 months (four, nine-month academic years). This amount would increase to $47,556 on August 1, 2009; $1,321 per month times 36 months.

25

VA consolidates the numbers of trainees who used the New GI Bill in 1985 and 1986 with Montgomery GI Bill users from 1987 forward.

26

Memorandum from T.A. Van Hintum, assistant director for program management, VA Education Service, July 3, 2007. As of Sept. 29, 2010, the number Mr. Douglass cites is 2,437,027. For helpful testimony on the role of community, junior, technical and vocational colleges and schools across the country in furnishing "convenient, low-cost, high quality, easy-access education and training" to the veteran and military student populations, see Committee on Veterans' Affairs, Senate, *Veterans' Education and Disability Compensation Legislation* (S. Hrg. 101-460), 101st Cong., 1st sess., 1989, 35, 231. (See Statement of Bernell C. Dickinson, Director, Office of Special Programs, North Carolina Department of Community Colleges, on behalf of American Association of Community and Junior Colleges.)

27

Veterans Benefits and Healthcare Improvements Act of 2000, enacted on November 1, 2000, as Public Law 106-419.

28

Department of Veterans Affairs, FY 2007 *Congressional Budget Submission*, 3A-17.

29

U.S. Department of Labor, Office of Assistant Secretary for Policy, "Special Report," http://www.dol.gov/asp/media/reports/credentialing/chapter1.html; (accessed October 29, 2006).

30

The National Association of State and Territorial Apprenticeship Directors promotes an effective national apprenticeship program. The Association promotes registered apprenticeships and its expansion as an economic asset to the nation. Notes the Association: "Shortly after World War II, a group of state apprenticeship directors met to discuss common problems encountered in the administration of their respective apprenticeship training programs. Included in the meetings were representatives of the federal Bureau of Apprenticeship and Training and the Veterans Administration." NASTAD, "An Overview of the NASTAD Organization," http://www.nastad.net; (accessed January 2, 2007).

31

Apprenticeship opportunities certified by the Department of Labor may begin while in the Navy and Marine Corps, for example, before the service member separates from the military and technically becomes a veteran, under the law. "More than 41,000 service members in 94 trades participate in the Navy's National Apprenticeship Program (NNAP). Almost 3,000 Marines are enrolled in apprenticeships in 27 trades." Current participation numbers most likely are dramatically higher. *Report of Congressional Commission on Servicemembers and Veterans Transition Assistance*, January 1999, 71.

32

Congressional Record, April 10, 2003, p. E752. This is the introductory statement by House Committee on Veterans' Affairs Chairman Christopher Smith on *Veterans Earn and Learn Act*. Joining as original cosponsors were Ranking Member Lane Evans, and Chairman and Ranking Member of the Benefits Subcommittee, Henry Brown, and Michael Michaud, respectively.

33

U.S. Department of Veterans' Affairs "Chapter 30 Rates–January 1, 2008," http://www.gibill.va.gov; (accessed February 12, 2008). The six-month monthly rates for the Selected Reserve Program are lesser.

34

Bill Stephens, interview by Kehrer (co-author), Arlington, VA, February 27, 2006.

35

Ibid.

36

Statement attributed to Secretary of Veterans Affairs Anthony Principi in address to Montvale (NJ) Business Association, fall 2005. Darryl Kehrer (co-author), eye-witness.

37

Congressional Commission on Servicemembers and Veterans Transition Assistance, *1999 Report to Congress*, 145.

38

Don Wilson, interview by Kehrer (co-author), Burke, VA, December 27, 2007. Some of Mr. Wilson's statements mirror his April 30, 2003, testimony before the Committee on Veterans' Affairs, U.S. House of Representatives on H.R. 1460, the proposed Veterans Entrepreneurship Act of 2003 and other legislation. p. 135. The published hearing record publication number is 108-10.

39

Mr. Wilson is quoting the "Small Business Success is Our Success" language that appears on the front cover/serves as the title of his organization's 2007 brochure. For information on America's small business development center network, see www.asbdc-us.org.

40

Ibid., 2.

41

Ibid., 3.

42

House Committee on Veterans' Affairs, Subcommittee on Benefits, Hearing on H.R. 1460, *The Veterans Entrepreneurship Act of 2003*; H.R. 1712, *The Veterans Federal Procurement Opportunity Act of 2003*, and H.R. 1416, *The Veterans Federal Procurement Opportunity Act of 2003*; and H.R. 1416, *The Veterans Earn and Learn Act. April 30, 2003*, 108th Cong., 1st sess., 2003, 135.

43

Ibid.

44

Ibid.

45

Ibid.

46

Executive Office of the President, *Economic Report of the President*, together with the Annual Economic Report of the Council of Economic Advisors, transmitted to Congress February 2007, (Washington, D.C., U.S. Government Printing Office), 61.

47

The primary authors were Representatives Bob Stump, Lane Evans, Jim Talent, Jack Quinn, and Bob Filner.

48

Walter Blackwell, interview by Kehrer (co-author), Washington, D.C., January 10, 2008. Some of the data in Mr. Blackwell's comments also are available at The Veterans Corporation, "Where Veterans Entrepreneurs Partner for Success," http://www.veteranscorp.org/abuntTVC.aspx; (accessed March 28, 2006).

49

President Blackwell also makes this statement at Annual Report, FY 2006, National Veterans Business Development Corporation, Page 9. The number for "The Veterans Corporation" is 866-283-8267.

50

Title of the enacting legislation was "The Veterans Entrepreneurship and Small Business Development Act of 1999." Public Law 106-50.

51

http://www.veteranscrp.org/GovernmentRelations.aspx, "State Fact Sheets," (accessed January 11, 2008).

52

Small Business Administration, Department of Defense, VetBiz.gov at Department of Veterans Affairs Center for Veterans Enterprise, and California Disabled Veteran Business Alliance. The Veterans Corporation has regional education sites that furnish face-to-face seminars, workshops, and multi-week programs in Boston, Flint, and St. Louis.

53

Veterans Business Development Corporation, Annual Report for FY 2006, 1.

54

Ibid.

55

Ibid. The actual number exceeds 325,982 because the number of service members and veterans served by the Virtual Veterans Resource Center were not immediately available.

CHAPTER 17:

1987-Winter 2008—

Effect of the Montgomery GI Bill: Developing the U.S. Workforce

1

Executive Office of the President, *Economic Report of the President, Together with the Annual Report of the Council of Economic Advisers,* Submitted to the Congress, February 2006, transmittal letter to Congress, (Washington, D.C., U.S. Government Printing Office, 2006), 5.

2

Milton Greenberg, *The GI Bill* (New York: Lickle Publishing, 1997): 12.

3

Department of Defense, Defense Manpower Data Center, "Separations from Active Duty (Fiscal Year 2006)," Unpaginated. The actual number is 179,292.

4

E-mail response from Dennis Douglass to letter request from Darryl Kehrer (co-author), June 30, 2006, in possession of Mississippi State University.

5

Representative Christopher Smith, former chairman of the House Committee on Veterans' Affairs, most likely was the originator of this statement, although others have used it, as well. Darryl Kehrer (co-author), eye-witness.

6

Letter, Representative Mike Simpson to Representative John Boozman, December 5, 2006. Letter furnished by Mr. Simpson's staff.

7

Title 38, United States Code, Section 3001 (6).

8

Senate Committee on Veterans' Affairs, Report on S. 12, 9-10.

9

Congressional Record, May 8, 1987, S6210.

10

Ibid., S6213.

11

Senate Committee on Veterans' Affairs, Report on S. 12, 9-10.

12

"Major academic journals in the field of labor economics and industrial relations are: *Industrial and Labor Relations Review; Industrial relations; Journal of Human Resources; Journal of Labor Economics; Journal of Labor Research; Labor History; and Proceedings of the Industrial Relations Research Association.*" University Libraries of Mississippi State University, "Guide to Go!," General Sources, Academic Journals, 2005,

not paginated but with internal identifier: J:/Ref handouts 05/Business/Labor B&I#5.doc;mg,update/ch; 02. http://library.msstate.edu.

13

General information by industry may be obtained from: *Forbes* "Annual Report on American Industry" (first January issue). Identifies major companies in each industry and describes the present condition and the outlook of 20 major industries; *Standard & Poor Industry Surveys* analyzes and present conditions and trends of over seventy industries. Includes graphs and tables and gives composite financial information for each industry; and *US Industry and Trade Outlook* contains statistics and financial information for more than 350 industries. University Libraries of Mississippi State University, "Guide to Go!," Industry Information, Business & Industry Resources No. 3, 2005, not paginated but with internal identifier: 1J:/Ref handouts 05/Business/Industry B&I#3.doc; mg/update by Ch 7/03.

14

World Business Directory contains four volumes. The directory gives detailed information on more than 140,000 businesses involved in international trade. It identifies top import/export companies, leading manufacturers, local niche companies, and small and medium- sized companies. University Libraries of Mississippi State University, "Guide to Go!," International Information, Business & Industries No. 4, 2005, not paginated but with internal identifier: 1J:/Ref handouts 05/Business/International B&I #4.doc; mg, ch 026/7/06.

15

On average, annual dischargees can reach as high as 220,000 when including Reservists and National Guard members. In any case, such numbers can vary dramatically from year to year. LTC U.S. Army Ron Howard (Ret.), interview by Kehrer (co-author), Washington, D.C., June 6, 2006.

16

House Committee on Veterans' Affairs Members Christopher Smith, Lane Evans, Henry Brown, and Michael Michaud convened a bipartisan press conference on Veterans as Unique National Resource/Competitive Business Asset on March 24, 2004. In addition to the convening officials, speakers included representatives from U.S. Business Roundtable, U.S. Chamber of Commerce, UBS Financial Services (formerly Paine-Webber), The Home Depot, Ford Motor Company, and others. The remarks of Representative Brown are his from the press conference.

17

U.S. House of Representatives, Committee on Veterans' Affairs, *Employing Veterans of Our Armed Forces*, 108th Cong., 2nd sess., 2004, 90.

18

Ibid., 89.

19

Ibid.

20

Ibid., 89, 90.

21

Ibid., 98 and 103. The letter from Subcommittee Chairman Henry Brown to Chairman Christopher Smith that encloses Dr. Klein's analysis appears at 95.

22

Hire Vets First (President's National Hire Veterans Committee), "Employer Testimonials - An Employer Speaks," http://www.hirevetsfirst.gov/emptestimonials/lutz.asp, (accessed February 20, 2006).

23

U.S. House of Representatives, *Employing Veterans of Our Armed Forces*, 9.

24

Ibid., 14-15. Mr. Poriotis is founder and CEO of the executive placement firm Wesley, Brown, and Bartle. He also is founder of the Center for Military and Private-Sector Initiatives and *Veterans Across America*, created with Dr. Ray Healy.

25

Ibid., 28.

26

Ibid., 30. Among People Soft's numerous corporate and government clients is the Army University Access Online program.

27

Ibid., 33. Mr. Crawford also noted in his testimony that "Our Chairman and CEO (Art Ryan), corporate controller, chief auditor, the head of our learning organization, and many more senior staff members, too numerous to mention, are veterans."

28

House Committee on Veterans' Affairs, "Veterans' Benefits: Obtaining Education and Job Training," http://www.house.gov/va/benefits/mgib.html; (accessed October 29, 2006.)

29

Evan Gaddis, interview by Kehrer (co-author), December 21, 2006. Indeed, Deere and Company testified at a public hearing to its identifying service members in various technical areas before enlisting so as to hire them after discharge from the military. Hearing on Employing Veterans of Our Armed Forces, March 24, 2004, 9.

30

The date of the *Los Angeles Business Journal* article is June 16, 2006. The date of the *New York Times* article is June 18, 2006. http://www.hirevetsfirst.G.V.o/news/la_bix_journal.asp and http://hirevetsfirst.gov/news/ny_times.asp; (accessed November 26, 2006).

31

Employer testimony furnishes the basis for the phrase "hiring veterans fundamentally represents a good business decision for our economy" as recorded in *Hearing on Employing Veterans of Our Armed Forces*, March 24, 2004. See note 17 above. The phrase itself is attributed in 2004 to Representative Christopher Smith, Chairman, Committee on Veterans' Affairs. Darryl Kehrer, eye-witness.

32

Klemm Analysis Group, Program Evaluation of the Montgomery GI Bill, April 17, 2000.

33

For background on Assistant Secretary Ciccolella, see http://www.dol.gove/vets/aboutvets/asec/ciccolella.html.

34

For the *2006 Economic Report of the President*, see http://www.whitehouse.gov/cea.crp06.pdf. For the 2007 and 2008 reports, see http://www.whitehouse.gov/cea/pubs.html.

35

See http://www.whitehouse.gov/news/releases/2008/-2/200080213-3.html for a transcript of the President's remarks when signing the bill.

36

Executive Office of the President, *2008 Economic Report of the President Together, with the Annual Report of the Council of Economic Advisers, Transmitted to the Congress February 2008*, (United States Government Printing Office, Washington, D.C., 2008), 18.

37

2007 Economic Report of the President Together, with the Annual report of the Council of Economic Advisers, Transmitted to Congress February 2007, (United State Government Printing Office, Washington, D.C., 2007), 17.

38

2007 Economic Report of the President, Washington, D.C., 33, 34.

39

Ibid., 62.

40

Such industrialized countries are Canada, France, Germany, Italy, Japan, the United Kingdom, and the United States. 2007 *Economic Report of the President*, 45-46.

41

2006 Economic Report of the President, Washington, D.C., 3.

42

Ibid.

43

Ibid., 51.

44

Ibid., 49, 50. For example, as noted at 52, "Unlike the share of people who have completed high school, the share of people aged 25-29 who have a bachelor's degree or higher has continued to rise. This share, however, is rising more slowly than it was 25 years ago. During the past 25 years, it rose 6 percentage points, from 23 percent in 1979 to 29 percent in 2004. In contrast, in the 25 years prior to 1979, it increased by about 13 percentage points, or more than twice as much."

45

Ibid., 62. Further the text notes: "Recent studies have found that community colleges do contribute to workers' earnings. A year of community college raises real earnings by around 6 percent. Community college also helps laid-off workers. According to one study, in the long term, a year of community college raises the earnings of long-tenured, laid-off workers by about 7 percent for men and even more for women, compared to similar workers who do not enroll in community college classes. The earnings gains are higher for workers who take technical, scientific or health-related courses, and lower for workers who take less quantitative courses."

46

2007 *Economic Report of the President*, Washington, D.C., 41.

47

Ibid., 45.

48

Ibid., 42.

49

Ibid.

50

This clause—beginning with "especially" and ending with "economy"—is quoted from the transmittal letter to Congress of the 2006 *Economic Report of the President*, 5.

51

Tony Zeiss, *Get 'em While They Are Hot*, (Nelson Business, 2005), 1.

52

U.S. House of Representatives, *Hearing on Employing Veterans of Our Armed Forces*, 88. Author Zeiss makes a similar statement in *Get 'em While They Are Hot*, at vii and an endnoted statement at 2.

53

Zeiss, *Get em' While They Are Hot*, 2, and footnoted in the text.

54

Ibid., and not endnoted.

55

Ibid., vii.

56

"What's Wrong with Vocational School," the *Wall Street Journal*, January 17, 2007.

57

Ibid., 3. President George W. Bush gave this speech at Central Piedmont Community College on April 5, 2004. The White House, "President Discusses Economy and Job Training in North Carolina," htgtp:www.whitehouse.gov/news/releases/2004/04/20040405-3.html; (accessed October 31, 2006).

58

We have used Mr. Gunderson's 2006 projection even though the 2006 date has passed. For example, during the spring 2007 "Career Day" sponsored by Mississippi State University on January 23, of the 140 employers participating, 66 employers were seeking engineers—electrical, chemical, mechanical, aerospace, industrial, computer, civil, systems, environmental, or biomedical. Scott Maynard, associate director, The Career Center, Mississippi State University, interview by Kehrer (co-author), Starkville, MS, February 5, 2007.

59

Ibid., 11. These remarks were made in a February 2004 speech to the Association of Community College Trustees.

60

Economic Report of the President, Together with Annual Report of the Council of Economic Advisers, Transmitted to the Congress February 2006, 63.

61

Ibid. Also instructive is the observation of House Minority Leader Nancy Pelosi: "The U.S. will graduate 70,000 engineers this year, while India will graduate 350,000 and China 600,000." See "R and D Democrats," *Wall Street Journal*, February 13, 2006. Additionally instructive is former President Clinton's observation that "What you earn is the result of what you learn." See "Will Your Job Survive?" *Washington Post*, March 22, 2006, Op-Ed by Harold Meyerson. Lastly, the *Wall Street Journal College Journal* said even prior to the February 13. 2006, Pelosi article that it thought the 350,000 and 600,000 numbers citied by others regarding India and China graduates were much inflated. *The College Journal* cited lower estimates furnished by the National Science Foundation and Rochester Institute of Technology/Carnegie Mellon University. "Outsourcing Fears Help Inflate Numbers," *WSJ.Com College Journal*, August 30, 2005, http://www.collegejournal.com/globalcareers/newstrends/20050830-bialik.html; (accessed June 8, 2007).

62

2006 *Economic Report of the President*, Washington, D.C., 57.

63

Ibid., 58. The report goes on to say at 58: "This decline may be the result of increases in training opportunities in other countries and visa restrictions for foreign students and scholars put in place in the United States following the September 11, 2001, terrorist attacks."

64

Tom Speicher, "*Getting Small Yields Big Opportunities*," One College Avenue (Pennsylvania College of Technology–Penn State University), Volume 15, No. 1 (winter 2005-6). 4.

65

Ibid., 5.

66

Ibid.

67

Ibid. Instructive is other everyday examples of emerging uses of nanotechnology, as listed at nanotechnology.com on August 16, 2006, for example: "Nanotechnology designed to (1) shrink ovarian cancer tumors, (2) develop new materials research in organic semiconductors, and (3) provide innovative solutions in homeland security nanoparticles."

68

David Gergen, "The Danger of Drift," *U.S. News and World Report,* May 29, 2006, 44.

69

Lt. Col. (Ret) Anne Campbell, Ph.D., is a graduate of the U.S. Air Force Academy and headed American and Policy Studies there before retiring in 2003. The House Committee on Veterans' Affairs selected Lt. Col. Campbell as a legislative fellow during summer 2002, where she served with distinction.

70

This language is taken directly from Mr. Montgomery's copy of the framed citation presented to him by the President on behalf of the United States.

INDEX

H

PHOTO CREDITS

CHAPTER 1

4 Vice President and Mrs. Bush with Sonny Montgomery, G.V. Sonny Montgomery Collection, Congressional and Political Research Center, Mississippi State University Libraries
13 Bill Cohen U.S. Senate: Office of the Senate Historian
13 *Sonny Montgomery: The Veteran's Champion* book cover By permission of the publisher
13 Sonny Montgomery serving during WWII, G.V. Sonny Montgomery Collection, Congressional and Political Research Center, Mississippi State University Libraries
13 Sonny Montgomery: Senior at MSU, G.V. Sonny Montgomery Collection, Congressional and Political Research Center, Mississippi State University Libraries
13 Montgomery and Bush: Freshmen in Congress, G.V. Sonny Montgomery Collection, Congressional and Political Research Center, Mississippi State University Libraries
14 Montgomery and President and Mrs. George H.W. Bush, G.V. Sonny Montgomery Collection, Congressional and Political Research Center, Mississippi State University Libraries
14 Montgomery with troops, G.V. Sonny Montgomery Collection, Congressional and Political Research Center, Mississippi State University Libraries
14 Montgomery, portrait Paul Gillis for NGAUS
15 Cohen, Thurman, Montgomery, G.V. Sonny Montgomery Collection, Congressional and Political Research Center, Mississippi State University Libraries

CHAPTER 2

19 WW II pilots, Air Force Magazine
19 Milton Greenberg, Milton Greenberg
19 *The GI Bill,* Lickle Publishing
19 WW II bomber, Courtesy National Archives
19 Mighty Eighth Air Force Museum, Mighty Eighth Air Force Museum
19 Harry Colmery plaques, The American Legion
20 *When Dreams Come True,* Potomac Books, Inc. (Formerly Brassey's Inc.)
20 John Rankin, U.S. House of Representatives: Office of the House Historian
20 Edith Rogers, U.S. House of Representatives: Office of the House Historian
21 Dewey Short, U.S. House of Representatives: Office of the House Historian
21 Robert M. Hutchins, Special Collection Research Center, University of Chicago Library
21 Ernest McFarland, U.S. Senate: Office of the Senate Historian
21 Champ Clark, U.S. Senate: Office of the Senate Historian
22 Newpaper article, Lickle Publishing
22 Roosevelt signing GI Bill, 1944, photo Courtesy National Archives
22 James Michener, U.S. Army photograph
22 General Douglas McArthur, Philippines Courtesy National Archives
23 USS Missouri, WWII, Courtesy National Archives
23 Cheering families, WWII, Courtesy National Archives
23 GI kissing girl, WWII, Courtesy National Archives
23 Carmbridge, England, cemetery, Courtesy of American Battle Monuments Commission
23 Veterans enrolling in school, Lickle Publishing
24 Anthony Principi, et al, Department of Veterans Affairs
24 University of Nebraska students, University of Nebraska Archives
24 GI's register for classes, University of Nebraska Archives

CHAPTER 3

27 Dr. Cloyd Marvin, The George Washington University Special Collections and University Archives
27 Selma Borchardt, Wayne State University Archives
27 Dr. James Conant, Harvard University Library
28 Nathan M. Pusey, Photo courtesy of Lawrence University Archives
28 GI's arrive on campus, Wayne State University Archives
28 1st Sgt. Messiah, et al Lickle Publishing
28 Clint Eastwood, World Wide Images
29 *The Second Wave,* Robert B. Williams, Kennesaw State University
29 Montgomery and Principi, Department of Veterans Affairs
29 Principi and veteran, Department of Veterans Affairs
29 Lt. Benjamin Callison, Family of Ben Callison
29 B-17 cockpit, Family of Ben Callison
30 Peter Drucker, The Drucker Institute at Claremont Graduate University
30 Suzanne Mettler, Oxford University Press
30 *Soldiers to Citizens,* Oxford University Press
30 Soldiers during Korean Conflict, Military Officers Association of America
31 Marines in Vietnam, Military Officers Association of America
31 POW, U.S. Army photograph
31 President Lyndon, Johnson Department of Veterans Affairs
31 President Gerald Ford, Darryl Kehrer, personal collection
31 President Jimmy Carter, Darryl Kehrer, personal collection
31 Honoring the fallen, Department of Veterans Affairs
31 Jessica Maulding, G.V. "Sonny" Montgomery Center for America's Veterans

CHAPTER 4

37 Speaker's rostrum, U.S. House of Representatives: Office of the House Historian
38 Charles W. Johnson, U.S. House of Representatives: Office of the House Historian
38 Voting station, U.S. House of Representatives: Office of the House Historian
40 Colin Powell, U.S. Army photograph

CHAPTER 5

43 Soldier in Vietnam, Courtesy National Archives
43 Vietnam POWs, Courtesy National Archives
43 Charles Moskos, Northwestern University
44 Darryl Kehrer, Darryl Kehrer, personal collection
44 William Westmoreland, U.S. Army photograph
46 E.C. Meyer letter, Darryl Kehrer, personal collection
47 T.B. Hayward letter, Darryl Kehrer, personal collection
47 Lew Allen Jr. letter, Darryl Kehrer, personal collection
48 Bob Barrow letter, Darryl Kehrer, personal collection
48 David C. Jones letter ,Darryl Kehrer, personal collection
49 Robert Pirie letter, Darryl Kehrer, personal collection
50 Mike Simpson, U.S. House of Representatives: Office of the House Historian
50 Maxwell Thurman, U.S. Army photograph
50 Edward "Shy" Meyer, U.S. Army photograph
50 John Wickham, John Wickham, personal collection
50 Bob Elton, U.S. Army photograph

148 *Pentagram* article, Joint Base Myer - Henderson Hall for *Pentagram*

148 Tom Turnage, Department of Veterans Affairs

148 Howard Baker, U.S. Senate: Office of the Senate Historian

148 Baker letter, G.V. Sonny Montgomery Collection, Congressional and Political Research Center, Mississippi State University Libraries

148 Cochran letter, G.V. Sonny Montgomery Collection, Congressional and Political Research Center, Mississippi State University Libraries

149 George H.W. Bush letter, G.V. Sonny Montgomery Collection, Congressional and Political Research Center, Mississippi State University Libraries

149 Ronald Reagan, Courtesy Ronald Reagan Library

149 Reagan signing Montgomery GI Bill, Courtesy Ronald Reagan Library

149 Reagan's signature on Montgomery GI Bill, Library of Congress

150 Montgomery GI Bill ceremony, Library of Congress

150 Col. Mike Meese and cadet, Courtesy U.S. Military Academy

151 Montgomery, et al G.V. Sonny Montgomery Collection, Congressional and Political Research Center, Mississippi State University Libraries

151 Montgomery, et al G.V. Sonny Montgomery Collection, Congressional and Political Research Center, Mississippi State University Libraries

151 Montgomery, et al G.V. Sonny Montgomery Collection, Congressional and Political Research Center, Mississippi State University Libraries

151 Montgomery, et al G.V. Sonny Montgomery Collection, Congressional and Political Research Center, Mississippi State University Libraries

151 Montgomery, et al G.V. Sonny Montgomery Collection, Congressional and Political Research Center, Mississippi State University Libraries

151Montgomery, et al G.V. Sonny Montgomery Collection, Congressional and Political Research Center, Mississippi State University Libraries

151 Montgomery, et al G.V. Sonny Montgomery Collection, Congressional and Political Research Center, Mississippi State University Libraries

151 Montgomery, et al G.V. Sonny Montgomery Collection, Congressional and Political Research Center, Mississippi State University Libraries

151 American Legion group G.V. Sonny Montgomery Collection, Congressional and Political Research Center, Mississippi State University Libraries

CHAPTER 15

155 NERA newsletter article, NERA (National Enlisted and Reservist Association)

155 *Navy Times* article, Copyright © 1988 *Navy Times*

156 House Veterans' Affairs Committee, press release, Darryl Kehrer, personal collection

156 Jim Holley, U.S. House of Representatives: Office of the House Historian

156 Montgomery, et al G.V. Sonny Montgomery Collection, Congressional and Political Research Center, Mississippi State University Libraries

157 Montgomery with troops, U.S. Army photograph

157 Bush with troops, George Bush Presidential Library and Museum

157 Soldiers, U.S. Army photograph

157 Mother and daughter, Department of Veterans Affairs

157 Washington Monument, Department of Veterans Affairs

157 Bush, et al, Department of Veterans Affairs

157 Norman Schwartzkopf, Department of Veterans Affairs

158 Victory Parade, Department of Veterans Affairs

158 Victory Parade, Department of Veterans Affairs

158 Victory Parade, Department of Veterans Affairs

158 Victory Parade, Department of Veterans Affairs

158 Victory Parade, Department of Veterans Affairs

158 Victory Parade, Department of Veterans Affairs

158 Richard Darman, George Bush Presidential Library and Museum

158 Ryan and Montgomery, Patrick Ryan, personal collection

159 Clinton at VA, Department of Veterans Affairs

159 Clinton, et al, Department of Veterans Affairs

159 Clinton, et al, Department of Veterans Affairs

159 Color Guard, Department of Veterans Affairs

159 Clinton and Montgomery, Department of Veterans Affairs

160 Clinton, Department of Veterans Affairs

160 Joint Chiefs, letter U.S. Army photograph

160 *Washington Post* article, Library of Congress

160 John Shalikashvili, U.S. Army photograph

161 Transforming Defense, National Defense Panel

161 Philip Odeen, National Defense Panel

162 Commission on Servicemembers report cover, CSVTA

162 Security report, Commission on National Security

162 Gary Hart, U.S. Senate: Office of the Senate Historian

163 Patricia Tracey, VADM Pat Tracey, DASD Military Personnel Policy

163 National Security report, Darryl Kehrer, personal collection

163 Montgomery GI Bill logo, Montgomery Institute, design Kim Gianakos/Ad Astra LLC

163 Nancy Gibbs, *Time Inc.*

164 *TIME* magazine cover, 12/29/03 © 2003 TIME, Inc. All rights reserved. Used by permission and protected by the Copyright Laws of the United States. The printing, copying, redistribution, or retransmission of the Material without express written permission is prohibited.

164 C-17 named for Montgomery, G.V. Sonny Montgomery Collection, Congressional and Political Research Center, Mississippi State University Libraries

165 Montgomery, et al G.V. Sonny Montgomery Collection, Congressional and Political Research Center, Mississippi State University Libraries

165 Montgomery and Evans, Department of Veterans Affairs

165 Michael Michaud, U.S. House of Representatives: Office of the House Historian

165 Henry Brown, U.S. House of Representatives: Office of the House Historian

165 Bob Norton, MOAA

166 AASCU public policy report, American Association State Colleges and Universities

166 Ed Elmendorf, AASCU

166 Michael McGrevey, G.V. Sonny Montgomery Collection, Congressional and Political Research Center, Mississippi State University Libraries

166 Kimberly Island, G.V. "Sonny" Montgomery Center for America's Veterans

166 *Washington Times* news article, *The Washington Times, LLC*

166 *USA Today* article *USA TODAY,* a division of Gannett Satellite Information Network, Inc.

167 *Washington Times* news article, *The Washington Times, LLC*

167 George Lisicki, VFW

167 *USA Today* article *USA TODAY,* a division of Gannett Satellite Information Network, Inc.

167 The Montgomery GI Bill Selected Reserve, Department of Veterans Affairs

167 The Montgomery GI Bill Active Duty, Department of Veterans Affairs

167 For Service to Your Country - Vet Benefits, Peter Gaytan, personal collection

167 Marine recruits at Parris Island, Paul Kehrer

CHAPTER 16

CHAPTER 17

ABOUT THE CO-AUTHORS

Darryl Kehrer

Darryl Kehrer is the former Public Policy Officer, Montgomery Center for America's Veterans, Mississippi State University. He concluded 37 years of public service in 2005 as staff director, Subcommittee on Economic Opportunity, Committee on Veterans' Affairs, U.S. House of Representatives. He formerly served as Executive Director, Congressional Veterans Claims Adjudication Commission; and as Panel Staff Director, Congressional Commission on Servicemembers and Veterans Transition Assistance. Kehrer is a 1992 Woodrow Wilson Public Service Fellow representing the U.S. Department of Veterans Affairs.

Michael McGrevey

Michael McGrevey LTC, USAF (Ret) is President, JBHM Education Group, Jackson, Mississippi. He is former Chief of Staff and Vice President for Finance and Administration, Mississippi State University, where he co-founded the Montgomery Center for America's Veterans. McGrevey served as President of The Montgomery Institute, a non-profit economic and leadership development firm in Meridian, Mississippi, and is a founding board member of Friends of Veterans of Mississippi. He is a Phi Kappa Phi member and an Eagle Scout.